Cruelty and Laughter

Cruelty and Laughter

FORGOTTEN COMIC LITERATURE AND THE UNSENTIMENTAL EIGHTEENTH CENTURY

Simon Dickie

The University of Chicago Press   CHICAGO & LONDON

The University of Chicago Press, Chicago 60637
The University of Chicago Press, Ltd., London
© 2011 by The University of Chicago
All rights reserved. Published 2011.
Paperback edition 2014
Printed in the United States of America

23 22 21 20 19 18 17 16 15 14   2 3 4 5 6

ISBN-13: 978-0-226-14618-8 (cloth)
ISBN-13: 978-0-226-14254-8 (paper)
ISBN-13: 978-0-226-14620-1 (e-book)
DOI: 10.7208/chicago/9780226146201.001.0001

The University of Chicago Press gratefully acknowledges the generous
support of the University of Toronto toward the publication of this book.

Library of Congress Cataloging-in-Publication Data

Dickie, Simon.
    Cruelty and laughter : forgotten comic literature and the unsentimental
Eighteenth Century / Simon Dickie.
        p.   cm.
    Includes bibliographical references and index.
    ISBN-13: 978-0-226-14618-8 (hardcover : alk. paper)
    ISBN-10: 0-226-14618-9 (hardcover : alk. paper)   1. English wit
and humor—18th century—History and Criticism.   2. Cruelty in
literature.   I. Title.
    PR935.D53 2011
    827'.509—dc22

                                                        2011004069

♾ This paper meets the requirements of ANSI/NISO Z39.48-1992
(Permanence of Paper).

For N.H.A.

CONTENTS

ILLUSTRATIONS

This book has three aims. First, I bring to light a vast but little-known archive of eighteenth-century comic texts, from pamphlets and short-lived periodicals to jestbooks, verse miscellanies, farces, variety shows, and comic fiction. Mainly from the three decades 1740–70, these texts seem almost oblivious to the humanitarian sensibilities we have come to associate with this period. Second, I contest some prevailing tendencies in eighteenth-century studies—the interpretive habits that have kept this archive at the margins of scholarly inquiry. These include the routine treatment of this period as a moment of transition to modernity, and the related emphasis on politeness, sentimentalism, and other "middle-class" values. Third, I offer literary scholars an expanded understanding of some major authors, including Gay, Goldsmith, Aphra Behn, Charlotte Lennox, Lady Mary Wortley Montagu, Richardson, Smollett, Sarah Fielding, Burney, Austen, and Sterne. I devote a central chapter to Henry Fielding, the midcentury author who most urgently engages with contemporary debates about the fragility of sympathy and the dubious joys of laughter.

The raw material of this book will often be distasteful, if not repugnant, to modern readers. Yet these texts reach out to us from such an alien world, and preserve such unfamiliar idioms, that it seemed crucial to quote freely from them rather than reviewing the evidence in more detached ways. For the same reason, I have retained eighteenth-century terminologies in place of preferred modern usages: *cripple, hunchback, dwarf* rather than the currently preferred *little person*; *deaf* rather than *person with deafness*. *Fat, ugly, hag, cuckold*: the brutal directness of such words itself tells us a lot about this world of feeling. Both the primary texts and this book's approach to them raise troubling questions. How should abhorrent aspects of the past be written about? Who should or shouldn't do it? Should they be discussed at all? However these questions are answered, the evidence itself remains, and it won't go away.

NOTE ON PRIMARY SOURCES, QUOTATIONS, AND REFERENCES

Primary sources are quoted exactly as they appear—with all eighteenth-century spellings, capitalization, contractions, and word division. Since it would occur multiple times on every page, I have foregone all use of *sic*. With more canonical texts, unmodernized editions have been used wherever possible (the Florida Sterne, Donald Bond's *Spectator*, Halsband and Grundy's editions of Lady Mary Wortley Montagu, etc.).

In light of recent arguments for the expressive significance of nonstandard punctuation, and because so many of these texts were produced to be read aloud, I have strived to approximate details of layout and typography. Of particular importance to this project, I have retained all italics. Punch lines are often set in italic type, and italic is everywhere used to point up ironies or innuendos that might otherwise be lost on modern readers. This practice, while never consistent, became especially clear in nonliterary sources like newspapers and the Old Bailey Sessions Papers, examined in chapter 5. One of the few disappointments of the Old Bailey digitization project is its romanization of all italic type; citations to this source have been verified against the originals. Unless explicitly identified as mine, all italic text in primary-source quotations is original.

Jestbooks and comic pamphlets are notoriously fugitive texts. They were messily and haphazardly produced. Large numbers give no date in the imprint, and their publishers used all the most artful puffing techniques, including wildly inflated edition numbers. Ongoing work at the *English Short Title Catalogue (ESTC)* is now revealing the extent and diversity of bibliographic guesswork that went on as these books entered collections around the world. Even with easier access to newspaper advertisements and book trade data, it has not always been possible to establish firm publication dates or confirm edition numbers. Perhaps half the relevant *ESTC* dates are conjectural, many of them derived from the old *British Museum Catalogue of Printed Books* and now repeated in *Eighteenth Century Collections Online (ECCO)*. I have used none of these estimates without external confirmation. Occasional corrections to *ESTC* are made silently, and noticeably suspect edition numbers are given in quotation marks. In several cases, it seemed preferable to specify the actual copy consulted.

French and Spanish comic texts are all quoted from contemporary translations: Urquhart and Motteux's Rabelais, Motteux's Cervantes ("the odious Motteux translation," as Samuel Putnam described it), Tom Brown's Scarron, and contemporary versions of Quevédo, *Guzmán*, and *Lazarillo de Tormes*. For all their defects as translations, these were the versions that midcentury authors read and emulated. Biblical quotations are from the King James Version; quotations from Greek and Latin are from Loeb Classical Library editions. With dates before 1753, January 1 is taken as the beginning of the year.

ACKNOWLEDGMENTS

It would be impossible to thank everyone—colleagues, students, librarians, and archivists—who has helped me with this book. My largest debts are to my Stanford mentors. Terry Castle first pointed me toward the forgotten byways of eighteenth-century culture and taught me more about writing than she can ever know. John Bender has been energetically involved with this project since the beginning; I can only hope that the finished product rewards his hopes. Without the example and encouragement of Hans-Ulrich Gumbrecht, I would never have plunged so deeply into a single historical moment. Also at Stanford, I owe many valuable insights to W. B. Carnochan, Maureen Harkin, and Suvir Kaul. The most scholarly of librarians, William McPheron was also an unrivaled critic of academic prose.

I first conceived this study during a fellowship at the Stanford Humanities Center; I thank Keith Baker and the center staff for that year in ideal surroundings. The book was then rewritten during two years at the Michigan Society of Fellows in Ann Arbor. For this period of intense intellectual dialogue, I remain eternally grateful to James Boyd White and my fellow fellows. Also in Ann Arbor I found Dena Goodman in history, Ross Chambers in French, and wonderful interlocutors in English, notably Julie Ellison, Lincoln Faller, Scotti Parrish, Adela Pinch, David Porter, Michael Schoenfeldt, Tobin Siebers, and Martha Vicinus. At Toronto, I am particularly blessed with colleagues in my field, including John Baird, Alan Bewell, Brian Corman, Richard Greene, H. J. Jackson, Tom Keymer, Susan Lamb, Deidre Lynch, Mary Nyquist, Carol Percy, and Dan White. All have generously responded to various parts of the manuscript.

Beyond these institutions, several colleagues have read large sections or the entire manuscript: Donna Andrew, John Beattie, Robert D. Hume, Paula McDowell, Nicholas Rogers, and Simon Stern. Only time prevents me from pursuing every one of their suggestions. An early version of chapter 5 was presented at New York University in April 2008 as part of the symposium "Writing Women, 1700–1800." I thank Paula McDowell and Bryan Waterman for their invitation, my fellow participants for valuable feedback, and Mary Poovey for her formal response. I wish I had kept a record of everyone else who has answered local questions, shared work in progress, or directed me to sources. I fear that the following list, compiled from memory, must make some dreadful omissions. For manifold scholarly kindnesses, I thank Paula Backscheider, Jerry Beasley, Toni Bowers, Marshall Brown, Jill Campbell, E. J. Clery, Alison Conway, Lennard Davis, Helen Deutsch, Jan Fergus, Todd Gilman, George Haggerty, Tim Hitchcock, Maya Jasanoff, Thomas Lockwood, Judith Milhous, Franco Moretti, Felicity Nussbaum, Ronald Paulson, Adam Potkay, James Raven, Claude Rawson, Pat Rogers, Laura Rosenthal, Peter Sabor, Kevin Sienna, Jane Spencer, Susan Staves, and John Allen Stevenson. For early advice, I am indebted to the late Roy Porter. Several wonderful research assistants have been especially involved: Andrew Bricker, Benjamin Heller, Claire Laville, Jap Makkar, and Sean Tommasi.

I thank everyone at Chicago: Alan Thomas for his consistent faith in the project, Randy Petilos for good-humored answers to my many questions, Sandra Hazel for enforcing production deadlines, and Joe Brown for his patient but exacting copyediting. I hope my two anonymous readers will see how much the final version owes to their shrewd and detailed critiques.

Portions of chapter 1 were previously published in "Hilarity and Pitilessness in the Mid-Eighteenth Century: English Jestbook Humor," *Eighteenth Century Studies* 37, no. 1 (2003): 1–22. © 2003 by The American Society for Eighteenth-Century Studies. Reprinted with permission of The Johns Hopkins University Press. Portions of chapter 4 were previously published in "Joseph Andrews and the Great Laughter Debate," *Studies in Eighteenth-Century Culture* 34 (2005): 271–332. © 2005 by The American Society for Eighteenth-Century Studies. Reprinted with permission of The Johns Hopkins University Press. For their editorial acumen, I would like to thank Bernadette Fort and Catherine Ingrassia.

This book would not have been possible without specialists at the British Library, the Guildhall Library, the Bodleian Library, Westminster City Archives, London Metropolitan Archives, and the British Museum Department of Prints and Drawings. I am especially grateful to Clive Hurst at the Bodleian and Sheila O'Connell at the British Museum. In North America I am indebted to Alan Jutzie and Steven Tabor at the Huntington Library, and to experts at the Getty Center in Los Angeles, the Lewis Walpole Library, and the Yale Center for British Art. For all the everyday courtesies that make scholarship possible, I thank the campus libraries at Stanford, Michigan, and Toronto. For friendship and sustenance of other kinds, I thank my family and Neville Austin, Helen Blythe, Ruchi Choudhary, Michael Golston, Mark Hutchinson, Anne Keary, Awino Kürth, Mia Lee, Miguel Lobo, Chris Matzner, Isabel McIntosh, Nicky Murphy, Amir Najmi, Arlo Upton, and Rasmus Winther.

The Unsentimental
Eighteenth Century, 1740–70

Eighteenth-century Britons—or a high proportion of them—openly delighted in the miseries of others. Women as well as men laughed at cripples and hunchbacks. They tormented lunatics and led blind men into walls. Wife beating was a routine way of maintaining order within marriage—"an honest Englishman hates his wife" went the catchphrase. Types of violence that would now count as rape were almost mainstream sexual behaviors. Social hierarchies were part of God's plan, and those less favored were habitual figures of fun. Gentlemen beat their servants and scoffed at the hungry peasants who crouched along the road outside every major town. Yet social equals were no more likely to sympathize. Useless old women, village idiots, starving paupers, bastard bearers from the next parish—none of them attracted much sympathy from their own kind. Ridiculing and inflicting pain were everyday amusements, and powerful forces were defending them. Violence, intolerance, and schadenfreude were all tolerated as unavoidable side effects of British liberty, if not its very foundation.

This is not, safe to say, our prevailing image of the mid-eighteenth century. Recent scholarship has created a much kindlier picture, stressing benevolence, polite manners, Enlightenment rationality, and an increasing idealization of women. Social historians have described a dynamic "consumer society," a world of coffeehouses, pleasure gardens, and concert rooms. Congenial accounts of the eighteenth century have come and gone over the years, from Saintsbury's nostalgic *Peace of the Augustans* (1915) to the first, mid-twentieth-century "Age of Sensibility" with its cluster of male lyric poets (Thomson, Gray, Collins, and the rest). The latest version clearly owes a lot to work on the urban commercial classes—the elusive "middling sort" that was for so long almost ignored by early modern historians. The gradual process by which this "class" gained a sense of identity and achieved a moral and cultural authority to match its economic power has been one of the three or four great questions of modern British history. The most influential answers have pointed to a self-conscious politeness and sentimentality that enabled the newly prosperous trading class to differentiate itself at once from the mob below and the corrupt aristocracy above. We now know more than ever about the large-scale charities that accompanied the new ethical norms: hospitals and institutions for orphans, reformed prostitutes, disabled soldiers, and the blind. We have found the new standards promoted by a rapidly expanding print culture—by conduct literature, moral periodicals, and fictional or dramatic genres specializing in virtue in distress.

Of course no one suggests that any of this happened overnight. The appalling inequalities, misogyny, and violence of the age are never far away—the beggar women who gave birth in the streets, the broken farm laborers who drank themselves to death, the Bridewells, workhouses, and press-gangs. The squalor of Hogarth's *Gin Lane* and the brutality of *The Four Stages of Cruelty* are close at hand. We know about the cockfights and bullbaiting, the xenophobic mobs, executions, and homosexuals stoned to death in the pillory. And we think of literary instances: the hyperbolic brutalities of Swift, Smollett, and Voltaire; the churchyard brawl in *Tom Jones* and the unforgettable old women's footrace in Burney's *Evelina*. New work on the history of disability has taught us much about what it was like to live with physical impairments in this culture. We are learning more and more about the belligerence of British nationalism and the atrocities that went on at the fringes of the empire. And more important to my purposes here, scholars of sentimentalism and politeness have consistently emphasized the contested and contradictory nature of both projects. Pity mingled with heartlessness in every context. Sentimental novelists were preoccupied with the weakness and unreliability of sympathy, even as they extolled it. Lawrence Klein has consistently emphasized the ambiguities and contradictions of politeness, beginning with problems in the Shaftesbury manuscripts themselves.[1]

But a cumulative impression has nevertheless emerged—an effect quite independent of the subtlety of individual studies. So much good scholarship on politeness, sensibility, the middling sort, and the forces of change has turned the British into a "polite and commercial people" (as Paul Langford's title puts it).[2] As so often happens, powerful analytic perspectives have over time become reified as aprioristic categories—as the expectations or presuppositions with which we approach the past. The term *politeness* has moved far beyond its specialist historical use for behaviors facilitating interactions between strangers and social unequals. So much good scholarship on sentimental literature has effectively created a countercanon (certainly it is hard now to put ourselves back into the situation Terry Eagleton described in 1982, when he wondered whether "we may now once again be able to read Samuel Richardson").[3] In anthologies, literary histories, and syllabi, the middle decades of the eighteenth century have switched wholesale from the old Age of Johnson into the new Age of Sensibility.[4] Exactly how all this happened—how changes in British history coincided with new directions in the history of ideas, evolving critical practices in English departments, and changing demands on the academy as a whole—is a fascinating but hugely complex question. The simplified answer is that the politeness-sensibility paradigm is a compound formation: a critical mass of scholars has now focused on this cluster of phenomena, just as a previous generation decided that Johnson was the defining or most interesting figure of his age.

However it happened, one now detects a growing perception that the paradigm may have spread too far. David Fairer opens his recent overview of eighteenth-century poetry by explicitly contesting the prevailing "idealized picture" of this culture. Ideals and exhortations are too often taken as descriptions, he warns. This was not a polite world but "an impolite world that talked much about politeness." The historian Helen Berry finds assumptions about politeness creeping back into the late seventeenth century.[5] By 2000, Langford himself was wondering whether politeness had become an overly "fashionable" topic, and offering a partial correction with his study of European attitudes toward the British. Eighteenth-century visitors to Britain found the locals fractious and uncouth. The men were drunkards and lovers of cruel sports, with gross manners and hideous attitudes toward women, but British women were themselves shockingly indelicate. Such criticisms seem like mere national prejudice until one notices that native moralists were saying the same.[6] These ruder traits have now been explored (for a later period) by Vic Gatrell's study of graphic satire between 1780 and 1830. Writing explicitly against the "politeness paradigm," Gatrell describes a coarse but exuberant world of violence, drunkenness, and sexual freedom. In the process, he offers a strikingly unfamiliar picture of middle-class life: a "rough, struggling world" of unpolished artisans and hard-headed shopkeepers.[7]

Cruelty and Laughter aims not to displace the current emphasis, but to qualify it and to explore the baffling coexistence of what to modern readers seem like inconsistent impulses. Politeness and sentimentality were powerful ideals, but they had to compete with older freedoms. Certainly the middling sort was on the rise, but its political challenge was slower, and widespread changes in manners and tastes were slower still. Campaigns for the reformation of manners were taking on deep-seated habits. Instructions about kindness to strangers had to compete with age-old mistrusts and the elemental pleasure of throwing stones. Sentimental representations of rape victims were everywhere to be found by the 1750s, but in everyday situations few believed a woman who claimed to have been raped, and convictions were all but impossible to achieve. To the extent that such phenomena lend themselves to statistical analysis, the numbers prove that sentimental ideals were far from dominant in literature or any other area of cultural production. In his most recent overview of eighteenth-century theater studies, Robert D. Hume wonders at the persistent "myth of sentimental dominance." Sentimental drama "was never by any definition even remotely close to dominant." Revivals of old plays formed the bulk of the repertoire; sentimental drama never accounted for more than 10 percent of performances, and usually much less than that. Looking back on his exhaustive trawl through eighteenth-century poetry, Roger Lonsdale marvels to find so many poets indifferent to the emerging standards of politeness and preromantic sensibility.[8] Women as well as men wrote curses, lampoons, bawdy epigrams, and demotic verses about boxing, farting, and throwing up. They wrote long, pitiless poems about old maids and hunchbacks in love. Hence one of the recurring themes of this book: the sheer slowness with which ordinary sufferings—the unheroic miseries of poverty, the humiliations of disease, the private trauma of a rape victim—became worthy of sympathy and serious aesthetic representation.

To expose the enduring heartlessness of this world is in no sense to remasculinize the eighteenth century—to return to an old male canon or to moribund historical perspectives that simply left women out. Beyond the chapter on Fielding, *Cruelty and Laughter* draws on now-canonized women writers as much as any of the old guard. The bulk of my sources—by men, women, and anonymous authors who could be either—will never be canonical. At the same time, however, our polite-sentimental impression of this culture does owe a lot to feminist theory and ongoing work to recover women as authors, readers, and central characters in fiction. For scholars of the mid-eighteenth century, this has meant looking at Richardson and the "modest" middle generation of early women writers—those who made authorship respectable for women after the scandal of Behn, Manley, and Haywood. Along with the earlier Bluestockings, novelists like Sarah Fielding, Sarah Scott, Frances Sheridan, and

Frances Brooke largely restricted themselves to accepted "female" subjects. They produced tracts on education and child rearing, conduct books, devotional texts, and fictional adaptations of these ideals like Fielding's *The Governess* (1749) and Scott's *Millenium Hall* (1762). One prominent body of fiction and advice literature focused on genteel courtship and the difficulty of marrying well without compromising one's virtue or disobeying one's parents. Said to be uniquely qualified for representing strong emotions, women writers produced tragic-sentimental seduction plots and reiterated confrontations with human evil like Fielding's *David Simple* (1744-53). These restrictions of subject matter were for midcentury women writers the "terms of acceptance," as Jane Spencer put it—the condition for being taken up by male patrons and publishers. No wonder so many early feminist scholars put aside these texts with disappointment, concluding that feminism had all but gone to sleep until the 1790s.[9]

For all its simplification of the range of women's writing and the experimentation of individual texts, the three-phase generational pattern has its descriptive value. Midcentury women's writing does look painfully restrained beside Wollstonecraft's *Vindication* (1792), Inchbald's *Nature and Art* (1796), or Mary Hays's astonishing *Memoirs of Emma Courtney* (1796). By the early 1740s, even Eliza Haywood was producing more right-minded fiction, none of it published under her own name. More to the point, these midcentury texts have now been so intensively studied that they can easily seem representational. So many domestic courtship plots—most of them focused on and addressed to the upper ranks of society—inevitably create a sense of narrowed possibilities. What sticks in the mind are the polished manners and propriety of speech, the exquisitely felt moral dilemmas of Sheridan's *Sidney Biddulph* (1767), or the David Simple circle weeping so helplessly at the villainies of the world. Exemplary acts of benevolence, uncompromising modesty, careful discussions of proper and improper reading: these are the predominant images of midcentury women's writing.

All the more reason to pay serious attention to recent historical work on the range of action and possibility for eighteenth-century women. Vigorously contesting old clichés about separate spheres, Amanda Vickery, Linda Colley, Charlotte Sussman, Karen O'Brien, and others have found eighteenth-century women leading visible and active lives, often intensely engaged in public and political debate. Among other things, these scholars confirm that women were present in all manner of public spaces: not just the assembly rooms, theaters, and pleasure gardens, but also the more mixed environments of fairgrounds and public parks. Women were at the assizes and Old Bailey sessions; they watched executions and floggings from carriages and upstairs windows. Far from delicate, Amanda Vickery's Lancashire gentlewomen were pragmatic and assertive, tough-minded managers of servants and household economies. They were stoic rather than helpless in the face of adversity and scornful of emotional self-indulgence. In turn, new research on book-trade data has now established the surprising range of women's reading matter. Women read everything I discuss in this book—all the lowest farces, jestbooks, and rascally "male" novels.[10]

This new historical work reminds us that all the cautions about delicacy, benevolence, sexual modesty, and the proper use of time would hardly be necessary if women were already following them. *Cruelty and Laughter* uses everyday humor and comic literature as uniquely rich illustrations of this gulf between precept and practice. From the constant dire warnings in the advice literature, one could easily assume that a collective anhedonia had descended on the entire female sex. ("Wit is the most dangerous talent you can possess," begins the relevant section of Dr. Gregory's gloomy *Legacy to His Daughters*.)[11] Throughout this study, I find women laughing at the same comic objects as men—all the hunchbacks, stutterers, and nasty old maids. Perhaps they do so with a parade of disapproval; perhaps they leave the room first, as many conduct writers suggest. But they laugh nonetheless and write to their friends about it. Crucial sources here have been the enormous number of unpublished writings that continue to emerge from the archives—diaries, letters, commonplace books, collections of family poetry, and the like.[12] The women who step out of such sources are unexpectedly protean, alternately sentimental and caustic, high-minded and bluntly unillusioned. Many agree that doing good was a great pleasure, but the impulse clearly came and went. Women send each other pitiless recollections of tedious social occasions and mock elegies for hated relatives; suddenly one finds them discussing the poor qualifications of various suitors and sending along caricatures or impromptu riddles. To go from *Millenium Hall* to the Montagu correspondence in the Huntington Library is to feel that Sarah Scott and her sister suddenly come to life. Alternating between a deeply Anglican morality, gossip, and strikingly unguarded jokes about sex, this and so many other manuscript collections bristle with inconsistencies that we have still to comprehend.

As we are often reminded, the point of print was a definite threshold for many of these women. Yet the more we dig around the margins of the women's canon, the more diversity we find, and the further we get from conventionally feminine styles and subject matter. One great surprise throughout this project was the volume and inventiveness of women's comic publications. Some of this qualifies as subversive or antipatriarchal humor and has therefore been studied, but at least as much resists feminist perspectives and therefore has no champions. Scholars have long discussed such limitations: the problems of how we read, and what gets left out, when our primary question with all women writers is their gender. In a recent state-of-the-field essay—an introduction to commemorate the thirty-fifth anniversary of the American Society for Eighteenth-Century Studies (ASECS) women's caucus—Laura Rosenthal wonders how this gender determinism may be hampering our understanding of such authors as Aphra Behn and Lady Mary Wortley Montagu. While both are now fully "recovered," Rosenthal finds both still treated in highly selective ways; neither is yet available in all her ambiguity and self-contradiction.[13] Probably it is no accident that Behn and Montagu were such major sources for this book. Both take up subjects that every modern reader, male or female, will find disturbing. Particularly shocking, both repeat and elaborate on some chilling patriarchal assumptions about sexual violence. So, unfortunately, do Haywood, Lennox, and, most surprising of all, Sarah Fielding. Discovering unpleasant secrets in justly admired authors was a challenge that arrived early on in this project and never went away.

*

To many historians, any analysis of changing manners, tastes, and gender norms falls naturally into a question of continuity and change: the perennial challenge of determining the balance of inertia and progress at each historical moment. How to separate out the strands or layers of history, all of them moving at different speeds—some racing ahead, others halting and contested but nevertheless moving on, and others so slow as to seem immobile? A commonsense materialist would point to the economy as the first thing to change, followed by social formations, discourse, and politics and only then by culture as broadly conceived. In practice, however, one finds constant exceptions and variabilities, all manner of ruptures, resistances, and unexpected causalities. Literature, as Raymond Williams reminded us, has an autonomy of its own, sometimes naturalizing a reigning ideology and at other times imagining new social identities or even bringing them into existence. And so it was with politeness and sensibility. New forms of wealth were clearly creating new social identities, conscious behaviors and tastes were following behind, and cultural activity was taking place at every point of the continuum, embodying residual, dominant, and emergent forces.[14]

Yet beneath such tangible developments lie habits and perceptions that are always slower to change. The base materials of my study—spontaneous pleasures, unquestioned assumptions and belief systems, almost automatic reactions like laughter—will always resist change more stubbornly than other areas of culture. Few people listen when someone tells them not to have fun. Indeed the strident reforming discourse of this age—all the charity sermons and periodical moralizing, the sentimental novels about helpless virgins and gloomy old soldiers—surely attests less to the triumph of sensibility than to its failures, to the endurance of older and less sympathetic pleasures. Inertias and resistances of this sort are historical forces as powerful as the momentums of change, but they are less often explored. Searching for models as I began work on this project, I found myself thinking back to the early *mentalité* historians: to Febvre and Bloch, and especially to books like Bloch's *Royal Touch* (1924), with its dazzling account of the persistence of monarchical superstition into the age of Descartes and beyond. For all their problems—generalizations about collective belief systems, speculations about lived experience, the perennial reluctance to talk about politics—these scholars still offer some of the best reminders of the layered nature of history and the inevitable lag as sensibilities and belief systems adapt to material, political, or cultural change.[15]

These distinctions are important because so much of the best recent work in eighteenth-century studies has stressed the new that was emerging, and this emphasis has tended collectively to speed up our perceptions of change at every level of culture. Again, this forward-looking bias starts to make sense once one looks back on the recent development of British historical scholarship. Just twenty years ago, eighteenth-century historians were routinely complaining that no one had looked seriously at the new commercial classes and the widespread changes they produced. The rise of the middle class was an ancient topic in economic history, but political and social historians were more interested in analyzing the stability that followed the settlement of 1688—the "Hanoverian peace" consolidated by Walpole and maintained by Lewis Namier's local oligarchs. The major challenge to this perspective came from Marxist historians, most influentially in E. P. Thompson's bipolar model of struggle between patricians and plebeians. But Thompson had no more to say about the middling sort than did Namier or J. H. Plumb.

After two decades of phenomenally energetic work, we now have a much fuller understanding not just of this emerging class but of all the momentous changes of the age—of economic growth, urbanization, and the beginnings of industrial production; of secularization and the rise of modern science; and of the rise of an assertive bourgeoisie, with consequent changes in gender roles and political discourse, and eventually, the emergence of humanitarian

sensibility and modern human rights.[16] At the same time, the base justifications we make as historians and literary critics have altered almost beyond
recognition. Exploring change now provides one of our most reliable arguments for the relevance of this period and its literature, one we all use with
students and skeptical laypeople. It is enshrined in the official mission statement of ASECS, with its emphatically upbeat promotion of "a time that has
profoundly influenced our world."

For literary scholars, forward-looking perspectives have offered a way of
escaping stuffy assumptions about Augustan values and the canon of Swift,
Pope, Johnson, Gibbon, and Burke, each of them treated as a sort of last stand
against modernity. By the mid-1980s, the old formalist ideals were themselves
dying out, and the field was shifting its attention to texts more intricately engaged with the changes of the age. The Foucauldian turn toward discourse
meant that texts could now be seen not just as reflections but as agents of
those changes—as emergent phenomena.[17] These developments have been
aided by progressively easier access to the vast and scattered archive of
eighteenth-century printed matter. Huge bodies of forgotten texts have now
been explored—literary periodicals, drama, travel writing, more poetry than
we ever suspected, and the extraordinary mass of sentimental fiction. Frac-
tured and deeply ambiguous, these last texts might have been tailor-made for
the new critical preferences, each one an endlessly analyzable artifact of contemporary conflicts about class, gender, and social change.

But it is worth pausing to consider the aggregate effects of so many forward-looking perspectives. Looking for elements of the new is both a selective
and a familiarizing perspective. What gets left behind are all the most unfamiliar texts, everything irrelevant to subsequent developments. One consequence of so many studies of emergence is an impression that the beginnings
of long-term changes were typical of the age as a whole. To be sure, this is a
cumulative phenomenon, not the intention of any one study. No one claims
that change was anything but contested and uneven. And in making these
cautions I am building on long-standing habits of self-criticism in eighteenth-
century studies. Our field has been singularly preoccupied with questions of
periodization. (Why 1700–1800 or 1660–1815? Why not 1667 or 1689? Why
not a long seventeenth century from 1603 to 1714 followed by a short eighteenth century ending in 1776, 1780, or 1798?)[18] Current scholars are pursuing these problems more intensely than ever, exploring the mingling of tradition and innovation at every cultural moment. We now have much clearer
demonstrations that satire and other public genres endured as the romantic
lyric was emerging, that Pope and Johnson remained influential well into the

nineteenth century, and so on. More important, eighteenth-century scholars have been warning against teleology for generations. Poetry specialists have repeatedly insisted that we will never understand mid-eighteenth-century poetry unless we stop looking for anticipations of romanticism. Scholars of early women's fiction long ago demonstrated that we have to put aside narratives about the rise of realism if we are make sense of Behn, Manley, Haywood, and other long-scorned authors.

This single-genre scholarship provides invaluable demonstrations that anyone aspiring to a genuinely historicist picture of the literary past must try to put aside, at least temporarily, their knowledge of what happened next. My focus in this study is not a genre but a slice of time, the thirty years 1740–70. The majority of my sources—literary and paraliterary texts, plays, letters, diaries, and newspapers—were written, reprinted, or restaged during these decades. In looking at reprints and restagings, I am clearly opting for the *parliament* model of literary history rather than the *parade*: I look at the full range of texts available at this historical moment, inherited as well as new.[19] My persistent questions are the following: What would this period look like if we didn't know about the rise of the middle class or the emergence of proletarian class consciousness? About industrialization, the French Revolution, or the Reform Bill? About Wollstonecraft or Victorian gender norms, emerging standards of politeness, or modern human rights? What would mid-eighteenth-century literature would look like if we tried not to think about romanticism or the triumph of novelistic realism? That these goals are unachievable goes without saying; inevitably, the chronological self-limitation works better with some subjects than others. But as a heuristic gesture, it has been immensely productive. A narrower time frame means a vastly expanded sample size. By concentrating on thirty years, I am able to explore minor as well as accepted canonical texts, newspapers and ephemera, and then move beyond print to manuscripts, material objects, and social practices. This period looks very different once one approaches it not for evidence of the new that was emerging, but as a richly textured world in which people lived, laughed, suffered, and read books.

Cruelty and Laughter presents the fruit of this experiment. For the moment I should like to emphasize two points. First is the self-evident fact that historical witnesses never experience change as it is retrospectively described ("the Fabrice syndrome" Eric Hobsbawm calls this phenomenon, after the uncomprehending hero of Stendhal's *Chartreuse de Parme*).[20] *Rise of the middle class, bourgeois revolution, industrial revolution*: these and other dialectical terms are the metaphors of nineteenth-century historians and vastly overestimate contemporaries' understanding of the changes through which they were living. This is not to say that no one noticed what was happening around them: social change was a recurring subject of urban print culture. But such educated sources are in no way typical of the age, and not even the most prescient can see into the future. In retrospect, politer manners and more sympathetic attitudes toward others seem like the way of the future, but many contemporaries dismissed them as passing affectations or fruitless attempts to undermine British manhood. The same cautions apply to literary history: a number of contemporaries did recognize the novel as a "new species of writing," but the genre's long-term dominance was far from obvious. Indeed, by the late 1750s many people thought the fad was over, as they watched fiction degrading into a mass of derivative texts.[21]

Second, dialectical history resolves apparent contradictions into old and new, and in speaking of static and dynamic phenomena I have done the same. But consistency is a culturally relative concept, and what we now think of as incongruous reactions were in the mid-eighteenth century alternate and even compatible possibilities. A starving widow or ruined maiden, a frail hunchback feeling her way along the pavement, a shoeless beggar crouching in a ditch, an old soldier with a wooden leg—the same sight made one person laugh and another cry. One person followed the Christian duty to relieve distress, while someone else triumphed and compounded that distress. Confronted with identical spectacles of suffering, the same individual might laugh one day and weep the next. The baffling unpredictability of such responses is one of the most perplexing of all human phenomena, in this or any other culture. Laughter and tears are proverbially interchangeable reactions, and beyond them one imagines myriad possible reactions to the same spectacle of suffering—horror, disgust, anger, sadness, delight, or even sexual arousal. In the mid-eighteenth century I am exploring a historical moment at which these instabilities were especially overt. Pity coexisted with indifference; sympathy was fleeting, unstable, and easily transformed into malice or delight. It is a strange and unsettling world of feeling; evoking its paradoxes without resolving them into old and new has been one great challenge of this project.

One can hardly go further without addressing the political implications of such a project. In British studies, at least, any proposal to suspend teleology inevitably recalls the most virulent disputes in postwar history. One thinks immediately of the row between revisionist historians of the early seventeenth century (Elton, Russell, and others who analyzed static moments and refused to relate them to what came next) and Marxist or narrative historians like Hill and Stone. (Narrative, said Hill, was "the only possible historical attitude"; anything else was "sentimental antiquarianism." Stone was still more emphatic: "If history is not concerned with change, it is nothing.")[22] In eighteenth-century studies, the continuity pole was occupied in very different ways by the old secular Hanoverian peace or the Whig supremacy and then by J. C. D. Clark's account of eighteenth-century England as a monarchical and religious society comparable to the Continental anciens régimes. Both positions have been contested first by Thompsonian Marxists and then by more recent work on commercialization and the middling sort. Several times attempting to ease the tension, Roy Porter stressed that there was nothing inherently conservative or radical about either perspective: analyzing static structures or long-term continuities can be politically progressive (as it is in the work of Perry Anderson).[23] And ultimately both perspectives are indispensable to a full picture of the past—the synchronic or spatial axis of experience as well as the diachronic or temporal one.

Beyond these national disputes, suspending teleology is one of the oldest and most useful of defamiliarizing tools, recommended by historians of every stripe. It was important to the *Geistesgeschichte* of Schleiermacher and Dilthey and is now central to the contextual history of ideas developed by J. G. A. Pocock and Quentin Skinner. Scholars of early modern religious writing have repeatedly emphasized the importance of getting back to a time before secularization and post-Enlightenment assumptions that this was a good thing. The gesture of cutting ties with the present has been equally important to more polemical historians. Thus post-Foucauldian projects focusing on historical moments at which gender identities or sexual practices were freer, or radical legal theories of the sort developed by Peter Goodrich, all of them striving to rescue failed potentials as the basis of contemporary critique.[24] Such perspectives now gain particular relevance from widespread perceptions of the impossibility of narrative. The collapse of the *grands récits*, we are often told, means that cultural history can be written only in disconnected episodes, as in the work of T. J. Clark or Denis Hollier's *New History of French Literature*.[25] Landscape, terrain, archaeology—these are the metaphors of so much of the most fruitful recent work in cultural history. In the strictest sense, one can never avoid presentism; "really dead" history, as Carlo Ginzburg once called it, does not exist.[26] But a working terminal date does at least discourage teleology. One can go a long way by avoiding forward-looking terms and especially the dialectical rhetoric that continues to proliferate in our field (*sentimental revolution, financial revolution, consumer revolution, explosion of print*, to mention only a few recent additions).

Attempts at synchronicity can be especially useful countergestures with moments traditionally taken as turning points. These potentials were long ago demonstrated by single-year studies like Jean Starobinski's phenomenological account of 1789 (which treats the Revolution as just one of a dozen or so significant "images" of that year) or Hans-Robert Jauss's famous seminar on 1857. The year 1857 has always been an iconic date in French literary history, the year of both *Madame Bovary* and *Les fleurs du mal*. Jauss and his students put Flaubert and Baudelaire to one side and explored the mass of forgotten writings that surrounded them. Sampling more than seven hundred lyric poems written in 1857, they were struck most of all by the overwhelming stagnation of belief and aesthetic practice.[27] Both projects have their problems (Jauss's generalizations about "the contemporary reader" being only the most obvious). But they do show what a refusal of teleology and a detailed contextualization can do to the orthodox structuring of historical time. *Cruelty and Laughter* focuses on a longer period, but the mid-eighteenth century is a watershed as important to Western historians as the Reformation or the French Revolution. Dates around 1750 still carry almost mythic force as transitions between old and new—moments of large-scale social and economic changes, scientific and technological discoveries, and literary innovations. A quick title search through any research library finds hundreds of recent monographs—in literary studies and social, economic, and political history—with 1740, 1745, 1750, 1760, or 1763 as either a starting or an ending date.[28] Few fail to comment on the arbitrariness of their dates, but cumulatively they create an impression.

So what does the mid-eighteenth century look like once one puts aside one's knowledge of what happened next? One finds everything irrelevant to the teleologies of mainstream history, everything that has not been handed down—"the rubbish-heap of history," Walter Benjamin once called it, everything that fell by the wayside as history moved on.[29] Texts without long-term influence, doomed belief systems, social practices or modes of speech that bourgeois manners would stamp out: all this becomes visible once one strives to avoid teleology. One finds masses of trashy ephemeral texts: failed experiments, ham-fisted novels that were read for a season and then forgotten. And one finds authors from the recent past who remained vital parts of mid-century culture. Tom Brown, Rochester, Scarron, Aphra Behn, Ned Ward, D'Urfey—all these humorists went through multiple midcentury editions or performances. In paying attention to such texts, I may at least intermittently address complaints, from Steven Zwicker and others, that the recent self-consciousness about crossing period boundaries has produced far fewer studies looking backward to the seventeenth century than looking forward to the nineteenth.[30]

Because they most forcefully struck me as left behind, this book focuses on an archive of forgotten comic texts. Some fall easily into recognizable genres—jestbooks, one-act farces, collections of drinking songs—but most are less definable. There are brief "memoirs" of celebrated wits and short-lived comic periodicals like *The Weekly Amusement, All-Alive and Merry,* or *The Jester's Magazine.* There are epigrams on one-eyed ladies of fashion and illustrated broadsides about rape or Welsh baiting. Women and men alike wrote masses of antisentimental texts: burlesque "she" tragedies, mock epistolary novels about communities of weepy rustics, epitaphs for hated wives who choke on fish bones, mock consolations addressed to syphilitics who lose their nose, every one of them making fun of the very possibility of tender feelings. Yet all this coexists with polite and sentimental texts. Wife-beating catches appear alongside the preromantic lyrics of Gray and Collins; *Clarissa* appears alongside clumsy novels about strolling players or hard-drinking smugglers.

*

Chapter 1 begins deep in the archive, examining more than two hundred midcentury jestbooks. An exploration of production, distribution, and reading practices leads me to affirm recent arguments about the diversity of female tastes in this period. Chapter 2 pushes the evidence from printed jokes about deformity to theaters and street corners and finally into the realm of everyday experience. Chapter 3 takes up an issue that can be avoided no longer: the distasteful class contexts of so much of this humor. By chapter 4, I have accumulated sufficient background to offer a densely contextual reading of Fielding's *Joseph Andrews,* a text that brings together so many of its culture's debates about the nature and ethics of laughter. In the process, I necessarily take up some of the thornier issues in Fielding scholarship. Chapter 5 attempts a very different challenge, exploring a large and deeply unsettling body of midcentury rape jokes. Since so many of these focus on the legal treatment of rape, I pursue the evidence into judicial contexts, where the impulse to scoff produced its most painful consequences. In the conclusion, I present a systematic analysis of a subgenre I have drawn on throughout: almost ninety forgotten comic novels published during the three decades of my study. Mingling tenderness and brutality, these texts are almost opaque to modern readers, but they were popular with male and female readers and at least as profitable as the now-familiar sentimental fiction of the age.

Cruelty and Laughter thus offers two detailed discussions of profitable but neglected comic genres (chapter 1 and the conclusion), one focused analysis of a canonical text (chapter 4), and three case studies that bring together literature and social history to expose the limits of sympathy in mid-eighteenth-century culture (chapters 2, 3, and 5). Rather than generalizing about this culture as a whole, each section explores a significant cluster of texts or a well-documented cultural phenomenon. At the same time, jestbooks, ramble novels, and burlesque rape trials are not marginal phenomena. They are not eccentric "anecdotes" of the sort associated with the new historicism (and recently reaffirmed by Stephen Greenblatt and Catherine Gallagher as the very key to their method).[31] Nor are they deliberately archaic phenomena—the "hindrances" or "resistances" of Annales historians. I do not discuss scold's bridles or superstitions about dwarfs; there is no mention of badger baiting or shin-kicking contests (although one finds ample evidence of all these things). My focus on London sources was partly a practical matter, but it also enabled me to confront presumptions that less sympathetic pleasures could have survived only in isolated parts of the country. Dancing cripples, little ditties about hunchbacks, and five-shilling comic miscellanies published every Christmas were part of the metropolitan entertainment economy. They were commercial entertainments as popular and as profitable as the music parties, operas, and high-minded dramas. How polite and well-heeled consumers reconciled pleasures that seem so incompatible to us remains a central question at every point of this book.

CHAPTER ONE

Jestbooks and the Indifference to Reform

What did British people laugh at in the mid-eighteenth century? The literary record offers a partial answer in the corrective laughter of Augustan satire, the cuckolds and sex plots of stage comedy, and the familiar cast of Irish idiots and *soupe-maigre* Frenchmen. The tortured distinction between true and false wit is an ancient topic in eighteenth-century studies. Historians of popular culture have told us much about the humor of protest. But what did people laugh at in everyday situations—in streets, coffeehouses, and polite assemblies? One might begin, like a good ethnographer, with a few jokes:

> A Man being very much diseased and weak, was bemoaning himself to his only Son, whom he loved very well: For, *Jack*, says he, if I stand, my Legs ach; if I kneel, my Knees ach; if I go, my Feet ach; if I lie, then my Back achs; if I sit, my Hips ach; and if I lean, my Elbows ach. Why truly Father, says he (like a good dutiful Child) I advise you to hang yourself for an Hour or two, and if that does not do, then come to me again.[1]

> One Day in the Grove, [Beau Nash] joined some Ladies, and asking *one* of them, who was crooked, whence she came? She replied, *Strait* from *London. Indeed, Madam*, said he, *then you must have been confoundedly warpt by the Way*.[2]

> One observing a crooked Fellow in close Argument with another, who would have dissuaded him from some inconsiderable Resolution, said to

his Friend, *Prithee let him alone, and say no more to him, you see he's* bent *upon it.*[3]

A Welchman begging upon the road came to a farm-house, where they fill'd his belly with whey, that it made his guts to ake: Hur prays to St. Davy for comfort; an owl being at roost in the barn, as he held up his head a praying, the owl shit just in his mouth. *O thank good St.* Davy, *for hur desired but a drop, but hur hath given hur a mouthful.*[4]

One *Easter Monday*, an arch Rogue meeting a *blind* Woman who was crying Puddings and Pies, taking her by the Arm said Come along with me Dame, I am going to *Moorfields*, where this Holliday-time, you may Chance to meet with good Custom. Thank'e kindly, Sir, says she. Whereupon he conducted her to *Cripplegate* Church, and placed her in the middle Isle. Now, says he, you are in *Moorfields*: which she believing to be true, immediately cried out, *Hot Puddings and Pies! Hot Puddings and Pies! come their all Hot!* &c. which caused the whole Congregation to burst out in a loud Laughter, and the Clerk came and told her she was in a Church: You are a lying son of a Whore, says she. Which so enraged the Clerk, that he dragged her out of the Church: she cursing and damning him all the while, nor would she believe him 'till she heard the Organs play.[5]

A young Man married to an ill-temper'd Woman, who not contented, tho' he was very kind to her, made continual Complaints to her Father, to the great Grief of both Families; the Husband, no longer able to endure this scurvy Humour, bang'd her soundly: Hereupon she complain'd to her Father, who understanding well the Perverseness of her Humour, took her to Task, and lac'd her Sides soundly too; saying, *Go, commend me to your Husband, and tell him, I am now even with him, for I have cudgell'd his Wife, as he hath beaten my Daughter.*[6]

Modern readers will be struck by the callousness of these jokes, their frank delight in human misery. All take it for granted that one laughed at illness, disability, hunger, and domestic violence. The blind pie vendor, the battered wife, the sickly old man, the starving Welsh migrant sheltering in a barn: the victims of these jokes are as helpless and vulnerable as it is possible to be. Those who mock them are delighting in their superiority and good fortune; they are indulging the "Sudden Glory" that Hobbes describes in his famous analysis of laughter, the rush of glee caused "by the apprehension of some deformed thing in another, by comparison whereof they suddenly applaud themselves."[7] Yet it is all surprisingly genial: the fellow who torments the pie seller is "an arch Rogue." In countless similar jokes, the tormentor is introduced as "a good impudent fellow," a "diverting wag," or "this facetious gentleman."

British jestbooks of this period are full of jokes about cripples, hunchbacks, blind men, and desperate beggars. One finds an almost encyclopedic range of jokes about the deaf.[8] Some texts even separate out their deformity jokes into categories—"Of Crookedness and Lameness," "Of Noses," "Of Deaf Folk," "Of Faces and Scars."[9] Noselessness was evidently a particularly amusing affliction—perhaps because it reduced one to an animal state (man, it was said, was the only being with a true nose).[10] God bless your eyesight, says the joker to someone with no nose, because you certainly couldn't wear spectacles. The prank about a melancholy old father is typical of many in which sickly old folk are told to go and kill themselves. The joke against the blind pie seller is one of the most frequently reprinted of all jestbook anecdotes (one owner of *The Complete London Jester* identified it as a particular favorite, with a large inky spot in the margin).[11] Judging by *The Nut-Cracker* (1751), the profitable jestbook he compiled for John Newbery, Christopher Smart was particularly fond of stuttering jokes:

> An Arch Boy, belonging to one of the Ships of War at *Portsmouth*, had purchased of his Play-fellows a Magpye, which he carried to his Father's House, and was at the Door feeding it, when a Gentleman in the Neighbourhood, who had an Impediment in his Speech, coming up, *T-T-T-Tom*, says the Gentleman, *can your Mag T-T-T-Talk yet? Ay Sir*, says the Boy, *better than you, or I'd wring his Head off.*[12]

This one appears alongside jokes about famous stutterers (D'Urfey, Addison, Lord Strangford) in almost every eighteenth-century jestbook. The wife-beating joke is one of thousands. A man who "us'd to divert himself now and then by beating his wife" begins another joke from Smart's *Nut-Cracker*.[13]

The waggish insults already demand some major efforts of historical understanding. But it gets much worse. Large parts of every book are devoted to more brutal cruelties—blind men led into walls, dwarfs tossed out windows, lame matrons tumbled into ditches. Many of these are elaborate practical jokes, like the following:

The lord Mohun and the earl of Warwick being on the ramble, they took notice of an old woman, who early and late was boiling codlings [apples] near Charing-cross; one day they bought some of her, pitied her poverty, and promised to send her a bushel of charcoal for nothing. I thank your honours, replied the old woman. In the morning a porter brings a bushel of charcoal, at which the old woman was very joyful: but their lordships had filled up the hollow of the charcoal with gunpowder, and sealed up the ends with black wax and stood at a distance to see the effect of their project. The old woman's fire beginning to decay, she supplied it with the charcoal which was sent her. In a little time, bounce went the charcoal like so many crackers, down went the kettle into the street, and away flew the codlings about the old woman's ears; and she getting no hurt, their lordships were well pleased with the frolick.[14]

Slangy and gleefully circumstantial, this is one of many anecdotes about a waggish aristocrat tormenting a cripple or starving pauper before a delighted mob. (So much for plebeian class consciousness.)

It is all strikingly at odds with emerging sentimental standards. Jestbook humor seems oblivious to contemporary debates about the nature and ethics of laughter, not to mention inherited Christian injunctions to feed the hungry and care for the sick. The cruelty of certain types of humor was a recurring subject in Shaftesbury, Addison, Hutcheson, Akenside, Lord Kames, and almost every other moral philosopher. Scores of anonymous periodical essays dealt with the subject, and there were dedicated treatises like Whitehead's *On Ridicule* (1743) and Corbyn Morris's *Essay towards Fixing the True Standards of Wit, Humour, Raillery, Satire, and Ridicule* (1744). Eighteenth-century satirists all felt compelled to refute the charge of malice, to establish their own good nature and the righteous didacticism of their verse. Comic dramatists routinely added prologues insisting on the corrective functions of their humor.[15] Above all, it was becoming unacceptable to laugh at the defects and sufferings of others: sympathy was the proper response for these misfortunes. Nothing shocks us more, wrote Adam Smith in the opening pages of *The Theory of Moral Sentiments* (1759), than an absence of sympathy. "It is natural," insisted James Beattie, that "pity should prevail over the ludicrous emotion."[16] To Hume, anyone without sympathy was hardly human: "All his sentiments must be inverted, and directly opposite to those which prevail in the human species." Adopting a different tone for her young female readers, Hester Chapone warns anyone who laughs at sickness or old age: "[C]all it seriously to mind, when you are confessing your faults to Almighty God: and, be fully persuaded, that it is not one of the least which you have to repent of."[17]

NASTY JOKES, POLITE WOMEN

Jestbooks have generally been categorized as "popular" texts. And certainly one's initial reaction is to see them as artifacts of low culture, examples of the vulgar taste from which the "polite" classes were self-consciously separating themselves. Laughing at hunchbacks or blind men seems more like the humor of the stables or the servants' hall. One instinctually associates such jokes with the cheaper forms of print: the Dicey chapbooks or even smaller comic pamphlets sold by itinerant peddlers and the shabbiest booksellers on and around London Bridge. Among higher classes, they are the sort of jokes one might associate with urban roués, madcap Oxbridge students, idle young gentlemen from the Inns of Court—generally the hangover of a premodern barbarity that was soon to sink into oblivion.

The problem is that none of these nasty witticisms comes from the cheapest or crudest forms of print. Most jestbooks were produced for middle- and upper-class readers: at 1s. 6d., 3s., or even 5s., they were far beyond the reach of a popular audience. They were produced in enormous quantities, with dozens of new volumes appearing each year. Swift and others might have scorned *"Six-peny-worth of Wit,* Westminster *Drolleries, Delightful Tales, Compleat Jesters,* and the like,*"* but they were a profitable part of the eighteenth-century book market.[18] Packed with cruel jokes, they surely force us to qualify our assumptions about levels of sentimentalism and about the rapid sharpening of social divisions in midcentury Britain. Polite anxieties about cultural distinctions would seem to have been less widespread than we have assumed. These texts and their readership offer further raw material for ongoing debates about the strength of class divisions in eighteenth-century Britain and certainly about the viability of the popular/polite distinction, with its emphasis on differences rather than continuities and its simplification of the infinite gradations and mutations of the British social hierarchy.[19]

Above all, this readership forces us to look seriously at recent critiques of the last two decades' work on the middling sort. So much good work on the commercial middle classes has collectively reified this category, even if most scholars stop short of talking about class consciousness. In a meticulously researched study, the social historian H. R. French lays out the overwhelming heterogeneity obscured by terms like *middling sort*: vast differences between educated professionals (physicians, lawyers, minor clergymen) and artisans or shopkeepers (with further hierarchies between "clean" and "dirty" trades). Talk of a national middling sort also flattens out regional differences, conflating the "chief inhabitants" of rural communities with the bourgeoisie of provincial towns and the "big bourgeoisie" of the metropolis. In all these contexts, French insists, identities were contingent and multiple: like everyone else, middling people behaved and thought of themselves differently in different contexts. This was already evident in the very different pictures of middle-class life presented by such historians as Margaret Hunt (who describes a thrifty, industrious, and domestic middle class) and others (like Peter Borsay) who concentrate on leisure and consumption. Middle-class life was by definition a combination of work and leisure.[20] At the same time, jestbooks also point to activities and pleasures that cut across classes: one finds very similar jokes in expensive texts and in the crudest broadsides or farthing pamphlets. Several of the most fashionable jestbooks were abridged as chapbooks or published in weekly parts for lower readers.[21]

Given that these texts have received so little scholarly attention—and that they have so often been treated as popular texts—it seems important to discuss them and their social distribution in some detail.[22] The only truly popular jestbooks were chapbook versions produced by the Dicey family and other printers and, beneath them, all sorts of even more diminutive pamphlets of perhaps a single quarto sheet, the work of ephemera publishers and provincial booksellers. *Joaks upon Joaks*, *The Penny Budget of Wit*, *Pills to Purge Melancholy*, *A Whetstone for Dull Wits*: these and other perennial favorites were poorly printed on cheap paper, with perhaps a couple of crude woodcuts. They sold for no more than a few pennies and provided barely literate readers with a short assortment of traditional humor: comic insults (calling someone an ass, goose, or blockhead) and all the tripping, scalding, and head knocking of early modern practical jokes. In these texts one meets the most traditional victims of folk humor: scolds and cuckolds, droning parsons, Puritans, Catholics, and the ubiquitous idiots of the Celtic fringe (Sawney the Scot, Taffy from Wales, and so on). There are laxatives and itching powders and all sorts of fun with human excrement. A barmaid pisses into a pot of beer; a boy makes a shit pie for his mother's lover. One finds all the usual bawdy tales, marital rows, and nocturnal mishaps in the corridors of coaching inns. Many favorite chapbooks relate the rudimentary life story and pranks of native tricksters like Tom Thumb, Tom Tram, Swalpo, and Robin Goodfellow—a succession of violent or scatological tricks against mean widows, Puritans, gypsies, and assorted other dupes. The Dicey chapbooks were printed in vast numbers, sometimes ten thousand or more, and circulated far more widely than any other printed matter in eighteenth-century England.²³ They provide the clearest evidence of popular tastes and of the overwhelming stagnation of popular humor from the Middle Ages into the early nineteenth century, when the chapbooks finally declined and traditional popular humor was consigned to oblivion or cleaned up as children's literature.

These texts have now been widely studied, but we are still far less familiar with the duodecimo jestbooks and comic miscellanies put out by mainstream London booksellers—those producing the classics, sacred literature, expensive scientific or philosophical works, and what we now think of as polite literature. One of the largest jestbook publishers was the firm of Hawes and Hitch in Paternoster Row, which also published editions of *Clarissa* and *Sir Charles Grandison*; of Locke and Virgil; New Testaments in Greek and Latin; and many extremely expensive belletristic texts. For most mainstream booksellers, jestbooks seem to have been a source of steady income comparable to almanacs. Most are well printed on good-quality paper, and they are frequently decorated with engraved frontispieces and rococo ornaments.

Each season saw reprints of favorites (*Coffee-House Jests*, *Laugh and Be Fat*, *Joe Miller's Jests*) and perhaps fifteen or twenty new texts. In spite of their extravagant boasts of originality, these new titles were invariably plagiarized wholesale from previous books, hastily thrown together by minor actors or printer's hacks who were down on their luck. These were often attributed to some famous wit: *The Jests of Beau Nash* (1763), *Nancy Dawson's Jests* (1761), *The Celebrated Mrs. Pilkington's Jests* (1764; fig. 1), *Lord Chesterfield's Witticisms* (1773). Many were attributed to famous actors: *Quin's Jests* (1766), *Colley Cibber's Jests* (1761), *Spiller's Jests* (1730), *Garrick's Complete Jester* (1779), and the most famous of them all, *Joe Miller* (1739). Such texts were clearly published without permission, usually appearing shortly after the wit's death. They might provide a handful of jokes associated with the historical figure—a few of Beau Nash's most celebrated bons mots, Chesterfield's famous prank against John James Heidegger—but generally did little more than reprint hundreds of old jokes from other jestbooks. Still other texts were published under droll pseudonyms: Luke Lively or Tom Gaylove, Humphry Frolicksome or Sir Toby Tickleside. Even popular literary characters demanded their own jestbooks: Polly Peachum, Roderick Random, or Tom Jones, "the most impudent man living," as he was called in midcentury editions of *Joe Miller*. The *Tristram Shandy* craze produced a torrent of jestbooks attributed to Sterne, Yorick, or Tristram himself.²⁴

A sizable number were addressed to particular groups of readers: to young men about town (*The Choice Spirit's Pocket Companion*; *The Buck's Pocket Companion; or, The Merry Fellow*) or students (*College Wit, Oxford Jests*). There was a *Sailor's Jester* (1788), offering "strange Adventures and dangerous Escapes" as well as the usual puns and insults—the whole being "a diverting Friend between the Watches." *Woman's Wit* and *The Female Jester* (subtitled *Wit for the Ladies*) were clearly targeted at women, although they print the same range of material as the rest.[25] Whole jestbooks were devoted to particular types of humor: to Irish jokes, numbskull tales, jokes about macaronis or actors.[26] Later in the century, one finds a fad for intensely topical jestbooks: *The Balloon Jester; or, Flights of Wit and Humour* (ca. 1784); *The Comet; or, Meteor of Mirth* (1772); *Shakespear's Jests; or, The Jubilee Jester* (ca. 1777); *The Lottery Jest-Book; or, Fun Even for the Losers* (1777).

Most, however, sought to capture as much as possible of the print market, offering a wide variety of contents and recommending themselves to different groups of readers: to Londoners and countrymen, to melancholics in need of uplift or scholars in search of diversion, and to women as well as men. His jokes were collected at both "St *James's*" and "St *Giles's*," boasted the editor of *Polly Peachum's Jests*, and were "suited alike to the Capacities of the Peer, and the Porter."[27] *Jack Smart's Merry Jester* is dedicated to all ranks and both sexes—to dukes and ladies as well as carters and milkmaids.[28] However strongly they insisted that everything was "entirely new"—that they reprinted nothing out of *Joe Miller* or *Tom Brown's Jests*—one finds the same jokes repeated ad nauseam. At the lower end of the market, one finds great blocks of text and even entire signatures transferred from other books. The same joke is attributed in one book to Swift, in another to Rochester; here to Nancy Dawson, there to David Garrick. "Pointed axioms and acute replies fly loose about the world," as Johnson found when trying to authenticate anecdotes for his *Lives of the Poets*, "and are assigned successively to those whom it may be the fashion to celebrate."[29]

The typical book gathers several hundred jokes, in no particular order, followed by a dizzying array of other amusements. Short comic tales are often included—"Merry Adventures," "Frolicks of Wit and Humour"—followed by witty epigrams or drinking songs. (Vocal miscellanies are a closely related genre and were published in similar quantities.) There were whimsical "country tales" about idiot rustics named Hodge or Margery. Many books boasted special attractions: a "droll dialogue" between a lady of fashion and a Thames waterman or an extended swearing contest between Oysteria and Welfleta, two Billingsgate fishwives.[30] *Rochester's Jests* offered "*A learned Dispute between two* Welshmen"; another text appended "A Drunken Oration,

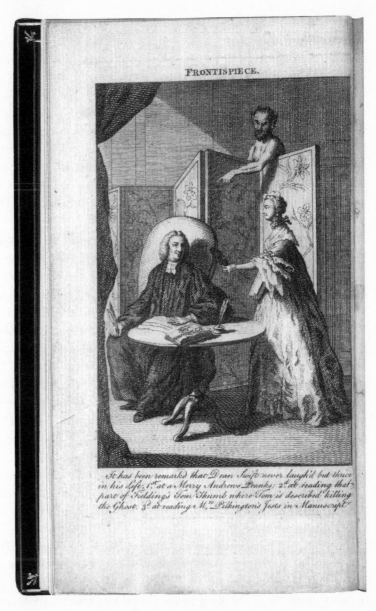

FRONTISPIECE.

It has been remarked that Dean Swift never laugh'd but thrice in his Life, 1st at a Merry Andrew's Pranks; 2d at reading that part of Fielding's Tom Thumb where Tom is described killing the Ghost; 3d at reading Mrs Pilkington's Jests in Manuscript

FIGURE 1. Frontispiece and title page from *The Celebrated Mrs. Pilkington's Jests*, 2nd ed. (London, 1764), one of many jestbooks attributed to famously witty women, real or fictional (cf. Sally Salisbury, Nancy Dawson, Polly Peachum), and offering a miscellaneous jumble of puns, riddles, bawdy tales, and extremely rude jokes about flatulence and defecation. The book and its high-quality frontispiece play on Mrs. Pilkington's early connection with Swift, and

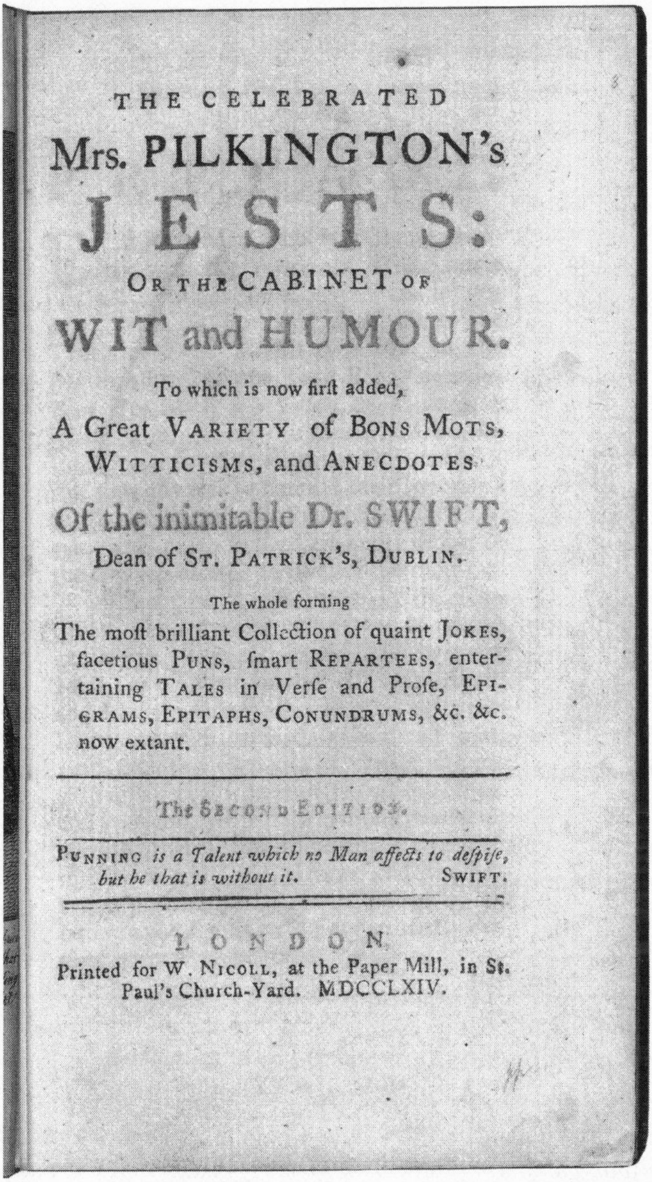

THE CELEBRATED

Mrs. PILKINGTON's

JESTS:

OR THE CABINET OF

WIT and HUMOUR.

To which is now firſt added,

A Great VARIETY of BONS MOTS,
WITTICISMS, and ANECDOTES

Of the inimitable Dr. SWIFT,
Dean of ST. PATRICK's, DUBLIN.

The whole forming

The moſt brilliant Collection of quaint JOKES,
facetious PUNS, ſmart REPARTEES, entertaining TALES in Verſe and Proſe, EPI-
GRAMS, EPITAPHS, CONUNDRUMS, &c. &c.
now extant.

The SECOND EDITION.

PUNNING *is a Talent which no Man affects to deſpiſe,
but he that is without it.*　　　　SWIFT.

LONDON.
Printed for W. NICOLL, at the Paper Mill, in St.
Paul's Church-Yard. MDCCLXIV.

the commonplace that the dean had laughed only twice in his life. There was a third time,
this frontispiece playfully informs us: when he read *Mrs. Pilkington's Jests* in manuscript. The
illustration shows Pilkington presenting him with her text, encouraged by the devil behind
the screen. Reproduced by permission of the Huntington Library, San Marino, California
(288788).

as it was performed at the Theatre Royal in Covent Garden, by Mr. Shuter."[31] One unexpected feature is a collection of epitaphs, serious along with comic. All this might be combined, still more incongruously to modern readers, with proverbs, maxims, or didactic fables. *Joe Miller's Jests* was regularly issued with a concluding selection of "moral sentences." Inconsistency, it becomes ever clearer, is a culturally and historically specific concept.

This variety of materials reached its greatest extent in the comic miscellanies that seemed to swell with each bookselling season—*The Wit's Miscellany*, *The Merry Medley*, and dozens more. These were often annual compilations, published around Christmas and intended, like *The Merry Medley*, to "drive the cold Winter away with Mirth and Melody" (fig. 2).[32] The largest of them extended to several volumes, sold for 3s. and even 5s. a volume, and combined hundreds of jests with every conceivable humorous genre. There were animal fables, fustian love letters between hopelessly mismatched lovers, repulsive stories about vomit and rotten food, and absurd tall tales (like the one about a lobster killing a hare on Salisbury Plain). One finds epigrams and apothegms; bawdy songs and music for country dances; riddles, rebusses, and puzzles; and instructions for parlor games, juggling, and legerdemain ("To make Flames of Fire issue from an Egg").[33] Remedies for ringworm or the colic rub shoulders with didactic and even devotional materials; there are instructions for courting modest countrywomen and rules for dream interpretation.

Taken together, midcentury jestbooks offer a promising introduction to the accepted comedians of eighteenth-century culture. At the bottom of the scale were a range of demotic tricksters: the "arch boys" and insolent apprentices of so much jestbook humor; smart-mouthed beggars and old crones who tell people to eat their poo. Droll prostitutes and orange wenches show up in every text, as do bawds (Mother Needham remained a routine figure for decades after she was stoned to death in May 1731).[34] The witty ripostes of Nell Gwyn continued to be printed, and London editors evidently took pride in keeping up with contemporary courtesans like Kitty Fisher and Fanny Murray. Kitty Clive, Peg Woffington, and other leading actresses are all there. Quacks and charlatans remained entertaining even as the medical establishment was denouncing them—thus *The Merry Quack Doctor* (ca. 1775), subtitled *The Fun-Box Broke Open*.[35] There are hard-drinking bucks and fat drunken squires of the Mr. Western sort. Famous judges sport with terrified footpads as they send them to the gallows. More surprising is the range of genteel and aristocratic women. Mean or smutty jokes are attached not just to fabled figures like Frances, Lady Vane (ca. 1715–88), or Etheldreda, the outrageous Lady Townshend (ca. 1708–88), but to all sorts of otherwise respectable noblewomen.

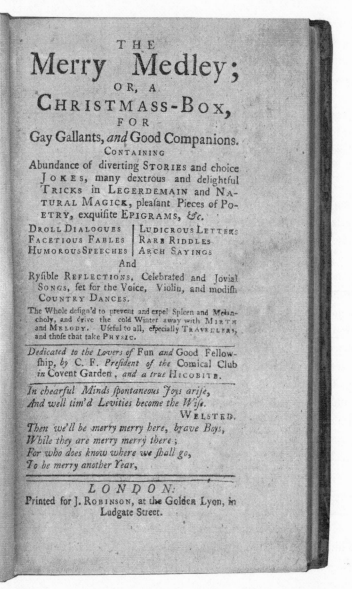

FIGURE 2. Title page from *The Merry Medley* (London, ca. 1750). At four hundred pages or even more, comic miscellanies were expensive texts selling at 3s. or even 5s. *The Merry Medley* appeared every Christmas for decades and exemplifies the familial audience of so much minor comic literature—a mixed group around a winter fire. The annual miscellanies offered a jumble of several hundred jests, comic monologues, exchanges of love letters between rustic idiots, and humorous tales of the fabliau sort. There are songs and instructions for country dances, riddles, puzzles, and directions for parlor tricks. Reproduced by permission of the Huntington Library, San Marino, California (123464).

We find the Duchess of Marlborough joking about farting and various less identifiable grandees (Lady C——, the Duchess of B——) doing even worse. Lower down the hierarchy, brassy "gentlewomen" repeatedly invite people to kiss their arse:

> A Gentlewoman being a Horseback, and having a Hole in her Dust-Gown, a Country fellow seeing it, says, Mistress, Mistress, you have got a Hole in your Arse. *I know that*, says she, *and you may come and put your Nose in it.*

Young women of fashion show up with all sorts of lewd innuendos. Calmly urinating against a house, a gentleman looks up to find two young ladies laughing at the window. What was so funny? *"O Sir*, said one of them, *a very little Thing will make us Laugh."*[36]

Certainly no one can ignore the hoariness of so much jestbook humor: alongside cruel taunts to hunchbacks and blind women, one finds extremely rude sexual and scatological jokes. "Eat my poo," "kiss my arse," even the vilest practical jokes: upper-class versions were just more periphrastic. A little French pastry cook just can't get the recipe right for his shit tart (a joke that comes complete with a specious moral about the simplicity of British cookery and the folly of trying to go against nature).[37] The following, repeated in every possible venue, provides a fascinating insight into the bounds of politeness for those who could afford these books:

> Some unlucky Boys, the Scholars of Dr. *Busby*, at *Westminster*, besmeared the Stairs leading to the School with something that shall be nameless; the Doctor, as it was designed, befoul'd his Fingers very much in it; which so enrag'd him, that he cry'd out; He would give any Boy Half a Crown, that would discover who had a Hand in it; upon which, an arch Boy immediately told him . . . *"Why then . . . you had a Hand in it, or it would not have been so besh——t."*[38]

Here the joke is somewhat modified by a play on words, but potty humor is a primitive pleasure, and one finds much more elemental jokes, sometimes lifted wholesale out of *Till Eulenspiegel*. A waggish gentleman amuses himself by shitting on a table and leaving it for the innkeeper to find. Another mad spark, forced to share a bed with a parson, wakes early and defecates on his side of the bed, telling the hostler on the way out that he couldn't stand it any longer—the parson had befouled himself in his sleep.[39] Or consider the one

about Jo Haines (the Restoration actor) and Tom D'Urfey, who was notorious
for his vile breath. Haines picks up a turd ("Sur-reverence") with the end of
his sword. "Now, Sir, said he, keeping [D'Urfey] at Arm's Length, I can talk to
you, and we are pretty much upon a Par." Along the way, this joke tells us a lot
about the physical environment in which such humor could be so mainstream
(a suitable turd just happens to be available).[40]

The marital bed appears as the locus of many jokes:

> A merry fellow being in Bed with his wife, let a rousing fart: hearing his wife
> laugh, he said to her, In truth wife you have but a small cause to be so merry,
> for if the wind holds, we are like to have very foul weather. He falling asleep,
> she raised her arse to his Neck, and piss'd very plentifully upon him, so that
> it ran down his Back to his heels: He awaking, says what a pox Wife are you
> doing? *No Harm, Husband, what I did was to prevent that terrible storm
> you said might come; for they say a little rain will allay a great wind.*[41]

The actors in this little drama, and many others like it, are not filthy laborers
but members of the London commercial classes. A jovial young man farts on
his wedding night. "Alas, my dear," he tells his wife, "when a fortress is besieg-
ing, the cannons must roar in making a breach. *By my faith, husband, you need
not put yourself to this trouble for the breach was made long since by my father's
journeyman.*"[42] One finds extremely frank sexual innuendos, suggesting an
exuberant and guiltless enjoyment of bawdy that we too often forget. "Lady
C——g and her two Daughters, having taken Lodgings at a Leather-Breeches
Maker's in *Piccadilly*, the Sign of the *Cock* and *Leather Breeches*, was always
put to the Blush, when she was obliged to give any Body Directions." She asks
the tradesman to alter his sign. "I'll tell you how you may please both me and
my Daughters; *Only take down your* Breeches, *and let your* Cock *stand.*"[43]
In "Melesinda's Misfortune," we find a semipornographic tale about a genteel young woman dreaming of sex by the fireplace when her smock catches
fire. "Misfortunes will, I see, betide, / When maidens throw their legs too
wide."[44]

The effect could hardly be more incongruous to modern readers. *The Jests
of Beau Nash* is an expensive text from which I have taken Nash's joke about
the "crooked" lady; it alternates between this sort of nastiness and the politer repartee for which Nash was famous. It offers explicit obscenities and
filthy quips about arse kissing.[45] In the midst of *The Merry Medley*, one of
the more expensive Christmas miscellanies (fig. 2 above), one finds a young
gentleman caught defecating in St. Paul's churchyard, with his face to the wall

and his backside in full view. He couldn't turn the other way, he explains, for "that's the Way to be seen: every Body knows my Face, and no Body knows my A——se." A few pages later, one learns about some young blades and their violent revenge on an aging bawd: having stripped her naked, they cover her with tar and feathers and march her through the streets, all of it "to the great Diversion and Surprize of the Mob."[46] Expensive jestbooks offer almost the same uncomplicated cruelties, the same ribald or scatological tales, the same cast of scolds or cuckolds, and the same stale deformity jokes as the crudest chapbooks.

On the basis of price alone, mainstream duodecimo jestbooks were clearly produced for those with considerable disposable income—even artisans or small shopkeepers would have struggled to scrape together the necessary shillings. These books appealed to readers very different from those who bought the Dicey chapbooks. Many jestbook situations are specific to urban readers with money: jokes about gentlemanly debts or tailors' bills, about stupid footmen and filthy cooks. There is much topical metropolitan humor: accounts of celebrated "frolics" and "humbugs"; jokes about the London stage and high politics, about famous courtiers or men of fashion. There are learned puns, literary in-jokes, and jests that demand knowledge of history or the classics. The very terminology of these books—readers are offered "bons mots" and "smart repartees" rather than the "bulls," "pranks," or "merry adventures" of the chapbook tradition—clearly appeals to a higher audience.

Actual ownership is predictably harder to establish. Jestbooks rarely show up in the great sale catalogs of this period, with their familiar lists of belles lettres, history, theology, and scientific works. But they do show up in lesser catalogs, and personal inscriptions or circulating library stamps point to significant constituencies of polite readers. We know that Walpole, Wilkes, and Boswell owned jestbooks; Goldsmith had his "*ana*" and "*facetiae*." Later in the century, we find Parson Woodforde buying *Laugh and Grow Fat* from a peddler. New work on sources is now starting to reveal just how much major authors lifted from these texts.[47] Fielding plagiarized all manner of material from jestbooks, including the Nell Gwyn anecdote in book 11 of *Tom Jones* and Fitzpatrick's Irish bulls in book 10 ("If she be in the House, do carry me up in the Dark and shew her to me," etc.).[48] Sterne's library contained many volumes of "wit and humour," and we are now able to identify certain direct borrowings.[49] Increasingly empirical work in book history is now telling us more and more about the everyday use of these texts. Returning to her sources on the east Midland book trade, Jan Fergus finds jestbooks circulating widely in the provinces—*The Muse in Good Humour, Joe Miller, Tom Brown's Jests, Jemmy Buck's Jester, Winter Wit,* even specialty scatological productions like *The Button-Maker's Jestbook* (ca. 1771; *making buttons* is one of many smirking noneuphemisms for defecation). Records for the years 1740–74 show the Clay family, booksellers of Daventry, ordering jestbooks both for stock and for lending. They also made special orders for very different sorts of readers, from artisans to the grandest landowners like Mr. Knightley of Fawsley, who ordered thirteen jestbooks in 1770 alone.[50]

Less expected, this new evidence shows jestbooks being widely consumed by women as well as men. In Daventry, again, Fergus finds Mrs. Brooke from the Wheat Sheaf inn ordering *Lord Chesterfield's Witticisms* (1773). A Miss Rush orders *The Macaroni Jester, Timothy Grin's Merry Jester,* and *Tom Gay's Comical Jester* in a single visit (1774). There are also grander ladies like Maria Cave, the daughter of Sir Thomas, who places several orders over the years. Closer to the metropolis, Mrs. Thrale owns several jestbooks and comic miscellanies. We have to imagine middling and wealthy women buying up these texts, ignoring or even scorning the polite injunctions just as even grander women would collect the filthy graphic satires recently discussed by Vic Gatrell. Odder still, even those texts that make explicit appeals to women do not modify their contents in any way. *The Complete London Jester* was designed "for the Amusement and Improvement of both Sexes" but nevertheless prints familiar jokes about blind pie vendors or rape plaintiffs laughed out of court (of which more in chapter 5).[51] Historians of reading have now repeatedly demonstrated just how wrong we were to attach so many genres—usually on the basis of content alone—to male or female readers. We now know that men and boys read romances and sentimental courtship novels. Contrary to all expectations and the antinovel hysteria of the age, men were often the largest body of subscribers at circulating libraries. One single-library study actually shows men to be the primary consumers of fiction, including novels written by women. (Still more counterintuitively, we find men reading explicitly targeted productions like *Light Summer Reading for the Ladies* [1768] and *The Ladies' Magazine* [1770–].) Women, conversely, were more consistent readers of magazines than novels and were therefore accessing much fiction in the form of extracts.[52]

That women were buying so many jestbooks only confirms this growing evidence of the overwhelmingly cross-gendered nature of eighteenth-century reading. Of course women always had some access to the libraries of fathers, brothers, and husbands, but new scholarship on diaries, letters, and commonplace books encourages us to put the matter more positively.[53] For all the warnings of clerics and moralists, large numbers of women bought, borrowed, and read whatever they liked. Neither circulating libraries nor bookshops divided their stock along gender lines. Women borrowed *Peregrine Pickle*, *The English Rogue*, and plays by D'Urfey or Vanbrugh. Cautions about the unsuitability of Fielding or Sterne only prove how consistently women were reading these authors. Husbands and wives read a diverse range of material to each other. Women sat in mixed groups listening to newspapers, satiric essays, or semistaged readings of English plays. Probably theater attendance should always have shown us just how wide the bounds of propriety could stretch. "There are few English comedies a lady can see, without a shock to delicacy," Dr. Gregory warns his daughters, but in practice there were few restraints.[54] Genteel women saw all the naughtiest farces, heard their bawdy epilogues, and invariably had trouble leaving before the farting Harlequins came on. As early modern historians have now been saying for some time, the fullest understanding of women's experience would look at the tastes and perceptions women shared with men, as well as those that kept them apart.

HOW TO BE A WAG

How were jestbooks used? One easily identifies three discrete reading practices, which in turn offer rare glimpses into manners and venues. First, we know that chapbooks were bought from itinerant peddlers and read aloud by the literate members of small communities and that larger jestbooks were used in similar ways.[55] *Fun for the Parlour; or, All Merry above Stairs*, *The Merry Medley*, and other annual miscellanies all imagine a collective audience, often illustrated as a group around a table or winter fire, guffawing over a copy of the jestbook (fig. 3). Comic dialogues or droll speeches, songs, parlor games, puzzles, and riddles were all designed to be performed or chortled over in company. Even dialects were rendered phonetically, suggesting their importance to a good performance ("A certain Welsh Shentleman"; "By my shoul and St. Patrick," as every Irish idiot cries).[56] Many texts claim to be compiled by clubs or groups of friends that gathered at coffeehouses for conversation and telling jokes. *The Diverting Muse; or, The Universal Medley* (1707) is apparently compiled "by a Society of merry Gentlemen, for the Entertainment of the Town," and on the final leaf one finds a paragraph inviting contributions:

> If they please to communicate their Instructions to the Persons concern'd
> in this Miscellany, which will be continued Monthly, by a Society of Merry

Gentlemen, they have it done gratis, and inserted herein; also if they have anything of their own, that they are willing to make publick, if it be judg'd proper for our present undertaking, it shall be carefully admitted, as aforesaid: if they please to direct for Mr. George Dagonstaff, to be left at Mr. Hogarth's Coffee-house in St. John's Gate.[57]

The more buckish of these texts imagine a disorderly male gathering— exchanges of jokes in the back rooms of taverns or after dinner at private houses. Such texts as *The Buck's Bottle Companion* and *The Frisky Jester* are typical of many that combine jokes with rowdy drinking songs and almost in- finite lists of lewd toasts ("The best **** in Christendom," "To the stubborn soldier who forces his way into a narrow breach").[58]

Such texts offer further and unmistakable evidence of the raucous and im- polite nature of male sociability in this period—the bawdy catches, protracted innuendos, toasts to well-known women of pleasure, urinating in corners, and spewing out windows. Recalling his youth in 1770s–80s London, Fran- cis Place made it clear that Addison and Steele's descriptions of coffeehouse sociability were never more than a "delightful ideal." Recent monographs by Brian Cowan and Markman Ellis systematically demolish any lingering ideal- ism about these venues. The boorish excesses, drink, and foul language were continually condemned, but this condemnation evidently did little to diminish it. It won't do to argue that such behaviors were "an increasingly outmoded position"—that they were temporary eruptions of older freedoms or deliber- ate acts of resistance to the newer standards. No doubt some were, but much of this was guiltlessly enjoyed well into the nineteenth century.[59] Jestbooks also force us to recognize the continuities between more disorderly drinking parties and the high-minded literary and scientific societies that historians of Enlightenment sociability have described. Post-Habermasian discussions of the public sphere have inevitably emphasized the philosophical, scientific, political, and commercial discussions that went on in such contexts. But it is worth reminding ourselves of the staggering levels of alcohol consumption in all these clubs—the gallons and gallons of port and punch and the disorder and foul language that clearly accompanied them as the evening wore on.[60]

Second, and not at all inconsistently, jestbooks were also intended for soli- tary reading. Jestbooks and miscellanies offer themselves, in this period when solitude had far fewer positive associations, as substitutes for good company. For travelers and others forced to be alone, a jestbook provided "jovial" or "agreeable" companionship. *The Merry Medley* was "for Gay Gallants, and Good Companions." Subtitles such as *The Facetious Man's Pocket Companion*

Frontispiece.

Ha! ha, ha. He, he, he!

FIGURE 3. Frontispiece and title page from *Jemmy Twitcher's Jests* (London, 1770), a collection attributed to the famously depraved and witty Lord Sandwich (1718–92). Puns, comic tales, drinking songs, and extended accounts of fashionable "humbugs" are combined with filthy double entendres, of which the title page gives a sample. The illustration of a boozy circle guffawing over a copy of the jestbook is common and gives some indication of how these books were used. Photograph © The British Library Board (12316.bb.46).

Jemmy Twitcher's Jeſts:

OR,

Wit with the Gravy in it:

COLLECTED

By a MEMBER of the Beef-Steak Club;

And now firſt publiſhed

By DANIEL GUNSTON.

Interſperſed with Variety of entertaining Articles
from his own Budget;

The Whole conſiſting of

Tales,	Jokes,	Humbugs,
Repartees,	Double Entendres,	Catches,
Conundrums,	Epigrams,	Glees,
Bulls,	Puns,	And

Every other Species of Wit and Humour.

So that every perſon who is pleaſed with a *Jeſt*, may
have a large Quantity by paying a Shilling *earneſt*;

If a *Bull* has any Charms for him, let him *buy* this
little Volume, and he will find that we have *given*
him a great *many*;

If a *Double Entendre* can afford Delight, we appeal to
the Ladies, whether we have not a juſt Claim to
their Approbation, and we are willing to *ſtand* or
fall by their Verdict. In ſhort, we flatter ourſelves
that this Performance abounds with every Species of
Wit; and we have the Satisfaction to ſay, what none
of our Predeceſſors can, that theſe Jeſts are entirely
new, and have never appeared in any other Jeſt Book.

N. B. This little Volume, as its Contents have never
been broached, may properly be ſaid to be a *Maiden One*,
and may be had, Price One Shilling *ſtitched*.

LONDON,

Printed for T. Evans, at No. 54, and J. Smith, at No. 15,
in Pater-noſter Row; and ſold by all other Bookſellers.
[Price One Shilling.]
MDCCLXX.

or *The Wit's Vade Mecum* make it clear that these small books were carried about in pockets, a rough handling that is evident in surviving copies and accounts in part for their exceptionally low survival rates. *The Jests of Beau Nash* opens with an anecdote that suggests the role jestbooks might have played in gentlemanly libraries. The "Gentleman of great Genius and Learning" who had induced Nash to produce his collection of jests, we are told, used

> to provide himself with all the Books of Jest and Merriment that made their Appearance, which he threw promiscuously into a large Bag in one corner of his Library to obviate Melancholy, or relax his severer Studies. Whenever he was tired with Reading, or a dull fit took him, he immediately went to his Bag, and dipping in his Hand, laid hold of that Companion which Chance threw in his Way.[61]

For all the fine recent work on the history of reading, we still know too little about these occasional and recreational reading habits, about the bags in corners and messy piles of unbound volumes.

Third, and finally, jestbooks were produced, in this age when dullness was the worst of social vices, as how-to manuals for those wanting to shine in company. And here, having mentioned the all-male venues (drinking parties, urban rambles), it seems important to emphasize how much of this humor envisages a mixed or entirely female audience and how many of the implied speakers are female. Women as well as men read jestbooks before social events. "I fancy, madam, you have been reading a jest book this morning," says Mr. Burchell to an unusually witty Mrs. Primrose in *The Vicar of Wakefield*. Still in the late 1820s, the shy young Philip Henry Gosse tried to ease his social life by learning jokes and riddles from *Joe Miller's Jests*.[62] Prefaces offer instructions about how to recite or perform such jokes "so as to engage the Attention of the Audience, and excite in them Mirth and good Humour." *The Nut-Cracker* begins with a long introduction advising readers how to recite a joke ("crack a *Nut*") with success. Don't tell a joke that has nothing to do with the conversation, Smart advises. Liven it up with a few "cheerful Looks and whimsical Agitations"; use a funny accent.[63] Evidence of this practice comes in the marginal annotations of many surviving copies. Asterisks and crosses identify favorite jokes, as do miniature pointing hands ("manicules," as William Sherman so nicely calls them) and one particularly common mark, two concentric circles surrounding an inky dot, a sort of miniature bull's eye.[64] Lists of pages or joke numbers identify favorite jests out of the random sequence of hundreds. On a larger scale, there were book-length guides for would-be wits, with appropriate jokes for different contexts.[65]

We also know that people kept commonplace books of jokes, collecting favorite jests from the books and from conversation. Pepys's *Diary* offers glimpses of this practice, as, a century later, does Mrs. Thrale's *Thraliana*—her repository for "all kinds of Nonsense," as she called it. With some of this she was clearly just amusing herself, but one also finds her stocking up to entertain the Johnson circle.[66] George Bubb Dodington (ca. 1690–1762)—Pope's Bubo, "the egregious Bubb," roly-poly counselor to Frederick Prince of Wales—used to pore over a great commonplace book of witticisms before he went into company.[67] One fascinating manuscript jestbook survives from the mid-seventeenth century, a compilation of almost seven hundred jokes collected by Sir Nicholas LeStrange, the elder brother of the Restoration censor.[68] Jestbooks, then, taught their readers to be witty in an original way. Anyone could sneer at an old hunchback or someone with no nose; it took a real wit to ask the hunchback whether she had come "straight from home" or to tell the noseless man he had nowhere to hang his spectacles. Such taunts were evidently a regular way of promoting good cheer in company. Jestbook insults correspond to habitual witticisms, the sort of waggery that earned one the reputation of a wit or "droll fellow." Chesterfield thought it vulgar to tell stories in company, but clearly few others agreed. Having a fund of jolly tales, readers were advised, would make them the life and soul of any company.[69]

Many jestbooks boast of real-world sources: their jokes were recorded in the "Politest Drawing Rooms" or the "Genteel Resorts of the Beau Monde." *The Jests of Beau Nash*, its editor informs us, records repartee "between [Nash] and Personages of the first Distinction" in the assembly rooms of Bath.[70] Of course, there is no evidence that Beau Nash ever told a hunchback that she must have got *"warpt by the Way"*; this and most of the other jests attributed to him in this collection seem to be plagiarized from earlier jestbooks. Books published so soon after a person's death could not have been totally off the mark, but the most that one can say with certainty is that this was the sort of joke that readers might plausibly associate with a celebrated wit like Nash. Yet these compressed witticisms ring with authenticity. They are anchored in concrete milieus: named London streets, taverns, and coffeehouses; theaters and law courts; even the Grove at Bath, that archetypal locus of polite culture. Particularly suggestive are the number taking place in Holborn, Covent Garden, Drury Lane, Lincoln's Inn Fields, Fleet Street, and the Strand, all of them places of encounter between riotous young gentlemen from the

West End or Inns of Court and the canaille.[71] In their very uniformity, these jokes seem to reflect everyday situations. "Honest *Joe Miller*, going one Day along *Fleet street*. . . ." "One *Easter Monday*, an arch Rogue meeting a *blind Woman*. . . ." "One meeting an old Man all trembling on his Staff. . . ."[72] Their formal condensation—the sheer self-evidence of what are to us the obscurest conceits—suggests everyday attitudes.

At this point, every professional historian will take several steps backward—and qualifications are clearly required. First, I am not making a holistic claim. Malicious jokes were becoming problematic in many contexts. Neither pious dissenters nor the politest middle-class women would have bought *The Merry Medley* or *The Jests of Beau Nash*. They would never have laughed openly at cripples and blind men nor at the bawdy and excremental humor that sold so well. They would not have recited such jokes in company. Levels of sympathy varied enormously between individuals and in different contexts: no one could deny that the forces of reform were gathering steam in mid-eighteenth-century Britain. Indeed, an increasing number of jestbooks seem to reflect these changing standards, at least claiming to eschew malice and vulgarity. A number offered themselves specifically to polite readers: publications like *The Prudent Jester* (1756), *The Polite Companion* (1750, 1760), and *The Delicate Jester*, subtitled *Wit and Humour Divested of Ribaldry* (1760, 1772, 1780, etc.). They were accompanied by cleaned-up songbooks—*The Delicate Songster* (1767), *The Ladies Polite Songster; or, Harmony for the Fair-Sex* (ca. 1775).

These claims were increasingly common, as one would expect, with jestbooks marketed to women: *Woman's Wit* is billed as "freed from that load of indelicacy which has hitherto disgraced all the books of this kind." But once one opens the book, one finds all the standard jestbook fare.[73] *The Delicate Jester* has been edited, we are assured, "with such particular Care as not to offend the Ears of Chastity, or infringe on the Rules of Morality, Decency, and good Manners." Soon, however, we find a beggar with two wooden legs who follows a gouty old gentleman for almost a mile, repeatedly asking for a handout. Punch line: "You miserly hopping son of a ——, I would not change legs with you for all you're worth."[74] The editor of *The Female Jester* gravely warns away those looking for "profane Oaths, coarse Expressions, or indecent Allusions"; anyone wanting such things "will probably deem this but a dull Collection." A few pages later, however, we meet a duke with a stutter and then the usual hag inviting people to kiss her arse.[75] It is hard to believe that such things still passed for delicacy. What is striking is how easily, and for how long, women readers and those who supervised them were reassured with a denial on the title page and at most some superficial censorship.

Other texts manifest an occasional sensitivity about cruelty. Beau Nash was a little "too apt to say cruel Things, and to sacrifice Decency and Good-nature to a Jest," concedes his editor, who goes on, however, to give us the usual jokes about blind men and hunchbacks.[76] Readers are intermittently reassured that the victims of violent pranks are not seriously wounded. The old apple seller is not actually blown up when Mohun and Warwick put gunpowder in her charcoal. An old maid with one eye is only bruised or covered in mud by her fall into the kennel. Jokes about the deformed, certain jestbooks claim, were corrective rather than malicious: it was not the person's physical misfortune that made people laugh but the affectation that things were otherwise. "Altho' the Infirmities of Nature are not proper Substance to be made a Jest of," declares the compiler of *Joe Miller's Jests*, "yet when People take a great deal of Pains to conceal what every Body sees, there is nothing more ridiculous." This justification (of which more in chapter 2) was, by midcentury, an accepted defense for every satirist. "He spared a hump or crooked nose," wrote Swift in his "Verses on the Death of Dr Swift," "Whose owners set not up for beaux."[77]

But justifications are rarer than one might expect. They are usually unconvincing, if not flagrantly insincere. Most midcentury jestbooks offer even the rudest and nastiest of their jokes without qualification. Many, indeed, boast that their humor had not been refined away, that they preserved the "meat" or "marrow"—the essential, nourishing part of the jest. *Wit with the Gravy in It* is the subtitle of *Jemmy Twitcher's Jests*, a popular collection of malice and doubles entendres that first appeared in 1770 (fig. 3 above). Title-page declarations that a jestbook is "free from Obscenity" or contains "nothing that could offend the chastest Ear" are usually ironic. They are part of the joke, a thumbing of the nose at overrefinement or puritan humorlessness. Thus *Rochester's Jests* (London, 1766), in which the pranks of this culture's most notorious libertine are preceded by pious protestations about their decency and didactic force. Often, indeed, the disapproving reader is simply told to like it or lump it: "All those that do not like of this Epistle," declares the author of one popular miscellany, "Let them lay down the Book, and go and whistle."[78] Cruel and filthy humor was a profitable commodity to the booksellers and continued to be enjoyed at all levels of society.

Of course a joke is a hugely complex speech act, and a printed joke is different again. To read a jestbook, even to read its jokes out loud in company, is not the same thing as laughing at a cripple or tormenting a blind woman on the street. Many jokes, now as in the eighteenth century, are funny precisely because they violate standards of decency or taste. In many contexts, one imagines, jokes about cripples or excrement must have encountered the same sort of groan that allows modern academics to enjoy cruel or tasteless jokes, all the time demonstrating that they are appalled. The increase in jestbook production during this period could suggest that printed texts or readings from them were providing substitutes for pleasures that could no longer be openly indulged. Certainly scholars of politeness have tended to argue this way, casting enduring libertine behaviors as isolated reactions to changing tastes rather than inherited behaviors that politeness was struggling to curtail.[79] In this sense, the widespread enjoyment of such jokes does not disprove the rising tide of politeness so much as confirm it.

Supporting this view are the formal qualities of these jokes, the verbal play that distinguishes many jestbook witticisms from the crudest chapbook humor. Freud's famous theory of humor points to the punch line as the crucial mechanism of the "joke-work"—the means by which the joker is able to express some socially unacceptable sexual or aggressive impulse. Verbal humor, says Freud, allows us to evade repression, to indulge instincts that, "because of obstacles standing in the way, we could not express openly or consciously."[80] In many eighteenth-century jestbook witticisms, a low comic situation is somewhat refined by a play on words. Framed as a pun, the joke about Dr. Busby with his "hands in it" makes it into a polite jestbook where chapbook-style scatology might not. The blatant bawdiness of traditional popular humor is often elaborated into a complex double entendre. Sneers at physical deformities frequently appear as instances of verbal wit. Arguably, then, such jokes were acceptable in polite society only because of their verbal framing, just as the circumlocutions of Augustan poetic diction—Pope's "imbrownings" and "sable streams"—made it possible to discuss base or repugnant things without violating linguistic decorum.

Yet many crude or malicious jokes appear without the barest linguistic sophistication. The pranks against the pie vendor and the apple seller are typical of any number of situational jokes that appear with little, if any, verbal cleverness. Transhistorical theories of humor—whether Freud's drive-discharge theory or the various incongruity theories—find their limits with such materials. For Freud, the success of any joke depends on its novelty or verbal inventiveness, yet many early modern jokes are purely situational. Perhaps verbal framing became more important in later stages of the civilizing process, as a mechanism for controlling the obscene or aggressive content of a joke.[81] Concluding puns are noticeably less important, for example, in Tudor and Stuart jestbooks, with their "Merry Jests of Blind Folks" and uninventive cruelties to old maids. At any rate, verbal play is never simply obfuscating. Like euphemism or periphrasis, a pun signifies even as it claims not to. So many eighteenth-century punch lines work less to obscure a basic comic situation—the humor of sex or shit or physical deformity—than to enrich it, adding an extra layer of wit. By framing their cruel jokes as inventive *jeux de mots*, the jestbooks turned age-old comic scenarios into the sort of witty conceit that would amuse polite society. But the malicious kernel of the joke remains. The reformers did little to reduce the production of cruel jestbooks. Not until 1836 did *Joe Miller's Jests* drop the nastiest of its jokes (49 of the original 247)—in deference, the editor informs us, to "the greater delicacy observed in modern society and conversation."[82] Further refinements led to *The Family Joe Miller*, subtitled *A Drawing-Room Jest-Book* (1848)—and by then Byron, Hazlitt, Thackeray, and others had looked back nostalgically on the eighteenth century as an age of open humor and freedom in speech.

Still, the question of gender remains pressing. Could eighteenth-century women really have laughed at such jokes, let alone repeated them? The rudest jestbook humor does provide a context for older anecdotes like the one about Lady Mary Wortley Montagu's bespoke chamber pot with "Pope" and "Swift" painted on the bottom, which even years after their deaths offered her the satisfaction "of shitting on them every day." The sharp-tongued gentlewomen who step out of these texts help us make sense of fictional characters like Richardson's Anna Howe or the unforgettable Charlotte Grandison, so fond of remarking that her brother "still kept his Maidenhead."[83] But beyond Charlotte Grandison are historical women like Lady Bradshaigh (probably Richardson's model) and many, many others. Take the four Lennox sisters, daughters of the second Duke of Richmond. They were characteristic mid-century aristocratic women, says Stella Tillyard: they "rode to hounds, told dirty jokes, flirted, [and] argued vigorously in drawing rooms." From here one thinks naturally of the fast set around Henry Fox (who had married Caroline Lennox in 1744). Banter and sexual teasing went on in mixed company at the Fox household, with impromptu verses and scatological riddles shared across gender lines. Regular visitors included Elizabeth Vesey, always the quirkiest of the early Bluestockings, and Frances Greville, Frances Burney's godmother and the probable model for Mrs. Selwyn, the brash and vocal widow who makes plot happen in volume 3 of *Evelina*.[84]

With its scandalous freethinking streak, the Fox household was hardly typical, but it was not anomalous either. The more secure one's status in this society, the less one needed to keep constructing it, and the more fun it was to repeat dirty or outrageous jokes that social inferiors would never dare to make. Certain women were so grand, as Johnson said when the Duchess of Northumberland published her rhyme about a buttered muffin (1775), that they could get away with anything.[85] At the same time, this did not mean that humbler women could not make the same types of jokes. So long as a bawdy joke was listened to or repeated with the right display of tutting disapproval, all was well. Standards of sexual modesty were certainly repressive, but in this as in any other culture, repression only led to more innuendo. The same could be said of the cruelest jokes. Women's conduct literature is full of warnings about the unchristian malice of ridicule. The spiteful great lady became a stock figure in sentimental fiction, beginning with Lady Davers in *Pamela* (1740) and Lady Spatter in *David Simple* (1744). Differentiating oneself from such women was no small part of the performance of middle-class femininity.

Yet here again the class differences begin to collapse. Genteel women's private writings—now more accessible than ever—are full of spiteful remarks about the ugliness of some acquaintance or her new suitor. Often these are framed by evasions or cushioned by a mass of disapproving padding. Yet now and then one finds a blast of unguarded joy about someone's illness and its ruinous effects on his or her looks. Witness Elizabeth Shackleton (1726–81), the waspish provincial matriarch at the heart of Vickery's *Gentleman's Daughter*. There is no sex in Shackleton's letters, but otherwise she minces no words. Some of the clearest insights into everyday comments and perceptions come, inadvertently, in the finer distinctions of conduct literature. Never let anyone actually see you laughing at them, Hester Chapone insists at one point: at the very least, leave the room first.[86] If any of this seems counterintuitive, recent work on Jane Austen may be more familiar—all the revisionist scholarship that draws on Austen's letters and juvenilia to create a tougher and less sentimental figure. This Austen jokes about physical misfortunes (blindness, crossed eyes, obesity), hilariously incongruous marriages, and, in one notorious instance, a miscarriage. All this only in the papers that Cassandra did not destroy.

Having said all this, the issue of humor in eighteenth-century women's writing does tend to resolve into a repeated pattern. Again and again, one finds the text's comic energies displaced or split off from the author or heroine onto women who somehow get away with it while simultaneously embodying negative assumptions about the type of woman who laughs. One thinks immediately of Burney's Mrs. Selwyn (altogether too "satirical," as the heroine keeps saying) or Austen's Mary Crawford with her sodomy joke in

Mansfield Park. But such figures crop up in every genre of women's writing: take Mrs. Mary Singleton, the garrulous persona of Frances Brooke's periodical *The Old Maid* (1755–56) or the witty old nurse who tells the stories in Sarah Scott's *Journey through Every Stage of Life* (1754). The satiric voice of *David Simple* is entirely displaced onto the witty Cynthia, an outspoken Bluestocking figure. Maria Edgeworth's *Belinda* (1801) offers two of these licensed yet satirized women: the sparkish Lady Delacour and the wonderful Harriet Freke, who stalks through the book with her "horse laugh" and love of mischief. Arranged more or less chronologically, from Sarah Fielding's Cynthia to Harriet Freke and Mary Crawford, these figures grow progressively more shocking. They have rightly been linked to increasing anxieties about women's authorship and women writers' own growing discomfort with a vocal and public role. But the sudden, eye-popping vitality that these characters bring to each text points to some insistent comic energies and the difficulty of constraining them.

*

A final plea. Given their prominence in the eighteenth-century book trade, jestbooks and related comic imprints are now extremely rare. One repeatedly finds references—in newspapers, bookseller's catalogs, end-page advertisements, and printers' ledgers—to texts of which there are now no records. Even if one assumes high levels of puffing, the number of lost texts is phenomenal. More starkly than most print genres, jestbooks remind us that survival rates are never a reliable guide to the original prevalence and distribution of any book.[87] They also invite us to reflect on the accidents and processes by which less appealing historical documents survive or perish. At the most basic level, the scarcity of jestbooks is a material phenomenon: sold in sheets and carried about in pockets, they were read to the point of disintegration. But at least as important, such publications were hardly ever collected, in any of the multiple senses of that term. They were obviously disdained by the great copyright libraries, then building up their collections of belles lettres and national historical documents. They had little of the quaintness or folkloric interest of the Roxburghe ballads or the early collections of Bagford and Strutt. Among comparable categories of publication—almanacs, newspapers, halfpenny ballad sheets, Nonconformist tracts, economic pamphlets—ephemeral comic texts may be the least likely to have survived. (Compare the fate of didactic or religious texts, preserved from the very beginning in public collections and invaluable private ones like Dr. Williams's Library.)

Early modern jestbooks have survived only because they were treasured and gradually accumulated by reclusive and cranky bibliophiles—figures as diverse as Francis Douce ("constitutionally irritable," as his obiturist tactfully put it), Henry Huth, Robert Hoe, and W. C. Hazlitt (that "antiquarian bumbler" Samuel Schoenbaum dubbed him for the spectacular mess he made with Shakespeare). The obscure hero of this project is Walter Newton Henry Harding (1883–1973), a cinema organist and music-hall pianist from Chicago who amassed almost three hundred early jest- and songbooks and left them to the Bodleian Library. *Cruelty and Laughter* would have been immensely more difficult without them.[88] In 2011, however, one might be more sanguine about this and other long-standing gaps in the human record. Databases and digitization projects now offer ever easier access to rare and scattered texts; the remaining barriers are more institutional and disciplinary. Nondramatic comic literature has never had much status in professional contexts. In bibliographies, databases, and library catalogs, minor comic texts are still buried under deadening categories. Classifications like *wit and humor* reliably trivialize anything they touch. The term *satire* implies a comparison to higher examples and an instrumental purpose—anything to avoid just being funny. The worst of all these terms must be *ephemera*, which by definition casts texts as cheap and unimportant. Archivists and scholars are only beginning to appreciate how wrong this is.

CHAPTER TWO

Cripples, Hunchbacks, and the Limits of Sympathy

Constant jokes about hunchbacks or blind men almost compel one to look for more, and to speculate about the world that produced them. The first generation of disability scholars—those who put the subject on the map— were understandably reluctant to explore the evidence of cruel torments. Laughing at cripples has generally been cast as something that more humane or scientific perspectives were leaving behind, along with superstitions about dwarfs or clubfeet. But tormenting the disabled remained ubiquitous and automatic in eighteenth-century culture; printed epigrams and stage routines were profitable parts of its entertainment economy. Distasteful as they are, these materials reach out to us from a stubbornly unfamiliar world; my task in the opening sections of this chapter is simply to gather the lost and scattered evidence. I have intentionally ranged as widely as possible. The obvious risks of this approach seemed far outweighed by the need to establish the fullness and variety of the historical record. Ultimately, I hope that the exercise might address the recurring complaint that we still know too little about the lived experience of disability in eighteenth-century culture—about what it was actually like to live with bodily defects or impaired functions.

Deformity and *disability* as I use them in this chapter are deliberately inclusive categories, embracing all manner of physical disabilities, impairments, or "defects," whether congenital or acquired. Of necessity, I leave aside modern debates about who is or is not disabled (whether the deaf are disabled or a linguistic minority, to mention just one example). This is not to say that very distinct afflictions were perceived or treated in the same way. The modern understanding of *disability* as a unified category—at least sufficiently unified to be used by activists and legislators—did not exist.[1] One would also be quite wrong to posit significant solidarity between different deformed groups— between the blind and deaf, dwarfs, hunchbacks, or the elderly. What unifies these disparate conditions, for my purposes in this chapter, is the comic reaction they evoked—even as they also evoked pity, fear, malicious triumph, and scientific curiosity. With this perspective, I have tried to follow recent tendencies in disability studies, where the older "medical model" of disability, emphasizing individual impairment, is combined with a "social model" that stresses perceptions of that impairment and the prejudices or limitations they create.[2]

DEFORMITY GENRES

Jestbooks are the tip of an iceberg. One finds the same cruel humor in countless other contexts. Daily newspapers often included a section of droll anecdotes—usually variations on old jokes about the blind man who comes *to see* someone or the hilarious misunderstandings of a deaf man.[3] Even the blank spaces of almanacs and cookbooks were filled up with jokes: someone tells a hunchback he can't "set him straight" or "do him right." It's no use arguing with you, says a coffeehouse wag to someone with scoliosis: "I can see you're all on one side."[4] Short-lived comic periodicals—*All-Alive and Merry*, *The Weekly Amusement*, *The Monthly Merry Maker*, and others—combined these old jokes with noticeably newer ones like the increasing number about glass eyes. (An Irishman buys himself a new glass eye, only to return the next day and abuse the oculist because he can't see out of it.) Exchanges of insults between two deformed people—the ancient *tu quoque* scenario—recur in every form. "A Man, blind of one Eye met his hunchback'd Neighbour. . . ." A man with one eye sneers at a squinter—he'd rather have one good eye than two cocked ones like that.[5] Old folktale versions extend the humor to many stanzas: a blind man and a cripple go begging together, each exploiting the other's disability. But there were also protracted contemporary versions: a gout sufferer takes a long coach journey beside a blind and deaf man who keeps knocking his gouty feet but hears no cries of pain.[6]

These materials were a profitable part of the expanding print market, important content in newer genres as well as the familiar jestbooks and miscellanies. Canting dictionaries, for example, delighted in deformity jokes and lovingly collected every possible nickname for squinters or people with bandy legs. Francis Grose ventriloquizes the scene when a hunchback stepped into the street:

> "Did you come straight from home? if so, you have got confoundedly bent by the way." "Don't abuse the gemman," adds a by-stander, "he has been grossly insulted already: don't you see his back's up?" Or some one asks him if the show is behind; "because I see," adds he, "you have the drum at your back."

It continues: a soldier asks him whether he's joining their troop, since he's already wearing a knapsack.[7] Then the nicknames: a lame man was "Mr. Hopkins," "Hopping Giles," or simply "Giles" (the patron saint of cripples). "An ugly blind man," says Grose, was a "Groper" or "Blind Cupid" (proverbially blind and often painted with a blindfold). And one finds much that was more topical. Miscellanies published short "lives" of celebrated wits who torment lunatics and toss dwarfs out windows. There are illustrated broadsides with verses about the latest freak show or the new dwarf waiter at a certain coffeehouse. Look, he's already forty-four and still hasn't grown up; at this rate he'll live for ever.[8] That little hunchback is rude, says one gentleman to another. No he's not, replies his friend: look at that nice *bow* he's making.[9] A well-known hunchback dies after falling from his horse—and soon the magazines were full of commemorative verses.

In all these contexts, verbal wit alternates with accounts of pitiless physical pranks. Someone kicks a cripple's crutch from under him or grabs hold of a sailor's wooden leg. Dwarfs are thrown down chimneys or dunked in horse ponds. One of the more commonly excerpted episodes from Ward's *London Spy* evokes the goings-on at a Billingsgate tavern—a smoky cellar full of rakes and foulmouthed sailors. Two seamen walk in with "a little crooked fiddler." Soon they spot a hook above the fireplace, "which they immediately converted into a very comical use":

> Laying violent hands on my little Lord Fiddler by the hind slit of his breeches they hung him upon the tenter. In this condition, pendant like a play-house machine or a brazen cherub over a church branch, he hung sprawling, begging with humble submission to be set safe upon *terra firma*. At last, by wriggling, he broke the string of his breeches, and down came our broiled scraper into the ashes.

This put the company, Ward concludes, into "an extravagant fit of laughter" and the "angry homunculus" into a characteristic dwarfish fit. His only revenge is to torment the company with a hideous tune, after which "he cocked the arm of his humped shoulder on his hip, and away rolled the runlet [little barrel] of gall, turning his back upon the company."[10]

Such incidents—along with the "proof" of collective laughter—were mainstream fare in early modern comic fiction. Certainly they are unavoidable in the picaresque and antiromance traditions. Only a few pages into *Lazarillo de Tormes*, we find the hero punishing a malignant blind beggar. Lazarillo leads the old man along the worst roads, over sharp stones and through filthy ditches. He throws up in the man's face and finally leads him into a post before abandoning him, his head split open, in the winter rain.[11] The hero of Quevédo's *The Swindler* spends a night in an almshouse for crippled beggars and delightedly describes their struggles to dress in the morning.[12] Everyone recalled the misfortunes of Ragotin, the unfortunate little dwarf in Scarron's *Roman comique*, who is remorselessly beaten and humiliated and finally drowned in a river. All these texts were widely read and translated throughout the eighteenth century; combining with native traditions in texts such as *The English Rogue* (1665–80), they remained vital parts of English fiction.[13]

More important, these scenarios continued to appear in the new comic fiction of the age. Smollett's *Peregrine Pickle* (1751) seems to work almost systematically through the established scenarios—invalids, hunchbacks, lame matrons, wooden legs, nonsensical conversations with the deaf. Commodore Trunnion's marriage to Mrs. Grizzle—he gouty, one eyed, impotent, and hideously scarred across the nose, she "a squinting, block-faced, chattering piss-kitchen"—is a glorious practical joke against the groom. The hero's hateful younger brother is a tiny cripple nicknamed "Crookback" or "my Lord" who is subjected to a long sequence of torments before being thrown out a window into "a parcel of hogs that fed under it." Mr. Keypstick, the German schoolmaster, is another shrunken hunchback who does his best to look presentable and therefore cries out to be exposed. Peregrine strews his way with bean shells (the eighteenth-century equivalent of the slapstick banana skin), with the result that "his heels slipped from under him, his hunch pitched upon the ground, and the furniture of his head fell off in the shock; so that he lay in a very ludicrous attitude for the entertainment of the spectators."[14] This concluding formula is typical of Smollett's deformity humor: all ends "to the infinite satisfaction of the spectators." Another victim "roared hideously with repeated bellowings, to the unspeakable enjoyment of Peregrine and the lady, who laughed themselves almost into convulsions at the joke."[15] In the syntactic fluency of these formulas—their utterly satisfied sense of comic closure—one suddenly senses the guiltless, intoxicating pleasure of tormenting the disabled in early modern culture.

These incidents were also profitable ingredients of the minor comic fiction of the age. *Miss C——y's Cabinet of Curiosities* (1765) is one of several dozen nonsense fictions that appeared in the wake of *Tristram Shandy*. Early in the book, we find the extended story of a clever young woman walking along behind an Irish hunchback:

> "Holla!—You!—My Lord HUMP!"—cried a fine Young Girl, of about seventeen, to a little, deformed, old Fellow of about fifty-seven, twenty-five Days ago, as he was walking slowly along the *Strand*, in *London*.
>
> The Man, however, did not hear her at first, he being, it seems, somewhat deaf.
>
> "Holla!—You!—My Lord HUMP!"—iterated the fine Young Girl, as PADDY from *Cork* was passing along very unconcernedly, and whistling the Tune of the *Black Joke and Belly so white*.

The girl, it turns out, is an accomplished tormentor, able to keep a straight face even as the old man is looking directly at her to see who called. She repeats her call six times, each time "looking as grave as an old Woman at a Christening." The whole incident is imagined in an actual London topography, as the man and his tormentor walk along the Strand and stop at a pastry shop on Catherine Street (where Paddy asks for "a Rawspery Tart") and into Exeter 'Change. "HOLLA!—You!—My Lord HUMP!" concludes the girl, as she reaches home: "My Lord HUMP!—HUMP!—HUMP!—HUMP!" This time, however, Paddy smokes her out, turning his head "just at the very Instant the Word *Hump* was proceeding from her pretty Mouth."

> "Oh, oh," cried he, "but its you that have been making Game of me all this Time, is it?—I'll hump you immediately."

In true Sterneian fashion, the chapter now breaks off: the narrator is unable to tell us whether Paddy puts his threat into execution, as he had a lunch engagement. He will take up "the Cause of hunch-backed People being called in Derision my Lord or Lady," he tells us, "in my seventeenth Volume."[16]

Ubiquitous as these episodes were in fiction, the net volume of "deformity poetry" must be far greater. We are still only beginning to appreciate the vastness of the eighteenth-century poetry archive and its dazzling variety of forms, subjects, tones, and points of view.[17] Even in the 1760s, poetry still accounted for one in seven printed texts, as compared to one in twenty-five for prose fiction.[18] Deformity poetry appeared in every genre. Epigrams and lampoons, for example, are everywhere: condensed, clever, and immensely self-satisfied verses about someone else's facial defects or two hunchbacks in love. A garrulous old woman loses an eye—why wasn't it her tongue? An alewife loses her last four teeth to scurvy:

> When Gammer *Gurton* first I knew,
> Four Teeth in all she reckon'd,
> Comes a damn'd Cough, and whips out two,
> And t'other two a second.

What must be emphasized is the ongoing creativity of this poetry, its continuing adaptation of existing verse forms, and its obvious delight in form-content analogies. The cough is there in the sudden spondee and hard consonants of line 3; the last two teeth drop out in a splutter of dentals. But never mind, the poem concludes—the old woman doesn't need teeth to pour a jug of beer.[19] At its most ingenious, deformity poetry comes close to pattern or shape poetry. The title of Wycherley's "To a Little, Crooked Woman, with a Good Face and Eyes, Tho' with a Bunch Before, and Behind" itself imitates a sequential act of perception. The poet notices the generally small physique and beautiful face, but then sees the projecting belly and finally the hump on her back, the whole confusion bunched up together in the alliterative final words. The contorted versification that follows then imitates the impossibility of making love to a hunchback:

> Because your Crooked Back does lie so high,
> That to your Belly there's no coming nigh,
> Which, as your Back's more low, more high does lie. . . .

This poem was reprinted, with or without attribution, in dozens of comic miscellanies.[20]

One finds verses written from the sufferer's point of view, almost malignant as they imagine what it must feel like to lose a leg or go deaf. Thus "A Reverend D——r's Lamentation for the Loss of His Hearing":

> Deaf, giddy, helpless, left alone;
> To all my Friends a Burden grown.[21]

Laconic as it is, this couplet manages to capture the sudden loneliness of the deaf in a world of hearers. Yet one struggles to define it as either cold or empathetic—especially when it ends by consoling the doctor that at least he would never hear a woman's voice again. Behind this example are hundreds of mock consolations, in a baffling range of tones. An old debauchee is comforted after losing his nose to syphilis. At least the little hunchback wouldn't have to bend over when he got into a coach. A deformed woman was truly blessed: she would have no trouble preserving her chastity. Less malicious, perhaps, are the short "laments" addressed to a man who loses his favorite glass eye, or an amputee whose housemaid accidentally burns his wooden leg in the kitchen fire.

At the same time, one finds a range of extended narrative poems. Consider one peculiarly popular travesty of William Shenstone's "Pastoral Ballad" (1733) by a minor Shrewsbury poet named Samuel Johnson (ca. 1738–98; no relation). A one-eyed Irish shepherd named Phelim O'Gimlet describes his torments courting Margaret (Moggy) Timbertoe, a wooden-legged shepherdess. Moggy is also deaf, dumb, and one eyed. They are very well suited, he tells her: "We have two pretty legs here between us, / And a very complete pair of eyes." Moggy plays hard to get, and Phelim finally wins her heart only with a new glass eye and an elegant cork leg. She signifies her acceptance by squinting toward the church, where they are stitched together by a drunken parson.[22]

What is most surprising, given our routine division of texts into popular or polite, are the continuities between the cheapest and the most expensive examples of this genre. The same scenarios and the same poetic devices migrate easily between broadsides and costly miscellanies. The *deformed wedding*, as one might call it, shows up in the tiniest comic pamphlets (a few pennies at most) and in *Peregrine Pickle* (12 s. for four volumes). Blind men suffer in identical ways whether the text is a chiastic epigram on classical models or a folk rhyme like the following, chanted during games of Blind Man's Buff:

> Blind man, blind man,
> Sure you can't see?
> Turn round three times,
> And try to catch me.[23]

This and other folk rhymes offer the clearest proof of the elemental humor of deformities and speech impediments, across all boundaries of class or education:

> The girl in the lane, that couldn't speak plain,
>   Cried, Gobble, gobble, gobble:
> The man on the hill, that couldn't stand still,
>   Went hobble, hobble, hobble.

Or consider the following, which may still be used as a skipping rhyme in parts of England:

> There was a crooked man, and he walked a crooked mile,
> He found a crooked sixpence against a crooked stile;
> He bought a crooked cat, which caught a crooked mouse,
> And they all lived together in a little crooked house.[24]

The tone here is elusive, with regular hexameters so easily obscuring the subject and the cuteness of the second couplet leaving a sense of happily ever after. Such ambiguities enabled nineteenth-century folklorists to explain away cruelties as political allegories, just as they cleaned up folktales for a juvenile audience. Everyone knows how the three blind mice became Ridley, Cranmer, and Latimer, burned at the stake by Bloody Mary (farmer's wife, carving knife). The same process was applied to deformity rhymes: the crooked man is General Leslie, one of the Scottish Covenanters; the sixpence is Charles I; and the crooked stile is the border between Scotland and England. Like most of the political allegories, this one is far-fetched (the recognized experts have no time for it), and the frank nastiness of other rhymes casts suspicion on all attempts to soften:

> As I was going to sell my eggs,
> I met a man with bandy legs,
> Bandy legs and crooked toes,
> I tript up his heels, and he fell on his nose.

Compressed, rhythmic, and immensely self-gratified: this verse allows no explaining away.[25]

One scenario—the miseries of a disabled market woman—moves especially easily between demotic and polite contexts. The following appeared in numerous versions well into the nineteenth century:

> There was an Old Woman,
> Sold Puddings and Pyes.
> She went to the Mill,
> And Dust blew in her Eyes.[26]

In turn, this street scene and its simple experience of discomfiture helps make sense of one of the most perplexing moments in more canonical poetry. No one has much to say about the story of Doll the deformed apple seller (her neck "warpt beneath autumnal loads") in book 2 of Gay's *Trivia* (1716). In the midst of his extended account of the great frost fair of 1715–16, Gay suddenly pauses for an elegy to Doll, who sinks through the ice and loses her head:

> The cracking crystal yields, she sinks, she dyes,
> Her head, chopt off; from her lost shoulders flies;
> Pippins she cry'd, but death her voice confounds,
> And pip-pip-pip along the ice resounds.

The final line initiates one of Gay's Virgilian allusions (Doll's speaking head compared to that of Orpheus, torn from his body by the women of Thrace but still calling for Eurydice as it floated down the river Hebrus). Yet the allusion should not obscure the malicious fantasy of these lines or their very contemporary contexts—the decrepit apple vendor at Charing Cross, the blind pudding-pie woman in Cripplegate Church, and their like. In all the substantial criticism on this poem—studies of Gay's play with Georgic convention, of his complex satiric persona and the influence of Swift or Pope—one finds almost nothing said about the peculiar flippancy of this episode.[27]

Doll the twisted apple vendor, "Lord HUMP" the Irish hunchback, "my little Lord Fiddler," "the girl in the lane, that couldn't speak plain"—one could extend the list of victims ad infinitum. One finds droll rhymes and anecdotes about every conceivable physical anomaly. Bowlegs, clubfeet, cleft palates, harelips—every one of these conditions had its corresponding witticisms. Scurvy, jaundice, rickets, and other malnutritive illnesses all cried out to be laughed at. There were jokes about diabetes, consumption, asthma, epilepsy, and rheumatism; about strokes, tremors, incontinence, and the manifold humiliations of old age. Some of the language involved will be legible to modern readers. A judge tells someone he has a very *lame* case; a hunchback was "camel-back" or "mountain-back."[28] A woman with one eye was Gorgonia or Miss Cyclops. An asthmatic was Mr. Wheezy; Chicken Hams or Mr. Crook-Shanks were nicknames for people with bandy legs. Someone scarred by smallpox was Stub-Face or Mr. Pocklington.

But so much of this stuff—puns, riddles, nicknames, and odd explanations—will be more obscure. A toothless geriatric with a prominent nose and chin was Nutcracker-Face. A man with one eye must have just got up: he still had one of his windows shut. Didn't he know it was three in the afternoon?[29] The following was one of dozens of clever ways of insulting someone with a badly set nose:

> A Person having a wry Nose, another told him he knew what his Nose was made on, and what it was not made on; why, said he, how is that? It is not made of *Wheat*, 'tis made *a'Wry*, replied the other.

The same pun reappears as a riddle or conundrum:

> Why is a crooked woman like a country brown loaf?
> Because she is made a-wry.[30]

And there were thousands more in the same vein:

> Why is a lame Man like a good Clock?
> Because he never stands.

> Why is a sparrow like a man with one leg?
> Because it hops.

> Why is a Wig like a blind Beggar?
> Because it is Cur-led.[31]

At a distance of 250 years, one wonders how anyone could have laughed. From Dennis and Addison to Chesterfield and beyond, generations of commentators railed against puns and other forms of "false wit." But the British were evidently addicted, reliably amused by groaning homonyms, enigmas, and riddles, all of them printed by the hundred at the ends of miscellanies and songbooks.

These materials were not hangovers from the past: they continued to be produced, in greater numbers than ever. One of the many forgotten pastimes of this culture was "cross-reading": cutting out single lines from old newspapers and juxtaposing them for humorous effect. This began as an activity for rainy days in the country, but by the 1750s one finds particularly amusing examples reprinted in newspapers and jestbooks:

> Friday a poor blind man fell into a saw-pit,
>
> . . . .
>
> to which he was conducted by Sir Clement Cottrell.[32]

The antiquarian Sir Clement Cottrell (1686–1758) was a wise old man about town; the idea that he might lead a blind man into a hole was a bit outré but not completely preposterous. And there is much more where this came from: lumbering paradoxes and similes that confound modern readers but must have been clear enough to work comically in this culture. A man with a very bright or "ruby" nose walks into a tavern; some wag opines that now they could do without candles. Someone's warped spine "was enough to make anyone an atheist, convincing him that the world was made by chance."[33] One finds prolonged analogies with contemporary events, fashions, even pieces of legislation:

> After the Fire of *London*, there was an Act of Parliament to regulate the Buildings of the City; every House was to be *three Stories* high, and there was to be no *Balconies* backwards: A *Gloucestershire* Gentleman, a Man of great Wit and Humour, just after this Act was passed, going along the Street, and seeing a little, crooked Gentlewoman on the other Side of the Way, he runs over to her in great Haste, Lord, Madam, said he, how dare you walk thus publickly in the Streets? Walk publickly in the Streets! and why not, pray Sir? answered the little Woman. *Because*, said he, *you are built directly contrary to Act of Parliament; you are but two Stories high, and your* Balcony *hangs over your House of Office.*[34]

If we accept that a successful punch line must justify the length of the joke, we must conclude that the simple image of taunting a hunchback compensated readers for the labored complexity of the analogy. One everywhere encounters these painfully distended analogies, along with wry explanations for particular deformities. A hunchback must have been nursed by a camel. No wonder that old scold has no teeth: her tongue wore them away.[35] A knock-kneed person must be trying to grind mustard with his knees. Was he from Durham (famous for mustard)? Smallpox scars: Satan must have walked across your face in hobnailed boots. As for a squinter, his mother must have given birth in a hackney coach, looking out both windows. Was he born midweek, looking both ways for Sunday? Young Miss Squint would make a great cook—she could always keep one eye on the pot while the other looked up the chimney.[36] Her brother Master Squint was destined to be a scholar: he could read both pages at the same time.[37] Where did bowlegged people buy their boots? Crooked Lane. Where did they get their socks? Bandy-Legged Walk. Their legs must have grown in the night, unable to see straight.[38]

In classic comic texts as well as newer productions, readers gloried in extravagant and far-fetched similes. Potbellied hunchbacks like Hudibras and Aesop were shaped like the letter Z or the number 5. Hudibras bore his buttocks above his head like Aeneas carrying Anchises from the ruins of Troy.[39] Ned Ward meets a man with a harelip "that had drawn his Mouth into as many corners as a Minc'd-Pye." The midcentury master of these metaphors, unsurprisingly, was Smollett. Someone with a bowel disorder is "bent into a horizontal position, like a mounted telescope"; an old man hangs from his crutches "like the mummy of a felon hanging in chains."[40] With their allusions to new optical technologies and the recently extended practice of hanging in chains (25 Geo. 2 c. 37), both examples demonstrate the contemporaneity of these mental habits.

A related convention was the extended deformed portrait, another set piece that both reached back to Rabelais, Cervantes, and Scarron and continued to attract modern authors. Here, characteristically luxuriating in the language, is Peter Motteux's description of Maritornes, the stunted servant wench whom Don Quixote takes for a lord's daughter:

> A Broad-fac'd, Flat-headed, Saddle-nos'd Dowdy; blind of one Eye, and t'other almost out . . . not above three Feet high from her Heels to her Head; and her Shoulders . . . having too much Flesh upon 'em made her look downwards oftner than she could have wish'd.[41]

When Hogarth engraved this description—as he did with Hudibras and other well-known fictional grotesques—he had only to follow the instructions. Fielding and Smollett continued the tradition in midcentury fiction. Again and again, the narrative suddenly stops for a virtuoso portrait of ugliness: balloon-shaped women like Mrs. Tow-Wouse and Slipslop (short, fat, tiny eyes, monstrous nose, cowlike breasts, pimples, and one leg shorter than the other, "which occasioned her to limp as she walked").[42]

The continuing demand for such stuff was partly satisfied by collecting and adapting older depictions of the deformed. Images were cut out and pasted into commonplace books, collected by antiquarians like Francis Douce, and eventually made their way into collective biographies like Granger's *Biographical History* (1769) and Caulfield's *Remarkable Persons* (1790–95). The same figures show up again and again, always described in the same odd tone of appreciative disgust. Deformed fortune-tellers, for example, were always ambiguous. Thus Robert Nixon, a Jacobean fortune-teller ("a short squab fellow [with] a great head and goggle eyes [who] used to drivel as he spoke").[43] Or Mother Shipton, a late medieval Yorkshire fortune-teller who remained a byword for hideous ugliness (a real Mother Shipton, "the very Counterpart of Mother *Shipton*"). Richard Head's late-seventeenth-century description exemplifies the luscious style of all these word portraits:

> Her Neck so strangely distorted, that her right shoulder was forced to be a supporter to her head, it being propt up by the help of her Chin, in such sort, that the right side of her Body stood much lower than the left; like the reeling of a Ship that sails with a side wind.[44]

This sort of stuff continued to provide good copy for midcentury periodical publishers. Flipping through the *London Magazine* for June 1753, one suddenly comes across an extended portrait of Bertholde, apparently a late medieval prime minister to the King of Lombardy:

> Bertholde had a large head, as round as a foot-ball, adorned with red hair, very strait, and which had a great resemblance to the bristles of a hog; an extremely short forehead furrowed with wrinkles; two little blear eyes, edged round with a border of bright carnation, and overshadowed by a pair of large eye-brows, which upon occasion, might be made use of as brushes.

The blazon continues: a "flat red nose, resembling an extinguisher," a huge mouth with teeth like boar tusks, donkey ears, great thick lips, a neck covered in warts and tumors. The metaphors are so overdone as to be almost kindly, and sure enough the description concludes with the usual consolation that nature might have been unkind with Bertholde's body, but had made up for it with a double dose of political cunning.[45]

Of course, laughing at personal defects had always been problematic in certain contexts. One finds intermittent cautions, for example, in the ancient rhetoricians and in Sidney, Bacon, and Renaissance courtesy literature. The unease was evidently spreading by the early eighteenth century, along with other worries about the nature of laughter. Dennis, Congreve, Addison, Steele, Blackmore, William Whitehead—all insist that comedy should laugh only at corrigible defects.[46] The subject soon received its most extended discussion in James Beattie's "Essay on Laughter and Ludicrous Composition," which singles out Smollett and his tricks against Hatchway, the one-legged mariner in *Peregrine Pickle*. "He who forgets humanity so far, as to smile at such a memorial of misfortune in a living person," Beattie declares, "will be blamed by every good man."[47] The tone of exhortation tells us that Beattie was denouncing widespread habits (and in fact readers loved Smollett's larks with the wooden leg, which were also frequently illustrated). Almost all attempts to curtail cruel laughter fall back on similar overstatements. No one but a "half-wit" would laugh at deformity, says Dennis; nothing was more "barbarous" and "ill-natured," says Congreve. Let "th'unthinking Crowd" laugh at hunchbacks and squinters, says Whitehead; a good man would restrain himself.[48]

In these circumstances, deformity humor relied more and more on the old "affectation" defense (and eventually on the still more evasive concept of "incongruity," which continues to dominate philosophical discussions of laughter).[49] Only a monster would laugh at "natural Imperfections," says Fielding in the preface to *Joseph Andrews*, "but when Ugliness aims at the Applause of Beauty, or Lameness endeavors to display Agility; it is then that these unfortunate Circumstances, which at first moved our Compassion, tend only to raise our Mirth."[50] One finds the same uneasy contrast in every context. "We are pitied, while we go lame because we can't help it," writes Wycherley, "but laughed at for pretending to dance, when we are obliged to hobble." "Pity those whom Nature abuses," says one of Vanbrugh's comic characters, "but never those who abuse Nature."[51] The insistent symmetries of these formulas obscure an untidy reality, but since deformed people understandably tried to avoid ridicule, they adapted themselves to every situation. Ragotin was a dwarf pretending to be a romantic lover, so perhaps he deserved the torments. Even the exchanges of insults could be justified in this way: "He who mocks a cripple should be straight himself" went the proverb—and behind it was the biblical mote and beam.[52] But what continues to surprise is the volume of deformity humor—all the magazine poetry, conundrums, little ditties in newspapers, and mainstream fictional episodes—that doesn't even bother with this defense. *Peregrine Pickle* shows almost no recognition that it might be problematic to torment a hunchback or toss a dwarf into a pigsty, and clearly many readers agreed.

DANCING CRIPPLES AND THE LONDON STAGE

Any cross-generic survey of deformity humor would be incomplete without at least a brief glance at the stage. For here, as with print, one finds an enduring taste for all the old taunts and torments—and at every level, from the patent theaters to fairground booths and variety shows. One remarkable illustration is the continuing popularity of John Vanbrugh's *Esop* (1697), which enjoyed regular performances into the 1750s. Aesop's deformity was a commonplace dating back to antiquity. He was portrayed on every frontispiece, including Samuel Richardson's adaptation of L'Estrange, as a twisted hunchback.[53] Vanbrugh's play takes the classic farce situation of a forced marriage but plays up the deformity humor, with the tyrannical Learchus trying to force his daughter Euphronia to marry the hideous old cripple. Esop is the court sage and eventually resolves the plot for the best, but there is ample room along the way for the old jokes. Esop beaten and boxed around the ears by a peevish widow, Esop coughing and hobbling about offstage, Esop the hunchbacked dwarf in foppish attire, doing his best to be handsome. Vanbrugh takes care to script out even the most standard vignettes:

Enter ROGER, *a Country Bumpkin, looks seriously upon* ESOP; *then bursts out a laughing.*
ROGER: Ha, ha, ha, ha, ha: Did ever Man behold the like? Ha, ha, ha, ha, ha.

Much of the play's humor consists in nasty references to Esop's appearance. "Monster," "Baboon," "half-Man, half-Monkey," "that ugly, ill-boding Cyclops," "the most deform'd Monster that Copulation ever produc'd." Esop is a "Crump," "Devil," "treacherous Piece of Vermin," "that unfinish'd Lump, that Chaos of Humanity." At times, the action stops entirely for a sequence of overblown insults: "Why, you pitiful Pigmy . . . you little, sorry, crooked, dry, wither'd Eunuch."[54]

Virtuoso abuse clearly made for good theater; Garrick used many of the same insults in *Lethe*, his satiric afterpiece of 1745, which transfers Aesop to the underworld as a wise man consulted by a sequence of fools. In Garrick's version, the best lines go to the fashionable Mrs. Riot: "You ugly Creature you"; "if I see any more of you, I shall die with Temerity." For all the satiric force of her character, the lady is a crucial vehicle for this incidental humor: "O you ugly Devil you!" "You old Fright!" "Nay, now I must laugh in your ugly Face, my Dear." "The wise think me handsome, Madam," Aesop gravely informs her—at which one cannot avoid the sound of collective laughter.[55]

Esop is only the best known of several "deformity comedies"—plays that revolve around some maimed or disfigured central character. The greatest midcentury producer of these plays was Samuel Foote, whose early successes included pitiless imitations of deformed contemporaries, culminating in his notorious takeoff of the one-legged Dublin bookseller George Faulkner in *The Orators* (1762). Everyone recognized the justice four years later when Foote lost his own right leg in a riding accident (heaven punished him "in the part offending," as Chesterfield joked to Faulkner).[56] Foote characteristically made the best of it, purchasing two wooden legs and quickly returning to the stage. The disability actually enhanced some of his greatest comic roles. The rheumatic Mother Cole in *The Minor* (1760) and Lady Pentweazle in *Taste* (1752) were both improved by a limp. Best of all, Foote could now imitate Faulkner with authenticity. His audiences were now larger than ever: ten people went to see Foote with one leg, said one contemporary, for every one who went when he had two.[57] Two of the great successes of his later years were dedicated deformity comedies. *The Devil upon Two Sticks* (1768) was a three-act adaptation of Le Sage, in which Foote played the title character to great effect. *The Lame Lover* (1770) was yet another comedy about a father trying to force his daughter to marry a deformed man. Foote played Sir Luke Limp, a one-legged social climber.

Of the many less familiar deformity comedies, I will mention only two, chosen as different ends of a spectrum. A late example of the genre came with John O'Keeffe's *The Little Hunchback; or, A Frolic in Bagdad*, first performed at Covent Garden in 1789 and frequently thereafter. Crumpy, the little hunchback, is a jovial prankster figure (court dwarf to the bassa of Baghdad) who nevertheless suffers all the usual humiliations. By the end of the play he has been dropped down a chimney, thrown down a flight of stairs, stunned by a falling flowerpot, and almost choked on a fish bone. *The Little Hunchback* was sufficiently well-known, and sufficiently benign, to be included in William West's "Toy Theatre" collection of 1815—one of the earliest cardboard cutout sets produced for children.[58] At the opposite end of the spectrum, and surely the most objectionable of all these plays, is *Trick for Trick* (1735), a two-act ballad opera by the amateur playwright Robert Fabian (formerly a footman in the royal household). As with *Aesop* and *The Lame Lover*, *Trick for Trick* centers on a threat of marriage to a deformed person. In this case, a greedy old man is tricked into agreeing to marry a hideous dwarfess named Estifania, described before her appearance with characteristic embellishment:

What pity it is this amiable Lady should be not above three Foot high; that her back shou'd have the Curiosity to rise and peep over her Head; that her Nose should be so unfortunate as to be loaded with a Wart as big as a Pomegranate; and that her Face should be perfectly out of Countenance, for want of an Eye.

In a stunning instance of the adaptability of deformity humor, the joke here is not on the dwarf but on the old suitor. The orchestrator of the joke is Estifania's father, and his daughter is apparently delighted to use her defects in this way. The play ends with the usual burlesque wedding scene, with the bridegroom pompously approaching the sedan chair containing his "Phoenix of Virgin Loveliness," only to be horrified when the "deform'd little Creature" steps out. Everyone "bursts outs into a loud laugh," and Estifania herself joins in the teasing. "Why do you turn your eyes so inhumanely from your languishing bride?" she purrs. "I shall break my heart to see my husband unkind to me on my wedding-day." She completes his humiliation by dancing around him and singing the following ballad (to the tune of "Chevy Chase"):

> Some demon, sure, to my disgrace,
> Has made your lordship blind;
> Or you, to such an air and face
> Would blush to be unkind.
>
> If you this single eye survey,
> Such beams will strike your view,
> Your love to me will make you say,
> 'Tis well I had not two.

Her victim doesn't agree: "Death and damnation!—I'd sooner marry a She-Rhinoceros."[59]

Beyond these focused deformity comedies were countless others that had fun along the way. All the old jokes about blind men and hunchbacks show up as comic asides. Something was "as plain as the nose on your face." A hunchback is "bent upon it" or "has her back up," as in Vanbrugh and Cibber's *The Provoked Husband* (1728, and countless revivals). Deafness remained a routine source of farcical cross-purposes—in figures such as Corbaccio, the old miser in Jonson's *Volpone*, or Old Fumble in D'Urfey's *Fond Husband*, "very deaf and almost blind" and always answering absurdly.[60] John Hippisley, Dicky Norris, James Spiller, and other celebrated comic actors made their name in such geriatric roles. Onstage insult matches were an old tradition and remained ubiquitous in eighteenth-century comedy ("lame rogue," "blind knave," "pitiful limping Hag").[61] One prominent figure in many of these episodes is a disabled musician who comes on for a good beating and can respond only with a hideous noise on his instrument. An old blind fiddler comes on for a single scene in *The Devil to Pay* (1731), in which his sole function is to have the fiddle broken over his head by the termagant Lady Loverule:

FIDLER: O Murder, Murder! I am a dark Man, which way shall I get hence? Oh Heav'n! she has broke my Fiddle and undone me and my Wife and Children.[62]

No one really remembers the spectacular success of *The Devil to Pay*, but this riotous ballad opera about wife beating was the most-performed afterpiece of the eighteenth century. This means that the small detail of the blind fiddler was repeated literally thousands of times.

Alongside these scripted roles, we must also think about improvised deformity humor—the limps, trembles, and unscripted asides of so many performances. As automatic and as effortless as lewd innuendo, this aspect of performance is less often acknowledged in modern scholarship. Falstaff, for example, was often played with the infirmities of age. We know that Foote improvised with his leg all the time. "[W]here a piece has seemed to languish and flag," one contemporary recalled, "I have seen him, by a hobbling walk across the stage, accompanied with significant gesture and grimace, set the house in a roar."[63] Also inaccessible to the historian are all the spontaneous takeoffs on contemporary figures, a practice attacked in these lines from Churchill's *Rosciad*:

> Doth a man stutter, look a-squint, or halt?
> Mimics draw humour out of Nature's fault:
> With personal defects their mirth adorn,
> And hang misfortunes out to public scorn.

Little documentation survives, but theater critics' constant complaints about departures from the script point to a significant practice.[64]

Again, one finds intermittent concerns that it was all a bit nasty. By midcentury, Corbaccio became a stock example of improper comedy (although this concern did little to limit performances). Certain actors went too far with Falstaff, adding limps, gout, and rheumatic coughs.[65] One particularly illuminating discussion developed over Old Target, the stuttering lawyer cruelly impersonated in Steele's *Conscious Lovers* (1722). Steele himself was self-conscious enough to have the impersonator specify in advance why it was proper to laugh: "Nay, it would be an immoral thing to mock him, were it not that his Impertinence is the occasion of its breaking out to that degree." The critics would have none of it, but the *Whitehall Journal* repeated Steele's justification (anyone with a stutter should know better than to be a lawyer) and added that lawyers always deserved to be laughed at, stutter or no stutter.[66] Modern readers immediately detect the circular logic—deformed characters always pretend not to be deformed, and it was therefore always appropriate to ridicule them. But in its age, the defense evidently sufficed.

And one cannot stop here. Cripples, hunchbacks, and stutterers were also consistent objects of laughter in the nondramatic parts of every theater program. Deformed masks were always prominent in the commedia dell'arte, with its cast of stuttering pedants and wheezing fathers who came onstage to be kicked up the backside or powdered with soot. Everyone knows how quickly English audiences took to the hook-nosed, hunchbacked Pulcinella—who developed into Punch and had only to show his hump or monstrous nose at the side of the booth to set the audience roaring (and who knocks a blind beggar off the stage in most early versions).[67] Earlier English clowns had been dressed up as hunchbacks, and behind them stretches a tradition going back at least to the hunchbacked, hook-nosed, large-jawed Maccus and Bucco of Atellan farce.

One specialty performance was the "crutch dance," in which a group of hunchbacks and amputees danced about to a saltbox and homemade fiddle (or, in a version that further pointed up the contrasts, to minuets and rigadoons). Crutch dances were an established part of Brome's *Jovial Crew* (1641), which was much revived and adapted in the eighteenth century, including a popular ballad opera of 1731.[68] They featured in the staging of other low-life farces like Fletcher's *Beggars' Bush* (1622/61), Shadwell's *Squire of Alsatia* (1688), and Coffey's *Beggar's Wedding* (1729). Something similar is clearly intended in scripted novelty dances: dances of witches (Davenant's *Macbeth* [1664/74]), cuckolds (Wycherley's *The Country Wife* [1675]), and watchmen (Gay's *Mohocks* [1712], Fielding's *Tumble-Down Dick* [1736]). The tradition was still alive in 1795, when Henry Lucas included a beggars' crutch dance in his masque *Coelina*.[69]

Inevitably the evidence is spotty and some of the examples marginal, but 80 percent of mainstream theater programs also offered dancing as an interlude or afterpiece. We know far less about these performances than we do about other aspects of the eighteenth-century theater: both subjects and choreography were left to the dancing master, and few records remain. But we do know that the predominant subjects were comic and demotic rather than courtly or romantic. There were dances about domestic rows and national type characters, about beggars and drunken sailors. One finds advertisements for "wooden shoe" dances featuring rustic simpletons and "trade" dances—chimney sweeps, carpenters, market women, and knife grinders.[70] Disability or frailty is often part of the fun. Consider the following descriptions from Lambranzi's *School of Theatrical Dancing* (1716), a manual routinely used by dance historians to reconstruct what happened on the London stage:

> Here two old women enter and dance, half-walking, half-shaking, as far as possible to the extreme front of the stage. Then they scratch themselves before and behind, spin round and go back to whence they began, with their backs to the audience, where they perform the same gestures. These goings backwards and forwards continue until the end of the first air. Meanwhile a youth enters who, on seeing the old women, laughs at them.

Artificial and performative as it is, the structure of feeling here cannot be ignored: the old women "half-walking, half-shaking," their personal filth, and the laughing youth, which one would have thought redundant but no doubt gave audiences a jolly-along. There are many more in this vein:

> Here is seen a blind man who, hearing the sound of music, sets his staff firmly on the ground and jerks his shoulders to and fro as if about to dance. But Harlequin enters and crawling between his two feet throws his hat into his face. Then the blind man gropes about and strikes the air with his staff.
>
> Harlequin creeps from under the blind man and, putting his hat on his bat, holds it in front of the face of the blind man, who, feeling himself touched, lashes out bravely with his staff. Thereupon Harlequin begins to laugh loudly and when he has performed divers strange *pas* from one side to the other they exit together.[71]

These may be the most detailed descriptions we have of a routine but usually unrecorded form of entertainment. They also oblige us to imagine all sorts of improvised performances that must have gone on with the disabled musicians who milled about backstage at every theater.

The same skits were mainstream entertainments outside the patent theaters. Midcentury Londoners still recalled the crutch dances at Martin Powell's puppet theater.[72] The newspapers are full of advertisements for novelty dances at the fairgrounds. Clog dances. Dances of tinkers or Scots (both proverbially bony and emaciated). Ned Ward describes the "elephant capers" of a grossly fat dancer ("as much flesh on her bones as a Lincolnshire heifer").[73] One Bartholomew Fair handbill advertises "A New Dance between Three Bullies and Three Quakers" and "A Cripples Dance by Six Persons with Wooden Legs and Crutches in Imitation of a *Jovial Crew*."[74] This scenario was deeply rooted in the early modern imagination and captured even in casual expressions. It looked like a crutch dance, one said of any group of middle-aged or impaired people trying to dance.[75] The celebrated Gelosi company once performed before the Duke of Mantua with a cast made up entirely of real hunchbacks. A similar entertainment is depicted in one remarkable print of the marriage festivities of Henri IV and Marie de Medici (1600). There are six dancers: two hunchbacks, one with no arm, one with a wooden leg, and another with a grossly distended belly (fig. 4).[76]

By far the most famous deformity dancer in midcentury London was "Monsieur Timbertoe," a one-legged performer in "Mrs. Midnight's Oratory," Christopher Smart's transvestite nonsense show that came and went at various venues throughout the 1750s. Timbertoe first appeared at the Little Haymarket Theatre in the winter of 1752–53 and quickly became the talk of the town. Every other entertainment would fail, one anonymous versifier predicted; Garrick, Foote, Clive, Pritchard, even John Rich would be ruined. Timbertoe would make a fortune, while "Both Houses, fighting, shall give up their Glory, / And curse the good Old Woman's Oratory."[77] No detailed records survive of these performances, but Monsieur Timbertoe was presumably an old soldier in French dress (he was not a foreigner, Mrs. Midnight insisted after her enemies stirred up anti-French sentiment, but an Englishman who lost a leg serving his country). His signature act seems to have been the hornpipe, that most acrobatic of popular dances. There were evidently other deformed entertainers amid the crazy nonsense of this show (harebrained monologues, clattering saltboxes, firecrackers, contortionists, performing animals). Many of Mrs. Midnight's later advertisements end with an invitation to anyone with some special trick or physical oddity to join her "Band of Originals" in return for "present Pay and good Quarters," a formula that tells us much about the economic arrangements and living conditions of variety-show performers.[78]

Similar entertainments are easily found. "At the New Wells at Clerkenwell," announces the *General Advertiser* in May 1746, the "wonderful little Polander"

FIGURE 4. Hunchbacked clowns and amputees at the marriage of Henri IV and Marie de Medici (1600), detail. Artist unknown. Crutch dances remained deeply rooted scenarios in the European imagination. The dancing cripple was also a proverbial representation of folly or affectation: a freak who thought himself handsome. Photograph © V&A Images/Victoria and Albert Museum, London (S. 1202-2010 [George Speaight Collection]).

(two foot ten and at sixty extremely old for a dwarf) would perform a country dance with "the tall Saxon woman, seven feet high."[79] The fairgrounds were evidently full of deformed entertainers. Ward's London Spy encounters a pair of "little flat-nosed comedians" at May Fair—"a couple of chattering homunculuses, dressed up in scaramouch habit."[80] There were farcical prizefights between one-eyed or one-armed boxers. At Southwark Fair in September 1761, Samuel Foote's booth offered a "whimsical Duel" between one "Col. Crackcrown" and "the purblind Major Blinco," who was clearly to be soundly beaten. The entertainment was fully dramatized, complete with the affront that provoked the battle and "the fortunate Conclusion of Peace, by a Methodist Cobler."[81] Not one of these was a vulgar entertainment, any more than crutch dances at the patent theaters. Mrs. Midnight's Oratory charged the regular theatrical prices of 5s. for the boxes, 3s. for the pit, and 2s. for the gallery; the house, her advertisements promised, would be "well air'd, and will be illuminated with Wax-Lights" to attract the "quality."[82] At the fairgrounds, Mrs. Midnight offered a separate entrance for the gentry and a special gallery lit with wax candles, and still charged between 6s. and 3s. for tickets. Foote's fight was offered not just to the fairground mob but to those who could afford a range of more expensive seats: 2s. 6d., 1s. 6d., 1s.[83]

When required, such entertainments were easily defended as artificial and highly stylized performances. Defenders of commedia had always made this argument: the limps, hunched backs, speech impediments, and funny noses were not real, insisted Andrea Perrucci in his treatise of 1699. "Although in real life they would be pitiful and apt to arouse commiseration," when counterfeited on stage these defects were "simply laughable."[84] And no doubt appreciation was as common a reaction at these performances as derision or triumph: disabled military men like Monsieur Timbertoe or Major Blinco were tough survivors, admired for their resilience and immunity to pain. Many deformed performers were admired for their agility and skill. Monsieur Timbertoe could do "more with one Foot, than others can with two."[85] Crutches, wooden legs, and distinctive limps enabled novel physical movements and produced enlivening percussive sounds not unlike all the dances of carpenters, shoemakers, or prisoners in their chains.[86]

But here, too, one can follow the defenses only so far. The "unreality" defense leans heavily on Aristotle's brief remarks on comedy. For Aristotle, famously, the proper object of comic laughter is some "fault" or "ugliness" that causes no pain, as exemplified by the masks of Athenian comedy.[87] Endlessly adapted into other contexts, this formula worked to obscure uneasy continuities between comic representations and the world. I have deliberately ended this section with the most manic and performative deformity entertainments because even these seem to refer to everyday situations. A blind man lashing about with his stick. Mrs. Midnight's robust old soldier on his wooden leg. Frail and dirty old women who scratch themselves in unmentionable places. Whether they are substitutes, rehearsals, or fond recollections of something seen, these scenarios correspond to everyday encounters.

STREETS AND COFFEEHOUSES

What evidence is there of this everyday laughter? As we now know all too well, the real is inaccessible, and none of us can get beyond language or representations. But however irrecoverable their experience, historical people lived in this world, read these books, and saw these plays. "Crook-Back,"

"Mr. Hopkins," "Mr. Nasty-Face": people used these and hundreds of other nicknames. They chanted folk rhymes and imitated limps or speech impediments. Their jokes circulated between oral and written contexts, mutating in and out of print. Deformity *events*, as one might call them, were reported in newspapers, memorialized in verse, illustrated in prints and drawings, and then adapted as practical jokes—which in turn were renarrativized in letters. Taken alone, each source has obvious limitations. Jestbooks are several removes from actual speech; exaggeration is the very logic of canting dictionaries. Folktales are hyperconventional genres, and even the most topical graphic satires drew on ancient traditions of caricature. Yet, tested against each other and then against more accepted historical documents, comic sources may take us closer to a world of feeling. I make no holistic claims and weigh the evidence in exploratory ways. I describe not typical behaviors or opinions but possible ones—what was thinkable or doable for significant proportions of the population some of the time.[88]

Certainly such laughter is well documented at the bottom of the social scale. The mob's "standing Jest," says Whitehead, was "the Mountain back, or Head Advanc'd too high, / A Leg mis-shapen, or distorted Eye." And such taunts are recorded in one of the very few first-person accounts of deformity— the remarkable memoir of William Hay (1695-1755), a Whig MP and self-described hunchback. The moment he stepped into the street, says Hay, the insults would begin. Irish chairmen, beggars, linkboys, butchers—the entire rabble joined in the abuse. Someone would step up and address him with a mock-dignified title ("My Lord," "Your Grace"). Deformed people, he concludes, should avoid bear gardens, fairgrounds, masquerades, and other crowded places.[89] Eugenia, the pock-scarred hunchback of Burney's *Camilla* (1796), can hardly go into the local village without being abused by the market women and their children: she is a "scarecrow" or the "little hump-back gentlewoman." Only a handful of coins will shut them up.[90]

More violent torments are everywhere recorded. Lower-class boys delighted, everyone accepted, in confusing the blind and tumbling lame matrons into gutters. Pierre-Jean Grosley, the French visitor, describes the rough treatment met with on a London street by an elderly Frenchman with an ear trumpet.[91] Drunken apprentices set dogs on beggars or puked on them from upstairs windows. Late in life, the bookseller James Lackington (1746-1815) recalled all sorts of nasty pranks against a lame widow in Wellington: he and the local boys would jostle her about and kick her lantern to leave her fumbling in the dark. They fastened things to her coat and nailed up her front door. One of Lackington's satirists speculated that these "humorous stories and droll anecdotes" were actually supplied by someone else; if so, they offer yet further proof of the currency of such pranks, here relied on by the shrewd retailer to make himself more interesting.[92] All these cruelties were especially associated with holidays, hanging days, and seasonal fairs, when mobs of drunken apprentices surged through the streets breaking windows, tossing beggars in blankets, and knocking over market stalls. It is no coincidence that the prankish boy leads his blind pie woman into Cripplegate Church on Easter Monday. Such days, celebrated by labor historians as times of freedom and defiance, were hell for disabled beggars and street vendors, as they certainly were for the working women whose drunken husbands came home and beat them.[93]

One begins to detect a reality behind all those jokes about rickety apple women and blind fiddlers. Far from the picturesque figures of Victorian lithographs, eighteenth-century street hawkers were ragged, desperate, and usually severely disabled. They worked the streets only because they were too frail for any active trade.[94] Many became familiar figures on particular street corners, acquiring nicknames like "Blind Fanny," "Lame Cassie," or "Squint-Eyed Nan." These figures are everywhere to be found in the crowded street scenes of midcentury engravers: one-eyed ballad singers, frail hunchbacks disappearing round corners, beggars crouched in doorways. And now and then one finds them depicted with almost obscene realism—a harelipped oyster vendor, an ancient hunchback selling matches, a scrap-metal collector with a drooping shoulder and a rudimentary orthopedic device supporting his shorter leg. A historian of disability might do much with these scattered images—an accumulative study of the sort that David Dabydeen produced in *Hogarth's Blacks*.[95]

For the congenitally deformed, street music offered another recognized means of support. One-legged humstrum players, crippled drummers, blind fiddlers: such people were the producers of demotic music at every venue. The loftier humanitarianism of the European hospital-conservatories had its equivalent in Britain, where the London Foundling Hospital and local workhouses trained orphans, especially blind ones, on the violin.[96] No doubt a few of them gained semiregular work at theaters and pleasure gardens, but most joined the mass of street fiddlers, working intermittently in the vulgar entertainment business. Bandy-legged dwarfs blew horns or banged meat cleavers in front of fairground booths; they walked the streets with distributors of handbills. Crippled drummers silenced the audience at puppet theaters and announced the entrance of combatants at the prizefighting arenas.[97] Amputees seem also to have found a place in this milieu, working as musicians, bear wards, or wandering showmen. Samuel Butler develops an extended portrait in the figure of Crowdero, the one-legged fiddler and leader of the bearbaiting crowd in *Hudibras*.

Such figures were objects of mingled fondness and irritation. Disabled entertainers embodied a sort of defiant cheerfulness, a refusal to be brought down by circumstance; they stood for festivity and raucous pleasure. *Mist's Weekly Journal* tells the story of a man preparing to kill himself until dissuaded by the appearance of a one-legged man with three performing animals.[98] And of course one finds charity and solidarity. Families traditionally took care of disabled relatives; even in the desperate world of the London slums, one finds structures of reciprocity and neighborliness. Squatters helped each other out in tough times; they gave out scraps and took in lame beggars during cold snaps.[99] At the same time, musicians and street vendors also made an intolerable racket, the clamor so routinely complained of by visitors to London: the cacophony of cowhorns and bladder fiddles, the same few lines repeated ad nauseam in a tired croaking voice. People could be almost grateful to the nasty boy who tripped up the ballad singer and finally gave them some peace. Sympathies were fragile and inconsistent: the blind man might be allowed to sleep by the fire for two nights, only to be tossed out on the third. And any sort of kindness was so easily interrupted by the primitive urge to yank the wooden leg or bang the blind fiddler on the head.

Food sellers were similarly ambiguous figures. Fishwives were of course stinky and belligerent, but similar associations surrounded the vendors of other foods. Someone upsets a fruit cart: after the usual barrage of insults, the old woman picks the apples out of the gutter and dries them on her grubby shift. Smollett's Matt Bramble finds a London market woman polishing cherries with her own spittle.[100] The muffin man puts down his basket, defecates against a church wall, and then resumes his trade without so much as a rinse. Early versions of "The Old Pudding-Pye Woman" rhyme continue with eleven more verses about the woman's personal filth. She washed only three times a year. She scratched and spluttered, and her nose dripped into every pudding. Everyone loved pudding pies (custard tarts): they smelled wonderful, and having no bones they were perfect once your teeth fell out. But if they made you sick, you went back and threw the filthy hag into the sewer where she belonged.[101]

To be sure, the moralists were attacking such violence. Newspapers and periodicals are full of complaints. In the background of Hogarth's *Gin Lane* (1751), one finds someone beating a blind cripple with his own crutch. The staggering cripple aims a stool at his tormentor, and a crowd has gathered to enjoy the fun. Such satiric vignettes are easy to find: consider one of the lesser known "Cries of London," the "Blind Musician" (ca. 1740) by the German émigré artist J. S. Müller. Müller's blind musician appears with a series of didactic verses about the treatment he had suffered. A malicious buck ("Pamper'd Prodigal Unkind") had punctured his bladder fiddle while the usual gang of boys stood around laughing.[102] But neither of these examples is entirely controlled. The "official" reading of Hogarth's image is that taunting blind men was yet another corruption of a gin-soaked society, but taken out of context, the detail could just as easily be comic. Müller's musician makes a new hurdy-gurdy with an empty tea tin, his misery all but forgotten. The overturned market woman works in so many midcentury prints as an emblem of order overwhelmed by chaos, but it also recollected a familiar and reliably satisfying street scene. It exists alongside other vignettes that can only be comic, like the repeated detail of a dwarf or an old woman trying to fend off a dog—as if, like Richard III, they were so ugly that even the dogs barked at them.[103]

Midcentury newspapers collected and elaborated such public mishaps, clearly demonstrating their appeal at higher levels of society. An elderly woman is gored by a runaway bull "and besides being much bruised, had her Gown tore so that part of it hung by his Horn."[104] A little man with bandy legs throws a fit after someone accidentally knocks him on the head. The blind apple woman who stood at the corner of King Street was recovering after her run-in with a mad dog. The one-legged man with the monkey gets his wooden leg stuck in the pavement and falls into Fleet Ditch. Much nastier is the following, suffered by a disabled bear ward:

> As a lame Man was lately shewing Tricks with a Bear, over against Suffolk-street, near Charing-Cross, the Creature being hungry, or ill-humour'd, shew'd his Master such a Trick as he was like to have cost him his Life, for his Muzzle being somewhat loose, he bit him grievously by his Stump-Hand, and with his Paws tore his Arm and Face in a sad Manner.

Already in this example, with the angry bear "shew[ing] his Master such a Trick," one sees the physical misfortune being transformed into a verbal joke, a process that continued as the anecdote migrated from one paper to another, into scrapbooks, letters, and oral contexts.[105]

These narrativized events were collected from around the country. Someone writes from Chester with the story of a mischievous boy who ties two blind ballad sellers together with a bent nail, provoking a ferocious display of cursing and nose scratching. One finds a particular fascination for deformed marriages of various sorts:

> Tuesday a beggar, known by the name of Ben, who not having the use of his leggs begg'd about the streets with pattens fix'd to his knees, upon which with the assistance of his hands, he moved from place to place, was marry'd at St. Anne's Black Fryers to an agreeable young woman of 60£ fortune.[106]

There are countless variations, some probably true, but all of them cast as comic spectacles. Two disabled peddlers fall in love from opposite sides of the street. Francis Grose tells the story of a one-eyed, wooden-legged sailor with no arms who wants to marry the daughter of a blind man. He would have accepted the offer, says the father, "had not his daughter received some overtures from a man who crawled with his hinder parts in a porridge pot."[107] The marriage of a dwarf—or better still, two dwarfs—always aroused great interest. "A few days ago," reported the *London Chronicle* in February 1768, "was married Mr. Richard Mallard, the English dwarf, to Miss Mary Crow, the Irish Lilliputian."[108]

For certain sectors of the higher classes, the pleasures of reading such things extended into practical jokes. Tormenting the disabled was an established part of the drunken high jinks I discuss in chapter 3. Riotous young men spilled out of taverns and roamed the streets poking sticks at cripples, stealing dogs from the blind, and attacking the decrepit old watchmen that every parish employed to keep order at night (men "so feeble," as Defoe complained, "that a Puff of Breath can blow [them] down").[109] Almost by instinct, young bucks gathered a retinue of short ugly waiters, fiddlers, and linkboys ("a little knock-kneed link-boy" is one recurring formula), whose role was to be teased, tossed about, and trapped in high places. Stories continued to be told about Rochester's treatment of his hunchbacked fiddler, known only as "Your Honour":

> The late Lord Rochester being, upon a freak with some of his companions, at the Bear at the Bridge-foot, among their music, they had an hump-back'd fiddler, whom they called His Honour. To humour the frolic, they all agreed to leap into the Thames, and it came to Lord Rochester's turn to do it at last; but his Lordship seeing the rest in, and not at all liking the frolic, set the crooked fiddler at the brink of the balcony, and push'd him in, crying out—I can't come myself, gentlemen, but I've sent my honour.

Apocryphal as this example may be, it exemplifies some widespread habits, with a spontaneous prank further elaborated into a verbal joke.[110]

These were not just things gentlemen did when disinhibited by alcohol. Jestbook torments suggest a habitual impulse to sneer:

> A Gentleman entering into a Prison to visit a Friend of his, the Porter, who had a great Scar in his Face, demanded his Weapon. The Gentleman gave it him, saying, *Hold here, Friend, and see thou make much of it, for I assure thee, it is not it that did thee that Disgrace*, pointing to his Face.

One cannot overstate the pervasiveness of these spontaneous insults. People might go up to an ugly man and ask how he liked the hideous ballad woman across the road: didn't he think they'd make a fine pair?[111] Jonathan Swift once had enormous fun giving false directions to a madman. He was stopped in Pall Mall by the man, who obstinately insisted that the queen owed him £200,000; he had just been turned away at the palace and anxiously asked whether he should try again. The man is a lunatic, not a cripple, but what is interesting is how effortlessly Swift improvises his response, and how pleased he is to tell people about it:

> [I] begged him of all love to go and wait on her immediately; for that, to my knowledge the Queen would admit him; that this was an affair of great importance, and required dispatch: and I instructed him to let me know the success of his business, and come to the Smyrna Coffee-House, where I would wait for him till midnight.[112]

Of course we also know about Swift's complex sympathy for the insane. He hated filthy beggars and the street vendors outside his window in London ("I wish his largest cabbage was sticking in his throat"), but his biographers describe all sorts of quiet charities. In these inconsistencies—irritation combining with compassion, vitriol, and careless amusement—Swift may be more characteristic of his age than we might want to acknowledge.[113]

It should not surprise us, then, to find all the same types of deformity jokes in more domestic settings, in the presence of women as well as men. One of David Garrick's most famous dinner-table performances was his "Jack Pocklington" routine, an imitation of a man who came to offer himself for the stage with a speech impediment and a badly scarred face.[114] One finds gentlemen sending for their deaf housekeeper or the simpleton from the stables to entertain their friends; indeed, it was not at all unusual in this period to choose servants for some oddity that could be laughed at.[115] In this, one finds definite vestiges of older traditions: of household fools, madcap Renaissance courts like those of the Medici or the Estensi, the court of James I, or, especially unexpected, the household of Mme de Rambouillet (1588–1665), where the *préciosité* mingled with the antics of dwarfs, stutterers, acrobats, and hilariously bad poets.[116] The more eccentric wits of the age consciously surrounded themselves with cranks and oddballs, but even a country gentleman like Walter Shandy would hire a dropsical "fat foolish scullion" for her "simplicity."[117] One finds gentlemen hiring waiters with a limp or tremor who could then be berated and tossed downstairs for spilling the food. Gentlemen also organized "freak runs"—hopping races for lame or one-legged contestants, races between some very fat person and another on stilts. Another Garrick story has him offering an elaborate entertainment to Fox, Burke, Gibbon, Sheridan, Beauclerk, and Reynolds. The event "consisted in an old man and a young one running backwards and forwards between two baskets filled with stones, and whoever emptied his basket first was to be the victor." The octogenarians' footrace in Burney's *Evelina* offers a typically ambivalent insight into such amusements: as so often in Burney, unacceptable humor is provided at great length while all responsibility rests with characters who are themselves the objects of satire. The footrace appalls Evelina, but everyone else is amused; even the exemplary Lord Orville disapproves of the gambling rather than the frolic itself.[118]

In the same vein were comic assemblies of those with the same disability. In a well-known *Spectator* paper, Addison describes several possibilities, all of them attributed to "one of the Wits of the last Age." His first is a gathering of men with long chins. Then comes a dinner of "Oglers" or squinters, a great confusion of "cross Bows, mistaken Signs, and wrong Connivances." Finally, he gathers all the stammerers he can find and enlists a servant to sit behind a screen and write down their table talk. Naturally Addison announces his disapproval (there was "no Moral" in such entertainments), but he does so only after describing them at length.[119] And other versions seem to find it all harmless fun. Walpole attributes a stutterers' dinner to John, second Duke of Montagu (1690–1749), one of the most celebrated practical jokers of the age; according to other sources, the dinner ended in a brawl with each guest convinced that the others were mimicking him. Like so many other jokes, this one migrates about and attaches to different wits; few of the reports are verifiable. The important point is the fascination such scenarios continued to exert—the way they were reported, elaborated, reattributed, reenacted, and then again reported.[120] And they do have well-documented analogues in the great burlesque rituals of this age: mock processions, coronations, funerals, and the like. For several years in the early 1740s, the rake-wit Paul Whitehead (1710–74) organized a great travesty of the Freemasons' annual march along the Strand. These were phenomenally elaborate events: Whitehead would hire several dozen crippled beggars from the streets of Holborn to carry Masonic insignia and limp along beside the grand master's "coffin." The town was hugely amused, and the print shops put out large-scale illustrations on each occasion. The long-running mock election at Garrat in south London similarly engaged the ugliest and most deformed members of the community, who were dressed as candidates and given outrageous speeches to deliver before pulling the hustings down over their heads.[121]

POETRY AND POLITE LETTERS

Whitehead's procession, cripple races, dinners of stutterers, and such orchestrated events thrived in the immense gulf between the fashionable classes and the poor. The difficulty of sympathizing with one's social inferiors becomes a preoccupation in midcentury texts, baldly stated in every context. The only compassion that exists, says Booth in book 10 of Fielding's *Amelia*, is "Fellow-feeling only of Men of the same Rank and Degree of Life for one another, on account of the Evils to which they themselves are liable"; the great had almost no understanding of the "common distresses of Mankind." Sympathy, as Adam Smith defines it, was an imaginative response—and the imagination best assumes "the shape and configuration of the imaginations *of those with whom I am familiar.*" Blind beggars, broken farm laborers, and ragged street hawkers were as unfamiliar to those who lived their lives in comfort as it was possible to be.[122] Hundreds of London beggars did survive on handouts from passersby, but these handouts had much less to do with sympathy than we are apt to assume. As one commentator complained:

> If any person is born with any defect or Deformity, or maimed by Fire or other Casualty, or any inveterate Distemper, which renders them miserable Objects, their way is open to London, where they have free liberty of showing their nauseous sights to terrify People, and force them to give money to get rid of them.[123]

Such complaints are everywhere. You could hardly stop and greet a friend without some ragamuffin sticking her stump in your face and asking for money. A dirty crippled chimney sweep would sidle right up to you and just stand there until you paid him to move on.

But what about attitudes between genteel folk and their equals or supe-riors—attitudes toward those for whom sympathy was at least theoretically possible? Laughing at an enemy's deformities remained routine. The great Restoration satirists, with their guiltless laughter at physical misfortunes and their complex analogies between misguided political principles and deformed bodies, still offered authoritative models to mid-eighteenth-century wits. Tory attacks on the first Earl of Shaftesbury, for example, were still well-known one hundred years later. Almost disabled with gout and ague, Shaftesbury (1621–83) was nicknamed "Count Tapski" because of the copper tube that drained his hydatid cyst.[124] Dryden went so far as to delight that the disabled father produced a defective son—that the sickly second earl (1651–99) was "born a shapeless Lump, like Anarchy."[125] Even after Shaftesbury's death in 1683, his enemies were still laughing. The thought of him limping to his exile in Hol-land proved an irresistible occasion for chiastic couplets like the following:

> Nay, though no legs I had, my gait was fleet,
> Obliged to travel, though I had no Feet.

The old tap analogies now spawned many more: repeated comparisons be-tween the draining of Shaftesbury's cyst and William of Orange saving Hol-land by opening the sluices.[126]

Eighteenth-century satirists consciously harked back to these traditions. The analogies of Pope's enemies are well-known: his twisted spine was a mark of Cain or "Emblem of [his] crooked Mind" and some sort of correlative to the "crabbed Numbers" of his verse.[127] And the same imaginative habits con-tinued in countless less familiar contexts. Bishop Hoadly (1676–1761) was se-verely crippled and needed crutches all his adult life. His high church enemies delighted in pictorial representations of the "Criple'd Priest" and gloried in the predictable sneers about "crooked" arguments, his "lame" intellect, and doctrines so weak that they "like himself must be upheld by Crutches."[128] The Methodist preacher George Whitefield (1714–70) had a severe squint in his left eye; Foote mimicked him as Dr. Squintum, and the nickname stuck. The squint provided Whitefield's enemies with an irresistible emblem of hy-pocrisy: his right eye might look up to heaven, but the left looked about the earth with lust.[129]

Every satirist had an alibi if anyone objected: Hoadly and Whitefield were laughed at not for their deformities or illnesses but for their manifest danger to public morals. The fact that they were physically deformed was a coincidence—albeit an irresistible one. Pope himself got into all these arguments in successive versions of *The Dunciad*, and similar debates raged about the ethics of pictorial caricature.[130] Effective satire had to wound and inflict pain, it was often said: it had to strike where it hurt and make its object as ridiculous as possible. What is more remarkable, finally, is the amount of pitiless satire that appeared without any of these defenses. In this guiltless directness, high satire is often difficult to distinguish from the lowest insults. The same puns and analogies worked in both contexts. And in both contexts a simple insult alone would do just as well. A gentleman goes up to a dwarf and calls him a pygmy. Limping hag, blind cuckold: the jarring frankness of such insults remained a delight in polite society as it was below. Expensive jestbooks continued to print the joke about a cheeky linkboy who calls Pope a "crooked Son of a Bitch."[131]

Political disputes, doctrinal differences, literary rivalries, personal dislikes—all continued to take form in triumphant laughter about physical misfortunes. George, first Baron Lyttelton (1709–73), was born two months premature and remained frail and skinny all his life. He rejected Smollett's first literary effort (an unendurable tragedy called *The Regicide*), so Smollett satirized him as "Gosling Scrag"—a weedy little goose with a long neck. Hervey, Walpole, and many others were hugely amused by Lyttelton's lanky body and awkward movements. A narrow, skeletal figure, he is immediately recognizable in contemporary prints and sketches (juxtaposed, perhaps, beside some very fat figure like the Duke of Cumberland).[132] William Stanhope, the eccentric second Earl of Harrington (1719–79), was nicknamed "Peter Shambles" on account of his severely deformed legs and odd walk—and the face, said Walpole, was as twisted as the legs.[133] Everyone launched into Samuel Foote when he lost his leg in February 1766. Johnson coined a new word for the occasion, repeatedly joking about Foote's *depeditation*; the papers were full of puns and imitative verses with missing *feet*. And all this was compounded by the circumstances of the accident (which themselves offer a fascinating insight into upper-class practical joking). Foote had been boasting of his horsemanship, so his aristocratic hosts tricked him into mounting a particularly unmanageable animal. He was thrown within seconds.

Let us be precise about the experiences involved. Falling off a horse was unavoidable in early modern culture. Usually it was harmless, but at some point there were bound to be injuries, and by a certain age almost everyone had a limp or a wonky elbow from such accidents. Dislocations and broken bones were serious events, and in a definite percentage of cases they were fatal. For those who rode, falling from their horse was probably the most common non-disease-related form of death. Foote was terrified by his horrifying amputation and the dangerous burst artery that followed, not to mention the harrowing pain of it all. "I look upon my hold in life to depend upon a very slender tenure," he wrote to Garrick,

> and besides, admitting the best that can happen, is a mutilated man, a miserable instance of the weakness and frailty of human nature, a proper object to excite those emotions which can only be produced from vacant minds, discharged of every melancholy or pensive taint?[134]

For all his pluck in returning to the stage, Foote spent much of his final decade in excruciating pain. John O'Keeffe offers an unforgettable recollection of him leaning against a wall backstage, grimacing in agony as the false leg is being attached. Each performance left him wincing and panting with exhaustion.[135] None of this was difficult to imagine: everyone knew that amputation left extraordinarily sensitive wounds and the additional torments of a phantom limb. Pitiless mimic that he was, Samuel Foote may have been especially hard to sympathize with. But one finds the same well-informed delight at the miseries of Pope, Hoadly, Whitefield, and Shaftesbury. All these men were widely known to be gravely ill. Even as a young man, Hoadly needed help to get to the pulpit and read every sermon in a kneeling posture. Whitefield spent the last twenty-five years of his life vomiting blood after every sermon.

Satiric contexts offered partial justifications in each one of these cases, but in most circumstances no one needed permission to laugh at a cripple. If this still seems improbable, one need only look at some of the countless eighteenth-century descriptions of Bath, a venue that brought together fashionable people in search of amusement and invalids on the very point of death.[136] The crowds of lunatics, consumptives, barren wives, and paralytics in wheelchairs turned the streets into a national freak show. It is no accident that the deformed dinner parties of Addison and other wits were set in Bath, where a quorum could so easily be assembled. The steaming chaos of the King's Bath was a set piece in travel writing, fiction, and satiric poetry—a vile stew of dropsy, leprosy, jaundice, scrofula, and withered limbs. Alternately horrifying and hilarious, this spectacle was completely public. The bath sat right under the pump room windows "for the amusement of persons of a certain rank," as one midcentury physician complained, while spectators "of the lowest class" lined the railings on the other side and "divert[ed] themselves . . . as at a bull or bear-baiting."[137] A large part of the satirists' objection to Bath was its chaotic social mixing, the dissolution of rank and jostling bad manners that so appall Matt Bramble in *Humphry Clinker*. But like every other Bath satirist, Smollett keeps returning to the standard motifs of deformity humor. *Humphry Clinker* introduces grotesque couples like the "broken-winded Wapping landlady" with her brandy merchant "who stood by the window, prop'd upon crutches." In Smollett's descriptions, the town's famous balls become large-scale crutch dances, a spectacle of limping widows and decrepit tradesmen trying to "hobble country-dances and cotillions among lordlings, squires, counselors, and clergy."[138]

Almost all writings on Bath return to the same scenarios. The combination of steep streets and continual rain meant constant droll accidents—cripples spilling out of sedan chairs, lame soldiers knocked into cellars, the tumbling gout patients depicted with such relish by Rowlandson and other artists. Inevitably, different types of invalids are brought together for mutual torments: Bramble himself describes an encounter with an old friend, a former sailor who had lost a leg and was now almost blind: "[I]n saluting me, he thrust the spring of his spectacles into my eye and, at the same time, set his wooden stump upon my gouty toe."[139] His nephew Jery watches it all with glee: "[A] paralytic attorney of Shoe-lane, in shuffling up to the bar, kicked the shins of the chancellor of England, while his lordship, in a cut bob, drank a glass of water at the pump." The contemporaneity of such incidents can easily be lost on modern readers. The chancellor of England is Robert Henley (1708–72), first Earl of Northington. By 1771, Henley was tormented by gout and hardly able to walk. He had always been bad tempered, and this got worse with the gout. The encounter at the pump is thus a shorthand reference to one of Henley's famous tantrums. Smollett himself admired Henley, but this did not stop him enjoying the gouty rages along with everyone else. Perhaps this is why, for almost the first time in his oeuvre, Smollett shows a glimpse of recognition that it might not be appropriate to laugh at physical misfortunes. But Jery's tautology is only slightly uneasy: "I cannot account for my being pleased with these incidents, any other way than by saying, they are truly ridiculous in their own nature and serve to heighten the humour in the farce of life, which I am determined to enjoy as long as I can."[140]

One thinks back to all the mishaps and odd conjunctions of deformity poetry, which suddenly seem to commemorate historical people and actual encounters. Exactly how much of this poetry was genuinely occasional is impossible to say—we know nothing about any real person behind Wycherley's "Little Crooked Woman" or "The Reverend Doctor's Lamentation." But improvising epigrams was a fashionable parlor skill in this culture, like capping verses, "similitudes," or *bouts-rimés*. And the deformed offered obvious subjects, as in the following anecdote:

The ingenious Earl [of Rochester] meeting one day with a very deformed person ... was desired by one of his acquaintance to write a lampoon upon him, saying he was a very proper subject for it. To whom the earl presently replied.

> *There needs no calumny on him be thrown,*
> *Nature hath done the bus'ness of lampoon,*
> *And in his face his character hath shown,*
> *As clear as when the sun shines forth at noon.*

Again, there is no evidence that Rochester wrote these lines, which migrate about like so many other epigrams.[141] But he could easily have done so: thousands of impromptu deformity poems do survive—in print, copied into commonplace books, and in the scribal miscellanies first explored by Harold Love.[142] A foppish clergyman breaks his leg; a celebrated beauty loses an eye: a dozen versifiers were ready to memorialize the event, most of them delighting that the subject wouldn't be so proud any more. Other epigrams delight in odd coincidences ("On a young Gentleman and his young Mother, who had each lost an Eye").[143] One even finds "congratulatory" verses, a genre alluded to in Steele's "Ugly Club" papers, in which members compose poems to encourage ugly women to join their gatherings. Steele imagines lines in praise of smallpox, "a Panegyrick upon Mrs. *Andiron*'s left Shoulder," and "a Congratulatory Ode inscrib'd to Mrs. *Touchwood*, upon the loss of her two Fore-teeth."[144]

A number of poets seem almost to have specialized in these dubious commemorations. Witness the short career of William Pattison (1706–27), an impoverished hack who was sent down from Cambridge and promptly died of smallpox in Edmund Curll's attic. The following verses offer a fascinating glimpse into the university wit of his age. Pattison's subject is another student, a lame Latin poet ("Tom Hobblestart") who wrote mostly in elegiacs:

> For *This*, indeed, he seems cut out by Fate,
> Witness his rueful Look, and shambling Gait.
> His *Face* inspires him with Poetic-Woe,
> And his *unequal Legs* the *Measure* show.[145]

Pattison delighted in all the analogies and formal devices of deformity poetry—thus the trochaic substitution in line 2, with its sudden emphasis at the moment of witnessing. Walking paradoxes that they so often were, the deformed and disabled cried out for antitheses and chiastic antics: consider *"On hearing a very homely, and deformed Lady sing finely"* ("A Form so foul! such Harmony! . . . A sudden Taste of Heaven and Hell").[146] One of Pattison's more celebrated productions was a single couplet, *"Upon a lame Man, newly married,"* in which a lurching anapestic rhythm captures the man's hobble:

> *George Limpus* is lame, yet has gotten a Bride;
> He's lame, he can't walk; why then he may ride.

Here Pattison seems almost deliberately to reflect the history of English metrics, creating a sort of pseudomedieval alliterative meter with heavy caesuras in the middle of each line—a rude form in an age when the elegant norm was the heroic couplet, just as a crippled body was to proper human form. Such analogies were not at all far-fetched in eighteenth-century culture, and indeed the poem appears in miscellanies well into the nineteenth century, along with Pattison's imitations of Gay, Waller, and Pope's "Abelard to Eloisa."[147]

Firmer proof of all these pleasures is easily found in the private writings of the age. The great diaries and correspondences of this period—those of Walpole, Lady Mary Wortley Montagu, George Selwyn, Elizabeth Montagu, Frances Burney, and others—are full of nasty analogies or droll encounters with the ugly or disabled. So and so had developed a limp, but she bit your head off every time you mentioned it. Someone else came back from the Grand Tour with a huge scar across his face, and what was funnier, he was putting powder on it. Commonplace books are full of puns, mean little caricatures, and lampoons copied out of the newspapers—and this only in what survived the destructions of heirs and executors. There is also much sympathy in these contexts, but if there is anything we have learned from two decades' work on sentimentality, it is just how complex, contradictory, and self-deceiving even the simplest expression of sympathy can be. Sympathy cloaks all manner of less admissible impulses.

One naturally starts looking for these things in Walpole, and just as naturally one encounters powerful scholarly defenders. Walpole scholars spent much of the twentieth century repudiating Victorian attacks on the man and his circle as spiteful gossips.[148] But one can hardly avoid the old accusations in the group's descriptions of physical misfortunes. The comedy is mild enough in Walpole's accounts of Mme du Deffand—"an old blind *débauchée* of wit," as he describes her to Conway before an extended description of the comic confusion at her soirée (where the blind hostess systematically asks for a description of what everyone ate and then bellows the information at a former lover, by then eighty years old and "very near deaf").[149] A stronger animus is usually evident with Lady Mary Wortley Montagu, beginning with an early account of her still dancing at fifty-one, with greasy hair, filthy clothes, and a face scarred by smallpox. Yet all this pales beside a jeu d'esprit of 1741 in which Walpole follows Pope in adding syphilis to Lady Mary's ailments. Loosely imitating Horace's prayer to the vessel that took Virgil to Greece, Walpole writes "To the Postchaise that carries Lady Mary Wortley Montagu," concluding with a joke that her nose was so rotten that the slightest jolt might knock it off entirely:

> O chaise, who art condemn'd to carry
> The rotten hide of Lady Mary,
> To Italy's last corner drive;
> And prithee set her down alive;
> Nor jumble off with jolts and blows,
> The half she yet retains of nose![150]

It's a breathtaking composition, but only a more intricate version of hundreds of offhand remarks. Physical misfortunes excite a particular imaginative energy in Walpole and his friends. Tone and syntax acquire a sudden elasticity, moving between euphemism and flippant directness. A parade of reticence or sympathy is shot through with moments of pure malice—which then license themselves as references to the ancients or cross-linguistic puns, all of it enabling the writer to delight in his own cleverness.

Take Horace Mann's reports of Signora Gondi, a Florentine socialite whom Walpole had met on his Grand Tour. In Mann's first mention (September 1741), the signora is still a haughty beauty, scorning a "poor pale-faced *abbé*" who hovers at her elbow. By the following autumn, however, the unfortunate *dama* was disintegrating from scurvy: "There appears to be no remedy. Some days ago she spit out four of her teeth and last week, blowing her nose, [a] great part of the bone came away. . . . I pity the poor creature vastly, but you would laugh to hear all the ladies talk of the *scorbuto* with such compassion." The next summer, Gondi was going about "with her nose quite flat, and a whole false set of upper teeth"—and her abbé was still besotted.[151] This description is characteristic of so many more, swinging unpredictably between the misfortune itself and the comic circumstances that surround it, with self-gratifying snatches from foreign languages and sudden protestations of sympathy. But let us be clear about the disease Mann was describing: an advanced case of scurvy was one of the most wretched sights life had to offer. Debilitated, if not entirely paralyzed, the body was covered in huge purple spots and fetid bleeding sores. Gums rotted, teeth fell out, bones disintegrated; there were sudden hemorrhages and constant "extremely offensive" stools. Everyone had seen and smelled people dying of scurvy: the pallid or yellowing complexion, shallow breathing, dim sunken eyes, extreme "Dejection of Spirit," and famously, the simple longing to die.[152] Mann's description of the signora's disintegration is so brutally referential that it could seem self-defensive, a breezy way of detaching himself from the horror of it all. Perhaps he felt a certain admiration for a ruined beauty who went about with no nose. But one would be wrong to see much compassion.

Lady Mary's own descriptions of illness are no less elusive. Lord Townshend had consumption, she writes to the Countess of Pomfret in September 1738, and was "spitting up his lungs at the Gravel-pits." (Lady Townshend, meanwhile, was "diverting herself with daily rambles in town.")[153] One finds much more in this tone—bluff, slangy, and unsentimental but not exactly cruel. Everyone was amused by the spectacular failure of the Townshend marriage (and Lady Mary also reports, in her next letter, that Townshend had "renewed his lease of life").[154] Much odder is Lady Mary's report of the amour between the widowed Lady Holdernesse and Benjamin Mildmay (later Earl Fitzwalter). Quite aside from the age difference (Mildmay was fifty-two in 1724; Lady Holdernesse was twenty years younger), the lady was "sunk in all the joys of happy love, notwithstanding she wants the use of her two hands by a rheumatism, and he has an arm that he cannot move." "I wish I could send you the particulars of this amour," Lady Mary continues, "which seems to me as curious as that between two oysters, and as well worth the serious enquiry of the naturalists." Two lovers who could do little more than rub torsos like shellfish: this was only a more fashionable and elaborate version of a classic deformed marriage, the hilarity of Phelim O'Gimlet courting Moggy Timbertoe or Trunnion and Mrs. Grizzle at the beginning of *Peregrine Pickle*.[155]

Much of this laughter was surrounded with qualifications, implied if not stated. Walpole had his private grievances toward Lady Mary, although she thought he liked her.[156] Everyone deplored Lady Holdernesse's behavior, and Lady Mary was especially irked to have defended the woman. In many contexts, simply admitting that one disliked someone makes it acceptable to laugh at his or her physical misfortunes. "Miss Weston writes me Word that Sir Joshua Reynolds is going quite blind," Mrs. Thrale writes to Sophia Byron in August 1789; "you know how deaf he was long ago." Mrs. Thrale was not the only one spreading these rumors that summer (Reynolds was only partially deaf; his eyesight was weakening, but he never went completely blind). But she clearly recognizes her own schadenfreude, adding uneasily: "He and I never much loved one another, but I am sincerely grieved."[157]

Failing personal enmity, the old affectation defense was always available: periodical discussions make this all too clear. It was difficult not to laugh, says Steele, when someone has an ugly face but "thinks it an Aspect of Dignity" or spends time at the mirror trying to disguise it. In an act of self-loathing that still pains, Pope himself repeats the principle in *Guardian*, no. 91, his description of the "Short Club": "No man is ridiculous for being what he is, but only for the affectation of being something more." The Short Club's "laws" consist largely of punishments for those pretending not to be short. A particular poignancy comes in the fact that Pope *did* try to hide his deformities: he sat on a raised seat, used stiff corsets to straighten his spine, and wore extra stockings to plump out his spindle shanks. When Ned Ward and others scoffed at Pope's "false Calfs and padded Shoulders," they were doing so according to his own declared standards.[158]

Obviously all these correspondents were also capable of sympathy, for enemies as well as friends. By 1738, Lady Mary had fallen out with Lady Sundon, but the latter's throat cancer was "so dismal a prospect as would force compassion from her greatest enemies."[159] Walpole and Mrs. Thrale are different with each correspondent; Lady Mary's letters to the Countess of Pomfret strike a very different tone from those to her sister Lady Mar. Yet there is no avoiding the volume of entirely guiltless humor. As one final case, consider Frances Burney's habit of coming home after a tedious evening and venting her frustration in written form. The new, unexpurgated edition of her early journals and letters has restored some strikingly frank descriptions. Someone was the fattest, ugliest, most stupid booby she had ever met. Given that three members of the company were stone deaf, the conversation went round in circles for three hours. "Miss Dumpty" is her name for Marianne Davies (1743–1818), the "short, crooked & *squat*" glass harmonica player. Miss Betenson was "a fat, squab, ugly, vulgar Woman, yet, I am told, extremely proud, of her family!" "She is very little, ugly, & terribly deformed," Burney says of another acquaintance—but at least she could tell a good story. Katharine Read (1723–78), the fashionable portraitist, is mentioned numerous times in the journal, never without some comment on her physical misfortunes. She is "shrewd & clever," Burney acknowledges, but "most exceedingly ugly" and "so very Deaf" that it was hardly worth trying to talk to her. Read was a "very clever woman," she writes the following year, but had "a Countenance the most haggard & wretched I ever saw." She was wearing such odd and filthy clothes that she might as well have been "embraced by a chimney sweeper."[160] The novelist Frances Brooke was "very short & fat, & squints."[161] A few years later, Burney's sister Charlotte described her meeting with Hester Chapone: "She is deadly ugly to be sure;—such [an] African nose and lips, and such a clunch figure!" The anecdotist William Seward happened to be there as well: "*Poor Chappy*, she's so ugly you know!"[162]

I have explored these documents at such length because our focus on polite manners and epistolary communities has inevitably deemphasized the freedoms of genteel correspondence. This effect may be stronger still in our understanding of genteel conversation, dependent as we have been on conduct literature. Yet the snatches of real conversation that have come down to us are full of open jokes about sickness and deformity. Mrs. Thrale delighted in the sneers of George "Colonel" Bodens, resident wit at Streatham, recording them all at tedious length. A breathless asthmatic is "the Chelsey Waterworks"; the wealthy hunchback Dick Carver invites the inevitable comparison with Shakespeare's "crook-backed Richard."[163] Oliver Goldsmith was a famously unattractive man—with a face scarred by childhood smallpox, a protruding forehead, receding chin, and noticeably awkward physique. His biographers record constant cruel references to his "monkey face" and "grotesque orang-outang figure." A well-known story from the *Johnsonian Miscellanies* points not just to the acceptability of such comments but to their social currency—their value to everyday readjustments of the social pecking order. Asked to make a toast to the ugliest person she knows, a young lady raises her glass to Goldsmith. This so amuses a second lady that she reaches across the table to shake hands, "expressing some desire of being better acquainted with her, it being the first time they met." Johnson saw the point immediately: "Thus the Ancients, on the commencement of their Friendships, used to sacrifice a beast between them."[164]

Almost nothing was beyond the pale. People of fashion laughed at someone for having a hunchbacked wife or even for producing deformed children. Someone asks a painter how he creates such beautiful portraits but then has such hideous children (answer: "*Because I make the first in the Daylight, and the other in the Dark*").[165] One disturbing illustration of these habits is the fact that women evidently wore masks when they first came into company after a disfiguring accident or illness. This detail comes up in Fielding's *Amelia* and Lady Mary Wortley Montagu's "smallpox" eclogue, to mention just two well-known texts. It was partly, as in Lady Mary's case, to protect from oversensitivity to light. But other evidence suggests that wearing a mask was a way for women to avoid ridicule as they grew older or uglier, the practice referred to in yet another of William Pattison's compositions, "*Speak* Truth *and Shame the* Devil":

> Old *Olivia* wears a *Mask*
> > If any one the *Reason* ask,
> > This, Answer plain, reveals it:
> Her *Face* of late's so ugly grown,
> She does not care to fright the Town,
> > And so forsooth conceals *it*.

These lines still shock in their plodding directness. But there are many more just like them: mock-naive addresses to the "coy" mask, asking it to reveal its secrets, or, conversely, lines in praise of a mask that protects everyone from an ugly face.[166]

From this point it is a short step to the practical jokes of polite society—from impromptu torments to painstakingly orchestrated pranks. Everyone knew how to roast a deaf man, get a stutterer going, or provoke a gout sufferer like Chancellor Henley.[167] These habits help make sense of one repeated moment in the deformity comedies: the central character is heard wheezing or hobbling about offstage, and the rest of the cast gathers round to torment him. "Hark—I hear the old Baboon cough; away! Here he comes with his ugly Beak before him." Here he comes, says the heroine of Foote's *Lame Lover*. "I hear his stump on the stairs."[168] The blind poet Priscilla Pointon (ca. 1740–1801) herself describes one of these impromptu jokes, the reaction of an idiotic bachelor when she delicately announces that she needs to urinate after six hours drinking tea and punch. All the maids were out, he tells her,

> Then in contempt you came to me,
> And sneering cried, "Dear Miss, make free;
> Let me conduct you—don't be nice—
> Or if a basin is your choice,
> To fetch you one I'll instant fly."

Finally Pointon is led out by a kinder gentleman while the prankster and his friend "laughed aloud, / As if to dash [confound] a maid seemed proud."[169]

The nastiness of this trick is manifest, but other deformity pranks are much odder combinations of malice and joviality. Consider the recorded pranks

against John James Heidegger (1666–1749), the Swiss-born masquerade producer and a famously hideous man—Fielding's "Count Ugly," "the most ugly
man that ever was formed," as Mrs. Delany called him. Lord Chesterfield was
himself an odd-looking man—short like all the Stanhopes, with a huge head
and very bad teeth. (Hervey described him as "a stunted Giant," George II
called him "the Dwarf Baboon," and to the end of his life he remembered the
pain of being tormented as "Little Lord Stanhope.") None of this prevented
him from entering into a bet with Heidegger, who boasted that there was no
uglier face in London. After some searching, Chesterfield produced a hideous woman, but Heidegger put on her headdress and was then declared the
winner. (Other versions have Heidegger presenting a mirror to Chesterfield
and all versions, like the stutterer's dinner or the assembly of squinters, migrate about between different wits).[170] There are hundreds of Heidegger anecdotes, some of them clearly false, but others well documented, like the Duke
of Montagu's prank with a double of Heidegger, the cause of great havoc at
a masquerade attended by George II. This prank involved getting Heidegger
drunk at a tavern, at which point Montagu brought in a maker of death masks
to take a cast of his face. When the great day arrived, Heidegger ordered the
orchestra to herald the king's arrival with "God Save the King." But Montagu
was also there with his counterfeit Heidegger, who ordered them to play the
Jacobite "Over the Water to Charley." The subsequent confusion and Heidegger's hysteria were the delight of everyone.[171]

Since Heidegger was himself the first to make a joke about his appearance,
these last pranks must be distinguished from more elemental torments of stutterers or blind folk. But together they help us see the range of possibilities
in genteel as well as vulgar contexts. They confront us with all the inconsistencies of the age, the baffling alternations between cruelty and tenderness
and so many compound attitudes that lie between. We see Chesterfield, so
obsessed with the *bienséances*, sending his footmen out to find the ugliest
faces in London. The sincerities of Burney's fiction take their place alongside
the snobbery and meanness of her diary (licensed, perhaps, by the excuse
that it was a private context and no real harm was done). There is no end to
these incongruities. Christopher Smart, the sublime religious poet who collected so many deformity jokes. Walpole's relationship with Mme du Deffand,
such a perplexing muddle of affection, embarrassment, loyalty, and spite.
One finds people sympathetic toward one disease but disgusted by another.
Sharp-tongued, increasingly bad-tempered, and certainly capable of all the
nasty jokes attributed to him, Beau Nash was also famous for his philanthropy

and largely responsible for establishing Bath's general hospital—an act commemorated to this day in Prince Hoare's statue (1751) with Nash holding the hospital's plans in his right hand.

DAMAGED LIVES

However complex our understanding of reactions, early modern scholars have still learned little about the lived experience of disability. Historically focused work in disability studies has, in general, taken different directions from the modern disability movement. We have for the eighteenth century nothing like the blunt and confrontational books of which modern activists have made such powerful use—books like Kenny Fries's *Staring Back* (1997) or Simi Linton's *Claiming Disability* (1998).[172] William Hay's *Deformity: An Essay* (1752)—now widely cited and available in a modern scholarly edition—is the exception that proves the rule. This silence itself tells us a lot about the experience of internalized stigma: even compared to other historically disadvantaged groups (women, sexual minorities, Afro-Britons, laborers), the first-person records of disability are strikingly thin. Thus it is that Priscilla Pointon's poem offers such a sudden countervoice. Yet this poem about being taunted also sets one wondering about the evidentiary value of comic texts—texts written from the opposite perspective and recording the appalling pleasures of scorn rather than the anguish of being scorned. Repugnant and usually offering no more than the most oblique perspective on the disability experience, all the comic newspaper reports, perfectly pointed epigrams, and elaborate practical jokes do at least refer to populations that are otherwise lost to history. For the most part, these are negative references, but together they tell us something about the anonymous mass. And now and then one senses, with a jolt, a lived misery.

In making this move, I hope to open up some new directions. The paucity of evidence, combined with a post-Foucauldian stress on discourse, has meant that eighteenth-century scholars have written mainly about ideologies and representations of disability. We now know that the eighteenth century was a distinctly transitional moment in changing understandings of disability. Premodern fears and superstitions were being replaced by scientific study; marvels and curses became pathologies or natural "wonders."[173] Lennard Davis has written extensively about the eighteenth-century "invention of disability"—its increasing discursive presence and the development of institutional and medical structures to segregate and "fix" the disabled.[174] One particularly rich vein of research has explored the psychic effects of perceiving physical anomalies—the charged combination of fascination and unease that so destabilizes personal identity. These spectatorial experiences have been the focus of work from Leslie Fiedler's *Freaks* (1978)—subtitled *Myths and Images of the Secret Self*—to recent studies by Dennis Todd, Marie-Hélène Huet, and others. Thanks to Felicity Nussbaum, we now know a lot about the changing discursive connections between deformity and race, gender, and national identity.[175]

The eighteenth-century fictional record has been a rewarding source. The novels have their share of evil dwarfs and one-eyed moneylenders, but at the same time novelists were beginning to experiment with idealized deformed characters, whose deformity became a mark of virtue. These figures appear in early texts by Behn and Haywood and then increasingly from the mid-eighteenth century: Fielding's Amelia, Harriot Trentham in *Millenium Hall* (1762), and Eugenia in Burney's *Camilla*. Later came Scott's *Black Dwarf* (1816), the crippled Mrs. Smith in *Persuasion* (1818), Victor Hugo's Quasimodo (1831), Esther Summerson in *Bleak House* (1852–53), and then a long line of disabled children or childlike innocents.[176] These examples do at least attempt to represent the psychic experience of disability, but their value to a historian must be limited. Fiction can model a normative interaction, but it offers no evidence that such reactions were enacted or could be enacted in the world. That virtuous deformed characters first emerge in prose fiction is no accident: no genre enables a more detached representation of physical anomaly. By the end of *Amelia* or *Bleak House*, one has all but forgotten about the heroine's deformity. When I return to literary examples at the end of this chapter, it is not to fiction but to drama, where full embodiment was unavoidable and the limits of sentimentalism become unmistakably clear. One looks in vain for anything like these sentimental representations on the late-eighteenth-century stage. Indeed, it is hard to think of many idealized deformed characters anywhere in the canon of mainstream drama (Rigoletto, Verdi's wronged and pitiable hunchback, is an isolated exception in a genre in which the music does the work). Dramatic and fictional representations of deformity strike their limits at very different points.

Scholars have come closer to experience with the sizable group of early modern authors who were disabled or visibly "defective" in some way. Milton, Pope, and Johnson are three key figures, the last two discussed in richly imaginative books by Helen Deutsch. Much written about, and herself describing the experiences of smallpox and aging, Lady Mary Wortley Montagu has long been important to disability scholars and is now a central figure in the emerging field of feminist age studies. Joshua Reynolds's self-portraits, with their increasingly obtrusive references to deafness and poor eyesight, offer another fascinating source. Felicity Nussbaum has explored the special case of Duncan Campbell (ca. 1680–1730), a deaf-mute Scottish fortune-teller who became all the rage in early eighteenth-century London.[177] In a fascinating article on Pope and William Hay, Roger Lund has described the struggle of two disabled authors who experienced the sting of ridicule even as they accepted the aesthetic and theological arguments that licensed it.[178]

Perhaps the bluntest of all first-person accounts of disability comes in the work of the lesser-known women poets brought to light by Paula Backscheider, Roger Lonsdale, and others. It is an astonishing corpus: hundreds of poetic responses to illness, aging, and disability from authors who just twenty years ago were completely unknown. At one end of the spectrum are the hymns and devotional lyrics of Susannah Harrison (1752–84), who was disabled at twenty and spent her entire adult life expecting to die.[179] In Priscilla Pointon's career-long reflections on her disability, we see her struggling—as William Hay had done in prose—to find a silver lining:

> Tis an advantage, truly, to be blind;
> No tempting objects, and no joys impure,
> Can then our souls to vice so soon allure.

The blind avoided horrific sights. Nature had taken away their sense of sight, she writes to a blind musician who set one of her poems to music, but granted them higher levels of insight. Finally, like Hay and Susannah Harrison, Pointon submits to the divine will.[180] Like so many other disabled women poets, Pointon also reveals a particular fear of hostile readers. Any woman who dared to write must expect hostility, wrote her contemporary Esther Clark (ca. 1716–94), "every blemish, every fault, / Unseen before to light is brought." But disabled women faced the additional prospect of nasty analogies. Pointon's "To the Critics" begs the reviewers not to "frown indignant on [her] night-struck strain." Mary Chandler, the hunchbacked milliner-poet from Bath (1687–1745), is equally concerned about the "snarling Critics" and their inevitable talk about "crooked verse" or "lame designs."[181]

The more one looks at these women's poems, the more one detects a distinctively caustic perspective on the disability experience. Mary Chandler's imaginary gravestone inscription typifies this ruthless unsentimentality: "Here lies a true maid, deformed and old, / Who, that she never was handsome, need never be told." One of Chandler's later compositions is a droll account of receiving a marriage proposal from a rich country gentleman who had fallen in love with her verse ("Fourscore long miles, to buy a crooked wife!").[182] Women created their own genres of deformity poetry, each of them a surprise for anyone who picks up these texts with presumptions about appropriately feminine subjects. Lady Mary Wortley Montagu's "Satturday" is one of many verse reflections on smallpox and the horror of losing one's beauty overnight (a subject that hardly exists in the canon of male poets).[183] Equally unique to women poets are mirror poems. The little-known Elizabeth Teft (fl. 1741-47) of Lincoln looks in the mirror and wonders whether Nature had been in a hurry when she made her—or maybe all the finer materials had been used to create "some perfect she," leaving nothing for her.[184] One even more astonishing mirror poem—and a companion piece to Pointon's poem about being laughed at—comes from Mary Barber (ca. 1685-1755), a protégée of Swift and the Delanys. At the age of forty-four, crippled by gout and rheumatism, Barber looks in the mirror and sees a "Gorgon's head." In true Swiftean style, she imagines the reactions of others. "Witty coxcombs" simply announce "Rot that old witch—she'll never die." Young women look at her with terror or turn aside and gaze at themselves in the mirror ("'Surely,' say you, 'this lovely face / Will never suffer such disgrace'").[185]

These stunning texts deserve far more attention than I am able to give them here. But one still wants to put a finer point on it: the experience of literate, reflective, and usually privileged people still tells us nothing about the vast majority of the deformed and disabled—the impoverished mass of one-legged soldiers, blind fiddlers, lame beggars, and dirty pie women of so much deformity humor. Who were these people, and how did they get that way? In pursuing these questions, I am inspired by a group of British historians of poverty who complain that the "linguistic turn" has narrowed their subject to a study of discourses. If one can never get beyond discourse or representations, and those at the bottom of society left no discursive records, the history of poverty inevitably becomes a history of representations or ideas about the poor. In reaction, these scholars have turned to less orthodox sources, including workhouse records, petitions to parish authorities, settlement and bastardy hearings, clemency pleas, coroner's records, postmortem inventories, and even graffiti—anything that gives some insight into lived experience. This work has its critics, and certainly my own materials resist its determined optimism—its consistent stress on the strategies, resourcefulness, and solidarities of the early modern poor. But this hugely energetic movement does at least show us what a careful use of nontraditional records might add to our knowledge of the past.[186]

My sources are as elliptical as any of these fragmentary documents. But consider the other major body of evidence for the low and illiterate disabled population—the large antiquarian collections that provided an obvious starting point for historians of disability. Freak show advertisements and semi-scientific writings about dwarfs, giants, conjoined twins, and other marvels were already being collected in the eighteenth century, and later antiquarians like Daniel Lysons and John Fillinham assembled enormous scrapbooks. I have deliberately avoided these sources: fascinating as they are, they tell us little or nothing about the vast and anonymous majority of deformed and disabled. Moreover, they tell us very little about the freaks themselves. Handbills and newspaper advertisements were written by canny showmen hoping to lure the crowds to see their "little Marvel of Nature." Dwarf show advertisements say nothing about the severe illnesses of most dwarfs or the distinctly unsympathetic atmosphere of most shows. They tell us nothing about the vast majority of dwarfs who were far too misshapen to exhibit—those referred to only negatively in the showman's boast that his particular dwarf was "entirely straight-grown," "straight and well-proportioned in every way," nothing like the "shocking monsters" of other impresarios. Dwarfism of any sort is an extremely rare condition (even the rate for achondroplasia, the most common cause, is less than one per twenty-five thousand live births). And so the question remains: What about the ordinary hunchbacks, deaf fruit vendors, and blind beggars who loom so large in eighteenth-century comic sources?

It is hard for us to imagine the almost phantasmagoric array of deformed bodies encountered every day on the streets of mid-eighteenth-century London. Bodies twisted by hernias. Spines bent by rickets or tuberculosis. Noses eaten away by disease. Rotting gums and pockmarked faces. The inescapable sound of coughing, wheezing, and choking. Periodicals and polite correspondences persistently complain about the swarms of deformed beggars on every city street. Maybe some of them deserved help, conceded a correspondent to the *London Journal*—but they should be kept out of sight, not "suffered to wander the Streets exposing their distorted Limbs and filthy Sores." It was disgusting to everyone and all too often caused "the worse consequences to Women with Child." In Paris, by contrast, there was hardly a beggar in sight.[187] This overstated comparison with other European cities was a set piece of polite travel writing. The streets of Rotterdam, says Lady Mary Wortley Montagu, were entirely free of all the "loathsome Cripples so common in London."[188]

It goes without saying that we have no accurate statistics for any of these conditions. Social historians have made some headway with the Bills of Mortality, hospital archives, and surviving workhouse documents (which sometimes record reasons for the inmates' inability to work). One local study of early modern Norwich suggests that around 25 percent of poor men and women were severely disabled by the age of sixty, and that the probability of disability increased exponentially every year beyond that age. Modern statistics for congenital defects might tell us something about the familiarity of conditions that are now routinely treated in developed countries. Clubfeet appear in one to two out of every thousand live births; cleft lips and palates (*harelips*, as the eighteenth century called them) occur in similar proportions. But such statistics are noticeably less helpful with skeletal disorders like bowlegs or curvature of the spine. The vast majority of skeletal disorders were acquired rather than congenital, the result of poor nutrition, aging, hernias, fractures, consumption, and other diseases.[189] Blindness could of course be congenital, but it was more often a consequence of disease, above all diabetes (still the most significant cause of blindness in developing countries). Amputation was far more common than we might expect: the result not just of major injuries but often of minor fractures, shallow wounds, or the gangrene that came with diabetes. Scurvy, smallpox, tuberculosis, rickets—these diseases are all now preventable, but in the eighteenth century they almost always left one severely disabled. Burns, flesh wounds, broken bones—all of these left damage that could not be rectified. There were cruel jokes about all these conditions. One finds a surprising number, for example, about advanced diabetes, evidently a particularly embarrassing condition since it required such frequent urination.

Disabled soldiers and sailors made up a large proportion of the vagabond population throughout this period. One late eighteenth-century survey of two thousand beggars found 18 percent to be former soldiers and sailors.[190] No wonder starving half-pay officers and one-legged sailors become such archetypal figures in sentimental literature: they were everywhere. But they were also distinctly problematic objects of sympathy, figures in whom a justifiable claim on one's charity combined with deep-seated comic associations about amputees and wooden legs. From Adam Smith to Goldsmith, James Beattie, and countless lesser authors, the man with a wooden leg becomes almost a master trope for testing the possibilities and limitations of sympathy. These men had been wounded in the service of their country, but there were just too many of them—and, anyway, who could possibly look at someone with a wooden leg and not burst out laughing?[191]

The biggest gap in our understanding, it seems to me, is just how many deformities were the predictable consequence of labor. Many were so inevitable as to be proverbially attached to different occupations. Baker's legs or baker's knee was the knock-kneed condition that all bakers eventually acquired from their constrained position while kneading bread. (A woman's tongue and a baker's legs, went one proverb, neither of them ever went straight.)[192] Tailors and shoemakers developed hunchbacks from stooping over their work. Sitting cross-legged for long periods left many tailors weak and sickly. Nine tailors make a man, ran one catchphrase, and the same debilities show up in rhymes about tailors or weavers who flee in terror from a snail.[193] Such associations were strengthened by the fact that particular trades not only produced specific deformities but also were seen as appropriate occupations for those congenitally deformed in certain ways. A knock-kneed boy was "born to be a baker"; a young hunchback, it was said, would make a fine tailor.

These and other occupational deformities are fully described in medical treatises and at least one full-scale text, Bernardino Ramazzini's *Treatise of the Diseases of Tradesmen*, translated into English in 1705 and expanded throughout the century. Most blacksmiths went bleary-eyed, Ramazzini tells us. Braziers, who spent all day hammering brass, went deaf and developed hunchbacks. Porters and coal heavers suffered hernias and ruptured vessels. In time, most developed a permanent stoop, nature having taught them "that they bear Burdens upon their Shoulders better with their Breasts bended, than when the Body is raised upright"; their habit of using one shoulder rather than both further twisted the spine. Leadworkers, plumbers, glaziers, and painters became increasingly paralyzed from lead fumes. The eyesight of needleworkers, compositors, and watchmakers grew progressively worse, and most were nearly blind by old age. Potters ended up "paralytic, lethargic, splenetic, cachectic and toothless." Ditch diggers, coal miners, knife grinders, bricklayers, sugar boilers—Ramazzini describes the characteristic diseases of all these groups. It all adds up to an unforgettable account of long hours in confined spaces, constrained postures, and constant noise, heat, and toxic fumes.[194]

Obviously the experience of occupational deformity varied widely. The prosperous watchmaker who lost his sight lived out his last years in very different circumstances from a broken brickmaker or myopic cutler. Journeymen tailors might do well, but they worked their parish apprentices into the ground. A few long-established urban trades (e.g., tanning and tallow chandling) were still governed by guilds that regulated conditions and provided limited help in tough times. Families helped up to a point, but a disabled or elderly relative was a bore and an economic burden; recent findings about extraordinarily high suicide rates among the elderly offer chilling insights into these circumstances.[195] "It is impossible," writes the historian Susannah Ottaway, "to exaggerate the desperate misery" of the aged poor. Those without familial support were reduced to lower and lower occupations and finally to the wretched choice between the workhouse or begging.[196] Along with the disabled street vendors and musicians, worn-out tradesmen and laborers died on street corners or froze to death in ditches. They were the anonymous, wretched victims of the consumer society so lavishly evoked by recent historians (and the same might be said for mutilated military men, cast-off by-products of the colonial expansions that were driving economic growth).

The genteel reaction to these consequences was the predictable jumble of concern, indifference, and disbelief. Ramazzini clearly wanted to improve the health of workers and artisans, but his reasons were political and economic at least as much as they were sympathetic. Dr. James (of Fever Powder fame) was even more explicit in his preface to the 1746 English edition of Ramazzini: those who fed and clothed the people were the basis of national prosperity; every Briton should be concerned about population levels. This was the Age of Charity, as scholars have lately reminded us: workhouses, almshouses, institutions for the blind and deaf, royal hospitals for soldiers and sailors, were all established out of a combination of older Christian motives and the modern economic ones. But we've also learned how selective and severe these institutions were and how insufficiently they dealt with the problem.[197]

Almost every discussion of occupational diseases ends up admitting that there is little to be done. "I freely own," says Ramazzini after several pages on the maladies of bakers, "I cannot think of any effectual preservatory Caution for these Workmen." A linen mask wouldn't stop the smallest particles of flour. Regular emetics might clear out the passages and at least delay the onset of lung disease—but apart from this he has nothing to suggest. Cobblers and tailors should try to stretch their legs on Sundays.[198] Dr. James's favorite advice is to work shorter hours. But wages remained low, and workers had no choice but to put in the hours in hazardous environments. No new legislation was introduced to regulate working conditions.[199] It was accepted that laborers in the most physical trades would be entirely broken within a few years; child laborers were often deformed before puberty. Chimney sweeps quickly developed skeletal defects and serious lung diseases; they lost their teeth in falls and suffered burns from insufficiently cooled chimneys. Battered, filthy, and literally nauseating since they collected night soil as well as soot, sweeps died young and were still hardly human when Blake took up their cause in the *Songs of Innocence* and *Songs of Experience*.[200] Perhaps more surprising are the presumptions about bodily deterioration that surrounded many mainstream trades. A London carpenter, says Adam Smith, was finished after eight years (usually immobilized by constant hernias).[201] Where they say anything about laborers' diseases, most medical treatises condense it into a laconic list at the end of the text. "Blacksmiths are blear-eyed." "Stone-cutters die of Asthmas, from the subtile Powder of the Stone."[202]

Blindness, hunched backs, and lung disease were obviously found at every level of society. But acquired disabilities, the consequences of toil, were associated with the laboring classes in the way that gout and the vapors were genteel diseases. The leisured classes took it for granted that manual laborers became deformed, often in specific and recognizable ways. One rather disturbing illustration of these associations is the games of Trades that were widespread throughout early modern Europe. Trades was a guessing game, with one side having to guess the trade imitated by the other (cobbler, blacksmith, sawyer, tailor, baker) and penalties for failing to guess correctly or, conversely, for a poor imitation.[203] A successful imitation would capture the worker's characteristic posture and skeletal abnormalities as well as his or her actions. One also finds collections of cards and single-sheet prints depicting workers with the tools and usual body type of their trade, with verses underneath challenging viewers to guess what that was.[204]

At the same time, however, this blithe and amused acceptance of occupational deformity coexisted with an almost willful refusal to recognize. Traditional mistrusts of beggars as idle frauds were increasing in this period, not falling away. A beggar's infirmities were usually faked, said Fielding. Good health was the natural condition, "the happy portion," of the poor.[205] Everyone had heard stories about a "blind" cripple found playing cards or a "lame" man who jumps to his feet when he sees a cart about to run him over. The club of false beggars was a set piece of comic literature: a jovial gang who come home, take off their blindfolds, and toss aside their crutches. They had slings and ties for simulating amputation and detailed techniques for painting on false sores (flour and sheep's blood for gangrene; lime, soap, and rust to make it look like you'd been kicked by a horse).[206] Most of this was fanciful, reported second- or thirdhand like modern urban legends ("a gentleman of my acquaintance," "a friend of my cousin"). But the stories were compounded by the handful of false beggars who were caught: one man with a false beard pretending to be lame; others pretending to be blind or dressed up as old women.[207] Distinguishing false from real beggars became a recurring preoccupation for second-generation sentimental novelists. "Lying is . . . my profession," the beggar tells Harley in Mackenzie's *Man of Feeling* (1771). And Mackenzie himself delighted in stories of fraudulent Edinburgh beggars. One man pretended to lack feet but then went on to enlist as a soldier; another made his living "acting convulsions to the life" on the doorsteps of charitable gentlemen.[208]

These mistrusts combined with increasingly powerful fantasies about physical work as healthier and psychologically more satisfying. For all its progressivism, Diderot and D'Alembert's great *Encyclopédie* (1751–72) emphatically idealized the lives of artisans, casting manual labor as a major source of human happiness—one differentiated from the stimulus of mental activity as the steady contentment of marriage compared to the sudden thrills of an affair.[209] It comes as no surprise to find deformities absent from the *Encyclopédie*'s famous occupational engravings: lauded as these are for their advanced realism, images of spacious and orderly workshops bear no resemblance to the cellars and garrets where weavers and metalworkers practiced their trade. Other occupational images were also getting less realistic, further and further away from the individuals they represented. Prettified bakers or fishwives were engraved onto household objects, sculpted in porcelain, and transformed into children's books, accompanied by rudimentary verses for those learning to read ("B is for baker"). Even in more realistic "Cries of London" like those of Laroon the Elder, one cannot help feeling that the stoops and twisted spines are there for compositional reasons, as adaptations of a *contrapposto* pose, for example.[210] And thus we find ourselves talking again about the complex of genteel attitudes, the irreducible confusion of sympathy, amusement, pragmatic concerns about population or the national wealth, and disgust, indifference, or disbelief. But perhaps we may now be moving toward a clearer idea of ordinary disabilities, how they developed, and what it was like to live with them.

DISABLED BODIES AND THE INEVITABILITY OF LAUGHTER

Psychohistory has a bad name, and rightly so. The tangle of human motives—fears and pleasures, realism and fantasy, instincts indulged or resisted, internal compulsions and societal or religious constraints—is obscure enough in any circumstance. Nevertheless, it seems important to discuss three historically specific impulses behind so much eighteenth-century laughter at the deformed. First, as should now be clear, these jokes were not always malicious. Between friends, at least, witticisms about deformity could be almost amiable. When William Hay's friends congratulated him "on [his] emergence from an Eclipse of a Sirloin of Roastbeef, or of a Bowl of Punch, that stood between us," he took it as no more than a "little innocent Pleasantry."[211] It was malicious to say that Pope's body was as twisted as his verse, but, in certain circumstances, the analogies might be kind. You could tell Pope was a great poet, says a friend, because he was "*in and out* like the lines of *a Pindaric ode*."[212]

Such good-humored jests were certainly possible, as they still are, between those who shared the same affliction. Mutilated soldiers dubbed each other "lank sleeve," "Timbertoe," "Stumpy," or, almost fondly, "*Stumpibus*."[213] Consider the following joke about Theophilus Cibber, one of the most famously ugly figures of the London theatrical scene:

> Quin, Cibber, and some more brother comedians, were one night at the Shakespeare, when each other's infirmities were the subject of their raillery. Said Quin to Cibber, "What in the name of wonder could ever make you think yourself a proper figure for the stage—a snuffling fellow without a nose, and a pair of bandy legs." "As to my nose (replied Cibber) that I give up, but I'll lay a bottle of claret there's a worse leg in the company than this," producing his right leg. Every one gave a contemptuous smile, thinking it an insult to accept the challenge—"Why then, said he, producing his other leg, there's a worse," which sure enough it was. This unexpected stroke from Cibber secured him so completely the laugh, that there was no farther attempt made upon his personal imperfections that evening.[214]

There were countless jokes about Cibber's spindly legs and crushed nose, many developing on the original accident at Drury Lane more than thirty years earlier, when Cibber had fallen and broken his nose during a pantomime. A sympathizer worries that Cibber has "*spoilt his face*." "By G——d, [says] Quin, that's impossible, for *any change must be for the better*."[215]

Cibber and his friends enjoy a *joking relationship*, as cultural anthropologists would call it, a special rapport in which one person is permitted to make fun of the other, who is in turn required to take no offense. The classic joking relationships work to diffuse tension, and one surely detects something like that here.[216] Cibber is here invited to make fun of his appearance, and his good-humored acknowledgment serves to discharge the topic. One wonders whether this acknowledgment—a recognition of the unavoidable body that stared everyone in the face—worked in this society as a necessary preliminary to social intercourse, something to get out of the way. This may be difficult for us to understand, living as we do in a culture in which the uncomfortable facts of disability are silently or euphemistically avoided. No reader of Erving

Goffman's *Stigma* can forget his evocation of the range of reactions of the "normal" to the disabled:

> The familiar signs of discomfort and stickiness: The guarded references, the common everyday words suddenly made taboo, the fixed stare elsewhere, the artificial levity, the compulsive loquaciousness, the awkward solemnity.[217]

Modern disability activists have argued eloquently about the effects of euphemism, its intolerable denial of physical presence. They have begun to reappropriate insults like *crip* or *gimp* and to reject politically correct language in favor of old descriptive terms like *deaf* and *blind*.[218]

A corollary to this movement within academic circles is the energetic debate about whether disabled people are better off now than they were in the past. Conclusions vary, but all this work shares a polemical determination to demolish modern self-satisfaction about our humanity. Lennard Davis acknowledges that premodern societies were hardly kind to the disabled, but at least, he insists, the blind and deaf remained "part of the social fabric." The sociologist Michael Oliver points to industrialization as the moment that marginalized the disabled with its dependence on normal bodies, both for mass production and for the manufactured goods themselves. James Trent's *Inventing the Feeble Mind* makes parallel arguments about mental retardation. Once "an expected part of rural and small town life," "simpletons" and "fools" were until the nineteenth century kindly cared for by families and the community.[219] Such comparisons can never be conclusive, but these studies at least warn us against imposing modern ethical judgments on the past.

Equally unfamiliar, I suspect, are early modern associations of ugliness and disability with festivity or mirth. These associations are clear in traditional leaders of merriment like King Carnival, usually the ugliest man of the community, with his train of hunchbacks and grotesques. Traces of this role appear in the figure of J. J. Heidegger, grotesque Lord of Misrule at his Haymarket masquerades. Enormous rotting bawds were almost folkloric figures in this culture, recognized leaders of brothel merriment, and a prominent drag role on the London stage—figures like Mother Punchbowl in Fielding's *Covent-Garden Tragedy* (1732) and Foote's wooden-legged Mother Cole.[220] Horrific and feared as they definitely were, certain diseases or impairments also carried festive associations in early modern culture. Gout and syphilis were "gay diseases," says Mikhail Bakhtin, the consequences of license and overindulgence.[221] Rabelais's boozy gout sufferers and groaning-laughing syphilitics are well-known examples, but the same sensibility appears in the mingled cheerfulness and pathos of Ned Ward's "No-Nose Club," formed, we learn, by a merry old fellow with no nose who "had often hazarded his own Boltspit, by steering a Vitious Course among the Rocks of Venus." One finds historical syphilitics acting out the role: ugliness, even grotesque and morbid ugliness, overlapped with mirth in early modern culture in ways we have forgotten.[222]

The same elusive attitudes appear in many group caricatures of the age, especially "Dutch"-style gatherings of cheerful deformed folk drinking at a tavern.[223] The "ugly club" or grotesques' drinking party was a powerful imaginative scenario long before Addison and Steele wrote their *Spectator* essays on the topic. A gathering of very deformed people was itself a terrific comic spectacle, but there was also assumed to be an element of camaraderie about it. Steele's "Ugly Club" was founded, he tells us, by one Alexander Carbuncle, with the aim of "composing and quieting the Minds of Men under all corporal Redundancies, Deficiencies and Irregularities whatsoever; and making every one sit down content in his own Carcass." Thus stated, the project has sometimes seemed kindly or even "humane," and there is evidence of several real ugly clubs, including one that came and went in midcentury Liverpool and left its ledger for the years 1743–53 (complete with full physical descriptions of members). Even so, the center of gravity in all these "ugly club" essays is their luxuriant word pictures of hideous faces and the humiliations and confusions that occurred in any gathering of disabled people.[224] William Hay has no time for Steele's recommendations: "I never was, nor ever will be, a Member of the Ugly Club." A gathering of deformed people just "doubles the Ridicule."[225]

Nevertheless, it is remarkable how many of the most celebrated wits of this age were somehow singled out by nature. Thomas D'Urfey was famously ugly, with a huge hooked nose, small, deep-set eyes, a protruding jaw, and an oversized forehead. He also had notoriously foul breath and stuttered uncontrollably, a misfortune that made him the object of many cruel lampoons.[226] "Beau" Nash was "a very ugly man," said the diarist Dudley Ryder, with a "black-brown" complexion and a "grim," "ill-tempered" look that seems to have licensed his particular blend of charisma and tyrannical rudeness. Vanbrugh's *Esop* is often said to be based on the youthful Nash's abortive attempt to court a young heiress, who rejected him with scorn.[227] Further examples come easily to mind. Short and fat, Samuel Foote was almost typecast as a comic performer, an effect that was only compounded once he lost his leg. Christopher Smart was a short, ugly, and pot-bellied man, ideally suited to his drag persona, but the most improbable shape for a religious poet. Smart's "round and stubbed form" made one think of "a common dealer behind a common counter," Frances Burney recalled. He hardly looked like a "votary of the Muses."[228] Mrs. Thrale had no doubt that George Bodens's ugliness was half the reason for his reputation as a wit:

> The enormous Weight of flesh, the stammering & sore Leg are all to his Advantage as he contrives them; & people are so accustomed to connect the Ideas of Drollery & Bodens together that they seem resolved to find humour in every thing he does or suffers.[229]

This final verb suddenly acknowledges—almost as an afterthought—that the very defects that qualified Bodens as a comedian also made it hard to sympathize.

Second, and almost antithetical, are the manifest defensive functions of so much laughter about disease and deformity. Noses shriveled by syphilis, leg-less beggars, consumptives making their feeble way along the street—these were horrifying sights, and laughter is one of our greatest analgesics. Bergson's famous formula may still put it best: laughter depends on "a momentary anesthesia of the heart," a temporary silencing of affection or pity that helps us avoid empathy with every horror we meet.[230] This was a world in which everyone faced the decrepitude and pain of old age, in which everyday accidents crippled one in an instant and a mild conjunctivitis could blind one for life. In such circumstances, there must often have been something therapeutic or compensatory about the laughter of witnesses. For laughter so often depends, as David Morris tells us in a fascinating reflection on comedy, on a "ghostly trace" of pain—the laugher's memories of pain and fears of future pain. To sneer at the deformities and disabilities of others could discharge for a moment one's own fears of physical degeneration, one's own sense of the proximity of disease and the near certainty of a miserable old age.[231]

Western culture has long noted the parallels between laughter and tears. From Andromache's simultaneous grief and joy, to Montaigne, to Figaro's "I laugh that I may not cry" and Byron's *Don Juan*, the peculiar substitutabil-ity of these reactions has been perpetually wondered at.[232] As psychological and even physical experiences, laughter and tears are strikingly similar—both of them impulsive reactions to extreme phenomena and both manifesting in a distinctive combination of facial spasms, rapid breathing, and involuntary sounds from the throat. Both are sudden discharges of tension and experi-ences in which the mind for a moment loses control of the body.[233] From this perspective, one easily finds in so much laughter at deformity a recognition of the physical fate that one shared with the miserable body before one's eyes, followed by or coexisting with a comic disarming of that recognition.

At the same time, however, one would be wrong to overestimate the element of foresight and identification in eighteenth-century laughter. Empathy has its limits in any culture. "When we look at the image of our own future provided by the old," notes Simone de Beauvoir in her fascinating essay on aging, "we do not believe it: an absurd inner voice whispers that *that* will never happen to us—when *that* happens it will no longer be ourselves that it happens to."[234] These defenses—this impulsive and instantaneous refusal to see one's own future in the afflictions of others—may well have been stronger in early modern culture. Such differences could never be proved, but the boldest historians of Western emotions certainly encourage us to think this way. Norbert Elias describes a much greater emotional volatility in preindustrial societies—sudden leaps from grief to joy, from intense aggression to extreme self-denial, all of them less constrained by pragmatism or self-control. Nietzsche's *Genealogy of Morals* offers a caustic account of the same process: the "immense labor" of instinctual renunciation by which the West developed ethical scruples to moderate impulse.[235] Eighteenth-century laughter so often seems like a present-tense phenomenon, a confident and thoughtless triumph at physical misfortunes, quite aside from the fact that one was likely to suffer a similar fate. This is not to suggest that the reaction was somehow raw or socially unmolded, but certainly it was less restrained by forethought and empathy. Eighteenth-century life was painful and uncertain. You took your pleasures where you could.[236]

Third, however, we are still left to explain certain deep-seated cultural assumptions that made the deformed and disabled such automatic figures of fun, assumptions that go far beyond the mere acceptability of malicious laughter. At the most abstract level, as Roger Lund has recently argued, laughter was licensed by aesthetic and theological ideologies like the argument from design.[237] But what about more immediate or impulsive reactions? What, precisely, made people laugh so freely and unreflectively at a twisted spine or a peculiar gait? It is not simply that cripples and hunchbacks were such easy targets: certain bodies seem to have been unavoidably comic in early modern culture. Any physical peculiarity, any disability or incapacity, any stutter, lameness, or blindness made one a standing joke—a reminder, perhaps, of the hilarious intransigence of nature, of the physicality that lay behind all attempts at human dignity. Bergson's theory of laughter again comes to mind.

We laugh, says Bergson, when an orator sneezes at the most pathetic moment of his speech, when the astronomer stumbles as he is gazing up at the stars— all of them moments when a person's self-conception is interrupted, when the body "takes precedence of the soul."[238] This elemental humor of clumsiness or incapacity is clear from the many traditional games that rely on temporary handicaps. Blindfolded wheelbarrow races, hopping races, and the like were important parts of eighteenth-century revels. (And approached from the comic archive, such games start to feel uncomfortably close to street incidents, especially blindfolding games like Blind Man's Buff or Muffin Man, in which a blindfolded man has to grab hold of or guess who is beating him.)[239]

One was defined by one's body in eighteenth-century culture. Dr. Squintum, Count Tapski, Miss Dumpty, Hopping Giles, My Lord Hump—these and all the other nicknames effectively limited a person's identity to his or her most visible attribute. Think of Joshua "Spot" Ward (1685–1761), the dodgy quack, defined and named all his life by the large birthmark on one side of his face. Hundreds of these nicknames were in active use, distinguishing between physical peculiarities that we would not now differentiate: Skinny Jaws, Plump-Cheeks, Beetle-Brows, Hatchet-Face, Pancake Face. There were Cock Eyes, Gimlet Eyes, Goggle Eyes, Gooseberry Eyes (dull like boiled gooseberries), and blear or gravy eyes (inflamed and running, a common and long-term complication of smallpox). Brandy Face, Brazen Face, Cream Face, Bacon Face, Bug Face, Muffin Face, Pock Face—these are just a few of the scores of names for different complexions. Most abundant of all are the terms for different noses. We now distinguish no more than a handful of noses; in the eighteenth century, there were dozens. Bottle Nose, Saddle Nose, Razor-Nose, Copper Nose, Ruby Nose, Pug Nose, Dub Nose, Potato Nose. Someone was Mr. Chin, Mr. Snout, "One-ey'd Simon," "Bow-legg'd Bob," "Squinting Dick," or "Stutt'ring Roger." "I will not be *blinking Sam*," Dr. Johnson told Mrs. Thrale after seeing Reynolds's portrait of him straining over a book.[240]

Such nicknames are condensed signs of a thoroughgoing *body determinism*, as one might call it. Contemporary accounts of accomplished disabled or ugly people invariably describe a moment at which one suddenly saw that they were not *just* a hunchback or hideous cripple. "Beau" Nash was hideous, everyone agreed, but then he opened his mouth. Oliver Goldsmith was just another awkward ugly hack until *The Traveller* convinced people that he was a great poet: "I never more shall think Dr. Goldsmith ugly," said Mrs. Cholmondeley to Johnson.[241] Or consider one entirely sympathetic account of the poet Mary Chandler. She was dreadfully deformed, says her biographer, but after she had spoken a few words one "immediately lost every disgust towards her, that the first appearance of her person tended to excite."[242] As so often, Jane Austen's juvenilia exposes her society's perceptions with uncompromising clarity. Here, for example, from "Frederic and Elfrida" (1787–90), are the heroine's raptures on her new acquaintance, "the amiable Rebecca":

> Lovely & too charming Fair one, notwithstanding your forbidding Squint, your greazy tresses & your swelling Back, which are more frightfull than imagination can paint or pen describe, I cannot refrain from expressing my raptures, at the engaging Qualities of your Mind, which so amply atone for the Horror, with which your first appearance must ever inspire the unwary visitor.[243]

There was no ignoring physical anomalies in this culture: they were "as plain as the nose on your face," as we still say. Early modern aesthetic philosophers—Addison, Hogarth, Hutcheson, and Shaftesbury—all presume that beauty and ugliness are immediate, almost involuntary perceptions. Anyone would laugh when someone came into the room with huge shoulders or an enormous mouth, says Steele. William Hay is similarly blunt: deformity was always "an obstruction in the Way to Favour"; the deformed person must labor to change the perceptions he invariably arouses (but at least people were always pleasantly surprised, he adds, ever alert to any possible "advantage" to deformity).[244]

Of course one also finds constant condemnations of the prejudices and the laughter. Hobbes was direct: laughing at the imperfections of others was an act of "Pusillanimity," the petty comfort of those least favored themselves. Religious objections themselves came in many forms. To judge people for defects they could not help was a violation of every Christian principle. Physical anomalies were part of the infinite variety of creation; it was sinful to laugh at any of God's creatures. An evil mind was the thing to judge, not a deformed body. But all too often these defenses are themselves risible: the fun of laughing at disability was actually enhanced by absurd claims that anyone could overlook appearances. Thus Vanbrugh's Learchus, attempting to convince his daughter to marry Esop:

EUPHRONIA: But Esop is so ugly, Sir.
LEARCHUS: His Soul has so much Beauty in't, your Reason ought to blind your Eyes.[245]

This particular absurdity itself produced its own genres: mock-didactic epistles, dialogues, and many more. One midcentury miscellany included a lengthy "Dialogue *between Miss* Louisa *and Miss* Maria: *against ridiculing personal Defects.*" "How could you be so barbarous, Sister, to ridicule Miss *Moliere*'s Shape, and mimic her limping Steps when she was hardly got out of the Room?" And "especially in one of her affable Disposition, and excellent Understanding." Besides, the elder sister continues, the Almighty would not let it go: "You know *Jenny Flounce* broke her Leg, in the very Action of mimicking her lame Mistress; and *Miss Titter* has ridicul'd her purblind Sister, till she is grown stark blind herself."[246]

Perhaps the most exaggerated example of this comedy is *Nothing Irregular in Nature; or, Deformity a Mere Fancy* (1734), a short quarto of hideous caricatures copied from Heemskerk, the Restoration genre artist.[247] Each is accompanied by mottoes and clumsy verses deploring the habit of judging from appearances. Number one is a toothless old man with an enormous hook nose, dripping and covered in carbuncles, accompanied by the usual directive to look beneath surfaces: "Of what e'er frame or hue the Face is, / The Mind may have ten thousand Graces" (fig. 5). The collection ends with a mock-sympathetic defense of old women. They might be hideous witches, but they were as chaste as could be (after all, "The added Length of Nose and Chin, / Permit no Kiss to come between"). This mock admiration for kindness or prudence—all the smirking talk about the "advantages" of deformity or ugliness as the best preservative for chastity—was a reliably productive comic situation. Christopher Smart characteristically tops them all with Mrs. Midnight's "Dissertation on the Dignity, Benefit, and Beauty of Ugliness." Even a woman with no principles at all can resist temptation, says Mrs. Midnight, if she is blessed with ugliness. A good deformity would make her the favorite of every other woman, a situation Mrs. Midnight ventriloquizes in a young woman's earnest praise for her less fortunate acquaintances:

'Tis true, Ma'am, says *Flirtelinda*, Mrs. *Hoppertail* is Hump-back;—but then she has all the Prudence and Discretion conceivable. Miss *Jingumbob* is to be sure very homely, but 'tis the Charms of the Mind that strike me, and tho' *Gorgonia* squints, has black Teeth, bandy Legs, and is Pot-bellied; yet all the World allows she is an exceeding good Sort of a Woman.[248]

Here, overstated as it is, we find an early version of the condescending "triumph over adversity" trope, *handicapism* as modern activists might call it.

Even those most optimistically committed to the sentimental project—those who lauded the didactic functions of sentimental drama or put their faith in sympathy as the glue of an enlightened human society—concede that

●◎◎◎◎◎◎◎◎◎◎◎◎◎ ◎◎◎◎◎◎◎◎◎◎◎◎◎◎◎◎◎◎

The Mind's the Man.

WHEN manly Wit, in ſhort Eſſays,
　　Refin'd the Beaux of *Anna's* Days;
When the polite Spectator reign'd,
And Vice was pleas'd to be reſtrain'd;
On *Iſis* Banks the *Muſes* warm'd
A virtuous Band, by Nature form'd,
In Mind, with ev'ry Art to pleaſe,
In Face and Body, worſe than theſe.
　　What powder'd Fop, or noiſy Spark,
Who travers'd *Hide*, or *James's* Park,
Could boaſt an *Addiſon* his Friend?
Would *Steele* to ſooth him condeſcend?
Yet *Steele* and *Addiſon* the Sage,
The joint Reformers of an Age,
When in the Ugly Club enroll'd,
Were * proud to have their Honour told.
　　Learn ye Male Belles, ye He-ſhe Things,
Where Virtue lies, whence Honour ſprings.
Dreſs, ſpark, and powder all you can,
'Tis to be Boys.—The Mind's the Man.

　* *Spectator.*

FIGURE 5. Poem and engraving from *Nothing Irregular in Nature; or, Deformity a Mere Fancy* (London, 1734). This startlingly frank mockery of the idea that one could overlook deformity in favor of moral or intellectual qualities also obliges us to detect a skeptical paratext around other exhortations on the subject. The didactic verses on the left are overtly contradicted by the grotesque image on the right. The two engraved figures embody the now-obscure concept of jovial ugliness. Courtesy of Research Library, The Getty Research Institute, Los Angeles (92-B22226).

Of what e'er frame or hue the Face is,
The Mind may have ten thousand Graces.

2

the deformed were unreliable, if not impossible, objects of sympathy. Pity, insists Adam Smith, is excited not by physical but by mental suffering: nothing would be more ridiculous than a tragic hero with a wooden leg.[249] Diderot is characteristically humane about deformity and the absolute relativity of beauty and ugliness; he has nothing but contempt for crude superstitions about hunchbacks or clubfeet.[250] But this did not mean that the deformed were easy to pity, as he bluntly tells us in the *Paradox of Acting* (1773). Empathy was difficult enough at the best of times. It might be achieved in the theater, but in everyday circumstances there was always some impediment. Think of a weeping woman with some facial blemish, he says: you're more likely to laugh than feel sorry for her. She might as well have a comic accent or wave her arms about in some coarse and sullen manner (*ignoble et maussade*).[251] Such observations come up with startling frequency in Enlightenment aesthetics, and nowhere more appallingly than in Lessing's *Laocoön*. "A mole on the face, a harelip, a flat nose with prominent nostrils [*plattgedrückte Nase*], a complete lack of eyebrows": Lessing simply announces that these defects interrupted any finer feelings.[252]

The predominance of the theater in these discussions is no accident. Drama is probably the central imaginative scenario in most discussions of sentiment.[253] More to the point, the theater was also an environment in which physical presence could not be ignored, and therefore the one in which the limits of pity become clearest. In a fascinating recent article, Judith Milhous gathers instances in which an actor's body becomes too anomalous for serious roles. Non-European features were pretty much out, she finds—even roles like Othello were always played in blackface until Ira Aldridge took the stage in the 1830s.[254] As they grew older, most actresses were confined to funny old women (something that was not true to the same extent for men). Samuel Sandford, the late Restoration actor, was famously lank and crooked and therefore confined to villains and ludicrous old men—not "by Choice," as Colley Cibber put it, "but from Necessity." Charles Coffey—creator of *The Devil to Pay* and *The Beggar's Wedding*—was a hunchback and therefore made a first-class Aesop.[255] Richard Arne, the brother of the composer, was a dwarf: he did Tom Thumb, Ariel, a series of servants and Cupids, and the dwarf bride in *Trick for Trick*, but then disappears from the records.*

---

* Why Arne disappeared is an old mystery in drama history. This was not because he was a dwarf, as some have speculated. The unfortunate truth is that he was implicated in one of the most horrific sex crimes of the century. In July 1735, he was one of a drunken gang of fourteen

Audiences evidently overlooked significant departures from physical ideals if they were compensated by strong acting or a good singing voice. Elizabeth Barry's skill made up for her irregular features and twisted mouth. Short and fat, with an oversized head, beady eyes, and a "pock-fretten" face, Thomas Betterton nevertheless became a celebrated tragic actor. Even Mary Porter managed to return to the tragic stage after her accident in 1732, using her cane to add emphasis.[256] Garrick is himself a prime example of these limits. At five foot four, he was a noticeably small man and himself recognized that he must never attempt such roles as Cato; his harsher critics insisted that he was entirely unsuited to tragedy. Charles Macklin was famously ugly and largely confined to villains like his celebrated Shylock. Fielding delighted in the joke of casting Macklin—"that ill-looked Dog"—to play the equally hideous Theophilus Cibber in his revival of *The Authors' Farce* (1734). Contemporary discussions of Macklin make a fascinating case study of these limits. Everyone agreed that the long, craggy face was hideous: he made a perfect Shylock, but what about Iago, who had at least to *seem* honest?[257]

Might one explore the question more positively? How did certain deformities actually qualify one as a comic actor? A remarkable number of the most celebrated eighteenth-century farceurs relied on some sort of defect. Dicky Norris was "a tiny man with odd face and voice"—"that little comical toothless divell," James Thomson described him. He was "form'd by Nature" to be a cuckold, said Anne Oldfield of his role in *The Amorous Widow* (1706). Spiller was blind in one eye but used the defect to great effect in his most celebrated roles (Jebson in *The Devil to Pay*, Hob the rustic idiot, and a succession of eccentric old men). With his squashed nose, grating voice, and skinny legs, Theophilus Cibber was perfectly qualified for farce and pantomime. He was a celebrated Pistol, played Abel Drugger and Fielding's Mock Doctor, and in the months before his death appeared as Mynheer Von Poop-Poop Broomstickado—presumably some sort of mock-Dutch bassoon-playing precision farter—in Mrs. Midnight's Oratory.[258]

Or consider, finally, the wildly popular John Hippisley, who was disfigured by a great burn scar. "The left Corner of his Mouth, and the Extremity of his

---

who raped a widowed fishwife in a privy off Mercer Street. Three of the gang were convicted at the September sessions and executed ten days later. Arne's father, Thomas, a Covent Garden upholsterer and theater servant, had been following these trials from the Old Bailey brandy shop but fled when it emerged that he had tried to bribe a witness. Arne Senior was soon back at his shop, but his son never returned to the stage. See *R. v. Togwell and Mattews, R. v. Whitney*, 11 September 1735 (OBSP t17350911-55-56).

Chin" were "very near Neighbours," said Foote. His "Risible Grimace," said Chetwood, "seemed greatly to aid the Comic parts he performed"—the usual range of clowns, Welsh bumpkins, and dotards like Corbaccio. Hippisley's scar was a long-running joke in the London theater world. His *face* was itself a *farce*. When Hippisley announced that he was going to bring his son onto the stage, Quin is said to have joked that it was now "high time to burn him." And unusually for theatrical portraits, likenesses of Hippisley freely represent his defect since this was such a major part of his success. Audiences "would clap him heartily, and fall a laughing at him as soon as he appeared upon the Stage," Tom Davies recalled—"before he had opened his Mouth to speak one Word."[259]

Still operating in some form was the traditional distinction between "natural" fools, whose defects destined them to play the fool, and "artificial" fools, who merely impersonated folly for a living.[260] Many of the greatest comic performers of early modern Europe were distinctively scarred or misshapen. Tarleton, the Elizabethan clown, had relied on his flattened nose, which he would poke through the tapestries at the back of the stage. Tiberio Fiorillo, the great Scaramouche—wildly popular during his visits to London in the 1670s and a huge hit performing trios with a dog and parrot—was "short-sighted, deaf in his left ear, [and] withered in one shoulder." Fiorillo was so hideous, in fact, that he played his signature role without a mask, merely dusting his face with white powder. Belleroche, the great seventeenth-century Crispin, was an inveterate stutterer; his son and grandson, inheriting the stutter, continued to play the same role.[261]

Burn scars, mutilated faces, hunched backs, or speech impediments seem not only to have drawn attention to an inescapable physicality—the great primal joke of the human body—but also to have dehumanized these actors. Comic performers had always obscured their regular facial expressions: with sooted cheeks in ancient Rome, red noses for medieval devils, grotesque masks in the commedia dell'arte, white bismuth and rouge in the English harlequinade. Such devices interrupted sympathy—anesthetizing the heart, as Bergson put it—and enabled audiences to laugh at all the humiliations and beatings. But sufficiently scarred performers had no need of masks and powders. They were already standing jokes.

CHAPTER THREE

Delights of Privilege

It is hard for modern scholars to appreciate how absurd it could still be, in 1740 or even 1800, to suggest that ordinary people had fine feelings. Early sentimental representations of peasants and housemaids were flagrant violations of inherited decorums. Apart from the idealizations of pastoral and Georgic, neoclassical aesthetics allowed common people to be represented only as objects of laughter. Traditionally, at least, only the comic genres allowed authors to go beyond the barest representation of humble environments, everyday speech, and ordinary food or clothing—and then only because these things were amusing. Foolish servants, village drunkards, rustics in love, grubby porters and draymen: these were the familiar representatives of common life. In most genres, they spoke the lowest forms of the language. They talked in unseemly detail about food, sex, and money. The great parodic genres of early modern literature—all the mock epics, burlesque tragedies, and satiric romances—worked precisely by transposing the action from castles to inns or hovels and transforming nobles into ordinary folk who belch, fart, and declare their love in dialect.

Then sentimental authors started asking readers to care about socially inferior characters and their everyday sufferings. Melancholy old soldiers, housemaids struggling to preserve their virtue, honest rural families on the brink of starvation: suddenly these people became objects of pity. Former comic settings—hedgerows, cheap lodgings, street corners, even brothels and madhouses—now became the sites of sentimental encounters. Eventually, unheroic protagonists in ordinary milieus would be used to explore the profoundest questions. How this happened is one of literary history's grandest stories (and after sixty years it may still have no greater chronicler than Erich Auerbach).[1] But the transvaluation of ignoble into sentimental was gradual and still problematic in the early nineteenth century. "The Idiot Boy" was a fine poem, said Coleridge, but Wordsworth had not "taken sufficient care" to prevent disgust—to stop readers laughing at a grubby simpleton and his doting mother.[2] These problems are still clearer in the early reception of sentimental literature. Indeed, many sentimental novels seem to make room for readers who needed to laugh: thus the odd tendency of sentimental charity cases to start telling lies or talking like village idiots. For all the fine research on the class contexts of British sentimentalism, we probably still need more work on this drift toward comedy.

My task in this chapter is to establish the persistence, in mid-eighteenth-century Britain, of the old comic representations of low life and the behavioral freedoms that went with them. Compared to the volume of comic-demeaning texts, sentimental representations of the poor were a minority phenomenon. No doubt some of these demeaning texts were reactions against emerging sensibilities, wishful reassertions of older hierarchies. But many more record habitual and unquestioned forms of fun—the casual pleasures of laughing at the ignorance, vulgarity, or poor personal hygiene of one's inferiors. For a significant proportion of the privileged classes, this sort of laughter heightened the joy of life. And more important for every scholar of the eighteenth century, these inherited attitudes continued to determine hierarchical interactions, from chance encounters and servant-master relations to poor law hearings and the justice system.

LAUGHING AT THE LOWER ORDERS

At the risk of flattening out individual texts, it seems crucial to review the full range of genres and scenarios, above all the less sympathetic ones. Alongside the usual footmen and fishwives were legions of now-forgotten plebeians. The "Wise Men" of Gotham were famous throughout the land, but there were thousands of other numbskulls—villagers who try to drown a basket of eels or dig a hole to bury a pile of earth.[3] Emerging images of rustic innocence had to compete with much nastier representations of village life—illicit sex, long-held grudges, brawls and cursing matches, spouses who torment each other to death. All these scenarios move between print genres and everyday perceptions. In genteel diaries and correspondence, the constant complaints about disobedient servants persistently develop into tales of plebeian stupidity. Hester Thrale seems never to have tired of recording the malapropisms of her own and other people's menials. A footman reports that her friend is "Lunatick" rather than "Rheumatic." "[It] is not *yet* got into an *Jest Book*, but *this*," she enthuses over another story: a maid delivers a request for "Three Oxen and a Hogshead" when her master asked for a Theocritus and a Horace![4]

The most reliable comic plebeians—and the most reliable murderers of proper English—were the idiots of the Celtic fringe. Dour hungry Scots, credulous Welshmen called Taffy (a corruption of Dafydd), and Irish simpletons named Paddy or Teague fill the pages of midcentury comic texts. Taffy is the most resilient of the three, always trotting along with a leek in his hat and asking for toasted cheese; he is also wonderfully gullible and prone to droll accidents. He is easily convinced that mustard is good for the eyes. Another story has him accidentally defecating in his pocket while trying to "do his business" off the side of a bridge.[5] Taffy is always hungry, and there is endless fun serving him plates of shit and omelettes of rotten eggs. Teague's specialty, at least since Tudor times, was the nonsensical Irish bull:

A person ask'd an *Irishman*, why he wore his Stockings the wrong Side outwards? *Because*, says he, *there is a Hole on the other Side.*

An *Irishman* having a Looking Glass in his Hand, shut his Eyes, and placed it before his Face; another asking him, Why he did so? *Upon my Shoul*, says Teague, *it is to see how I look when I am asleep.*

An *Irish* Servant being struck by his Master, cried out, Devil take me if I am certain whether he has kill'd me or no; but if I am dead it will afford me great Satisfaction to hear the old Rogue was hang'd for killing me.[6]

Alongside these jokes were thousands of more extended tales, from the benign one about an Irish footman who tries to dry wet candles in a fireplace to the more unsettling one about two Irish soldiers who accidentally blow themselves up.[7] For all their stereotyped structure, such jokes tell us much about the world that created them—a world in which masters routinely beat their servants, in which Celtic migrants were presumed to be ragged, hungry, and desperate. Irish paupers were evidently a particular nuisance in the capital (surveys suggest that 25–33 percent of London beggars came from Ireland). Thus the market for compendia like *The Irish Miscellany* (1746). Complete with a dialect preface by Teague himself ("Bee Shaint Patrick, de Dee'l tauke me noow, but I caun remaumber de Time, vaan . . ."), this text went through five editions in as many years.[8] While regional accents still cut across social hierarchies in this period, certain dialects, or extreme versions of any of them, were always absurd. A Scotch accent, says Smollett's Matt Bramble, "gives a clownish air even to sentiments of the greatest dignity and decorum."[9]

Consistently satisfying were jokes about foul language or repulsive personal habits. Welshmen were identified not just by the ubiquitous leek but by their rags, dirty feet, and famously vile breath (all that toasted cheese?). Filthy cooks show up by the hundreds, descendants perhaps of the sooty cooks of Roman comedy. A mistress asks her maid whether she has put enough blood in the black puddings. "I think there is Blood enough," she artlessly replies, "for my Nose has bled this half Hour, and all dropped into the Bowl." Told to wash tripe with hot water, the same young woman "made Water upon it very plentifully and rubbed it in with great Care and Pains."[10] Butterwives were the filthiest and most foulmouthed of all market women, long before Nashe's scolding "butter-whores." There are always revolting accidents on the way to market. The butter falls into a swamp, a horse urinates in it. A neighbor's dog eats the lot, forcing the woman to hang the animal until it throws up (a quick stir and no one knows the difference).[11] Clearly all these stories presume that such people belong at the bottom of society, but pedantically spelling out the implication could also be funny. Take Jane Cave's poem to a brawling kitchen maid whom she dubs "Mistress Dishclout." Next time you feel like raising hell, the poem concludes,

> Pray let the scullery hear it all,
> And learn to know your fittest place
> Is with the dishes and the grease.[12]

Like so much of the best invective verse, Cave's insistent tetrameter lines and emphatic end rhymes leave no doubts. Gentlewomen's diaries are no less direct in their constant complaints about "dirty and ungovernable" servants, about the "impudent dirty Slut" who runs off with the stable boy, about unspeakable goings-on in the dairy or John Thomas in the pantry with his paws in the sugar pot.[13]

Beyond their casual amusement about ignorance and filth, comic representations betray stubborn assumptions that the lower orders were incapable of finer feelings. Even the most optimistic sentimentalists accepted that a rude and precarious life coarsened the nerves and therefore the feelings. "The skin, pores, muscles and nerves of the day-labourer," said Hume, are as different from those of a man of quality as his sentiments, actions, and manners.[14] These assumptions emerge with brutal clarity from contemporary comic writing—and perhaps most strongly of all from such condensed genres as ballads, epigrams, and catchphrases. Late in life, the diarist Francis Place recalled a mildly smutty ballad about a dirty linkboy who falls for the naked charms of Brick-Dust Nan. They court for fifteen minutes and spend their wedding night in a pigsty. Similar scenarios recur in every vocal miscellany. Joe the sandman and Bess the bunter; Will the porter and Cerissa the haughty fruit vendor ("M'ambitious soul detests such scum").[15] Or consider a droll "Marriage Certificate," often attributed to Swift:

> Under this Hedge in stormy weather,
> I joined this Whore and Rogue together;
> And none but he who made the Thunder,
> Can put this Whore and Rogue asunder.

To complete the joke, a footnote adds: "She was big with Child when the Ceremony was performed."[16]

Miniaturized and coarsened, such verses must stand for thousands of dismissive representations of plebeian affect. Every jestbook had pages of mock elegies and epitaphs for rustic simpletons and dirty pie women. Gay's *Shepherd's Week* (1714) exploits an established convention when he has two louts sing a dirge about a dead dairymaid named Blouzelinda ("But now, alas! these Ears shall hear no more / The whining Swine surround the Dairy Door"). The tone of this poem is famously elusive, with the mockery of Ambrose Phillips combined with intermittent appreciation of pastoral simplicity and even touches of pathos. But the final lines of the dirge could hardly be clearer as they show every higher sentiment drowning in drink, lust, and thoughtlessness:

> Thus wail'd the Louts in melancholy Strain,
> 'Till bonny Susan sped across the Plain;
> They seized the Lass in Apron clean array'd,
> And to the Ale-house forc'd the willing Maid;
> In ale and Kisses they forgot their Cares,
> And *Susan Blouzelinda's* Loss repairs.[17]

By the 1760s, the burlesque pastoral tradition so evident in these lines had merged into a prominent body of antisentimental writings, all of them mocking the very possibility of fine sentiments in peasants, servants, or urban laborers. There were hundreds of mock laments, like the "elegy" for an oversized Derbyshire breweress "who unfortunately smother'd herself in her own Mashing

Tub."[18] One finds mock-sentimental sonnets about the ardor of apprentices and shopgirls and mock-epistolary novels about rustic lovers. Fielding's *Shamela* is one of hundreds of mock-sentimental tales that turn weepy heroines into whores or melancholy housemaids who lean on mops and weep their eyes out. As usual, Samuel Foote outdid them all with *Piety in Pattens*, his travestic puppet show of 1773. *Piety in Pattens* is a hilarious send-up of the "whining, lackadaisical do-me-good comedies" of the 1750s and 1760s, specifically of *Pamela*-inspired productions like Bickerstaffe's *Maid of the Mill* (1765).[19]

Literary history falls so naturally into dialectical periods that we easily overlook the prominence of such contemporary parodies. Antisentimentalism so often seems like a late eighteenth-century phenomenon, with new comedies by Goldsmith and Sheridan, critiques by Burke and Wollstonecraft, burlesques by Jane Austen, and political upheavals making the whole thing untenable by around 1810. This sequential pattern inevitably deemphasizes the vast and energetic contemporary reaction. For all the midcentury parodies we know about—*Shamela* and *Anti-Pamela*, magazine spoofs, burlesque tragedies by Foote and others—thousands more have sunk without trace. "Cheshire Nell," for example, is one of many long narrative poems about simple young countrywomen who get ideas above their station. Nell has read too many tales of maids who marry lords and reasons: "If other Virgins thus could rise, / Why might not she expect a Prize?" Nell scorns every local swain, carefully guarding her chastity for a higher suitor. Eventually her foolish parents send her off to London to become a lady. Within a stage of London, however, Nell is brought firmly down to earth by a dreadful coach accident:

> Amidst the Pool of Mire and Clay,
> Poor *Nell* distress'd and breathless lay;
> Her lovely Limbs with mud o'erspread,
> Limbs worthy of a sweeter Bed!
> Her Dreams of future Wealth and State,
> All scatter'd by this Blast of Fate.

The rest is all too predictable. Nell takes shelter at an inn where she recuperates until her ambition returns. But alas, preparing to set out again, she discovers that she has lost her purse (as obscene a proleptic suggestion as it seems).[20] Unable to pay the reckoning, poor Nell has no choice but to stay at the inn and work as a chambermaid. There she toils every day, the object of lewd whispers, until at last "Her Pride grew less—she lost her Shame; / For Gain she sold her Virgin Name." Such is the fate, the tale concludes, of those who dream above their station: "Ambition is a dang'rous Guest." Along the way, the poem takes pains to establish the callous insensibility of every other person of Nell's class. Tumbled out of the coach, she arrives bruised, weeping, and covered in filth at the inn. No one cares:

> Heedless, the Folks the Story hear,
> Tho' grac'd with many a pearly Tear:
> Alas! She thought not all her Pain
> Was Joy to them—which brought them Gain.

As in so many midcentury comic texts, "Cheshire Nell" here extrapolates from local circumstance to a general comment on the base practicality of the lower classes, their stolid indifference to fine sentiments of any sort.[21]

Even more representational, it seems to me, are the many jokes about physical encounters between gentlemen and their inferiors. One of the most frequent of all jestbook scenarios involves a meeting between mounted gentlemen and some solitary peasant. "A Gentleman meeting with a Welshman thought to put a trick on him . . ."; three young Oxonians "met a Grave old Gentleman with whom they had a mind to be rudely merry . . ."[22] The joke can be as simple as an insult:

> Two Gentlemen riding between Stanstead and Bishop Stafford, overtook a miller riding very soberly, they being merrily disposed, were resolv'd to affront him. . . . So, said one to the miller, I prithee friend resolve me one Question, Whether thou art most Knave or Fool?[23]

Hundreds of jokes follow the same elemental pattern. Or perhaps the fellow might be told how much he stinks. In one oddly repeated scenario, the gentlemen find an old peasant woman delousing herself or defecating in a ditch. The following was reprinted in every edition of D'Urfey's *Pills to Purge Melancholy*:

> Underneath the rotten Hedge, the Tinker's Wife sat shiting,
> Tearing of a Cabbage Leaf, her shitten A—— a wiping;
> With her cole black Hands she scratch'd her A——
>> And swore she was beshitten,
>> With that the Pedlars all did skip,
>> And the Fidlers fell a spitting.[24]

Vagabonds, urban fruit vendors, anonymous hags on the side of the road—the sight of a plebeian defecating was evidently a routine sight (Fielding needs only the briefest reference to evoke Square's squatting posture in Molly Seagrim's garret).[25]

The meeting of a horseman and an earthbound plebeian was at once a routine and a deeply emblematic interaction, one in which the basic inequality in height and mobility confirmed social hierarchies, for both parties and with daily regularity. No wonder the scenario recurs so frequently in eighteenth-century landscape painting: gentlemen on horseback and peasants on their way to market or standing about their cottage door. These images go through every permutation—idyllic in Stubbs and Morland, comic and characteristically devoid of social critique in Rowlandson and Laroon the Younger.[26] For the comic depictions, at least, jestbooks would seem to offer a sort of verbal script. In one endlessly satisfying joke, the rustic is simply reminded how unlucky he is:

> A Countryman sowing his Ground, two smart Fellows riding that Way, one of them called to him with an insolent Air: Well, honest Fellow, said he, 'tis your Business to sow, but we reap the Fruits of your Labour. To which the Countryman replied, '*Tis very likely you may, truly; for I am sowing Hemp.*[27]

This time the countryman has the last word, but many jokes offer no more than a simple act of snobbish triumph. A decrepit old man will be tormented for his deformities or laughed at for having no teeth. In many instances, the yokel is teased or bewildered with foolish questions. "Miller," asks the gentleman in another joke, "can you chop Logic? No, says the Miller. Why then I'll teach you: Your Horse has eight Sides. How can that be? says the Fellow"—and so on.[28] Students, especially, are always keen to try out their paradoxes and conundrums, forcing some peasant to admit that he is a goose or an ass. They might play on the man's superstitions, warning him about ghosts along the road and demonstrating, at the same time, the irredeemable ignorance and credulity of the lower orders.

All this comes close to that favorite after-dinner entertainment, "quizzing" the servants—sending for some dim-witted kitchenmaid or stable boy who could be baffled in front of the company. An ostler might be asked to translate a line of Virgil, after which he could be dismissed and told that he deserved the station to which Providence had consigned him. *Coffee-House Jests* records the story of an "arch wag" who doesn't want to interrupt a game of cards to relieve himself. With a wink at the company, therefore, he sends for a young housemaid ("who was not above Fourteen Years of Age, and newly come out of the Country, and a very innocent poor Soul") and asks her "to go into the Yard and make Water for him":

> With that the Girl began to blush; but her Mistress (to keep up the Humour) kept her Countenance, and said to the Girl, Hussey, if you can, go and do it for the Gentleman; for you see he can't well come out himself. Truly, forsooth, says she, I can't indeed, for I made my Water but just now in our Back-kitchen: Which set them all a laughing, and the poor Girl a crying; but the Gentleman gave her Six-pence to pacify her.[29]

It is all too easy to imagine obscener versions of this joke set in all-male parties. What is striking about this version is the role of the girl's mistress, the hostess of the polite card party who happily plays along.

Jokes about servants and their foolish answers are ubiquitous. What happened to the new teapot? "It just came apart in my hands" was evidently the standard answer to such questions. Less familiar but at least as common is the scenario of a mistress interrogating her pregnant maidservant. Who's the father? No one, says the maid. "You whore, do ye think any Woman can be with Child without a Man?" From here it is not far to the innumerable jokes about official interrogations—paupers examined by parish officers, JPs, or trial judges. An unmarried pregnant woman is hauled before the overseer. Why was her belly swollen? She had drunk a lot of water.[30] Who was the father? She can't say since she was at it with two men at the same time. (Confusion reigns until it emerges that one of them was Welsh. The clerk waves a piece of toasted cheese in front of the child, which cries out in disgust; its father must be English.)[31] Other pregnancy jokes get comic mileage out of the woman's desperation for anyone to pay for her bastard. Who got you pregnant? It was Dicky in the stables. You're lying: Dicky was transported last year. OK, then, it was Roger, the tapster at the Red Cow. More absurdly, the woman tries swearing her bastard to some obviously incapable man—to a decrepit old fellow or, in more metropolitan forms of the joke, to the Chevalier d'Eon.[32] There were chapbook versions: a village wench tries to swear her bastard to the fool John Franks, who has no idea what he is accused of. "Hussey, you must seek another father for your child," concludes the JP, sending her away for a good flogging.[33] Cumulatively, at least, these jokes make fun of the very possibility that a simple young woman could be telling the truth.

Still others spell it out in different ways, focusing more directly on her bad character:

> A gentleman was accused for getting his maid with child, and that he went into his maid's bed to do it: he to excuse it, swore he never went into his maid's bed, for the bed was his own.[34]

More obviously, and more distastefully, than most jokes, these constant pregnancy jokes were performing powerful cultural functions. A lower-class woman is put back in her place; her accusation collapses, and her reputation is ruined. Along the way, they also point to the JP's parlor and the parish vestry as recognized comic venues.

By far the most discomforting plebeian jokes are the staggering number about capital trials. With only a handful of exceptions, the defendant exposes his guilt, offering some ludicrously improbable defense:

> A *Welshman* hearing a Malefactor, that was tried before him, say, concerning a Mare he had stole, *that he had brought it up from a Colt*: When he came to be examined about a Sword he had stolen, swore, by St. *Taffey, it was hur own, for hur had brought it up from a Dagger.*

Or consider the following, printed under the title "The Thief's Destiny":

> A Fellow being tried for his Life before a Judge, alledged for himself, that he could not avoid it, because it was his Destiny that he should steal: If so, said the Judge, know also 'tis your Destiny to be hanged.

Yes, I did make off with the silver cup, says the defendant, but I certainly didn't mean any harm by it—it's just a silly custom I've got. Well, says the judge, "if it be your Custom to steal, it is also my Custom to hang up those that do steal."[35] The most ubiquitous of these ludicrous defense jokes—one that turns up in every jestbook—concerns a horse thief. I was just borrowing the bridle, he announces, and I hope you won't hang a man over a bit of rope. Soon, of course, he admits that there was a horse attached to it—and off he goes to the gallows. Horse thieves always offer absurd excuses. They found the horse. It must be an evil spirit, pleads another felon, "for I no sooner took the Bridle by the end, but the Jade followed me foot for foot, till I was come to my own door."[36] Other desympathizing jokes focus more squarely on capital punishment, which at first seems extreme but is gradually justified and finally seems natural and inevitable:

> Two Fellows meeting, one ask'd the other, Why he look'd so sad? I have good Reason for it, answer'd the other, poor *Jack* such a one, the greatest Croney and best Friend I had in the World was hang'd but two Days ago. What had he done, says the first? Alas! reply'd the other, he did no more than you or I should ha' done on the like Occasion; he found a Bridle on the Road, and took it up; What! says the other, hang a Man for taking up a Bridle? That's hard, indeed! *To tell the Truth of the Matter*, says the other, *there was a Horse tied to the other End of it.*[37]

It comes as no surprise to find *The Irish Miscellany* collecting multiple versions of this scenario.[38]

Judicial humor is prominent in every jestbook. Condemned men humiliate themselves as they plead mercy, speaking nonsense even as they beg for their lives:

> One being sentenced to die, fell on his Knees, and besought the Judge to spare his Life, for the sake of his *Widow* and his *fatherless Children*.

"I crave Mercy," says the thief who steals a lantern one night. "I was only going to snuff the Candle, that I might see to go along."[39] Still others introduce felons too stupid to understand that you don't come back after being hanged. What are you doing here, one felon asks his wife at the gallows? Get home and weed the vegetables, or we'll have nothing to eat this winter.[40] "Go home with a Vengeance, you nasty Baggage," says another to his wife as he is about to be strung up. "Look to your House, a Man had as good be hanged as be a Husband to such a lazy Slut." The related scenario of idiots making long-term plans on the eve of their execution produced its own subgenres, from droll "dialogues" to extended epistles ("A true Copy of a Letter that Patrick O'Flaherty sent his Mother at *Tipperary* the Night before his Execution"). Unsurprisingly, Irish idiots loom large in this family of jokes. Two Irishmen meet on a street corner. What happened to their old friend Patrick Murphy? "Arrah, now dear Homey, answered the other, poor Patty was condemn'd to be hang'd; but he saved his Life by dying in Prison." Pat had met with an unfortunate accident, sighs his friend in another example:

As he was standing on a *plank*, talking devoutly to a priest, at a place in London, which I think they call the Old Bailey, the plank suddenly gave way, and poor Pat got his neck broke.

Like so many Irish bulls, these plodding circumlocutions almost enact the presumed slowness of Irish mental processing. It is not difficult to imagine what this last joke—printed in Dublin—was doing for its Anglo-Irish readers.[41]

Having raced through the demeaning and desympathizing jokes, I must at least glance at the obvious exceptions: jokes in which underdogs get the last laugh or turn tables on their tormentors. Paupers too had their unmotivated pranks. A laborer refuses to open the gate for the genteel horseman, protesting that he is "unworthy of that honor." A ditch digger sends a gentleman through a swamp, assuring him that it was "hard at the bottom." The gentleman soon sinks up to the saddle:

> Why thou Whoreson Rascal, said he to the Ditcher, didst thou not tell me it was hard at the Bottom? *Ay*, replied the other, *but you are not half Way to the Bottom yet*.[42]

Others enact a sort of revenge for arrogance or mistreatment. Why don't you make yourself a set of stocks, says an arrogant gentleman to a tinker? Lend me your head and hands, replies the tinker, and I'd be happy to.[43] A gentleman punishes his footman with a good "Kick on the Breech," at which the Footman "let a great F——." "Out, you stinking Rascal, said his Master. *Why, Sir*, replied the Man, *as you are my Master, I must answer you at the same Door you knock at*."[44] Here and there one finds the satiric implications openly spelled out ("Three young conceited Wits, *as they thought themselves . . .*"). We'll prove you're a horse or an ass, say two Oxford scholars to the Yorkshire ostler. "And I can prove your Saddle to be a *Mule*," says the ostler. "A *Mule*! how can that be? *Because*, said the Ostler, *it is something between a* Horse *and an* Ass."[45] And beyond all these are thousands of more rudimentary replies. Say what you like, but your nose is falling off. Or simply that perennial favorite, "Kiss my arse."

Still striking after two and a half centuries are the number of exchanges between mounted gentlemen and defecating plebeians. Two young sparks come across the usual old woman doing her business under a hedge:

> So old mother, I see you have been emptying your self. *Sir*, said she, *you see more with your eyes, than you can carry away with your mouth*. But, said he,

why did you look back? *why, sir, said she, seeing of you coming, I looked to see whether there was enough for you both.*[46]

Turning around and looking at it is a recurring detail, one that takes us back to the minutest protocols of the plein air bowel movement. The same joke also occurs in the milder form of an inadvertent insult. Deaf jokes, for example, often follow this pattern:

> A deaf Fellow coming to *London* to sell a turkey, at *Hyde Park* corner had occasion to untruss a point [undo his breeches]; a gentleman passing by, intending to put a joke upon him; countryman, said he, there's a turd under you. The man thinking he asked the price of his turkey, said 4s. master. I say, there's a turd under you, said the other. It is as good as ever you eat in your life, said the fellow, either baked or roasted.

Behind these are hundreds of similar jokes in which the tormentor gets what he deserves. A nobleman amuses himself at the expense of a poor deaf man, finally smiling and wishing him "a thousand gallows and ropes around your neck." "My Lord," replies the deaf man, "I wish you twice as many."[47]

How subversive are such jokes? Ronald Paulson reads them as part of a "folk realization that under his dress and manners the great man is no different."[48] Certainly they demonstrate the enduring appeal of plebeian trickster figures—from butcher's boys to more literary types like the clever servant, a stock comic character at least since Plautus. But jestbooks were middle- and upper-class commodities; if anything, their jokes work to contain challenges to rank. The old laborer may tell the gentlemen they're going to be hanged, but the gentlemen ride on, and the laborer goes on sowing seed for them. The beggar woman may tell her tormentors to eat her shit, but she is still left with nowhere to live and nothing to eat; she would die in a ditch, and no one would care. A momentary defiance does nothing to alter basic inequalities. Indeed half the fun of insulting a stinky yokel or market woman was the gloriously vulgar response it provoked. Late in life, Henry Mackenzie still remembered a friend going up to a Billingsgate fishwife and insulting her fish. Result: the usual torrent of abuse followed by a rotten lobster before the man silences her with a verse of Homer.[49] The deaf turkey vendor may offer his tormentor the best turd he ever ate, but most versions of this joke add an additional punch line that casually informs us of the most likely consequence of insolence. "You rascal," says the gentleman, "I could find [it] in my heart to kick you soundly. Chuse, said the fellow, if you won't another will."[50] "Am I not a fool to do as

I did?" muses the gentleman in another jest. "Yes truly, sir," says his manser-
vant, "and a very great fool." Again, the violence is inevitable: "You rogue,
says his master to him again, though I call myself fool, I do not allow you to
call me so; and so kickt the fellow down-stairs."[51]

I hasten to repeat that these examples come from a broad range of sources
and reflect an even broader range of tones. *The Shepherd's Week* chortles gently at the baseness of rural laborers; other texts announce that plebeians were
innately dishonest and suggest that they would hardly notice if you hanged
them out of the way. A continuum of attitudes stretches from tolerant amusement at one end to suspicion or disgust at the other. But behind it all lie certain stubbornly consistent assumptions about the lower orders as ignorant,
absurd, and overwhelmingly physical beings. They existed in a deeply sur-
vivalist mode and were inured to hardship. Since they did not suffer like their
betters, sympathy was neither habitual nor appropriate. Perhaps more forc-
ibly than other genres, comic representations remind us just how immutable
inherited social hierarchies were assumed to be. Produced for a wide variety
of middle- and upper-class readers, these texts must also complicate our understanding of middle-class aspiration and the polite manners and tastes that
supposedly enabled it. Laughing at social inferiors was part of becoming a
gentleman, a mode of self-differentiation as potent as the self-conscious politeness we have learned so much about. For the middling readers who bought
so many of these books—who read the prefaces about how to tell good jokes,
who wanted to laugh like gentlemen, who were determined to disguise their
humble origins and the taint of trade—disdainful laughter was part of their
self-presentation. Becoming a gentleman in this culture meant acquiring the
right mixture of noblesse and indifference, of demonstrative generosity and
breezy disdain.

CONTEXTS FROM SOCIAL HISTORY

Some important caveats are in order. First, recent social historians have established nothing so strongly as the structural complexity of midcentury
British society. Any polarity between ruling classes and the poor would be
the crudest simplification of any local hierarchy, quite aside from all the regional differences and variations over time. London artisans drifted in and
out of poverty; tenant farmers went through periods of plenty and others in
which they needed parish assistance. Wherever one looks, one finds internal
conflicts, shifting factions, and changing allegiances—even within the most
stable social groupings. Structures of sympathy, assistance, tolerance, and

fear existed in a constant state of flux. The landed classes included old-style paternalists who gave out scraps at the back door and hard-nosed capitalists who teamed up with larger farmers to punish gleaners and wood thieves. As for the official interactions that loom so large in the comic sources, the actual hierarchical differences varied enormously. JPs had to earn £100 per year, but above that there was no consistency. One finds constant complaints that the great landowners—those presumed sufficiently disinterested to exercise the responsibility most fairly—were reluctant to administer local justice.[52] Several decades on from the heyday of Marxist history, we now know that the criminal law was never a simple form of class oppression. Even the lowest members of this society used the courts. In every context, as Peter King has written, the law was shaped by "layer and layer of negotiation opportunities and discretionary choices."[53] Vestries were open to all ratepayers; parish officers ranged from wealthy merchants and farmers down to low-middling sorts who were not much better off than the laborers who sought relief.[54] In short, exceptions are everywhere to be found; to the extent that I use class categories, I do so with acute self-consciousness. At the same time, class categories are not entirely useless. While not always the best label for the mutating mass at the bottom of eighteenth-century society, *the poor* does at least refer to an imaginative or ideological entity, one continually constructed and reconstructed in discourse and practice.

Second, laughing at one's social inferiors had always been ethically problematic and was becoming more so. Such laughter violated the most central Christian teachings of humility and equality before God. When Pamela tells Mr. B that "[her] Soul is of equal Importance with the Soul of a Princess," she is repeating the inconvenient but unavoidable message of the Gospels. These leveling tendencies could be qualified with more providentialist accounts of rank, but there was no avoiding the essential element of the Christian story: God's incarnation on earth as a human being of humble station who performed miracles among artisans, innkeepers, prostitutes, and fishermen. In the history of representation, as Erich Auerbach reminds us, the Judeo-Christian tradition positively favored humble life: in both the Old Testament and the New, momentous spiritual events take place in conspicuously ordinary environments.[55] By the early eighteenth century, these traditions were combining with emerging benevolist ones to make older forms of laughter problematic. Even Aristotle's hallowed theory of comedy proved hard to justify. In most midcentury discussions, Stuart Tave finds the philosopher "given a short paragraph at the beginning and gently dismissed": explaining laughter as a reaction to the base or ugly "seemed to hang too close to Hobbes."[56] These concerns were keenly felt by every satirist. Along with all their other charges of malice, Pope's enemies attacked *The Dunciad* for delighting in the poverty and hunger of his dunces. Pope, wrote James Ralph, seemed to assume that "the want of a Dinner made a Man a Fool."[57] In these contexts, jokes about poverty and vulgarity can easily seem like substitutes for an increasingly unacceptable laughter, a form of upper-class retrenchment against new restraints.

Third, and most important, high-low humor cannot be detached from the conflicts and challenges so richly documented by British labor historians. In retrospect it seems obvious that elite mistrust of the poor was growing in this period. Letters and pamphlet literature are full of complaints about insolent servants and apprentices, weary observations that the old structures of deference were no more.[58] New research on parish law and local justice is now showing us just how consciously and successfully the poor manipulated these systems. Many understood the legal requirements for a "settlement" in the parish and carefully tailored their answers to the authorities. Starving laborers, disabled widows, and unwed mothers all maintained firm beliefs in their right to relief. They knew that the parish was legally obliged to help them, and appealed to magistrates if the overseers turned them away. A proper display of submission was part of this manipulation: bastard bearers knew that a bit of weepy contrition would force the parish and/or the alleged father to support their child.[59] Even beggars had a powerful range of strategies: established rights to beg at Christmas and other holidays, to ask for scraps at kitchen doors, and to stand outside churches on Sundays. They expected a handout after weddings and funerals. They sussed out potential benefactors and adapted their appeal accordingly: from the rhetoric of Christian charity to pitiable tales of seduction and betrayal or how they lost their limb. They made the baby cry or did their rasping cough routine. And if appeals to higher sentiments failed, they could flash their sores or reach out to soil your clothes.[60]

Jokes about stupid, dirty, and docile paupers can easily seem like defusals of all these demands. To return to one specific example, jests about bastardy hearings reflect widespread concerns that respectable citizens were being forced to pay large sums on nothing more than the word of a lower-class woman. The mother had only to name a father under oath, and any justice could issue an arrest warrant. It was just about taken for granted that such a woman was lying. Maybe she was desperate for any source of subsistence. Maybe the accused had rebuffed her, and going before the justice was a way of getting back at him or forcing him to marry her (as often happened). Whatever the circumstances, the charges were difficult to rebut—it was usually easier, as *The Gentleman's Magazine* complained, to shell out the £10–£12, buy the overseers a good dinner, and be done with it.[61] All those trial jokes may register similar anxieties. Endless jokes about dim-witted thieves who easily betray their guilt surely reflect concerns about the failures of the justice system, particularly its inability to check rising levels of property crime. Jokes about jovial judges who make everyone laugh as they send a rascal to the gallows seem like wishful fantasies at a time when courtrooms were disorderly and a plebeian crowd was a force to be reckoned with. In trials across the country, malicious prosecutors were shouted down, and verdicts were disputed. Harsh sentences were met with stamping, booing, or even violence.[62]

One would be wrong to underestimate these levels of conflict or the elite fears they produced. Midcentury periodicals continually bemoan the violence and lawlessness of the age. Even increasing execution levels and the additional terrors of anatomization and hanging in chains failed to awe the populace, which treated hanging days as festivals. The peace of Aix-la-Chapelle (1748) brought thousands of demobilized soldiers onto the streets. Highwaymen menaced every road out of London; vicious smugglers ruled large territories near the coast. It was a time of "rapine and assassination," Smollett recalled. The criminals were more desperate and savage than ever. "The whole land was overspread with a succession of tumult, riot, and insurrection."[63] The poachers, grain rioters, London house-breakers, rebel weavers, and coal heavers so lovingly brought to life by Marxist historians were a force to be reckoned with, an unparalleled threat to property and social stability.

The official reaction to these threats—the panic, draconian statutes, and frankly bloodthirsty rhetoric—is well-known. At an opposite pole, escapist idealization of the poor lived on in neoclassical pastoral and the Claude-Poussin line of landscape painting. Only slightly more realistic were the English Georgics of Thomson and Dyer and, in painting, the native picturesque tradition with its cheerful hardworking cottagers. It is still hard to disagree with first-wave Marxist accounts of these idealized representations as determined effacements of instability and conflict. But between the detached fantasies at one end of the spectrum and the ruthless pamphlets at the other stretched a range of more elusive representations: representations that engage with contemporary social problems in less definable ways. Always uneasy and ironic in its treatment of the poor, sentimental fiction has now been much studied. But one also finds large numbers of ambivalent comic texts—texts that directly confront the new threats, rather than merely repeating old assumptions about the poor as ridiculous but harmless.

One particularly suggestive example—at once droll and caustic to the point of malevolence—is an anonymous *Elegy Written in Covent-Garden*, put out by the fashionable West End bookseller John Ridley and much anthologized. It is one of several dozen contemporary parodies of Gray's *Elegy* (1751), most of them benign exercises in wit. In this case, however, the villagers of Stoke Poges are replaced by the dangerous rabble of the London streets:

> Beneath those butchers stalls, that pent-house shade,
>> Where rankling offals fret in many a heap,
> Each in his nasty stye of garbage laid,
>> The dex'trous sons of *Buckhorse* [linkboys] stink and sleep.

Gray's villagers are preserved by their obscurity from the crimes of the great; this parodist's urban paupers are cunning and brutal. They are nimble pickpockets who cluster outside playhouses or linkboys who lead customers into dark alleys. All beggars are rogues in disguise: they shed artful tears but then bludgeon you with their crutch. Gray's famous "Epitaph" is replaced by four sneering lines:

> Here fest'ring rots a *quondam* pest of earth,
>> To virtue and to honest shame unknown,
> Low-cunning on a dung-hill gave him birth,
>> Vice clapp'd her hands and mark'd him for her own.

It was better, the poet concludes, to hang them all out of the way: "Full many a rogue is born to cheat unseen, / And dies unhang'd for want of proper care."[64]

The offhand savagery of these lines still shocks, but there is much more where they came from: all sorts of nasty riddles and epigrams, vengeful fantasies about workhouse discipline or mass executions. Bitter, brutal paupers curse and spit and frighten nice ladies. Reflecting wryly on England's alleged suicide epidemic, one midcentury satirist told the story of a charitable lady who bequeathed a large sum "for erecting and endowing a Gallows for the Poor to hang themselves on Gratis."[65] Frustrated by the increasing prettiness of recent *Cries of London*, the watercolorist Paul Sandby in the late 1750s painted twelve counterimages showing the urban poor at its most vicious and confrontational. Instead of cheerful flower girls and rag collectors, Sandby depicted belligerent whores, menacing drunkards, and aggressive street vendors. A hideous fishwife terrifies customers who peek timidly from their doorway.[66]

Still, even these mordant burlesques must be distinguished from the purer ferocity of contemporary pamphleteers. A burlesque structure—the very possibility of a literary or pictorial conceit—implies a level of assurance. In Sandby, as in Ridley's *Elegy in Covent-Garden*, one finds a mistrust that has not completely hardened into hatred: one that is still capable of amusement, if only at the diversion of an artistic in-joke. And further along the spectrum one finds levity and contempt combined in widely varying proportions. Even the most desperate and criminal poor—the vagabonds and pickpockets of contemporary pamphlet literature—could be represented in amused or appreciative ways. Scathing accounts of beggars as thieves alternated with equally powerful traditions about harmless drunkards whose lies were transparent and whose curses were colorful rather than threatening. As merry as a beggar, went the catchphrase; "who so merry as he that hath naught to lose?"[67] This was not a complete fantasy. A droll patois—a skillful combination of flattery, cajoling, insults, and tall tales—was one of a successful beggar's strategies, one that benefactors rewarded for its sheer entertainment value. As we learn more about the very poor in eighteenth-century Britain, we are finding beggars tolerated or appreciated as well as despised, living almost as permanent fixtures in both rural and urban communities. The village drunkard with a cheerful word for everyone, the broken chimney sweep at a certain street corner—these people were part of the social fabric.[68]

Here one thinks of the tone of *Trivia* or *The Beggar's Opera*, where serious social problems are evoked but comically contained so that the final effect is a wry acceptance. Pickpockets and highwaymen were obviously a nuisance, Gay seems to be saying, but life would be awfully dull if everyone washed, renounced alcohol, and obeyed the law. One finds the same mixed perspective in picturesque-burlesque images like Reynolds's *Cupid as Link-Boy* and *Mercury as Cut-Purse* (both 1774 and hugely amusing the rakish third Duke of Dorset, who bought them to hang at Knole). It is there in the compositional conceits of Nathaniel Hone's *Brickdust Man* (1760) with its John the Baptist references or Zoffany's *Beggars on the Road to Stanmore* (1770), where the central group recalls the holy family and St. John. That such images are anodyne goes without saying: John Barrell's arguments about British painters' effacement of rural conflict apply as much to these jeux d'esprit as to the artificiality of pastoral. Unlike more idealized representations, however, burlesque images by definition engage with reality; their humor consists precisely in the contrast between high iconography and a base reality. As such, they reflect an enduring elite confidence, a sense that rank may be challenged but is not yet in danger—a sense of the ultimate harmlessness, or at least the manageability, of the very poor.

Such representations caution us, more clearly than fanciful or simply derisive ones, not to overstate levels of elite discomfort. We now see that class conflict was growing in the mid-eighteenth century, but the poor law and the legal system would long remain stacked against the poor. Insubordination, as Peter King sums up the situation, "was a nuisance, not a menace." One would be wrong to underestimate the strength of the landed classes or, indeed, of the Georgian state; aristocratic dominance may even have been increasing in this period as it adopted newer methods of control.[69] One should be able to make these points without falling back on old clichés about Hanoverian stability. I am not reviving Harold Perkin's "Old Society" or J. C. D. Clark's English "ancien regime," both of which so downplay dissent that they end up repeating the elite's own image of itself and society.[70] Few historians, after E. P. Thompson's later work, would deny that genteel hegemony required constant concession, compromise, and role-playing. The genteel and middling sorts who ran the poor law and justice systems could not do whatever they liked. They had to maintain certain levels of goodwill, respect traditional rights, and fulfill traditional obligations.[71] However presciently contemporaries were describing an escalation of social conflict, their unease coexisted with much older habits and a confidence that would be around for long to come. Historians from below have so often described the humor of protest that one easily loses sight of this immensely less appealing laughter of elites at their social inferiors, a laughter that worked to maintain social structures rather than subverting them.

FROLICS, HIGH JINKS, AND VIOLENT FREEDOMS

What can one learn about interactions beyond the texts? What of practical jokes? One particularly telling scenario involves a gang of rowdy gentlemen coming across a drunken laborer or beggar sleeping on the side of the road. They drench him, fire their pistols to wake him in terror, or simply gather round for a good kicking. In jestbooks marketed to students—*Oxford Jests*, *College Wit*, and the like—the joke was to rob the sleeping pauper and use the proceeds for a drinking binge:

> Some waggish Scholars walking out one Day from the University of *Oxford*, espied a poor Fellow, near *Abingdon*, asleep in a Ditch, with an Ass by him laden with Earthenware. . . . Says one of the Scholars to the rest, If you'll assist me, I'll help you to a little Money, for you know we are bare at present.

Naturally they steal the ass and sell it at the next market town, but since there was always more fun to be had with a rustic, one student stays in the ditch to test the old man's credulity. He puts the bridle in his mouth and the panniers on his back. His father was a necromancer, he announces when the fellow wakes up, and had punished him by transforming him into an ass. There follows a long sequence of torments before the student joins his friends at the alehouse.[72] Such "frolics" were not just imaginary scenarios: one routinely comes across them in elite diaries and letters. Rambling around Hampshire in the summer of 1733, the Duke of Richmond and his chums find some "game" in the form of a drunken pauper dozing under a hedge outside Petersfield. They pick his pocket "without wakeing him," the duke later boasts to his friends, leaving the poor man with only "a few half pence and a tobacco stopper." Then it is on to Portsmouth, where they have a riotous time with the spoils.[73] One struggles to understand a world in which it could be funny to rob a pauper of his last resources, to torment an indigent with nowhere else to sleep, defecate, eat, or make love. And yet it was so.

Violence was never far away in any hierarchical interaction. Gentlemen always carried a horsewhip or a stout cudgel and regularly used them on obstreperous inferiors. Coachmen, porters, and Irish footmen all had to be beaten since violence was the only language a rascal would understand. Swift was constantly having problems with Patrick, his feckless Irish footman. After one particularly trying day, he writes to Stella: "I went up, shut the chamber door, and gave him two or three swinging cuffs on the ear, and I have strained the thumb of my left hand with pulling him."[74] These scenarios are casually introduced in many contexts: "A Gentleman having cudgell'd his Page for a fault . . . ;" "A Nobleman gave an old Servant of his two Boxes on the Ear . . ."[75] Smollett twice flogs difficult servants in his *Travels through France and Italy* (1766), and *Peregrine Pickle* offers a long line of vicious "punishments." Two London chairmen demand more than their fare and warrant a particularly elaborate revenge. Tom Pipes, the hero's sidekick, loads himself with heavy weights. Both chairmen get infuriated trying to carry him, and it ends in a vicious brawl. "Peregrine, who followed at a distance, enjoyed the pleasure of seeing them both beaten almost to a jelly."[76]

The presumptive right to beat inferiors was certainly being challenged in these years, and along with all the charges of insubordination appeared complaints that servants were refusing to submit to physical correction. The hot-tempered Charlotte Lennox was well-known for abusing her servants and once had to defend herself at the Middlesex Sessions, where she was prosecuted for assaulting a former housemaid.[77] Such prosecutions might succeed if a permanent injury could be shown to the court; occasionally one finds crowds hissing at particularly violent employers. But the legal right to strike servants endured until 1861, and even then complaints still had to be supported by two JPs.[78] Tailors who insisted on being paid, cheating bawds, and demanding prostitutes all risked a good beating. James Boswell intuitively starts knocking about a "little profligate Wench" who demanded more than sixpence. One of the first reactions to a diagnosis of syphilis was to go back to the brothel, beat the whore, and knock around the bawd who had passed her off as a virgin.[79]

More unfamiliar torments include vigorous shakings, nose tweaking, and pulling by the nose, all of them hugely satisfying ways of punishing insolents. Mutilations or threats of mutilation long remained part of the lexicon of aristocratic bullying, one of the swaggering threats one made to any officious inferior who dared oppose one's will. Such things became illegal in 1670, after a band of courtiers mutilated the MP Sir John Coventry, but the scenario retained its fascination right through the eighteenth century. Frustrated in his attempt to abduct Anne Bracegirdle from Drury Lane (1692), Lord Mohun threatened to mutilate anyone he could lay hands on.[80] "I would certainly have cropped one of his ears," wrote Swift after yet more trouble from Patrick—except that Bolingbroke was on his way.[81] Richardson's Lovelace naturally assumes "a right to break every man's head [he passes] by" and talks repeatedly about ear chopping. "I must have this fellow's ears in my pocket," he says of poor Hickman. "Thou wilt highly oblige me," he tells Belford of the officious Mr. Brand, "if thou'lt find him out and send me his ears in the next letter." Even Anna Howe delights in these scenarios. Clarissa should send Betty Barnes over, she jokes; she'd teach her to mind her manners. Did the Coventry Act apply to women? It would be nice to chop Betty's nose off. At the very least, she concludes, she would send her home "well soused in and dragged through our deepest horsepond."[82] Closely related is all the droll talk about the judicial mutilations that were then disappearing. The last official mutilation occurred in June 1731, when the forger Japhet Crook lost both ears and nostrils before the lunchtime crowd at Charing Cross (a grisly event repeatedly referred to in Pope's later satires).[83] Yet jokes about ear clipping remain uncomfortably common well into the nineteenth century. An executioner tries to chop the ears off, only to find that the man has none and is wearing papier-mâché replacements. Where was his left ear? The last time he saw it, the felon replies, it was "nailed to the pillory in Bristol."[84]

Much of this malicious fantasizing presents itself as a natural reaction to the annoyance of disobedience. But knocking around one's social inferiors could also be hugely enjoyable in itself. Stuck for something to do, upper-class men could always head outside, insult a few laborers, and then cudgel them for their insolent replies. Such violence was also a routine way of venting frustration. Angry at a letter from Mrs. Sinclair, Lovelace relieves himself by beating the messenger. "I retreated to my own apartment with my heart full," he tells Belford after another difficult conversation with Clarissa. "And my man Will not being near me, gave myself a plaguy knock on the forehead with my double fist." Will himself bears the marks of many beatings; appearing incognito before Clarissa, he is forced to stuff a handkerchief in his mouth lest she see the missing teeth ("the tethe which your Honner was pleased to bett out with your Honner's fyste," as he writes to Lovelace).[85] Behind all these habits lay half-serious assumptions that sturdy plebeians didn't feel pain, anyway. So solid were their boneheads that you were more likely to break your cudgel than do any damage. *Hob; or, The Country Wake*, one of the most popular of all eighteenth-century farces, consisted of little more than a series of repeated beatings and cudgelings suffered by the hero, a sturdy native clown who each time gets up with puppetlike recovery.[86]

The most notorious of these violent behaviors were the drunken high jinks of midcentury men-about-town. Newspapers and periodicals are full of complaints about gangs of "bucks" who spilled out of taverns in the early hours, skirmishing with the watch, overturning milkmaids, cudgeling apprentices, and tossing beggars in blankets. This became a standard scenario in every genre, so familiar that the most compressed references would do. It is there as a standard phase of youthful vice in *Roderick Random*, in Fielding's Mr. Wilson and the Man of the Hill, and in MacKenzie's more sentimental *Man of the World* (1773). Plate 3 of *The Rake's Progress* shows Tom Rakewell lolling at the Rose Tavern with an unsheathed sword and a watchman's broken lantern. William Kenrick's *Fun*, a "Parodi-Tragi-Comical Satire" of 1752, provides a useful synthesis of the usual tropes. A London blood named Bullyboy is advising his country cousin how to "be witty the right Way." "Your Country Jokes are nothing," Bullyboy tells him:

[Y]ou must learn to bully, pull people by the Nose, trip up their Heels, break their Heads and so forth. . . . And to be truly humorous you must . . . bilk Taverns,—tumble the Waiters down Stairs,—break all the Glasses in your Way,—sally into the Street,—take all the young Women you meet for Whores, and kick the old ones into the Kennel,—knock down the Watch,— lie all Night in *Covent-garden Round-house*, be carried before the *Justice*, where you have nothing to do but to prove your Father a *Gentleman*, and the old Dog his Worship will stand by you in abusing all the World.—This, my Boy, is true Humour.[87]

For all the satiric overstatement, Kenrick does describe an established set of behaviors, a ready-made script for young men of means. The imaginative representations correspond to a mass of more verifiable evidence—court documents, newspaper reports, letters, and biographical records. One finds gangs of high-spirited young gentlemen causing mayhem at theaters and pleasure gardens. Thus the repeated disorders at Vauxhall Gardens in 1764, when bands of up to fifty bucks went roaring about, insulting modest women and barging into private supper boxes.[88] At the theater they damned plays, tossed oranges across the pit, and even came onstage—like the Irish gentleman who started groping Peg Woffington while she was trying to do Cordelia's tender soliloquy to the sleeping Lear.[89] Marauding bucks broke windows, smashed lamps, stripped naked, and made bonfires of their clothes. They started riots at fairgrounds and "beat the rounds" of the brothels, tossing furniture onto the street and kicking the whores downstairs (already operating outside the law, bawds and prostitutes were powerless to complain).[90]

The newspapers thrived on exaggeration, and many reports seem entirely fanciful—little more than rehearsals of old stories about Mohocks, Scowrers, and Hectors or Roaring Boys before that. Stray anecdotes floated about and attached themselves to the most infamous rakes of the moment. A droll lord hires a bear and lets it loose in a chophouse or takes a blind horse into a china shop. A group of bucks throws an alewife out the window and has her put on the bill—a prank attributed to many midcentury wits, including the comic orator George Stevens (ca. 1710–84).[91] Probably drunken bucks did occasionally let loose a bull from Smithfield market or nail up a watchman in his box. Perhaps they occasionally rolled someone downhill in a barrel ("Matrons, hoop'd within the Hoghead's Womb / [And] tumbled furious thence," as Gay prettily put it).[92] But there is little evidence for periodic reports of organized gangs with mock-serious rules and rituals—gangs like Steele's "Sweaters," who surrounded pedestrians and pricked them with their swords, or the "Tumblers," who dragged women into side streets and forced them to walk on their hands, their skirts falling over their heads.[93] Still less plausible are reports of horrific mutilations and specialized terminologies for them: slitting noses, chopping off ears, and the like.

Yet behind the hysteria lay well-documented patterns of upper-class roistering. New research into the Mohock scare of 1712 finds little evidence of a formal club, but plenty of Mohock-like violence. Historians have found routine attacks on the watch, window breaking, sackings of taverns and bawdy houses, assaults on whores, and—most interestingly—a pattern of random and unprovoked violence in which there is no theft and thus no financial motive. At a time when only a fraction of breaches of the peace were reported, this density of evidence is significant.[94] New work on newspapers and court documents is bringing to light further instances, and violent misrule is certainly well represented in the archives of universities and the Inns of Court.[95] Biographers of the more notorious midcentury dissolutes—Francis Dashwood, Paul Whitehead, John Wilkes, George Selwyn, and others—provide abundant and verified accounts of their nocturnal roistering, all of it attempting in some measure to match the exploits of earlier generations of rakes. This was not just a passing stage of late adolescence, as some historians have suggested. Frederick, Prince of Wales, was still breaking windows in his thirties, once being shot by a retainer of the Duchess of Buckingham after smashing all her windows in the early hours. Dashwood, Whitehead, and their Hell-Fire chums went on with their drunken high jinks into their forties and beyond.[96]

Street violence cut across social hierarchies in eighteenth-century culture. Window breaking, arson, attacks on market women, and scuffles with the watch were plebeian male behaviors as much as aristocratic ones. Bands of drunken apprentices roamed the streets as mischievously as any of the buckish gangs. Dueling might have been an aristocratic practice, but boxing was practiced at every level of society. In their violence toward woman and animals, as Anna Clark reminds us, aristocratic and working-class masculinity shared important parallels into the nineteenth century.[97] Still, one would be wrong to deemphasize the specific class contexts: the immense and largely unquestioned sense of privilege behind upper-class forms of misrule. Scholars have been far quicker to acknowledge the sexual freedoms of early modern libertinism than the equally important freedoms of violence and destruction. Yet these may tell us more about the inner experience of privilege, its obscure and immensely unappealing mixture of subconscious impulse and more demonstrative action.[98] On the one hand, brutal high jinks show us just how automatically these men delighted in their superiority and good fortune—how intuitively they assumed their right to knock around inferiors, destroy private property, and do what they liked with women. On the other hand, such excesses often seem like deliberate demonstrations of contempt for the burgherly values of prudence, sobriety, regular hours, and sympathy for others. The reports of formal clubs also record some deep-seated imaginative structures. Upper-class men in this period did go about in bands, whether hunting, drinking, going to the theater or to a brothel across the street. They formed semiformal clubs almost automatically—from literary and scientific societies to blasphemous drinking clubs. Rituals, arcane oaths, and ludic terminologies all had roots in public school and university life.

Class differences manifested themselves most clearly in the legal consequences of violence. "Us mad fellows as are above all law," Lovelace describes his gang—and this was close to the truth.[99] We now know that everyone used the eighteenth-century legal system, from cottagers to princes. In practice, however, the bucks had little to fear: any plebeian bringing an assault charge against a social superior was bound to fail. The young buck's insolence to a magistrate is a ubiquitous comic incident. What did the young man have to say for himself? Nothing much, he replies—except that the justice had a shiny red nose. The young man just laughs as he is ordered to pay for the broken windows or buy a new lantern for the watchman. Perhaps he is browbeaten from the bench, but the judge soon changes his tune when he discovers the young man's connections. Scoffing at the judge seems to complete the joke in many frolics; the bucks' friends came to watch, and all competed with each other in impudence to different judges.[100]

More chilling are occasional glimpses of murderous frolics and the ways these were treated by the law. The worst that could be expected was a conviction for manslaughter (a relatively trivial crime for lords and gentlemen). Witness the minor flutter at Christ Church, Oxford in April 1747, after a college servant was found in the quad with a cracked skull. Lord Abergavenny, Lord Charles Scott, and two others had got the man very drunk and played all sorts of tricks that ended with him falling down Abergavenny's staircase. The Oxford coroner returned a verdict of willful murder, and for a while it looked like the lords might be tried for their lives. Relating events to Horace Mann, Walpole was sympathetic, but not for the dead man: "One pities the poor boys, who undoubtedly did not foresee the melancholy event of their sport." In the end, the grand jury refused to indict them.[101]

No doubt there was much wish fulfillment in so many representations of outrageous young men who somehow get away with it all. Attacks on aristocratic vice were increasing, and this climate inevitably affected older freedoms.[102] But change was slow. Midcentury England remained a venal oligarchy, and not even the most notorious excesses prevented men like Dashwood, Selwyn, Wilkes, or Sandwich from holding the highest public offices. Dashwood combined the drink, violence, and nocturnal mummeries of Medmenham Abbey with serious antiquarian research and an active parliamentary career. Louche and notoriously unprincipled, Sandwich nevertheless made an effective first lord of the Admiralty. This pattern had been set most famously by Lord Bolingbroke, who flaunted his vices and delighted in defying those who found them inconsistent with his political or philosophical principles. Everywhere enacted in more quotidian social contexts, these odd compatibilities are inevitably downplayed by recent studies of the refinement and intellectual functions of midcentury club culture. Upper-class misrule is too often explained away as a marginal phenomenon, a temporary rebellion against increasing politeness and feminization. Drunken frolics and high jinks were mainstream behaviors that coexisted comfortably with the more attractive aspects of eighteenth-century life. They were not disappearing.

Ultimately, the concrete evidence of such behaviors may matter less than their astonishing discursive presence—the mass of literary and artistic representations they continued to produce. Buckish misrule is indulgently treated, if not openly celebrated, in every genre. Hundreds of buckish songbooks survive from this period—titles like *The Muse in Good Humour*, *The Buck's Delight*, and *The Buck's Bottle Companion*, all of them packed with musical celebrations of street violence that enabled singers to rehearse their exploits before they went outside to enact them. The same tediously predictable scenarios recur in satiric guides to London. Particularly daring pranks might be celebrated in broadsides or one-off comic pamphlets. London bucks write breathless "letters" to friends in the country—slangy and dysorthographic accounts of riots at the theater and bonfires of wigs. Moronic as they may sound, these texts reflect considerable and ongoing creativity. One finds riddles, acrostic poems, and miniature epics that transform bucks into heroes. Beginners were pedantically shown the ropes in mock catechisms and spoof instructional texts like "The Buck's Grammar; or, Rudiments of Libertinism" (bucks preferred active to passive verbs; their favorite nouns were *blood, whore*, and *frolic*).[103] Alongside the text genres appeared an enormous range of graphic representations—from high-quality copper engravings to expensive oils like Hogarth's *Night Encounter* (ca. 1740). Commissioned by Gustavus Hamilton, second Viscount Boyne (1710–46), *A Night Encounter* shows Boyne cudgeling a watchman after a night on the town with his friend, Horace Walpole's unruly older brother Ned (fig. 6).[104]

Such representations were bought as celebrations by the young who were still up to such things and as mementos by those now past it. Worn-out rakes like Rochester's old debauchee were consoled by the excesses of a new generation ("Whores attack'd . . . Bauds Quarters beaten up . . . Windows demolish'd, Watches overcome").[105] More striking to social historians will be the array of lower representations: chapbook stories, ephemeral prints, even some of the crudest woodcuts that have come down to us. Buckish violence is

FIGURE 6. William Hogarth, *A Night Encounter* (ca. 1740). Oil on canvas. This painting is one of two "modern moral conversations" commissioned by Gustavus Hamilton, second Viscount Boyne. For the Whiggish Boyne circle, violence and large quantities of drink were evidently part of a robust British liberty. Private collection; photograph courtesy of Ronald Paulson.

there, for example, in the cheapest miscellany prints—in the "lottery" sheets of eight or twelve crude images put out by Bowles and Carver and other less fashionable print sellers. There, among the rudimentary milkmaids or hay-makers, one finds shrunken images of bucks cudgeling the watch, crude and heavily lined but in composition almost identical to Hogarth's painting (figs. 7–8). Odder still is the caption that accompanies these images: "The Beau's Frolic,—to cure the Cholic." Every spark knew that drink and riot were reliable ways of reviving the spirits (or, in this case, of relieving bowel spasms). In the catchpenny prints, however, this therapeutic violence is illustrated for a popular audience and appears, with shocking equivalence, alongside mundane illustrations of cats killing mice, fishing, or rural courtship. Buckish violence was one of the most emblematic images of the age, recurring at every level of artistic production. Reduced and schematic, the lowest versions work

The Beau's Frolic, —to cure the Cholic.

FIGURE 7. *The Beau's Frolic,—to cure the Cholic.* Detail from Bowles & Carver lottery sheet (fig. 8 below). Photograph © Trustees of the British Museum (1858,0417.9).

almost like ideograms, immediately recognizable images of the way things were, of something subliminally taken for granted.

Again, the freedoms and the fascination must be set against the profusion of complaints, from outrage in the Nonconformist press to aldermanly disapproval in *The Gentleman's Magazine* and urbaner satire in *The Connoisseur* or *The World*. In their different idioms, all make the same complaints about overindulgent parents, the brutalizing effects of a public school education, the terrors of walking the streets at night, and the bucks' scandalous immunity from prosecution. The more one reads of these texts, however, the more they seem to drift toward amusement. Sermons or condensed denunciations were one thing, but wherever the satire is allowed to expand, its moral clarities begin to break down. Even as they denounce buckish violence, Colman and Thornton's *Connoisseur* essays (1754–56) betray their mirth. *The Connoisseur* was famous for its lightness of touch, for exposing the follies of the age "without assuming the rigid air of a preacher, or the moroseness of a philosopher."[106] In their attacks on upper-class vice, the essayists' chief technique is a lofty sarcasm—a combination of arch understatement, ironic praise, and stylistic play that originated with Addison and Steele. Breaking lamps, sack-

FIGURE 8. Bowles & Carver lottery sheet. Copper engraving, ca. 1750; this impression and hand coloring, ca. 1790. At 1s. 10d. per hundred sheets, lottery prints were among the cheapest graphic materials on the market, offering multiple small images to be colored and cut out by children. The image of upper-class violence is here naturalized alongside such everyday sights as a milkmaid, a lamplighter, juggling, fishing, and that most natural thing of all, a cat about to kill some mice. Photograph © Trustees of the British Museum (1858,0417.9).

ing brothels, and tormenting the watch were "mighty pretty pleasantries," says Mr. Town, *The Connoisseur*'s chief satiric persona. Bucks were geniuses of invention, capable of the sublimest fancies! "Prevailing on an Irish chairman now and then to favour them with a broken head" or conferring the same "token of their esteem" on a waiter: these were extraordinary accomplishments! At least someone had a go at all these "dull sober fools, that are trudging about their business" and don't know how "to whore and drink like a gentleman."[107]

Why indulge so liberally in this language world? Many of the specific ironies go back to Steele's *Spectator* papers on the 1712 Mohock panic, in which the stylistic antics strayed even closer to amusement. *The Spectator*'s account of "sweating," for example, only barely restrains its fascination with buckish cant. Steele positively distends the malicious analogy. "Sweaters" would surround some terrified inferior ("the Patient") with drawn swords and begin their "Operation." "That Member of the Circle, towards whom he is so rude as to turn his Back first, runs his Sword directly into that Part of the Patient wherein School-boys are punished." Spinning around in terror, the victim turns his back on someone else, who "punishes" him in the same way. And so it goes on until "the Patient is thought to have sweat [bled] sufficiently," at which point he is "very handsomely rubb'd down [cudgeled] by some Attendants."[108] The sardonic eulogizing, mock-Homeric epithets, and mock-decorous circumlocutions all survive in midcentury periodicals, where they continued to help essayists avoid priggishness. In 1712, the ironies also helped Steele poke fun at all the exaggerated Mohock stories and suggest partisan motives behind those exaggerations.[109] Yet, himself something of a rake in his younger days, he was clearly drawn to the stories, even as he knew he must deplore them.

The same fatal instability of tone, this time without partisan contexts, persists in midcentury satires on buckish violence. The bucks were "exalted geniuses," "knights errant of mirth."[110] Still more telling is the way midcentury authors went on inventing new comic scenarios: a deaf watchman who can be beaten for not listening; a lewd exchange between the buck and a milkmaid before he knocks her over and spills the milk. Long after the Mohock scare, humorists kept coming up with new clubs like the "Bold Bucks" (motto "Blind and Bold Love"), who went about assaulting women of all ages, from flower girls to grandmothers. Wits wrote rules for fictive organizations like the "Kicking Club" ("each Member was in turn to kick every Man he met, and on refusal to forfeit a Flask of *French* Claret for the Benefit of the Club").[111] And these imaginative habits easily adapted to every new discourse. In July 1764, Henry Woodfall's *Public Advertiser* published "A Description of the Animal

Called a Buck," the whole thing written in the language of Enlightenment natural history. The animal walked on two legs, had hands, arms, and feet like a man, but exhibited a monkey's love of mischief. There seemed to be two species: one in the country and another one in town. Populations of the latter had increased greatly in recent years, "which is owing to so few of them being hanged."[112]

Arch, sardonic, and pedantically drawing out its conceit, this essay may be of its time, but no one can deny its flaws as a piece of satire. After five paragraphs, the author himself seems to recognize that something has gone wrong and concludes with an extreme and therefore more stable instance of buckish cruelty. The sheer extremity of this example—a vicious attack on a defenseless pregnant woman—suddenly reveals how far one had to go to arouse reliable sympathy for a social inferior. The routine victims of upper-class violence were hard to pity. Bawds and prostitutes were depraved and blamed for being depraved. They charged too much and spread pox through the land. Waiters were uncooperative cheats ("Coming Sir!"). Landladies were notorious for watering down their beer or thinning it out with chicken poo. Everyone knew that the watchmen and linkboys were in league with the footpads. Ballad sellers might look frail and desperate, but they were probably teamed up with pickpockets, who worked the crowds that gathered.[113] It was still hard to feel sorry for any underling—which is why neither Walpole nor anyone else had much to say about the dead college scout at Christ Church.

LOVELACE AT THE HABERDASHER

For all its brutal childishness, buckish misrule remained an insistent fascination at every level of eighteenth-century society. At least as much as plebeian tricksters—those familiar and far more likable orchestrators of collective laughter—riotous upper-class men were acknowledged comedians in eighteenth-century culture, figures to whom this culture had tacitly granted the privilege of poking fun.[114] They were drunks, blasphemers, and overgrown schoolboys, but at least they added some color to life, like a runaway pig or rain during a picnic. All but the most shrill and compressed attacks begin to waver. Witness "The Bucks Have at Ye All" (1754), one of the most popular theatrical epilogues for almost fifty years, with its half-serious, half-indulgent criticism of buckish mischief at the playhouses. The shrieking, roaring, tossed wigs, and lewd interjections were things many people enjoyed about the theater. In this context as in so many others, bucks were acting on behalf of their society, creating its favorite forms of fun.[115] Kicking an apple woman, telling a blind man to "go and look" for something, burning someone with hot coals: these were established jokes, cruel and predictable as they were.

One cannot overstate the force of this indulgence. Stories were told and retold about legendary rake-humorists: about Rochester and his Merry Gang, about Sedley, Buckhurst, Buckingham, Etherege, and Wycherley. Even Philip Herbert, the vicious seventh Earl of Pembroke (1653–83), remained famous as a wit—a man who had killed three men in duels or drunken scuffles and was pardoned every time. Later came Philip, Duke of Wharton (1698–1731), Edward, sixth Earl of Warwick (1673–1701), and his friend the fourth Lord Mohun (ca. 1675–1712), another aristocratic street fighter. All these men were notorious, but they were also celebrated humorists. Swift despised Mohun ("little better than a conceited talker in company"), but others admired him; Delarivière Manley left two extended portraits of the man and his "exalted Wit."[116] Mohun, Warwick, and Pembroke are still listed on the title pages of midcentury jestbooks—along with Wilkes, Garrick, Ben Jonson, and Joe Miller—as the country's greatest humorists. The story of Mohun and Warwick blowing up the apple seller is one of the most common of all eighteenth-century jokes. One repeatedly comes across the tediously protracted tale of Warwick tricking a drayman into scalding himself in a pot of boiling water.[117]

Then there is Rochester, the most famous of them all. While his reputation as a poet was clearly in decline by the 1750s, fascination with the man endured—Rochester the penitent seducer of Burnet's *Passages of the Life and Death* and Rochester the humorist and practical joker.[118] The earl's comic exploits were repeated in every possible context: in histories of the Restoration, in salacious memoirs like those of Anthony Hamilton (1713/14, 1750, 1760), and onstage in the figure of Dorimant, rake hero of Etherege's *Man of Mode*. They were there in large-scale reference works like the Shiels/Cibber *Lives of the Poets* (1753). Almost every eighteenth-century edition of Rochester reprinted biographical matter like the spurious "memoir" attributed to St. Evremond, while the poems were illustrated by quite unconnected engravings of his pranks. Everyone knew about Rochester's love of disguises—his singular ability to pass as a beggar, porter, sickly old woman, or city merchant. Everyone knew that he once set up as an astrologer on Tower Hill and that he and Buckingham once disguised themselves as innkeepers at Newmarket. Rochester long remained famous for "the agreeable manner of his chiding his servants," as John Dennis put it. Etherege's *Man of Mode* begins with an extended instance of this wit, with Dorimant abusing a sequence of underlings: from servants to Tom the drunken shoemaker and Foggy Nan the bloated orange woman ("double Tripe," "Flasket of Guts").[119]

Much of this—including the astrologer episode, where Rochester most explicitly performs the role of public entertainer—continued to be fictionalized in *Peregrine Pickle* and other comic novels. Otherwise unsubstantiated stories proliferated: the one about him tossing his dwarf into the Thames and many more. Rochester remained a figure in every jestbook: turning puns, insulting aging courtesans, or furnishing some sort of pedigree to low insults like the "kiss my arse" quip in *Tom Jones*.[120] Perhaps the most repugnant of all these stories is the following, here in Thomas Hearne's version:

> Once the wild Earl of Rochester, and some of his companions, a little way from Woodstock, meeting in a morning with a fine young maid going with butter to market, they bought all the butter of her, and paid her for it, and afterwards stuck it up against a tree, which the maid perceiving, after they were gone, she went and took it off, thinking it pity that it should be quite spoiled. They observed her, and riding after her, soon overtook her, and as a punishment, set her upon her head, and clapt the butter upon her breach.

It is hard to imagine a clearer enactment of contempt for the necessary toil and thrift of the peasantry. As it happens, there is no other evidence that Rochester did this. Like so many other comic anecdotes, this story migrates from one wit to another. Hearne's taste for the salacious clearly increased as he aged.[121] But true or false, such stories reveal a persistent fascination with the lordly freedom to squander in a culture of scarcity and torment one's inferiors simply because one could. And this fascination showed no signs of dying out: *Rochester's Jests*, an elegantly produced volume of 1766, went through at least four editions; soon came *The Whimsical Jester; or, Rochester in High Glee* (1784 and two more editions). The stories were repeated in umpteen bastard editions of Burnet's *Passages of the Life and Death*, in which humorous and amatory exploits far outweigh the homiletic content that licensed the book as virtuous reading. As late as 1818, one finds large-scale entertainments like *Rochester; or, King Charles the Second's Merry Days*, a "Comic Historical Burletta" at the Olympic Theater.

More surprising is the persistence of these stories in much cheaper publications—in the chapbooks and even cruder pamphlets put out by the Dicey family and a handful of provincial booksellers. These texts continue to print the same old anecdotes about Pembroke, Warwick, Rochester, and Mohun. The butterwife joke shows up (attributed this time to Pembroke) in *Joaks upon Joaks* (ca. 1770), a tiny octavo pamphlet put out by the Worcester printer Samuel Gamidge.[122] A still more disgusting version shows up in late-eighteenth-century chapbooks, now attributed to the Jacobean courtier Sir James Percy. "O thou wicked covetous Wretch!" Percy cries when he spots the woman gathering up her butter, "art thou robbing me before my Face?"

> And so throwing her down, in spight of all her Pleadings, That it was pity good Butter should be spoiled. . . . He so bedaubed her Buttocks and Thighs, calling for his Hounds, which immediately came in full Cry, he caused them to lick and take it off, while the poor Woman cry'd out most lamentably, expecting every Moment she should be devoured, and in the Bellies [of] those loud-mouth'd voracious Curs; but he suffered them not to hurt her, only sending her away with a greasy Pair of Buttocks.[123]

No one would now take such stories as evidence of a popular *mentalité*. Like the Bowles and Carver prints and other popular genres, chapbooks are top-down phenomena, produced in London, and distributed by a complex system of middlemen and peddlers. The number of reactions that made their way back to the Diceys must have been close to zero.[124] At the same time, we know nothing about how these texts were used or "appropriated" by ordinary readers.[125] But we do know that low readers went on buying the chapbooks, in enormous quantities, well into the nineteenth century. Whatever appropriations or local resistances were going on, stories of aristocratic frolics continued to entertain. One would be hard-pressed to find more than the odd hint of protest in any comic chapbook of this period—a few folk heroes take on the great, but if anything the chapbooks are more conservative than politer jestbooks, more reliant on old stories about the Restoration wits and Tudor and Stuart monarchs. They do nothing to challenge the ideology of a hierarchical and deferential society.[126]

However authentically it was accepted, the role of the upper-class prankster continued to be played. Attacked as they were by reformers of all stripes, these men long retained their charisma. Even the canonical literary record is vast, stretching from the wits of Restoration comedy to clumsier sots like Goldsmith's Tony Lumpkin, from Burney's Captain Mirvan to Sir Thomas Bullford in *Humphry Clinker* (Sir Tummas Ballfart, Win calls him). One easily finds historical figures alongside the fictions: boorish sea captains, madcap country squires, dissolute student-wits, and gay templars with time on their hands. These men enacted all their society's favorite pranks against accepted figures of fun. They plucked wigs, dragged fops by the nose, and made horses bolt by putting nettles under the tails. They set up trip wires and dug booby traps full of manure. They stole in on sleepers, picking pockets and stealing clothes; they sprinkled sneezing powders and quietly emptied chamber pots into the bed. They put soot in the soup and encouraged everyone to take great helpings of sharp mustard. They made people throw up after dinner, convincing them they had eaten roast dog or rat fricassée. They put laxatives in the wine and then laughed themselves silly when their victims made a mess in church.

Upper-class pranksters also had access to a unique range of ingredients, combining traditional folk knowledge with more expensive stuff from the apothecaries. Local plants had all sorts of uses. Burdock and goosegrass had sticky burrs; crushed rose hips made a wonderful itching powder. The common cuckoo pint (wake robin, Jack in the Pulpit) had an extremely corrosive root. This "will make excellent sport with a saucy sharking guest," one botanist informed his readers: even a small piece "will so burn and prick his mouth that he shall not be able to eat any more, or scarce speak for pain."[127] The contemporary medicine chest supplied even better ingredients. Cowhage or cow-itch (the stiff hairs of a tropical bean) was widely prescribed for intestinal worms, but it also made a fantastic itching powder. And best of all the itching powders was stone or Roman alum. Diluted alum was a popular astringent, but the full-strength powder, sprinkled on sheets or underclothes, was irritating to the point of torment.

In this as in every other area of life, these men strove to outdo each other. Any schoolboy could say boo to an old woman or start shrieking about mad dogs on the loose; gentlemen-pranksters raised comic terror to a fine art. Thus the folkloric figure of Daniel Pearce of Salisbury (d. 1762)—"the Great Dowdy," as he was known across the country. This man's specialty was pretending to be an escaped madman. Assuming a "tatter'd garment" decorated with straw, trailing "rattling chains," and smearing his face with blood, Pearce would burst into rooms at the Golden Lion inn and pursue his victims "thro' windows, up chimneys, and even over the tops of houses, [as they sought] to escape the fury of a supposed raving, mischievous Bedlamite, intent on their destruction." This trick was sufficiently famous to be exhibited before the Prince of Wales and to earn a casual reference in book 6 of *Tom Jones*.[128] A real wag also knew how to improve on the old tricks of ghost noises and firecrackers down chimneys. John Wilkes once had terrific fun with a baboon in a chest. There were sacks full of screeching tomcats. Goats, bears, and donkeys were dressed up with bells and let loose in the corridors of coaching inns. There were elaborate Satan costumes: a goat's head on a broomstick with a cloak of bloody animal skins. With a bit of money, you could make it glow in the dark with liquid phosphorous from Ambrose Godfrey's manufactory in Southampton Street.[129]

The classic nocturnal terror trick was a false fire alarm, an age-old device for creating mayhem and getting everyone out of bed with nothing on. The literary and dramatic versions of this prank are too common to warrant discussion, but consider one contemporary enactment. After seeing his London house burn to the ground in 1748, the poet Thomas Gray lived in mortal fear of fire. By the winter of 1755–56, he was so afraid that he had a rope ladder attached to his window in Cambridge. Gray's peculiarity became well-known, and it was only a matter of time before someone had a lark at his expense. Early in March 1756, as one older don recorded the incident, Lord Perceval and some of the commoners at Peterhouse were going hunting before dawn, and "determined to have a little sport before they set out, and thought it would be no bad diversion to make Gray bolt, as they called it, so ordered their man Joe Draper to roar out fire." Gray ran to the window in terror but soon discovered the truth and returned to bed. The actual joke went no further, but local rumor soon had the fastidious Gray clambering down the ladder, drenching himself in a tub of water, and having to be carried back to his lodgings by the college porter. None of these things happened, but they do offer striking insights into the humiliations that would have transformed a spontaneous whim into a really spectacular joke.[130]

What may not be clear from these examples is how naturally these high-colored gentlemen entertained their social inferiors. In rural areas, such men led the revels at fairs and village games as well as orchestrating the fun at the big house. Squires had always made their appearances at seasonal festivities, awarding little prizes for footraces and donating hogsheads of ale or roasted oxen. But young gentlemen in the country would evidently do anything to relieve boredom, and the more spectators, the better. They organized great duck-hunting or badgerbaiting events and hired itinerant showmen. They scandalized the community with dares of the sort made famous by the young Beau Nash, who once rode naked through a village on a cow and happily accepted £50 to pose as a beggar at the door of York Minster, clothed in nothing but a blanket. Any squire could put up £10 for the local alewife to fight a hefty cow woman or award a beaver hat to the man who broke the most heads at cudgeling. Particularly amusing was a grinning contest, in which the prize went to the person able to make the most grotesque faces—usually some grubby farm laborer with the worst teeth in the village (since showing teeth or opening one's mouth wide were indecorous in this society, grinning was by definition an enactment of vulgarity).[131] An ass race was reliably amusing since many donkeys would not move at all and there would be a glorious display of braying, clubbing, and foul language. In Clarence Hervey's pig and turkey race, Edgeworth's *Belinda* gives us a glimpse of all sorts of silly contests between farmyard animals.[132]

As one midcentury wag about whom uniquely rich evidence survives, consider Francis Delaval (1727–71), the rich, dissolute friend of Smart, Foote, and others in the fashionable-theatrical set. Each summer, Delaval gathered parties of friends at Seaton Delaval, his great house in Northumberland. Foote was often there, as were Macklin, Jemmy Worsdale the Irish parlor entertainer (ca. 1692–1767), the young Henry Angelo, and various local bores who were there to be laughed at. Afternoons were devoted to larks with the local peasantry: sack races and wrestling matches; a Holland smock for the winner of a maidens' running race; a pouch of tobacco for grinning. Festivities concluded with sparrow mumbling: hands tied behind their backs, the young men of the village tried to bite the head off a cock sparrow whose wings had been clipped. (It was terrific fun, said Francis Grose of this sport, with the contestant constantly flinching from "many pecks and pinches he receives from the enraged bird.")[133] These daytime diversions were succeeded at night by still more elaborate revels, of which the Delavals' modern biographer provides a summary:

> The assiduous host and his friends, candlesticks in hand, passed from bedroom to bedroom, stifling their laughter as they made things comfortable for their unsuspecting guests. Ducks and hens were put between the sheets, a bath of water placed beneath a remarkable bed that let down in the middle by means of pulleys, manikins like ghosts of ancient Delavals were set up in clothes closets, and a sleepy housemaid was pinched awake to take in the seams of a jilted baronet's suit of clothes so that when he awoke he would think love had given him dropsy. One guest was kept in bed three days by persuading him that it was still night.[134]

All this was reported in the London newspapers, and one marvels at the scale of it. In March 1753, the papers were reporting that Delaval had "upwards of four thousand ladies and gentlemen" at Seaton Delaval for a tumbling and rope-dancing performance.[135]

Such events—from the spontaneous larks to the elaborately orchestrated frolics—easily transferred to the capital. The youthful James Boswell once entertained the waiting audience at Drury Lane by imitating a lowing cow, later confiding in his diary: "I was so successful in this boyish frolic that the universal cry of the galleries was '*Encore* the cow! *Encore* the cow!'"[136] Young sparks raced their footmen in the park and hired chimney sweeps to race on asses. They wagered enormous sums on hackney-coach races or "freak runs" between limping watchmen. London was also the place for large-scale burlesque spectacles. The more partisan of these events—effigy burnings, anti-Jacobite processions, "funerals" for British Liberty, the Wilkesite festivals of 1762–63—are familiar to scholars. But one also finds less political skits like Bonnell Thornton's burlesque "Ode on Saint Cecilia's Day," performed at Ranelagh Gardens in June 1763 to the accompaniment of a hurdy-gurdy, Jew's harp, saltbox, and marrow bone and cleaver. As usual, travestic energies cannot be entirely detached from politics (Wilkes's presence added a certain charge to Thornton's "Ancient British Music"). But the memory that lingered for Samuel Johnson and other witnesses was the anarchic silliness of it all, Thornton's raucous challenge to all things elegant and orderly. What interests me is how naturally Thornton led the revels, how effortlessly a privileged young man assumed the role of lord of misrule.[137]

The London public was also the natural audience for a really good hoax, offering maximum exposure for the hoaxer and maximum humiliation for his victim. The repertoire of town hoaxes was well established: sending chairmen on false errands, summoning midwives or surgeons for those in no need of them, telling an old woman that one had dropped sixpence into a puddle and watching her grope around for it.[138] With no living to earn and nothing to do, young men about town delighted in spreading false rumors, from scandals about respectable women to matters of state. In August 1737, a "well-dressed" gentleman rode at a furious rate along the King's Road from Fulham, commanding all the turnpike keepers to throw open their gates as he was a messenger conveying the news of Queen Caroline's sudden death. The news spread like wildfire. Regiments interrupted their exercises and linen drapers spent fortunes on black cloth, while the "impudent Fellow" himself disappeared, having got all the way into town without paying a single turnpike.[139]

The best London hoaxes—*bites*, *roasts*, or *humbugs*, as they were called—increasingly employed the newest print media. Swift's Bickerstaff hoax offers a well-known early example, but by midcentury one finds practical jokers routinely using the newspapers to create a scene. *The Connoisseur* describes advertisements summoning all the wet nurses who wanted a place or calling old women to bring their tabby cats, for which they could expect a good price. One group of bucks allegedly advertised a vacant curacy, drawing a crowd of indigent parsons to St. Paul's coffeehouse, where "the Bucks themselves sat in another box, to smoke their rusty wigs and brown cassocks."[140] Mr. Town lays on his usual lofty sarcasms, but there are striking continuities between such amusements and the more "learned" hoaxes of the age: the antiquarians tricked into paying large sums for forged documents, the naturalists deceived by homemade marvels like baby mermaids or horned roosters.[141] William Hogarth was a lifelong hoaxer and enthusiastically joined his friends in the famous "Rembrandt Hoax" of 1751. Their victim was the irksome connoisseur Thomas Hudson ("Damn it," Hogarth allegedly said, "let us expose the fat-headed fellow"). Having been tricked into buying a forged Rembrandt etching, Hudson was invited to a lavish supper where he was humiliated in front of twenty-two guests. The main dish, literalizing the metaphor, was "an English roast"—a huge sirloin covered in identical copies of the "priceless" etching. The story went on and on, even being added to revisions of Foote's *Taste* (Drury Lane, 1752).[142]

The consummate hoaxer of the age, and the model for countless humbler pranksters, was John, second Duke of Montagu, whom we have met as the organizer of dinners for stutterers and squinters and the masquerade trick against Heidegger. There were many more stories. One finds him giving a dinner for grave professional men, furnishing his vestibule with wonky mirrors so that everyone set their wigs askew.[143] Another story has him taking the aldermen of Windsor out on the Thames, only to sink the boat and force them all to wade back through the mud.[144] He served an impossibly tough steak to the epicure Charles Dartiquenave, all the time lecturing the man on patience in adversity. In 1730, he invited the visiting Montesquieu to Boughton, his great house in Northamptonshire. "His singularity knew no bounds," Montesquieu recalled; "before I had leisure to get into any sort of intimacy . . . he soused me over head and ears into a tub of cold water." The prank became famous and probably inspired the dunking of Parson Adams in *Joseph Andrews* (unlike Fielding's parson, Montesquieu took it all in good fun).[145]

In town, Montagu's great accomplice was his cousin and neighbor the Duke of Richmond (1701–50)—Clarissimo and Magnifico, the pair were known to friends. Together they executed some of the most celebrated hoaxes of the age. In January 1732, they caused a riot at Drury Lane by politicizing James Miller's new comedy *The Modish Couple*. Shortly before Montagu's death in 1749, he and Richmond topped their previous bites by advertising that a man would enter a quart wine bottle onstage at the Little Haymarket Theatre. It was a fabulous exaggeration of the outlandish boasts of contemporary conjurors and contortionists; the enormous crowd satisfied the dukes' goal of proving that there was no end to public credulity. But there were consequences: the furious crowd destroyed the theater, which cost thousands to rebuild.[146]

Many, of course, found such antics puerile as well as low. "That most consummate puppy and unprincipled jackanapes," Chesterfield called Delaval.[147]
The Duchess of Marlborough was never more caustic than when talking
about Montagu, who had married her daughter at fourteen and remained a
thorn in her side for the next thirty years. His greatest talents, she complained
in 1740, were "to get people into his gardens and wet them with squirts, to
invite people to his country houses and put things into their beds to make
them itch, and twenty other such pretty fancies." Such tricks were "natural
to boys of fifteen, and he is about two and fifty."[148] Richmond's sense of fun
also had its critics: Queen Caroline thought him "so half-witted so bizarre
and so grandseigneur, and so mulish."[149] The mania for hoaxes was especially
deplored: what now passed for wit, as one essayist complained in 1751, was
"no better than what was 20 years ago called lying."[150] But modern definitions
of adult behavior were only beginning to emerge in this period, and other
contemporaries found all these jokes hilarious.[151] William Cole, bachelorly
antiquarian that he was, thought Delaval "the very soul of frolic and amusement." Walpole, Fielding, and many others liked Richmond greatly; no one
was so "cheerful and entertaining," said Lord Hervey.[152] The pranks of these
men were the talk of the town, the regular subjects of coffeehouse chatter and
gentlemanly correspondence; they were routinely reported in the papers.
Montagu's latest prank, the mad goings-on at Boughton or Seaton Delaval,
what Samuel Foote did last night at the Shakespeare's Head: these were the
constant topics of fashionable talk.

Perhaps more surprising to modern readers are the odd compatibilities
between these jokes and the sentimental benevolence with which we more
readily associate the age. Montagu was as famous for his benevolence as for
his odd sense of fun. He was an important early patron to Ignatius Sancho
and is said to have sponsored a Cambridge education for Francis Williams,
another former slave. Everyone knew about Montagu's errands of mercy: a
lavish handout for the gloomy beggar on his London street; roast fowl for
a starving widow; a living for a desperate curate. For his age, Montagu was
extraordinarily sentimental about animals, cherishing ugly lapdogs that no
one else wanted and for decades keeping a sort of geriatric hospital for retired
cows and horses. In spite of his "foibles," Walpole concluded, Montagu "was
a most amiable man, and one of the most feeling I ever knew."[153] One repeatedly finds this formula in accounts of famous wits. Delaval "overbalanced a
few foibles by a thousand amiable qualities." Beau Nash was a little "too apt
to say cruel Things," but he had the kindest heart imaginable; he was "rude
enough to make a jest of poverty, though he had sensibility enough to relieve

it."[154] Except for his murderous lunatic act, Daniel Pearce was "a pacifick and civil man." Richmond got carried away with his jokes, but in reality he was the "most humane and best man living."[155]

Taunting distress or relieving it, triumph or pity—these alternating reactions were not so much opposites as variations on the same structure of feeling. Both evince the same appalling thrill of having others absolutely in one's power, of determining their happiness or misery. These homologies become especially clear in mutating versions of one of Montagu's most famous charities. This time the beneficiary is a desperate half-pay officer, spotted many days in a row standing alone in St. James' Park. After making inquiries and bringing the man's family up from Yorkshire, Montagu invites the old soldier for dinner. The distinctive Montagu touch is his deferral of the reunion—his delight in toying with the man, telling him that he had invited him "to oblige a lady who had long had a regard for him" until the man protests he is being made a fool of. Only at this point does Montagu produce the soldier's family and allow the tears to flow. This story appears several times in miscellanies and magazines, and Sarah Fielding seems specifically to recall it with it with Lord Dorchester's charity to Traverse and his family in her *History of Ophelia* (1760). Like so many second-generation sentimental novelists, Fielding uses such episodes to reflect, with ever-greater subtlety, on the psychology of benevolence. Thus Dorchester obtrusively prolongs Traverse's misery— offering to help him on condition that he accept a commission in the West Indies, where the climate will certainly kill him—before revealing that he will make his fortune at home.[156]

And then it just keeps getting odder. The story also shows up in jestbooks, where it is explicitly introduced as "*The Duke of* Montagu's *Frolick*." One version reflects quite openly on the comic satisfactions of benevolence:

> We have often been amused with stories of the whims and frolicks that great men have exercised upon little ones, to the no small astonishment and perplexity of the said little men, and the unspeakable delight of themselves and their company. The late duke of Montague was remarkable for these atchievements of wit and humour; which he conducted with a dexterity and address peculiar to himself.

Only minor adjustments are required to transform a sentimental anecdote into a prank. It is the man's particular look of "mournful solemnity" that first interests the duke and makes him a fit subject for "the sport." Events unfold almost identically: the same riddling references to "a lady who had long had a particular regard for him," the old man's "foolish look of wonder and perplexity," the confusion enjoyed for as long as possible before the duke reunites the family and provides for them all.[157]

In conclusion, one canonical treatment of these behaviors cannot be avoided: Lovelace's unforgettable visit to the Smiths' shop in volume 6 of *Clarissa*.[158] In retrospect, Richardson's masterpiece seems to announce a monumental end to all the freedoms I have described—the utter obsolescence of the libertine tradition and its ways of treating women and social inferiors. It may also be the richest record we have of a tradesman's envious fascination with privilege. Short, fat, inadequate and humorless in conversation, so jittery and timid that he sometimes wrote letters to servants in the next room, Richardson poured into Lovelace all his most inadmissible fantasies—and not just the sexual ones.[159] Two months after the rape and just two and a half weeks before Clarissa's death, the shop visit should work as a final demonstration of villainy; certainly the heroine takes his "shocking levity" as proof that his contrition is feigned. Yet somehow it all slips spectacularly, almost marvelously, out of control. Lovelace of course arrives in the highest spirits: "[O]ff went their hats; Will ready at hand in a new livery . . . out rushed my honour; the woman behind the counter all in flutters." Knees knocking in terror, Mrs. Smith denies all knowledge of Clarissa's whereabouts. "Don't tell fibs, Dame Smith, don't tell fibs; chucking her under the chin." Poor Mr. Smith tries to be the man of the house. "Prithee, man, don't cry upon thine own dunghill." Does he have children? No? Then he'll have to be Master Smith or plain John.[160]

The easiest game soon appears in the form of Joseph, the bushy-haired bodicemaker who grins moronically in the corner with a huge mouth and teeth "as broad and as black as his thumb-nails." "Honest Joseph, slapping him upon the shoulders on a sudden, which made him jump, didst ever grin for a wager, man?" Suddenly Lovelace decides that Joseph's teeth would make good replacements for Will's missing ones (these were the early years of the "live" tooth transplant fad).

> Oh Lord! said the pollard-headed dog, struggling to get his head loose from under my arm, while my other hand was muzzling about his cursed chaps, as if I would take his teeth out.
>
> I will pay thee a good price, man: don't struggle thus! The penknife, Will!

Oh Lord! cried Joseph, struggling still more and more: and out comes Will's pruning-knife, for the rascal is a gardener in the country. I have only this, sir.

The best in the world to lance a gum. D——n the fellow, why dost struggle thus?

The subsequent description of clownish confusion reads like something out of theatrical biography, Spiller's Hob or Hippisley's Drunken Man:

> Joseph shook his ears; and with both hands stroked down, smooth as it would lie, his bushy hair; and looked at me as if he knew not whether he should laugh or be angry: but after a stupid stare or two, stalked off to the other end of the shop, nodding his head at me as he went, still stroking his hair, . . . and shaking his bristled head, added, 'Twas well I was a gentleman, or he would not have taken such an affront.

Even Joseph is soon enjoying the performance again, along with everyone else, as Lovelace steps behind the counter to play shopkeeper. One customer is too ugly and has to be sent away immediately. There is great fun fitting gloves for a footman. "Thrust, and be d——ned," Lovelace tells the man; "why, fellow, thou has not the strength of a cat." The gloves split open; he'll have to chop some fingers off. "Will, said I, where's thy pruning knife?" Soon a crowd has gathered, and everyone is laughing heartily, including the pious Mrs. Smith.

As a libertine's last burst of confidence—the desperate gaiety of a man who has destroyed his happiness—this is an astonishing piece of psychological realism. Coming immediately before Lovelace's great baroque dream of assumption and damnation, it seems all the more demented. But what cannot be avoided is how deeply Richardson inhabits the role, how effortlessly he follows and elaborates on the script. At eleven tightly printed pages in the original edition, the episode goes infinitely beyond the requirements of the book's multivoiced epistolarity. Even Lady Bradshaigh, elsewhere so dangerously amused by Lovelace, objected to this "illtim'd gayity," concluding: "[T]he whole is an absurdity." But Richardson cheerfully defended the scene and never did anything to revise it.[161]

This society's fascination with libertine-pranksters inevitably compromises even the most negative portraits. Certainly the role and the freedoms were being challenged by midcentury. The legendary figures became ever more notorious. With Rochester-Dorimant, a crucial turning point came at Drury Lane in October 1755, when *The Man of Mode* was "Much dislik'd and

Hiss'd." The audience was evidently hissing more about Etherege's obscenities than anything else, but the play was rarely performed thereafter.[162] Lord
Mohun eventually ended up as the sinister seducer of Thackeray's *Henry Es-
mond* (1852). But the demonization was very gradual. In his Glasgow lectures
of 1762–63, Adam Smith was unusually blunt. "There is in human nature," he
tells his students, "a servility which inclines us to adore our superiors, and an
inhumanity which disposes us to [contemn] and trample underfoot our inferiors." So powerful is this "natural disposition" that even the most despicable
behavior cannot displace it: we imagine, indeed, "that there is something respectable even in their follies."[163]

CHAPTER FOUR

Joseph Andrews and the
Great Laughter Debate

When he sat down in the spring of 1741 to write *Joseph Andrews*, Fielding was struggling to overcome his reputation for profanity, low humor, and spiteful personal satire. Transforming himself into a man of law and literary moralist meant distancing himself from the madcap dramatist whose burlesques had all but banished sense and decorum from the London stage. For the ten years to 1737, he had gloried in the wallops and smut of early modern farce and, in his last two seasons, had introduced increasingly vicious attacks on the Walpole regime. Along with this went a personal reputation—part truth and part exaggeration by his enemies—for swearing, brawling, scoffing at religion, and dividing his time between brothels and taverns. All Fielding's writings of this middle period had to deal with these charges. Contemporaries were struck by the sudden high moral tone of *The Champion* (1739–40) and such works as the "Essay on Conversation" (1743), a sort of courtesy book where Fielding set out rules for polite social interaction. In every context, one finds him preoccupied with post-Hobbesian concerns about the malice of laughter. Again and again, Fielding denounces slander, raillery, and cruel practical jokes and strives to develop a benevolent morality, distinguishing a true "Good Nature" from "Good Humour" as his society understood it.

The most prominent product of these years, *Joseph Andrews* (1742) returns repeatedly to the ethics of laughter and therefore offers a rich case study in midcentury debates on the subject. The preface finds Fielding "solemnly" protesting that readers would find no personal satire, and developing careful distinctions between "the true Ridiculous" and malicious laughter. "Affectation only" was a proper object of laughter, he insists, not misfortune or the imperfections of nature. Matters were evidently complicated by generic questions: by calling the novel a "comic Epic-Poem in Prose," Fielding was making a half-serious, half-facetious claim for respectability and attempting to place his fiction within the neoclassical taxonomy of literary kinds. Yet this hybrid genre created its own anxieties, since comedy introduced "Persons of inferiour Rank" and such persons traditionally appeared in neoclassical genres as objects of scorn. All these concerns are emphatically stated: "What would give a greater Shock to Humanity, than an Attempt to expose the Miseries of Poverty and Distress to Ridicule?" No one but a monster would laugh at "a wretched family shivering with Cold and languishing with Hunger" (although we might laugh if their cottage was full of finery).[1] These distinctions are then played out within the book, with prominent illustrations of wicked or inappropriate laughter—above all the "roasting" of Parson Adams, Fielding's most fully realized embodiment of "Good Nature." At the hands of the malicious squire and his retinue, good Parson Adams is first attacked by hunting hounds and then subjected to a long series of torments that end with him dunked in a tub of cold water.

Thus summarized, Fielding's intentions seem clear. What is interesting for my purposes—and still not sufficiently acknowledged by Fielding scholars—is how completely the satiric aims were lost on most contemporaries. *Joseph Andrews* was popular and sold well, but not for the reasons Fielding announced in his preface. Readers delighted in the squire's pranks, as Sarah Fielding complained, failing to see that "the ridiculers of parson *Adams* are designed to be the proper objects of ridicule (and not that innocent man himself)." It was almost impossible to convince people that an absent-minded idealist like Adams was not there to be laughed at. Most fixed their thoughts on his oddities of dress and behavior or "the hounds trailing the bacon in his pocket," entirely overlooking "the noble simplicity of his mind, with the other innumerable beauties in his character."[2] And these mistakes (if that is the right word) are typical of early reactions to the book as a whole: to a vast majority of its initial readers, *Joseph Andrews* was farcical and irreligious. Many simply ignored its claims to moral or literary seriousness, delighting in its comic brawls, beatings, and bawdy incidents at coaching inns. To its harsher critics, *Joseph Andrews* was irremediably "low," continually degenerating into "wretched Buffoonery and Farce."[3] Graver still, Fielding's treatment of Adams amounted to wholesale mockery of religion: in this "dry unnatural Character," wrote one critic, Fielding had "ridicul'd all the inferior Clergy."[4] Even the novel's more sympathetic readers saw the parson as little more than a well-drawn comic eccentric, a figure of "gay contempt," as Arthur Murphy put it.[5]

How could so many get a text so wrong? Most modern critics—like Fielding's contemporary defenders—have put it down to ignorance or malice. Either the early readers of *Joseph Andrews* were unable to separate Fielding from his reputation as a morally careless comedian, or they were political enemies determined to find fault with anything he produced. But an interpretation favored by a vast majority of contemporaries—and one that prevailed for more than a century and a half after that—surely deserves to be taken seriously. Fielding had many enemies by 1742, but his readers were also responding to a text. What is there in this text to enable so many to read so contrary to its author's announced intentions? Above all, why does Fielding make it so easy for readers to laugh at Parson Adams? No one could ignore Fielding's fondness for his good-natured parson. Muddleheaded, pompous, and never completely capable of following his own precepts, Adams is also a figure of impulsive kindness, one who dashes into the dark at the screams of a woman and skips with joy at the reunion of Joseph and Fanny. But when it comes to the parson qua parson, Fielding's handling is noticeably less assured.

The distinctive ambivalence of Fielding's writings is no new idea. Scholars have long noted that the extreme contrasts of his public life—swings from one side of the political spectrum to the other, transformations from careless libertine to campaigner against adultery, from satirist of Richardson to admirer—have their correlative in the internal contradictions of his fiction. Fielding, as Henry Knight Miller put it almost fifty years ago, was an author of "unresolved dualities." His repeated habit, as J. Paul Hunter observes, is to take up some "central contradiction," only to "wrestle" it "to a standoff." This habit is apparent in the most local stylistic details—the elusive "double irony" so acutely described by William Empson. In the early 1990s, Jill Campbell found similarly stubborn ambiguities in Fielding's tangled treatment of gender. Lance Bertelsen, most recently, has explored the muddle of conflicting motives in Fielding's later years at Bow Street—constant oscillations between benevolence and opportunism, public-mindedness and titillation or exploitation.[6] *Joseph Andrews* is less often mentioned in these contexts than obvious "problem" novels like *Amelia* or *Jonathan Wild*. It may still be too easy to take Fielding's preface as a reliable guide to the text, and to read *Joseph Andrews* as a fictional version of his periodical moralizing. This chapter begins by testing such intentional statements against the unruly details of the text. Finally and unavoidably, the topic leads me into the heated debate about Fielding's changing religious views. *Joseph Andrews* emerges as a record of unresolved internal debates about the morality of different sorts of laughter, about class and the separation of virtue from rank, and about revealed religion and the role of the clergy.

NARRATIVE FROM A HIGH HORSE

One must clearly start with the most extended treatment of these themes—the famous roasting scene in book 3. Its ostensible functions are all very clear and its details close to Fielding's didactic writings on the subject, above all his *Champion* essay on roasting (13 March 1740). The episode comes immediately after Joseph's speech on charity and "true" goodness, which therefore functions as a set of instructions to the reader. Anyone who scoffed at a genuinely benevolent person, says Joseph, "would be laughed at himself, instead of making others laugh" (234). In the encounter between mounted gentlemen and simple country folk on foot, Fielding seems deliberately to be exploring the temptations of privilege. Hunting provides a powerful metaphor for the cruel pranks that follow, and Fielding several times points up his parallel between the dogs that first attack Adams and the squire's band of "two-legged Curs" (238, 244). The squire himself is conspicuously introduced as a negative example, with a lengthy analysis of his vices; he is suitably punished when Adams drags him into the tub after him (271, 251). Fielding seems to take special trouble to distance himself from events, to warn readers that none of this was supposed to be funny. The narrator prominently informs us that his account of the scene is incomplete: Adams himself can't remember everything that happened, and the narrator has his information only secondhand, "from a Servant of the Family" (246).

The important point, again, is that so few early readers saw it this way. How did Fielding, by then an experienced and savvy literary producer, so seriously miscalculate his effects? The very structure of his satire immediately raises questions. Why choose narrative rather than direct or declarative satire? Given this culture's love of ridicule and knockabout pranks, dramatizing those evils at such length was no reliable way of stamping them out. Given that everyone made fun of clergymen, working up a long narrative satire of the vice was surely the riskiest way of trying to correct it. And since upper-class pranksters were such accepted lords of misrule, even the most negative portrait of this figure was bound to mislead. It was "like trying to put burglary out of fashion by making it ridiculous," as one nineteenth-century critic nicely put it.[7] There was a very real danger that readers would interpret the satire of inappropriate humor as yet further instances of that humor. By 1742, Fielding should have known better: his burlesques of contemporary theater had repeatedly been attacked as just more of the same. Large parts of his audience, he complained, failed to see that *The Author's Farce* and *Pasquin* were burlesques rather than yet further nonsensical entertainments of the *Hurlothrumbo* sort. Spectators at *Tom Thumb*, William Shenstone recalled, had persistently mistaken Fielding's burlesque "for the very foolishness it exposes."[8]

And the closer one looks at the extended roasting of Adams, the more uncertain or mischievous it seems. Consider the ingenuity that goes into the first of these pranks, when Adams is pursued by hounds. The scenario itself reflects some old stage routines: dogs trained to bite Pantalone on the backside or affix themselves to Punch's nose.[9] Fielding has his parson attacked by an entire pack of hounds, which snatch his wig, take great bites out of his cassock, and set him fleeing before he takes them on with a cudgel. The very tempo of this scene recalls the frenetic brawls and chases of farce. In this age when gentlemen shaved their heads, losing one's wig was the greatest of indignities and a stock humiliation in every comic genre. One cannot avoid a sense that Fielding is enjoying knocking Adams around, even as he pities him. The grimace of fright, the bald head, the terrified flight from the hounds—these are straight out of farce and are described at length.

Within certain bounds, of course, we are invited to laugh at Adams. The absentmindedness and physical tics are endearing enough. Adams can be proud, even when declaiming against pride; probably he does need to be shaken out of his naive faith in human goodness. At such moments he fits Fielding's prefatory account of affectation as a proper object of corrective laughter. But why all the stylistic antics? Adams "deliver[ed] his Head from his Wig," Fielding waggishly informs us, and "escaped likewise from at least a third Part of his Cassock, which he willingly left as *Exuviae* or Spoils to the Enemy" (237). There are extended mock-learned asides: a classical justification for Adams's flight from the dogs, a long invocation to the muse of biography, a mock-epic description of Joseph's cudgel. Fielding then offers a deliberately plodding excuse for not introducing a Homeric simile (with a glance at contemporary debates over whether they were really appropriate in the heat of battle). With its stylistic play, classical references, and topical references to fashionable society, this episode is manifestly addressed to educated, upper-class readers, including those who would delight in the terror of a shabby clergyman and two rustics in flight from a pack of hounds.

We need a clearer sense of Fielding's voice at such moments—of the perspective through which events are "focalized," as a narratologist might put it. Take the narrator's treatment of the hounds. No critic fails to notice Fielding's explicit parallel between hunters of men and those of animals, but this parallel could hardly be less stable. Fanny weeps at the cruelty of hare coursing, "the Barbarity of worrying a poor innocent defenseless Animal out of its Life" (236). The buildup of adjectives is our first clue that the narrator might not agree, and sure enough Joseph, a former whipper-in to Sir Thomas Booby, informs her that the hare was killed fairly. Fielding was himself an avid hunter, which no doubt explains his oddly affectionate descriptions of the hounds: Rockwood and Jowler, Thunder, Plunder, Wonder, and Blunder, and the shameful Caesar ("O eternal Blot to his Name!"), who runs away yelping (242).[10] Ringwood, the last dog, merits an extended lament: "*Ringwood* the best Hound that ever pursued a Hare, who never threw his Tongue but where the Scent was undoubtedly true"—as it was, presumably, in the pursuit of Adams (241).

All this comes strikingly close to the tone of eighteenth-century hunting diaries, with their tedious records of long runs and comic accidents along the way, of injured horses or dogs that lose the scent and have to be hanged. The dogs' names were standard choices for hounds and easily fall into a Rabelaisian rhyming list (Fielding may also be recalling one of D'Urfey's hunting songs).[11] Odder still is the obscure in-joke that follows: the information that one of the hounds, the bitch named Fairmaid, is a gift to the roasting squire from one of Fielding's friends and patrons, John Temple (1680–1752), and that this dog is saved (241). One early modern usage further complicates the parallel: the term *dog*, like *rogue* or *devil*, could be indulgent as much as critical. These words were all used in appreciative ways to refer to wags or practical jokers (*arch dog, sly dog, impudent devil*). References to the captain as a "devil" and the quack doctor a "mischievous Dog" are therefore freighted with ambiguity (249).

With his playful use of hunting slang and elaborate in-jokes for the hunters in his readership—those who understood the sport and loved nothing better than a pack of hounds in full cry—Fielding hardly offers the most critical or detached perspective on his evil squire. At certain points, he seems entirely to forget where his sympathies are supposed to lie and comes close to what must be the squire's perspective on events. Thus the inherent comedy of two young rustics caught canoodling in a field, or his chuckle at the weepy simplicity of Fanny, who doesn't understand the rules of hunting and wants to take the bunny home. All this is recounted from a sort of *high horse* point of view—a metaphor that remained close to its literal sense in the eighteenth century and perfectly captures the perspective of this scene.

A learned gentleman describing the trying but ultimately harmless adventures of his social inferiors: this narrative mode was always going to sound uppish. Claude Rawson has described Fielding as an author of essentially aristocratic disposition, one who consistently writes "*de haut en bas*" and maintains an element of "unconscious or self-concealed hauteur"—even as he disdains all forms of snobbery and attempts to dissociate virtue from rank. Rawson finds this hauteur in saintly characters of middling status like the Heartfrees in *Jonathan Wild*, but it seems equally apparent in the presentation of Adams, Fanny, and Joseph.[12] *Joseph Andrews* unfolds in a folkish, almost miniaturized world, a sort of toy village. An improbably priggish rustic is in love with a buxom dairymaid while the muddleheaded vicar warns them about the sins of the flesh. A cast of comic auxiliaries surrounds them: a randy widow up at the big house, a mean-spirited scold at the parsonage, and so on. This is the world of pastoral comedy and cheerful ballad operas about the minor trials of rustics named Harry and Doll: the world of *The Village Opera*, *The Country Wedding*, *Love in a Village*, and so many others.[13] It is a benign world of green fields and kitchen firesides, of reveries, pastoral songs, and miniaturized romantic passions—as when Fanny suddenly leaps up from the udder, packs a little bundle, and sets off to find her Joseph (144). Adams, with his grubby cassock, sturdy crabstick, and inherited stock of moral precepts, is at one with this world: a worthy country parson who discusses eternity with an innkeeper and debates "Points of Theology" with Mrs. Slipslop (25).

Even Lady Booby's visit to the Adams household, another of the novel's hypertrophic illustrations of unacceptable laughter, is streaked with patrician amusement. Fielding's satiric setup is clear enough:

> [Lady Booby] led them towards Mr. *Adams's* House; and as she approached it, told them, if they pleased she would divert them with one of the most ridiculous Sights they had ever seen, which was an old foolish Parson, who, she said laughing, kept a Wife and six Brats on a Salary of about twenty Pounds a Year; adding, that there was not such another ragged Family in the Parish. They all readily agreed to this Visit. (244)

In case we should miss the point, Lady Booby specifically uses the word *ridiculous*. But the critique soon scatters as Adams receives his guests. As one who always "preached up Submission to Superiours," Adams receives Lady Booby "with about two hundred Bows" (306, 312). Mrs. Adams gets into a housewifely flutter, protesting that "she was ashamed to be seen in such a Pickle, and that her House was in such a Litter" (312). The parson then tries to get his son, still dripping wet from his tumble into the river, to read a story for the visitors (*"Lege, Dick, Lege"* [314]). When the inevitable village wedding occurs a few chapters later, Fanny appears, like the winner of some fairground beauty contest, in Pamela's cast-offs: a "white Dimity Night-Gown" with that gloriously incongruous detail, "an Edging of Lace round the Bosom." No wonder Pamela and Mr. Booby guffaw their way through the ceremony and have to be "publickly rebuked" by Adams, "for laughing in so sacred a Place, and so solemn an Occasion." Once at the wedding feast, however, even Adams gorges on ale and pudding and "giv[es] a Loose to more Facetiousness than was usual to him" (342).[14]

It is all very affectionate, little more than a gentlemanly chortle at the inelegance and simplicity of country folk—at Joseph's prudery and Adams's parsonical self-importance, as at Joseph's garbled names of Italian painters (Varnish for Veronese, Hannibal Scratchi for Annibale Carraci). Nowhere do Adams and the young lovers come close to monstrous vulgarians like Mrs. Tow-Wouse or the semiliterate Slipslop. But they are simple country people, and there are limits to their social elevation. Joseph uses the £2,000 from Mr. Booby to buy "a little Estate in the same Parish with his Father," while Fanny

> presides with most excellent Management in his Dairy; where, however, she is not at present very able to bustle much, being, as Mr. *Wilson* informs me in his last Letter, extremely big with her first Child. (344)

Fanny starts off as an illiterate dairymaid, and a hardworking farmer's wife is about as far as she can rise. The little dairy is no upper-class plaything: it is where she belongs. And the narrator, in the clearest emblem of Fielding's overall perspective, now ostentatiously detaches himself, rising above the cozy routines of village life, of which he is informed only by periodic letters from Mr. Wilson.

In her valuable reading of *Joseph Andrews*, Judith Frank links the narrator's loftiness to genteel anxieties about the social upheavals of the age. Frank's *Joseph Andrews* is preoccupied with plebeians who ape their superiors and the threat of literacy as an engine of upward mobility. Like *Shamela* before it, *Joseph Andrews* works "to defuse the scandal of Pamela's literacy," with Fanny as a wholly illiterate anti-Pamela and Joseph only semiliterate.[15] Still, we might be wrong to overestimate the anxiety of it all. By the end of his career, Fielding would indeed become anxious about the poor; the later social pamphlets are openly repressive. But *Joseph Andrews* and *Shamela* are confident books that effortlessly reproduce old assumptions about social inferiors. *Joseph Andrews* is consistently amused by the coarseness of the poor, but it hardly doubts their irremediable lowness. This reflexive superiority appears in all sorts of local details. Consider the appearance—no more than a few sentences long—of the good postilion who lends Joseph his greatcoat while the other passengers would let him die in the ditch. With its allusions to the Good Samaritan parable, this episode is rightly acknowledged as one of Fielding's clearest attempts to separate virtue from status. But why the Irish bull with which he alerts the passengers? "He was certain there was a *dead* Man in the ditch, for he heard him groan" (52). The postilion could not be closer, at this point, to the proverbial stupidities of Irish numbskulls or the "Wise Men" of Gotham. A tone of patronage is apparent even on the level of style, as when we are told that Fanny is completely "hagged out" after a long day on the road (333). Obviously, then, Fielding's prefatory declarations that he laughs only at the affectation of the poor—that he has "carefully excluded" all burlesque from his characterization of inferiors—are not played out in the text (4). No doubt this failure suggests a deep-seated resistance to working-class aspirations. But it also reflects a much more confident indulgence in the pleasures (such as they were) of snobbery.

Back to the roasting of Adams. For Fielding's uncertainties about laughter and good characters of lower rank become unmistakable once the action shifts to the squire's house. The "Scene of Roasting" in chapter 7 reads strikingly like a one-act farce, with a cast of fools and practical jokers introduced to torment a harebrained old man. The whole thing has its own inevitable logic, with progressively greater humiliations followed by the departure of their sodden and irate victim. As one particularly close analogue, witness the mistreatment of a foolish squire named Noodle in *The Generous Free-Mason* (1730), a raucous ballad opera by Fielding's friend William Chetwood. Noodle, a ridiculous old lover, is subjected to every conceivable humiliation. Blinded with snuff, he and his servant Doodle run into each other ("You Son of a Whore!" says Noodle, "you have knock'd my Eyes out." "And you," replies the servant, "have beaten my Teeth down my Throat.") The pair are then doused with urine and beaten "like Eggs to a Pudding."[16] In one extended scene—and one that comes strikingly close to Fielding's roasting of Adams—the credulous Noodle allows himself to be "initiated" as a Freemason, in hopes of marrying a particular young woman. The pretend Masons bind Noodle to a chair, blacken his face, pick his pocket, and steal his rings before tying him up in a sack that they leave center stage. (At this point, predictably, Doodle enters and trips over the bundle. "You Son of a Bitch," cries Noodle from the sack, "you have kick'd my Nose off.")[17] And so it goes on, until Noodle is duped into marrying a whore. *The Generous Free-Mason* is one of many eighteenth-century farces in which some recognized figure of fun comes onstage for the simple purpose of being beaten and humiliated.

Adams is obviously no Noodle, but Fielding provides his readers with a strikingly similar sequence of their favorite stage pranks. Adams is mocked, mimicked, tumbled to the ground, and scalded with hot soup. The captain's firecracker trick repeats familiar practical jokes with squibs or pistols let off in confined spaces: terror, even mortal terror, was still funny in this culture. Fielding was ostensibly satirizing all these types of humor, but his imagination keeps straying. The farcical sequence of Adams's reactions (fury, terror, pomposity) is described in exhaustive detail. Adams, "believing that he had been blown up in reality, started from his Chair, and jumped about the Room, to the infinite Joy of the Beholders, who declared that he was the best Dancer in the Universe" (247). A moment of unavoidable lowness comes when the parson so proudly produces his half guinea ("I do not shew you this out of Ostentation of Riches" [248]). His gullibility is as exaggerated as any stage dupe's: repeatedly tricked by the squire and his gang of wags, Adams repeatedly forgives them. As so often in Fielding's fiction, innocence is a positive quality, a sign of unsuspecting goodness. But so extended is this series of humiliations that readers easily associated the parson with their favorite comic butts, with the legion of gullible old men who are deceived and knocked around in any number of farces, fairground drolls, and comic novels.

Scholars have still barely scratched the surface of this elusive scene. In the most sophisticated analysis we have, Jill Campbell reads the roasting scene as a self-conscious meditation on the ethics of different comic genres. The squire's house becomes a "dark House of Satire," a testing ground where Fielding stages exaggerated versions of his theatrical humiliations and thereby distances himself from his history of public satire.[18] More important, Campbell finds the narrator anticipating and striving to prevent readerly truancies. By insisting that he is working from an incomplete record, for example, Fielding detaches himself from events and obviates assumptions "that he has invented the pranks himself, or was in some sense a co-persecutor of Adams."[19] One wonders whether this interpretation places too much weight on one of Fielding's favorite narrative antics: claims that the documents are incomplete or the protagonists themselves unable to remember. Fielding consciously imitated this device from Cervantes and Scarron and also uses it—to cite just one of many examples in *Joseph Andrews*—to put an end to the hero's speech on charity. It appears again and again in *Tom Jones* and *Jonathan Wild*.[20]

Almost every narrative choice in this episode can be read in similarly antithetical ways. Each prank is fully described before it is perpetrated: we see the mischievous captain attaching the cracker to Adams's coat; we already know that the throne is balanced over a tub of water.[21] By fully exposing the gang's contrivances before Adams suffers by them, Campbell argues, Fielding destroys any sense of dramatic surprise. But might we not, being let in on the secret, become somehow complicit with the parson's tormentors? This sort of dramatic irony is, after all, a favorite mechanism of stage comedy (recall Malvolio's hoaxers in *Twelfth Night*, who keep reminding us of the humiliations to come). In Lord Mohun's gunpowder trick, we know what's up long before the unfortunate old woman.

Consider, finally, the parade of boredom with which Fielding lists the pranks. "Thus completed Joke the first," yawns the narrator. "Joke the third was served up by one of the Waiting-men." Fielding affects a tone of weary censoriousness: he won't record all the stale witticisms that were made at Adams's expense; the physical pranks were "none of the least curious," and he won't bore us with them (245–46, 243). But he does give us page after page of this ostensibly inappropriate humor. The squire's delighted quip that Adams was "the largest Jack Hare he ever saw." All the talk about "Parson-hunting" being "the best Sport in the World." Praise for Adams's "standing at Bay, which they said he had done as well as any Badger" (238, 244). Idiotic as it is—and "procured with the greatest difficulty"—the poet's "Extempore Poem on Parson Adams" is quoted in full, with its gleeful account of Adams's tatty appearance, stench, and terrified flight from the hounds (246). The persistent refusal to fill in the details thus works more like Chaucerian *occupatio*: feigning to pass over the subject, Fielding indulges and draws attention to it.

Adjudicating between intentionalist and self-sabotaging interpretations of these devices must remain speculative. But it cannot be irrelevant that Fielding's declared intentions were so lost on his contemporaries, or that by 1742 he had repeatedly experienced such responses. Critics of his earliest farces had objected, using one of Jeremy Collier's favorite arguments, that it was never clear whether Fielding's vicious characters were being ridiculed or indulged.[22] Fielding had defended himself as John Dennis had defended Etherege and Wycherley against Collier: "Why should any Person of Modesty be offended at seeing a Set of Rakes and Whores exposed and set in the most ridiculous Light?"[23] But the charge had continued to dog him: critics of *The Covent-Garden Tragedy* recognized that Mother Punchbowl, Lovegirlo, and Kissinda were dangerously engaging characters. And so it happened with Adams and the roasting squire. Much as he might claim to deride the evils of malicious laughter, Fielding invented the humiliations to which Adams is subjected and put the jokes into the mouths of his tormentors. And his readers laughed, delighting where they were apparently intended to deplore.

THE ETHICS OF RIDICULE

The complexities of this scene start to make sense once one reads it alongside Fielding's impossibly shifting views on different sorts of humor. By the early 1750s, he was denouncing all humor that lacked a corrective purpose and entirely abandoning his old conviction that laughter, provided it was not malicious, could be an end in itself. As a justification, astonishingly, he quotes his old enemy Richardson: "*Pleasantry*, (as the ingenious Author of *Clarissa* says of a Story), *should be made only the Vehicle of Instruction.*" But "when no Moral, no Lesson, no Instruction is conveyed to the Reader, where the whole Design of the Composition is no more than to make us laugh, the Writer comes very near to the Character of a Buffoon." He now scorns comic "Scriblers" like D'Urfey and Tom Brown and carefully distances himself from Rabelais and Aristophanes, the acknowledged muses of his Haymarket comedies. Their design was no more than "to ridicule all Sobriety, Modesty, Decency, Virtue, and Religion, out of the World."[24] This was the Fielding who had lost his true genius for humor, as readers of *Amelia* were so loudly complaining.

Getting to this point, however, was a slow and halting process. Fielding's early prologues offer the usual perfunctory justifications ("to divert, instruct, and mend Mankind"), but the plays themselves revel in the anarchic fun that came so naturally. They also reflect powerful contemporary ideas that laughter could be an end in itself—a cure for the spleen or one of nature's great gifts, like eating and sex.[25] For all the twentieth-century attempts to cast them as partisan satires, *Tom Thumb* and *The Author's Farce* (both 1730) come closer to "imbecile delight," as one modern commentary puts it.[26] More often, indeed, the younger Fielding thumbs his nose at any demand for instruction. Thus the lunatic "Prolegomena" he affixes to the published version of *The Covent-Garden Tragedy* (1732): here Fielding impersonates a dim-witted critic who feels compelled to find a moral. The result? "I cannot help wishing this may teach all Gentlemen to pay their Chair-Men." If anyone had any doubt, the play's final couplet confirms its tone of cheerful amorality: "From such Examples as of this and that, / We all are taught to know I know not what."[27] By the early 1740s, Fielding was denouncing all sorts of inappropriate humor, but the preface to *Joseph Andrews* nevertheless continues to recommend the therapeutic virtues of "Mirth and Laughter," which were "probably more wholesome Physic for the Mind, and conduce better to purge away Spleen,

Melancholy and ill Affections, than is generally imagined" (5). The hesitant phrasing points to uncertainties, but it would be years before Fielding was able to denounce noncorrective laughter with a straight face.

Because they so sharply expose his internal conflicts as he was writing *Joseph Andrews*—and because they so usefully exemplify larger debates—it seems important to review Fielding's nonfictional reflections on laughter from this period. The most personal of these is a well-known letter to his friend James Harris, written from Bath in September 1741. Fielding tells Harris about an experience of public humiliation in the pump room: a beautiful young woman catches him ogling her ("looking at her pretty earnestly"), at which she and her companion "both presently burst into an affected Laugh." He recalls Hobbes's theory and then muses more generally on the nature of laughter. "[I] am in doubt," he writes, "whether that laughter which entitles to the general Character of Good Humour, be not rather a Sign of an evil than a good Mind." What is interesting is that a personal experience of ridicule sets him thinking, and that he seems to be *working toward* his mature distinction between good-natured and malicious laughter. To Harris, at least, he openly acknowledges the difficulty of assigning "the just Bounds between these two Kinds of Laughter," concluding: "It is sufficient for me that I know them when I see them."[28] "I know it when I see it" is a proverbially useless ethical norm, one from which no practical standards can ever be derived.

The more public versions of these musings are only slightly less direct about the difficulty of developing workable distinctions. Like the preface to *Joseph Andrews*, Fielding's essays on laughter repeatedly fall back on extreme contrasts. Miseries and misfortunes are "no Subjects of Mirth," he insists, but "laughing at the Vices and Follies of Mankind is entirely innocent" and "may be attended with good Consequences."[29] It was utterly malignant to laugh at a cripple or a very ugly man, but "when Ugliness aims at the Applause of Beauty, or Lameness endeavors to display Agility," who could avoid it? No one would laugh at a ragged beggar, but if the man was trying to be grand, we "would then begin to laugh, and with justice" (9). Sharpest of all, because so plainly unnerved by the complexity of human motives, is the long "Essay on the Knowledge of the Characters of Men," first published in the *Miscellanies* of 1743. Read alongside other eighteenth-century discussions of laughter, with their perpetual search for kindly explanations, Fielding's essay is strikingly frank about the baser impulses at work. Hobbes was right, he now admits: laughter is an act of sudden triumph. Almost everyone is "pleased with seeing a Blemish in another which we are ourselves free from." Few can avoid laughing when some well-dressed person slips over "in a dirty Place." Laughter in these cases is an involuntary reflex, a sort of "convulsive Extasy," one of the "spontaneous Motions of the Soul" that few people even notice "and none can prevent."[30]

The important thing is what happens next: "[W]hen we come to reflect on the Uneasiness this Person suffers, Laughter, in a good and delicate Mind, will begin to change itself into Compassion." It never becomes clear whether this "Compassion" is a competing benevolent impulse or a civilized response; the heavy punctuation and constant qualification suggest that Fielding had not resolved the matter in his own mind. Certainly the final clause—with its echo of Shamela's "began to offer to touch my Under-Petticoat"—seems painfully unconvinced. As usual, then, Fielding returns to an overstated contrast: if the people in question really injured themselves in their fall ("a violent Bruise or the breaking of a Bone"), anyone "who should still continue to laugh, would be entitled to the basest and vilest Appellation with which any Language can stigmatize him."[31] The practical challenges of making these distinctions are all too clear. At what point did comic "uneasiness" become an injury at which none but the "basest and vilest" of the species would laugh? Perhaps it then becomes significant that Adams is tormented and humiliated by the roasting squire, but not physically harmed.

Behind these uncertainties, one detects Fielding's lifelong resistance to overrefinement and moralizing humorlessness; the famous puppet show episode in *Tom Jones* is one of many treatments of this subject. All his prescriptive writings on laughter are streaked with concessions that it was hard not to laugh, that no one could avoid all ill-natured raillery, and that he wasn't trying to stop people enjoying themselves. The "Essay on Conversation" admits that it probably requires "great Delicacy" and "niceness" to maintain his rules, and indeed that he has observed "numberless Breaches" of them. Even the best-natured men sometimes humiliate others "from Negligence and Inadvertency" (although they soon desist once they notice their nasty self-satisfaction). The slipperiness of these distinctions reminds us how counterintuitive such standards were in eighteenth-century culture, how easy it was to get it wrong. Fielding's *Champion* essay on roasting makes all the same concessions. Ridiculing or tormenting someone in front of others is a pleasure "as thoroughly corrupt and diabolical as can possibly pollute the Mind of Man." But at the same time, he has known "some of Sense and Good-nature too forwardly give in to this Diversion. Men who would by no means have consented to do any other Injury, reputing this innocent and harmless."[32] Fielding could be thinking of any of the great roasters of his age, many of whom he knew well. More than likely, he was thinking of the prankster dukes Montagu and Richmond, both as famous for benevolence as they were for hoaxes and humbugs. Both were important patrons throughout Fielding's career; Richmond was the subject and dedicatee of his poem "Of Good Nature" ("What is Good-nature? Gen'rous *Richmond*, tell . . ."). All the evidence suggests that Fielding was hugely amused by their antics. In book 3 of *Joseph Andrews*, the hero's cudgel is engraved with the first-night riot of Captain Bodens's play (240). At the end of the decade, he would openly delight in the dukes' "Bottle Conjuror" hoax.[33]

Fielding was clearly also thinking of the banter and conversational freedoms of more ordinary environments—of the taverns, coffeehouses, and drinking parties in which he spent so much time. His companions during the 1730s and early 1740s were all hard drinkers and sharp wits: William Hogarth and James Ralph the deist (d. 1762); Thomas Cooke the Hesiod translator (1703–56); Robert and Anthony, the profligate Henley brothers; Harry Hatsell (d. 1772), prodigiously fat but always in good humor; and the bullish John Ellys (1701–57), portrait painter and boon companion of prizefighters. Some of these men were still gathering in Southwark for a weekly "club of Wits" in the mid-1740s, and Fielding was a man who *"will drink with any body,"* as a ministerial paper put it in October 1740.[34] What we know of all-male drinking parties in this period, and even of more mixed environments, makes it clear what all the cautions were aimed at. The surviving records of one drinking club provide fascinating insights into the mutual "chaffing" that went on after a few glasses: "[I]f any member had a weak point, his faulty armour was speedily pierced. . . . If a man showed signs of wincing under the lash of sarcasm, or was nettled by a bantering he could not perhaps reply to, he became at once a butt."[35] What we know of Fielding and his circle suggests similar levels of verbal combat (someone who could neither take a joke nor give one was not going to be good company, he acknowledges at an unguarded moment in the "Essay on Conversation"). "Without being in reality ill-natured," wrote Sir Joseph Mawbey of Thomas Cooke, he was "blunt," "coarse," and "not infrequently dictatorial and assuming, which often disgusted strangers, and made him feared by many."[36] Even in this company, Fielding's sense of humor could seem unkind. His "Wit and Gayety give Life to the Company," wrote Anthony Henley to Cooke, "but I believe you'l join with me in this point, he is *too free* with his *friends*."[37]

One finds Fielding having similar trouble condemning the knockabout fun of contemporary conviviality. In the "Essay on the Knowledge of the Characters of Men," he evidently feels compelled to follow the courtesy tradition and distance himself from belly laughs and raucous horseplay. The problem was how to do this without being a killjoy. His solution combines the old parade of boredom with a legitimating glance at Pope (who was now embracing Field-ing as a fellow victim of Whig censorship). *"Gentle Dulness ever loves a Joke,"* Fielding begins:

> *i.e.* one of her own Jokes. These are sometimes performed by the Foot; as by leaping over Heads, or Chairs, or Tables, Kicks in the B——ch, *&c.* sometimes by the Hand; as by Slaps in the Face, pulling off Wigs, and infi-nite other Dexterities, too tedious to particularize: sometimes by the Voice; as by hollowing, huzzaing, and singing merry (*i.e.* dull) Catches, by *merry* (*i.e.* dull) Fellows.[38]

This sardonic perspective may also recall one of Steele's *Tatler* papers, where Isaac Bickerstaff lays on the same tone of bored sarcasm to describe the eve-ning fun at a London tavern ("five hours with three merry, and two honest, fellows").[39] But in 1743 as in 1709, this was a pretty close description of main-stream male sociability.

By 1742, Fielding officially disapproved of all these pleasures. But when he came to dramatize that disapproval in the mistreatment of Adams, many of the old satisfactions seem to have returned—and he continued to indulge them, all the while protesting that they were deplorable. Some of the closest analogues to Fielding's roasting scene are plays like Gay's *Mohocks* (1712) and Shadwell's *Scowrers* (1690), in which the announced purpose—to attack the violent libertines of the age—fades beside an amused and extended dramati-zation of buckish misrule. Gay's Mohocks capture the watch and force them to swap clothes, before marching them off to an unsuspecting JP to be tried for their own crimes (the truth is revealed in the end, with no harm done). In-evitably, the rowdy young men get the best lines in these plays, while parsons, constables, and honest citizens can only carp on about *tempora* and *mores.* The roasting squire and his retinue retained, for Fielding's early readers if not for Fielding himself, much of this inversionary energy—the inherent delight of Punch beating the constable and hanging the executioner, of the Keystone Cops and so many other instances of the "world upside down."

To what extent are these local countertendencies about Adams apparent in the rest of *Joseph Andrews?* Some corrective laughter is clearly important to the book's ethical aims: "as entirely ignorant of this world as an infant just entered into it," Adams needs to be shaken out of his naive trust in human goodness (23). To be effective in the world, Fielding insists, the virtuous must recognize the existence of human evil. Like the violence of *Don Quixote,* the physical violence and duplicity encountered by Joseph and Adams are forcible reminders of the way of things. Immediately before the roasting scene, the sheer artificiality of the spot—"one of the beautifullest Spots of Ground in the Universe," a "natural Amphitheatre" surrounded by woods and "spread with a Verdure which no Paint could imitate"—obtrusively reminds us of the naïveté of Joseph's ideas about human nature. The clearing is cloud-cuckooland, a perfect place, as Fielding pointedly informs us, to raise "romantic Ideas" (232). We are invited to laugh, similarly, at Adams's various faults and blind spots—his pomposity, vanity, and so on. In retrospect, the parson can be identified as an early "round character"—a mixture of faults and virtues, one who deserves satiric correction but also elicits sympathy and affection (Falstaff is a still earlier example).[40]

Still, there is far more laughter than any of these aims requires. Why keep emphasizing Adams's peculiar appearance and involuntary tics? We are repeatedly offered long, still-camera descriptions of the parson's eccentric dress. The torn and filthy cassock, constantly falling down below his coat; the nightcap he wears over an ancient wig: no one could claim that Fielding does much to dissociate his parson from the indignities of poverty (73, 132, etc.). The bacon in his pocket is partly a material context for his pursuit by the hounds (as Fielding himself informs us in a gratuitous footnote: "All Hounds that will hunt Fox or other Vermin, will hunt a Piece of rusty Bacon trailed on the Ground" [246]). But bacon was also the proverbial foodstuff of uncouth rustics, as in the insults *chaw-bacon*, *bacon-brain*, or simply *bacon* ("On, bacons, on!" Falstaff cries to the travelers at Gadshill).[41] No wonder Adams is so repeatedly mistaken for some sort of vagabond—a beggar, a pig dealer, a thimble and button man on his way to a neighboring fair, and worst of all a Welsh parson, that archetypal figure of ignorance and ragged desperation (162–67, 101, 312). Mistaken identities are invariably significant in narrative, proleptic suggestions of true identity. Fielding's more deliberate instances of the device work in these familiar ways (Tom Jones is repeatedly taken for a gentleman in disguise). But with Adams, the constant mistakes work more negatively, progressively corroding his dignity.

Then there are all the eccentric gestures, the twitches, sighs, and groans. Here, for example, is Adams offering his sermons to the bookseller: "He then snapt his Fingers . . . and took two or three turns about the Room in an Extasy" (79). At such moments, Adams comes alarmingly close to the aging pedants (*dottore*) of commedia dell'arte, with their stammering, confusion, and constant odd gestures. Even his good-natured expressions of joy seem deliberately bizarre: all the hand rubbing and finger snapping, the tears and spontaneous prayers of thanks, the leaping about "like one frantick" (310, 292). Endearing as they may be, the sheer density of these details inevitably recalls the ludicrous oddballs of the early modern farce, with their mutterings and facial tics.

No modern critic ignores these elements of slapstick, but they have uniformly deemphasized their effect. J. Paul Hunter lists Adams's comic deficiencies but concludes that the parson is nevertheless "usually effective" as a "purveyor of moral truth." Claude Rawson notes an intermittent "hint of patronage" in Fielding's presentation of Adams, but concludes that this "desolemnif[ies] without deflating": Adams is an "upward reformulation" of his Cervantic original.[42] The matter seems worth pursuing. Why so much emphasis on the parson's absentmindedness? These details reflect ancient jokes about bookish scholars and their ludicrous detachment from the world. The one about the geographer who gets lost in a wood. Or the logician who almost drowns and vows never to go near water until he has learned to swim. Or the astronomer who falls into a ditch as he is looking up at the stars (a joke that goes back to Aesop and Plato's *Theaetetus*).[43] Adams famously sets off for London to sell his sermons, only to discover that he has left them at home. But this sort of humor is constant and laid on thick. The parson soaks himself crossing a great puddle, only to see a footpath around the side. Standing directly in front of one, he asks a local for directions to the nearest alehouse ("follow your Nose and be d——n'd" is the rustic's response [96]). He proposes swimming across a river, until Joseph points out that there is a bridge ("Odso," Adams replies, "I did not think of that" [194]).

Why does Adams have to be such a ridiculous old man? The obvious answer is that Fielding is modeling his unworldly parson on Don Quixote, creating a Christian fool who goes through a world of rascals, passionately committed to his ideals. In spite of all his oddities, this Adams is the moral center of the book. Eventually, as Stuart Tave has demonstrated, Adams became one of the earliest of a long tradition of "amiable humorists" or lovable English eccentrics. One immediate problem with this argument is that Don Quixote was, for mid-eighteenth-century readers, not the lovable eccentric or noble idealist that he subsequently became, but a hilariously deluded old man and the deserving victim of so many brutal torments. This view was changing, and *Joseph Andrews* is one of several texts attempting to establish a more charitable understanding of the Quixotic type.[44] In 1742, however, Fielding was effectively inviting large parts of his audience to laugh when his subtitle introduced Adams "in Imitation of the Manner of Cervantes." Fielding's friend William Young, the "real" Parson Adams, was far from delighted to be memorialized in this way—to see his eccentric gestures, absentmindedness, and gluttony depicted in such exaggerated ways (in another context, Fielding presented Young as "Belchandwheezius"). According to one contemporary, Young was soon threatening to knock down anyone who addressed him as Parson Adams.[45]

Worst of all is the long series of violent humiliations to which Fielding subjects his parson: all the beatings and knocks on the head, the constant tumbles, drenchings, and soilings. Adams is knocked into a pigsty, tossed from his horse, doused in urine, and momentarily blinded by a pail of hog's blood. He may need to be shaken out of his ignorance of the world, but he does not have to be so constantly knocked around: there were far less violent, and far less ambiguous, means for making the point. Nor are all these torments perpetrated by vicious characters—which would make them yet further instances of the villainous cruelty of the world. As if by reflex, Fielding subjects Adams to his own, entirely needless accidents. At the beginning of book 3, for no apparent reason, he rolls the parson down a steep hill in the dark (a chapter entitled, in classic farce style, "A Night-Scene"). Had they been able to see the sight, Fielding tells us, Joseph and Fanny "would scarce have refrained laughing" (194). Even in the final paragraphs of the novel, Fielding gives us a last laugh at his grave parson, contriving to have him thrown from a skittish horse. In his joy at the favorable turn of events, Adams spurs his horse too violently, "which the generous Beast disdaining . . . immediately ran away full speed, and played so many antic Tricks, that he tumbled the Parson from his Back"—a mishap that affords "infinite Merriment" to the crowd of bystanders (340).

Fielding positively dwells on the indignities of such situations. Here, for example, is the parson drenched in urine and soiled by filth after a brawl:

> It is not perhaps easy to describe the Figure of *Adams*; he had risen in such a violent Hurry, that he had on neither Breeches nor Stockings; nor had he taken from his Head a red spotted Handkerchief, which by Night bound his Wig, that was turned inside out, around his Head. He had on his torn Cassock, and his Great-Coat; but as the remainder of his Cassock hung down below his Great-Coat; so did a small Strip of white, or rather whitish Linnen appear below that; to which we may add the several Colours which appeared on his Face, where a long Piss-burnt [urine-stained] Beard, served to retain the Liquor of the Stone Pot, and that of a blacker hue which distilled from the Mop. (270)

The portrait could not be more demeaning. As an unexpected analogue from elsewhere in Fielding's oeuvre, take the lampooning of Samuel Foote in the *Jacobite's Journal*. Fielding hauls "Fut" before his own "Court of Criticism." "The Judgement of the Court," the magistrate tells him, "is, that you *Samuel Fut* be p——ssed upon, with Scorn and Contempt, as a low Buffoon. And I do p——ss upon you accordingly." The Prisoner is removed from the dock, Fielding concludes, "while the P——ss ran plentifully down his Face."[46] Adams is obviously no Samuel Fut, but why douse and daub him in an equally degrading way? And Fielding's description of Adams—along with its opening inexpressibility statement and its almost labored level of detail—is typical of regular prolonged descriptions of the parson in humiliating situations. Judging by the illustrations that Andrew Millar commissioned for the third edition of the novel, these episodes were favorites with early readers and a considerable draw for buyers. Adams appears as a figure of fun in more than half of Hulett's engravings: wigless and bloody at the kitchen at the Dragon Inn; pursued by hounds; tumbled into the tub of water by the roasting squire; tied to a bedpost and lecturing Joseph on courage in affliction; welcoming Lady Booby to his cottage in his half cassock and flannel nightcap (fig. 9).

FIELDING'S PROBLEM WITH PARSONS

Anyone hoping to explain the ambiguities around Parson Adams must clearly venture into the bitterly disputed territory of Fielding's religious views. For all their complexity, most debates on this subject revolve around a single question: To what extent did Fielding abandon his freethinking sympathies and embrace mainstream Anglicanism? No one denies his early involvement in the deist-libertine circle around James Ralph and Thomas Cooke. Nor does any scholar deny his youthful indulgence in wine and women, his indifference to the regular observances of the church, or his boisterous resistance to all forms of authority. Judging by his plays, the young Fielding shared the deists' hostility to revealed religion and their skepticism about miracles, immortality, divine rewards and punishments, and anything else that flew in the face of reason. In their resistance to "priestcraft" and clerical authority over the scriptures, these texts come strikingly close deist critiques.

A conflict rages, however, over Fielding's continued adherence to these heterodoxies. Martin Battestin suggests that the freethinking phase "probably did not last long" (while acknowledging that Fielding remained on friendly terms with Ralph's circle into the 1740s).[47] Fielding clearly discovered, early on, that deism lacked any workable moral system: most people needed more

FIGURE 9. James Hulett, engraving for *Joseph Andrews*, 3rd ed. (London, 1743). Parson Adams is being pursued by hunting hounds, with tatty cassock and wig askew. Courtesy of the Thomas Fisher Rare Book Library, University of Toronto.

than an innate moral sense to act ethically. From the late 1730s, he began to express more and more orthodox views. In a series of *Champion* essays (1739–40), he attacked deism, stridently defended the clergy, and praised the Bible's moral teachings as summed up in "the excellent and divine Sermon on the Mount."[48] By the early 1740s, the death of his father and two children seems to have led him, at least temporarily, to the consolations of religion. In the last years of his life, we find him publicly defending even the most irrational Christian doctrines (thus the extraordinary *Examples of the Interposition of Providence in the Detection and Punishment of Murder* [1752]). At the time of his death, he owned a range of mainstream Anglican texts.[49] On the basis of such evidence, Battestin describes *Joseph Andrews* as a sustained illustration of latitudinarian principles, with Joseph and Adams as the moral touchstones of the book and the history of Mr. Wilson in book 3 as a fictionalized account of Fielding's own shift from freethinking to orthodoxy. In the mistreatment of Parson Adams, he finds the major fictional component of a sustained "program to check the public contempt of the priesthood."[50]

Other scholars have objected, for many years, to Battestin's interpretations. Claude Rawson has repeatedly dissented.[51] In a more recent series of writings, Ronald Paulson argues that Fielding never entirely overcame his early skepticism. Paulson accepts that Fielding early on recognized the ethical problems of deism and the social necessity of invoking heaven and hell, that he turned to religion at moments of personal crisis, and that he increasingly came to appreciate the great latitudinarians—Tillotson, Barrow, Clarke, and Hoadly. He is more careful to insist, however, on the distinction between Fielding's public positions as a barrister, magistrate, and periodical moralist and internal debates that he probably never resolved. By the early 1750s, Fielding was presenting Christianity as the only means of preserving a fragile social fabric from utter chaos. But this did not mean, Paulson insists, that he believed it: "Where pragmatism ends and belief begins is impossible to say."[52] The social necessity of Christianity for the masses was, after all, almost a mainstream Enlightenment position.

The conflict continues and will never be resolved. The textual evidence is contradictory, and one can only hypothesize about what Fielding the man actually believed.[53] In what follows, I offer my own contribution to this ongoing debate by exploring an insistent strand of anticlerical humor in *Joseph Andrews*—a vestige, one assumes, of his early freethinking. Before returning to the text, however, it seems vital to review the literary evidence of these youthful opinions and at least glance at their contexts in mainstream English anticlericalism. For Fielding's plays are full of depraved, absurd, or dictatorial priests: Firebrand, the ferocious priest in *Pasquin* (1736); Murdertext, the canting Presbyterian in *The Author's Farce*; and Puzzletext, the ludicrous Welsh chaplain who is knocked around in *The Grub-Street Opera* (1731). Firebrand plots to depose the reigning Queen of Common Sense and replace her with the "pious" Queen Ignorance, who believes anything a priest tells her. The Queen of Common Sense asks far too many questions, at one point even demanding proof of priestly infallibility. You can't have it, says Firebrand—the document got soaked when Phaeton's chariot plunged into the sea, making it illegible to anyone but a priest. "And do you think I can believe this Tale?" the queen objects. "I order you to believe it," Firebrand snaps, "and you must." True faith meant doubting nothing.[54]

Fielding's stage priests are not mainstream Anglicans. His public position, no doubt, was that he was attacking the misguided or heretical branches of Christianity. Still, everyone knew that anti-Catholic or anti-Puritan satire was a dangerous business, one that easily strayed into more pervasive sorts of skepticism. *Pasquin* offers very little, as even Martin Battestin acknowledges, to balance its portrait of dangerous priestcraft. As usual, said Fielding's contemporaries, he was besmirching the cloth and scoffing at all the mysteries of religion.[55] It must have been hard to think otherwise after plays like *The Old Debauchees* (1732), Fielding's salacious early farce about a scandal in the French church. The case of Father Girard—a Jesuit who used black magic to seduce a young woman in his care—was the talk of London society in the winter of 1731–32. Fielding's adaptation of the story was loose and altogether lighter, with the seducer foiled by a quick-witted heroine named Isabel (one of Fielding's many vehicles for Kitty Clive). Isabel shares the play with the larky Old Laroon, a sort of early Squire Western who hates priests and has the dirty Jesuit (here named Father Martin) dragged through a horse pond and tossed in a blanket. In the guise of an anti-Catholic satire, *The Old Debauchees* makes all the usual Protestant jabs at celibacy, infallibility, confession, and the rest. But there was also far too much generalized anticlericalism.[56]

Fielding was ready with his defense, abusing critics who construed his satire of "*Roguish Jesuits* as an Abuse on Religion and the English Clergy."[57] But the mistake was all too easy to make. Long before we learn anything about Father Martin, we have had scene after scene of Old Laroon's coarse and thoroughly English slurs on the clergy. "Dirty Priests," "greasy Priests," "rascally Priests," the "Regiment of Black-guards," or swarm of "black Locusts": the old man repeats all these standard anticlerical epithets.[58] "[T]here's such a fine consort of groans, you would think yourself at an Opera," he tells Isabel's credulous father about his trip down to purgatory. "Some Spirits are shut up in Ovens, some are chain'd to Spits, some are scatter'd in Frying-pans." "I have taken up a Place for you on a Gridiron," he concludes, with a horse laugh at the old man's terrors.[59] Fielding strays onto especially dangerous ground with his mockery of miracles and the virgin birth, both orthodox Protestant doctrines (at one point, Isabel tells Father Martin about a dream in which she gives birth to the pope).[60] *The Old Debauchees* almost openly suggests that miracles, the afterlife, and immanent deity were the inventions of a power-hungry priesthood. "Superstition, I adore thee," Martin soliloquizes early in the play, "Thou handle to the cheated Layman's Mind, / By which in Fetters Priestcraft leads Mankind."[61]

Yet for all the protests of his enemies, one would be wrong to think Fielding's impieties too different from the general anticlericalism of this age. Clergymen were always figures of prohibition and restraint. Most Britons were forced to listen to them, whether they wanted to or not. For all those who heeded the warnings and craved the consolations of religion, equal numbers found such things at least intermittently intolerable. In any largely Christian society, as Hazlitt argued in his famous essay "On the Clerical Character," a clergyman was always both "positive and disagreeable":

> He is proud with an affectation of humility; bigotted, from a pretended zeal for the truth; greedy, with an ostentation of entire contempt for the things of this world; professing self-denial, and always thinking of self-gratification; censorious, and blind to his own faults; intolerant, unrelenting, impatient of opposition, insolent to those below, and cringing to those above him, with nothing but Christian meekness and brotherly love in his mouth.[62]

Hazlitt characteristically takes his portrait close to caricature, but it surely tells us a lot about the mingled respect and detestation that surrounded any parson in early modern culture. "Lewd whispers, groans of contrition burlesqued, winking and coughing": this response to a sermon from Goldsmith's vicar of Wakefield seems to record familiar impieties.[63] The jestbooks are full of jokes about long, tedious sermons and preachers who put the congregation to sleep (Reverend Drone, Doctor Drowsy, and many more). Righteous moralist that he was, the local vicar cried out for deflating humiliations—nothing was funnier than stealing his wig or finding him in bed with the village whore. Priest-baiting was an old game in English comedy, most brazenly in a cluster of late-Restoration plays that continued to be performed: Dryden's *Spanish Friar* (1681), Crowne's *English Frier* (1690), and Shadwell's *Lancashire Witches* (1681), with its violent pranks against Teague O'Dively, a ludicrous Irish priest.[64] It is equally prominent in comic fiction—from Nashe and Quevédo to Scarron, Smollett, and the imitative comic novels I discuss in the conclusion to this book.

Proverbially desperate and shabby, a poor parson like Adams went about "with his Shoes out at Toes, and his Stockings out at Heels, wandering about in an old Russet Coat, or a tatter'd Gown, for Apprentices to point at and Wags to break Jests on."[65] For the upper-class men who controlled clerical livings, teasing a clergyman with false hopes was a routine form of fun. Rural boredom could always be relieved by inviting the curate for dinner but then sending him home after the first dish. Naturally the hierarchies also elicited more elaborate practical jokes—and naturally no one did them better than a legendary prankster like the Duke of Richmond. Traveling from Portsmouth to London in July 1733, the duke and his friends resolve "to do something handsome upon the Road."[66] A perfect opportunity presents itself when they learn that a carriage will soon be passing on the same road with the duchess and one Doctor Sherwin, canon of Chichester and a tiresome hanger-on to the Goodwood circle. Grave and gullible, Parson Sherwin—"the small Coal man," as the duke calls him in his giddy "confession" of the affair—is the perfect object for some sport. Grossly fat, he came close to that archetype of anticlerical wit: the glutton gobbling up his tithe pig. Having concealed themselves in a ditch, the duke and his friends suddenly surround the coach and draw their pistols. "Dam you," says the duke to Dr. Sherwin, "deliver!" The parson snickers and tries to put on a brave face until the duke fires his gun:

> [S]lap I lett fly my pop, tho not with the intention to kill the poor Dog neither, butt the slugs whistled pretty close by his ears, which putt him in a most confounded fright; "take all" says he, upon which I whypt my hand into his pocket, which I could hardly do for his paunch.[67]

The duchess recognizes her husband and somehow keeps a straight face, and Richmond and his chums eventually make their way to London, where they divide the spoils.

One thinks of prominent fictional analogues for the prank: Captain Mirvan's holdup of Mme Duval or Mr. B's treatment of Parson Williams, the robbing and dunking that so delights Mrs. Jewkes.[68] And the prank delights not just the duke's circle but the entire fashionable world. "Ye Joke I like," wrote Lord Albemarle, "and wish I had seen Sherwin in his fright." Lord Montague wrote from Cowdray. "I should have been vastly pleased to have seen the Doctor's phyz at the time," wrote Tom Hill, the duke's former tutor. "'*Os il-*

lud' [that face of his], at all times ridiculous, must have been ten times more so. I have the idea of it before me, but to be sure far inferior to the reality." By the following week, the robbery was the "talk of the town." "One of ye dayly papers published it in the morning, and the evening post as I am told has it tonight. I have been ask'd tonight in the Park fifty questions about it." To complete the joke, Sherwin never seems to have suspected the truth and went about boasting of his bravery—"tho he was in mortal terror the whole time." "Every mortal now in England butt the Doctor know the joke," wrote the duke. "There is no describing it half so ridiculous as it was. Scarron himself could not do it, and his lyes are beyond Sir John Falstaff's."[69]

Richmond's literary comparisons—so familiar and so effortlessly recalled— point to established connections between behaviors and literary models and invite us to contextualize Fielding's ambivalence about good Parson Adams. Sure enough, Adams is surrounded by all the conventional anticlerical jokes. When the lame dancing master tries to get Adams to take the woman's part in a dance, quipping that "his Cassock would serve as Petticoats," he repeats a standard slur (247). Fielding was sufficiently fond of it to repeat it in *Amelia*, where the blustering Colonel Bath spares Dr. Harrison a beating only because he is wearing a dress.[70] The final night scene in *Joseph Andrews*—in which Adams is first caught in bed with Mrs. Slipslop and then wakes to find himself in bed with Fanny without so much as "a rag of Clothes on"—is a fonder version of a standard anticlerical prank (331). Fielding would create a much blunter version by putting Square behind the curtain in Molly Seagrim's attic.

One would expect Fielding to be more careful, however, with the speech of his good clergyman. Why so much parsonical nonsense, all the pedantry and pomposity he puts into Adams's mouth? "When they grow lazy, and are inclined to Nonsense," Jeremy Collier had complained, playwrights invari- ably "get a Clergy-man to speak it."[71] And Fielding himself had already done too much of this, with Firebrand, Father Martin, Murdertext, Puzzletext, and another nameless Welsh parson in *The Tragedy of Tragedies* (1731), not to mention Tickletext and Parson Williams in *Shamela*.[72] The curious thing is that Adams continues to speak so much of the same nonsense. "What would it avail me, to tarry in the Great City," he asks Joseph on discovering that he has forgotten his sermons, "unless I had my Discourses with me, which are, *ut ita dicam*, the sole Cause, the *Aitia monotate* of my Peregrination?" He concludes, Fielding tells us, with "a Verse out of *Theocritus*, which signifies no more than, *that sometimes it rains and sometimes the Sun shines*" (93). His speech is peppered with pompous Latinisms and classical allusions. "*Nihil habeo cum Porcis*," he announces from his prone position in the filth of Trulliber's pigsty. "*Heus tu, Traveller, heus tu!*" he bellows in the dark to the party of sheep rustlers (163, 140). All this is dangerously close to Father Martin's Latinate mumbo jumbo or to Parson Williams ("O! What a brave Thing it is to be a Schollard and to be able to talk Latin," Shamela enthuses to her mother).[73] Later we meet Partridge, with his "Scraps of Latin" and bungled quotations from Lily's *Grammar* ("You have hit the Nail *ad unguem*").[74]

Adams's longer speeches are shot through with these and all the other standard absurdities. Tedious preachers are always very pleased with themselves, and so it is with Adams. "I would not be vain," he tells Joseph in the midst of his oration on public schools, "but I esteem myself to be second to none, *nulli secundum*" (231). His sermon on the impiety of grief is elaborately divided into subjects and full of logic-chopping distinctions (265). Joseph cannot get married until Adams has completed his sermon on the "very heinous Sin" of lust, all too obvious in its scholastic plodding:

> "*Joseph*," says he, "I wish this Haste doth not arise rather from your Impatience than your Fear: but as it certainly springs from one of these Causes, I will examine both. Of each of these therefore in their Turn; and first, for the first of these, namely, Impatience. Now, Child, I must inform you. . . ." (307)

All this, we must remember, is addressed to a semiliterate footman (clergymen wasted their time, Goldsmith once complained, trying "to address the reason of those who have never reasoned in their lives").[75] Most exaggerated of all is Adams's interminable ramble about classical literature at the Wilson household, ending with "a hundred Greek verses" delivered "with such a Voice, Emphasis, and Action, that he almost frighten'd the Women" (199). Fielding's readers would have recognized the Cervantic prototype behind this speech: Don Quixote's long ramble about his knightly mission that so bewilders the sober gentleman of La Mancha.

In structure and style, at least, Adams's speeches could hardly be further from plain latitudinarian preaching. South, Barrow, and Tillotson all eschewed hard words, rhetorical embellishments, and elaborate syntax. Abstruse reasoning and scholastic divisions just made a sermon sound like a lease or a legal contract, South insisted. Affectations of learning, gratuitous quotations, and constant "*Deus dixit*" or "*Deus benedixit*" had no place in a sermon (the only person who needs Latin, says Mrs. Slipslop in a local jab at these habits, is a clergyman, who "can't preach without it" [26]).[76] At times, indeed, Adams's speeches come closer to travesties of contemporary preaching. Although we have almost lost sight of these texts, mock sermons and parodic homilies routinely appear in early modern comic literature, and actual performances remained popular at fairgrounds and variety shows. They were also a favorite improvisational trick for upper-class wits: Sterne's spoof treatise on sermon writing provides a fascinating glimpse of this practice.[77] Lord Sandwich—the appalling Jemmy Twitcher—was said to have held burlesque services in his village church, once preaching a sermon to a congregation of cats. Mock sermons exaggerate the most detested features of contemporary preaching—all the mumblings, digressions, sudden crescendos, and impassioned pleading with sinners—and reach ludicrous conclusions. Here, for example, is a mathematical argument for sexual continence: "[L]et youth be represented by the right line a, b, and discretion by another right line c, d . . . and let the point of intersection, b, represent perdition. . . ."[78]

Fielding's oeuvre is full of ludicrous parsonspeak—far more than can be mentioned here. *Joseph Andrews* itself puts an extended mock sermon, this time developing a string of rhetorical questions, into the mouth of the Romish priest (197–98). *Jonathan Wild* devotes an entire chapter to absurd speeches from the Newgate ordinary (who is further humiliated by a urinary infection). Murderers should be grateful, the ordinary tells Wild, that their crime gave them such a fine opportunity to be hanged. This argument has no effect, but neither does his hellfire warning: "Where then will be your Tauntings and your Vauntings, your Boastings and your Braggings?"[79] Adams's essential goodness separates him from the ludicrous ordinary and the wicked Catholic, but he shares far too many of their stylistic habits. He quibbles over alleged mistranslations. It wasn't a camel that couldn't pass through the eye of the needle, he tells the Romish priest, but "a Cable Rope"—*kamilon*, not *kamelon* (253). Like the ordinary, he distorts the meaning of biblical texts by leaving out the inconvenient "latter Part" of a verse, enabling him to warn Joseph against all forms of desire, whereas the Bible clearly makes room for conjugal sex. A close comparison between Adams's speech and that of Fielding's corrupt clergyman reveals numerous direct repetitions—all bits of Fielding's ready-made shorthand for clerical discourse.

Every time Adams offers to speak, one can almost hear a collective groan from the dramatis personae. No one can tolerate a sermon from him, just as no one can tolerate one of Don Quixote's rambles on the codes of chivalry. It is not just Barnabas and the bookseller who object when Adams offers them "two or three Discourses" as a specimen of his collection (80). Wilson and Joseph narrowly escape his sermon against vanity—his "Masterpiece," he proudly informs them (mercifully, he cannot find it in his pockets [214]). As Adams begins his Euclidian demonstration of the folly of riches, everyone leaves the room except for the Romish priest (who is hoping for a handout), and the narrator reassures readers that he won't bore us with the details (253–54). It is just as well, then, that every sermon Adams does manage to begin is cut short in some way. "If you are a good Lad," he tells Joseph shortly before his wedding, "I shall give you a Sermon *gratis*, wherein I shall demonstrate how little Regard ought to be had to the Flesh on such Occasions" (307). This was the last thing any young man wanted to hear at such a moment, and Fielding duly puts an end to the speech after only one page (the same joke appears several times in *The Old Debauchees*).[80] The interrupted sermon was another ancient topos of anticlerical humor. Coughing fits, missing pages, memory lapses, or anything else to shut the man up. At the very gravest point of one lecture, Smollett's Mr. Jolter loses all control of his bowels for "a full quarter of an hour."[81]

If he is not interrupted, every word Adams utters is comically undercut in other ways: by the verbal and physical tics or prominent descriptions of his ludicrous attire. The old flannel nightcap functions throughout as a sort of improvised fool's cap, as it does in so much early modern comic literature.[82] As if we didn't get the point, Fielding has Adams give his heaviest speeches from explicitly demeaning positions—tied to a bedpost, covered in pig dung, or gravely standing in front of his "throne," preparing to play the part of Socrates. Now, none of this in itself implies skepticism: burlesque coexisted with belief in this culture, just as the church somehow tolerated mock liturgies and baptisms of piglets. Deflating dogma and book learning is a major theme of *Joseph Andrews* as a whole: every reader remembers how quickly Adams forgets his own advice about submitting to Providence once he hears that his son Dicky may have drowned. Even so, it is striking to see just how emphatically Fielding signals his distance from the doctrinal content of Adams's speeches. Fielding himself advocates orthodox Christian consolations in his contemporaneous essay "Of the Remedy of Affliction for the Loss of Our Friends," but he also makes it clear that talk about God's will being done was intolerable during the initial shocks of grief.[83] By his own explicit standards, then, Adams's advice to Joseph is shockingly inappropriate. "No Accident happens without the Divine Permission," he tells him as Fanny is about to be raped by the roasting squire. A good Christian must "peaceably and quietly submit to all the Dispensations of Providence" (265–66). As if to exaggerate the inadequacy of his consolations, Adams digresses at length on Fanny's plight:

It is true you have lost the prettiest, kindest, loveliest, sweetest young Woman: One with whom you might have expected to have lived in Happiness, Virtue, and Innocence. By whom you might have promised yourself many little Darlings, who would have been the Delight of your Youth, and the Comfort of your Age. You have not only lost her, but have reason to fear the utmost Violence which Lust and Power can inflict upon her.

"O you have not spoken one Word of Comfort to me yet" is Joseph's apt response to this bizarrely distended reflection (266). Odder still, Adams's consolations for the loss of Fanny are almost identical to the perfunctory orthodoxies put into the mouth of Mr. Barnabas, the punch-drinking vicar in book 1 (bk. 1, chap. 13; bk. 3, chap. 11). Unsurprisingly, then, the subject falters as Adams cites a string of classical authorities to justify his point. For some reason, Joseph then delivers a garbled soliloquy from *Macbeth*, and Adams makes one of his routine denunciations of the theater (267).

Equally striking, considering the moderate Anglicanism that Fielding was publicly adopting at this point, are Adams's periodic warnings of the torments of hell. "And dost not thou then tremble at the Thought of eternal Punishment?" he bellows at one jovial innkeeper. "As for that," replies the man, "I never once thought about it: but what signifies talking about matters so far off? The Mug is out, shall I draw you another?" As usual, the arrival of a stagecoach puts an end to the discussion (100). This and other fire-and-brimstone moments emphatically separate Adams from the great latitudinarian preachers. The innkeeper's reaction seems to reflect not just Fielding's habitual anticlerical reflex but a general reluctance to dwell on heavy matters when life was to be lived—if not an ingrained skepticism about the existence of heaven and hell.

Adams just has too many traits that Fielding found objectionable about the clergy. For all his virtues, he is a self-righteous authoritarian—the sort of cleric that even a reformed deist could barely tolerate. "Boy," he scolds Joseph, "it doth not become green Heads to advise grey Hairs." "Now, Child, I must inform you . . ." (310, 307). Something of the same pomposity would reappear in Allworthy's lectures; it returns even more clearly in Dr. Harrison, the insufferable castigator in *Amelia*. Still worse, Adams is a consistent railer against merriment in all its forms. He can be a prohibitive, almost Lenten figure—one of the *agélastes* or enemies of laughter that Rabelais so memorably abuses in book 4 of *Pantagruel*. (In this context, it is tempting to see in the mistreatment of Adams a parallel to Rabelais's punishment of moralizing bores like Tappecoue or Lord Basché.)[84] The hypocritical doctor knows exactly how to win

Adams over when he slyly moralizes on those characteristic Puritan topics, "Levity of Conversation; and what is usually called Mirth" (249). Adams has nothing but praise for a magistrate "who had exerted himself very singularly in the Preservation of the Morality of his Neighbours, insomuch, that he had neither Ale-house, nor lewd women in the Parish where he lived" (77).

Worst of all, Adams comes strikingly close to the Puritan antitheatricalists with whom Fielding had repeatedly fought in his years as a dramatist.[85] Plays are "nothing but Heathenism," he insists, berating Joseph for his London theatergoing. "I never heard of any Plays fit for a Christian to read, but *Cato* and the *Conscious Lovers*"—and these only because they contained passages "almost solemn enough for a sermon" (267). This all sounds far too close to Jeremy Collier, or Jonson's Zeal-of-the-Land Busy, or Fielding's own Murdertext, the red-faced Presbyterian who rails against puppet shows in *The Author's Farce*:

> Verily I smell a great deal of A——bomination and Prophaness—a Smell of Brimstone offendeth my Nostrils, a Puppet-Show is the Devil's-House, and I will burn it.[86]

On this matter, at least, Adams is only slightly less strident—horror of horrors—than Wesley and Whitefield, who were then riding around England fulminating against plays and other diversions. Adams repeats not just the sentiments but the precise idiom of early modern antitheatricality and of Fielding's enemies at the *Grub-Street Journal*.

Indeed, by the standards that Fielding himself set forth in his *Champion* essays, Adams is far from an ideal clergyman. Consider the early series of questions he puts to Joseph: "[H]ow many Books there were in the New Testament? which were they? how many Chapters they contained? and such like" (23). This is standard Sunday school stuff, unimaginative rote learning and nothing to do with the Bible's moral teachings. Stranger still, Adams's superstitions are repeatedly emphasized. He twice declares his belief in ghosts and apparitions (192–96). "Sure the Devil must have taken it from me," he insists on discovering the loss of his half guinea (254). The confusions of the night at Booby Hall could have resulted only from witchcraft. The suggestion that Mrs. Slipslop might be a witch makes its own wink at the reader, but the parson's superstition is prominently repeated. Only sorcery, he persists, could have put him in bed with Fanny: "He is an infidel who doth not believe in Witchcraft. They as surely exist now as in the Days of *Saul*. My clothes are bewitched away too, and Fanny's brought into their place" (332–34).

The other notably superstitious figure in Fielding's oeuvre is Partridge, who repeatedly talks of ghosts and black magic and trembles in terror at a performance of *Hamlet*. The pious reading that Adams applauds in the young Joseph includes not just the Bible and *The Whole Duty of Man* but all the fanciful miracles from Baker's *Chronicle of the Kings of England* (1643, etc.)— obvious rubbish about the devil carrying away the chancel in the middle of a sermon or *"how a Field of Corn ran away down a Hill with all the Trees upon it"* (24). An enormous folio of one thousand pages, Baker's *Chronicle* was a by-word for foolish superstition in this culture. Fielding would be openly scornful when he discussed the book in the *Covent-Garden Journal*. (A still clearer illustration of contemporary opinions appears in Coventry's *Pompey the Little*, where the dog hero is thrown out by a pious spinster after accidentally shitting on her copy of Baker.)[87] Fielding the former deist was obviously scoffing at such credulities, but by the mid-eighteenth century they had become risible to almost anyone who could pay 6s. for the two volumes of *Joseph Andrews*.

So many of these topics come together, irresistibly, in the roasting squire's final prank against Adams. Infantile as it seems to us, the elaborately ritualized "Ambassador" trick, in which Adams agrees to play the part of Socrates and seat himself on the booby-trapped "throne," was familiar at every level of eighteenth-century society. It figured in apprentices' initiation rituals, and was among sailors a favorite way of tricking gullible landlubbers. As such, it is one of the book's more prominent examples of inappropriate practical humor. Fielding's version deliberately refers to one of the most famous of all practical jokes, Montesquieu's dunking by John, Duke of Montagu (discussed in chapter 3 above).[88] The episode also consolidates some deep-seated conventions in the representation of folly or ignorance. In the long tradition of antischolastic humor, as in Augustan satire, personifications of nonsense were often seated on some sort of throne, from which they would make their idiotic speech. In the crudest instances, they speak from a chamber pot or *chaise-percée* (one of Pope's pamphlets pictures Edmund Curll, silly nightcap on his head, delivering his last speech from a closestool; Smollett develops the same situation toward the end of *Humphry Clinker*).[89] By the early 1730s, the dramatic situation of a levee at which an enthroned personification of ignorance held court was common.[90] Fielding himself had enthroned the Goddess of Nonsense in *The Author's Farce* and Queen Ignorance in *Pasquin* (this latter figure was played by a man, suggesting further elusive connections with Adams and his clerical "petticoats"). Pope may have been influenced by these plays when he enthroned Dullness in book 4 of the *New Dunciad* (1742).[91]

The tumble and dunking also had their associations, from folk practices like the ducking of scolds and dishonest shopkeepers, to fairground amusements of enduring appeal. Restoration and eighteenth-century farce routinely seated idiot orators on a collapsing throne or had them stand on a trapdoor that would open beneath them. Shadwell's *The Virtuoso* (1676) introduces a foolish meddler named Sir Formal Trifle. "I must confess, I have some felicity in speaking," he boasts (like Adams and every other conceited orator) before beginning a florid speech on the subject of a mouse in a trap. "Now I am inspir'd with Eloquence," Sir Formal begins:

> Hem! hem! Being one day, most noble Auditors, musing in my Study upon the too fleeting condition of poor humane-kind, I observed, not far from the Scene of my Meditation, an excellent Machine, call'd a Mouse-trap. . . .

More than twenty lines follow in the same vein before his antic auditors open the trapdoor and put an end to his fustian. This incident is better known through Dryden's allusion at the end of *MacFlecknoe*, where the last speech of Flecknoe is curtailed by the same trick.[92] No contemporary reader could miss the allusions as Adams, by now very drunk on adulterated ale, gravely accepts the role of Socrates (the game, he muses, "was indeed a Diversion worthy the Relaxation of so great a Man"), delivers a long sermon "to the great Entertainment of all present," and finally tumbles "over Head and Ears" in the water (250–51).

Obviously thinking of episodes like this, Fielding's post facto preface recognizes that his model clergyman has gone badly wrong. After all the musings on literary history and uneasy distinctions between different sorts of laughter, the final paragraph suddenly acknowledges the problem. Adams is "the most glaring" character in the whole book and is dragged through all manner of "low Adventures." Gentlemen of the cloth could easily be offended: Fielding can only state his hope that the "Goodness of his Heart will recommend him to the Good-natur'd." This rather desperate tautology shows him struggling to convince himself. As in all the madcap farces that preceded it, *Joseph Andrews* has no trouble demonstrating what a clergyman should not be: Adams is surrounded by six depraved, bigoted, or incompetent priests. But a positive portrait was a much greater challenge. It was one thing to describe an ideal clergyman in abstract terms (charity, humility, good shepherd caring for his flock) but quite another to flesh out the ideal in fiction. Throughout *Joseph Andrews*, the strain of trying to create a good clergyman seems to unleash all the old subversive mischief.

Yet over time, of course, Parson Adams did become a proverbial figure, almost a byword for good-natured eccentricity. He is still one of the few eighteenth-century characters to step out of their book and bear comparison with Don Quixote or Falstaff. As lovable as Parson Adams, one said; "he was a perfect *Parson Adams*," Coleridge once wrote of his father.[93] That this affection developed in spite of Fielding's internal confusions tells us much about how and why we love certain literary characters (and indeed certain types of people). The obvious explanation is that Adams's spontaneous goodness is so powerfully depicted. Fielding always knew what he meant by "Good Nature"—"that benevolent and amiable Temper of Mind which disposes us to feel the Misfortunes, and enjoy the Happiness of others"—and Adams is by far his most sustained illustration of this virtue.[94] The less palatable explanation is that Fielding humiliates and ridicules his own creation and invites us to do the same. Early nineteenth-century admirers may have understood this love-and-laughter effect more clearly than we. Mrs. Barbauld praised Fielding's skill at "making us laugh so heartily at a character and yet keeping it above contempt." Hazlitt was somewhat more searching: alongside his lovable qualities, Adams's absentmindedness gave readers a powerful ego blast, "gratifying [their] sense of superior sagacity."[95] A franker analysis would admit that this is a belittling sort of affection—a strange combination of fondness and schadenfreude, the fondness somehow bolstered by the opportunity to laugh so hard, which in turn excused itself by the protest that one also found him so very lovable.

CHAPTER FIVE

Rape Jokes and the Law

The scale and sheer genius of Richardson's *Clarissa* has ensured that debates about the feminization of eighteenth-century British culture pay special attention to sexual violence. And for all their sadoeroticism, sentimental rape plots do announce a new willingness to believe and admire "female" emotions, at least an initial assault on old misogynistic ideas about women as carnal, deceitful, and irrational beings. In fiction, as in the she-tragedies of the age, the tears of rape victims now worked as positive signs of moral superiority. All this, as we know, was accompanied by Enlightenment assertions about the moral and intellectual equality of women and campaigns for the reformation of male manners. Legal concepts were gradually changing from medieval definitions of rape as a property crime against male relatives to something more like our modern definitions. In doctrine, if not so often in practice, women were gradually being recognized as legal subjects with a right to control their own bodies.

These progressive tendencies have been so intensively studied that it has been easy to lose sight of the culture's less sympathetic attitudes toward sexual violence. We know about the extremer misogynist traditions and the brutal pornography of the age, and certainly about the dismal conviction rates in rape trials. But between sympathy at one extreme and horrific mistrust at the other lie all sorts of less definable attitudes—a murky continuum of ambivalence and inconsistency that will always be more difficult to understand. By looking at everyday comic perspectives on rape, I hope to fill in some of this obscure middle ground. I have ranged widely in the literary archive, but have also collected the scattered evidence of catchphrases, puns, offhand comments, fleeting remarks in letters, and the wry slant of newspaper reports on rape. Deeply offensive as it is, this material strikes a very different tone from the virulent satires explored by Felicity Nussbaum and others. It has little in common with the lubricious pornography of the age (which comes closer, in fact, to sentimental representations of rape). At once flippant and opaque, these unsettling comic representations appear in expensive and avowedly literary texts, in ostensibly sentimental genres as well as recognizably comic ones, and in texts by women as well as men.

A large proportion of this humor focuses on legal scenarios—on the doctrines and procedures that defined male behaviors as either criminal or benign. What comic sources might tell us about everyday judicial practice and, in turn, how legal history can help us make sense of literary sources, are primary concerns throughout this chapter. The statutes and learned commentaries on sexual violence are easy to find. Official documents such as capital trial proceedings have now been exhaustively studied. But the day-to-day operations of local summary justice—by far the most routine venue for rape hearings—have been harder to recover. The records are spotty at best, and here comic genres seem to offer precious evidence of a lost world of local justice: a world of threats, grievances, negotiation, and redress. By the end of this chapter, I am able to return with new perspectives to more official rape trial records.

Needless to say, this research raised many troubling questions, none of them more persistent than the problem of tone. Beyond the overt comic genres—jestbooks, bawdy verses, bedroom farces, comic fiction—how could one be sure that particular treatments of sexual violence were supposed to be funny? Moving from the literary archive to supposedly nonfictional genres, I began to notice a disturbing jokiness. Sometimes this was blatant, as with so many sardonic newspaper reports. More often it was a matter of local stylistic hints: cryptic asides, sly clusters of adjectives, everyday words taking on contrary meanings. Particularly troubling in this regard were all the unsuccessful rape trials reported in the Old Bailey Sessions Papers. Why the long passages of gratuitous dialogue? Occasionally even the plaintiff's stammering or confusion was reproduced. The original versions of these records (as opposed to the transcriptions now available online) often set such details in italic, effectively transforming them into punch lines.

Stronger confirmation came late in the project, with the discovery of a long-lost anthology of comic trials. *Humours of the Old Bailey* (ca. 1772) was projected as a multivolume "Collection of all the merry and diverting Trials for above these thirty Years." Only one volume has so far reappeared, covering the years 1720–27. But this one volume tells us an awful lot. The title

THE

HUMOURS

OF THE

O L D   B A I L E Y;

JUSTICE Shaking her SIDES:

Being a Collection of all the merry and diverting TRIALS
for above thefe thirty Years; particularly for Rapes and
private Stealing: Such as have made even the Judges
on the Bench forget their wonted Gravity; and caufed
Scenes of Mirth very unufual in Courts of Juftice.

Warm from the Heart the lufcious Tales arife,
And ftamp their Influence on the Hearers Eyes:
Warm from the Heart they reach the Rev'rend Bench,
While AGE remembers that YOUTH lov'd a Wench!

L O N D O N:

Sold by P. WICKS, No. 6, Water-Lane, Fleet-Street; and all
Bookfellers in Town and Country.

(Price ONE SHILLING.)

FIGURE 10. Title page from *The Humours of the Old Bailey; or, Justice Shaking her Sides*
(London, ca. 1772), the unique surviving copy of a widely circulated anthology (not yet in
ESTC). Along with prostitutes' thefts from their customers ("private stealing"), rape trials are
here singled out as potentially comic events. The book reprints verbatim from the Old Bailey
Sessions Papers, with no alterations being required to point up their humor. With their repeated
references to guffawing judges, the long subtitle and verses offer a chilling insight into the courtroom atmosphere on these occasions. Courtesy of Guildhall Library, London (A 8.4 no. 26).

page (fig. 10) singles out rape trials, along with prostitutes' thefts from their customers, as potentially comic events. And sure enough, every one of the acquittals I had discussed for these years is here, reprinted verbatim from the Sessions Papers. No changes were required to turn an official court record into a winter evening's amusement. In retrospect, such discoveries seem to affirm the promise of a careful balancing of official and literary sources, fraught with difficulties as this combination must be.

In doing all this, I am building on a phenomenally committed body of scholarship—from polemical studies like Susan Brownmiller's *Against Our Will* (1975) to historically focused work by Anna Clark, Randolph Trumbach, Antony Simpson, Garthine Walker, and many others. To look at comic representations is not to forget the untold miseries of thousands of women.[1] Taken as a whole, indeed, these disturbingly understated treatments of rape read like one determined attempt to minimize or obscure those sufferings, to assert the triviality or at least the remediability of sexual violence. Rape humor effaces consequences, persistently nudging situations across the divide between tragic and comic. But it does so only because there are ambiguities and contested meanings to exploit. These ambiguities are crucial to a fuller picture of early modern sexual practices—the mutating, deeply inconsistent complex of sympathies and prejudices about the opposite sex.

LAUGHTER AND DISBELIEF

Here is the eighteenth century's most common rape joke (and one of the most common of all eighteenth-century jokes):

A Woman prosecuted a Gentleman for Rape; upon Trial the Judge ask'd her, if she made any Resistance? *I cry'd out*, an't please your Lordship, said the Woman. *Ay*, said one of the Witnesses, *but that was nine Months after*.[2]

Compressed as it is, the joke takes us strikingly close to the circumstances of most eighteenth-century rape trials: to the situation of a plaintiff pleading her fruitless case before a sneering crowd and an incredulous male jury. The punch line reflects a crucial moment in every trial, and the moment at which most cases collapsed: a successful plaintiff had to prove that she had vigorously and vocally resisted her attacker. At this moment, the cross-examination was at its cruelest. The room was above the street—why hadn't anybody heard her scream? Wouldn't her clothes be torn if she'd really struggled? Did she kick him? Did she knee him in the groin? How could he hold her down, lift her petticoat, and unbutton his breeches at the same time? Did he have three hands? In this joke, the plaintiff's pregnancy implies either that she had slept with other men and could therefore not be "ruined," or that she had agreed in the end, according to a stubborn folk belief that women conceived only if they took pleasure in the sex act.[3]

An interrogation, whether in a legal context or some less official one, is the commonest form of rape joke. The woman accidentally betrays her consent. "How did he get into the house?" asks the defense; "I opened the door for him." Did he offer any violence? Yes, she replies: "[H]e bound my Hands, and would have bound my Legs, but I kept them far enough asunder."[4] In perhaps the most common variant of this joke, the woman is asked why she hadn't cried out and offers some absurd answer. She had thought about it but worried that "it would make me look so very foolish." Why didn't you scream while my husband was raping you? a gentlewoman asks her maid. "Indeed Madam, I made no Noise for Fear of waking you." This variant was famously exemplified by Rabelais's story of soeur Fessue ("sister *Fatbum*," as Urquhart and Motteux translate it). Grossly pregnant under her habit, Fatbum claims to have been raped by frère Royddimet ("Friar *Stifly-stand-to't*"). She didn't call for help, she tells the furious abbess, for "the Rape was committed in the *Dorter*, where she durst not cry, because it was a place of sempiternal Silence."[5] In many trial jokes, both defendant and plaintiff are clueless. How long have you been deaf? a judge asks the defendant. Ever since the rape, he replies—she screamed so loud I lost my hearing. "Which the Girl hearing, immediately told the Court it was false, for she made no Noise at all."[6]

Alternatively, the joke focuses on a plaintiff of evidently bad character—a prostitute or obviously unchaste young woman. Eighteenth-century jurists disagreed about whether such a woman could actually be raped. Hale and Blackstone insisted that even a "common strumpet" was entitled to legal protection. But in practice the mere suggestion of previous sexual license was enough to end the case; a large proportion of cases revolved precisely around the issue of virginity. Even Blackstone's wording suggests that the case could stand only when the "strumpet" had unequivocally renounced her "unlawful course of life" before the attack.[7] William Kenrick's *Fun* (1752) characteristically presents the scenario in its most exaggerated form. A syphilitic whore named Peg Brindle has charged Riot, a young blood, with rape:

JUSTICE: Well, Mistress, who are you? What have you to say?
MRS. BRINDLE: My name is *Brindle*, if it please your Worship,—this young
    Gentleman here is a vile Fellow, and last Night broke into my Bed-chamber

and ravish'd me, *without giving me any Thing for it*;—which your Worship knows is a cruel Thing.

"I beg your Worship," she goes on, to "make out a *Mittimus* and send him to *Newgate*, and have him scragg'd." The justice turns sternly to the accused: "Do you know, Sir, the Consequence of a Rape?"

RIOT: The Consequence of a Rape, old Boy!—a Bastard, a Bastard, or two at most—but there's no Danger with *Peg* there; she'll breed nothing but the Consumption of Mercury.

Unsurprisingly the case is dismissed, and Mrs. Brindle herself risks imprisonment for bringing a false charge.[8] If not a whore, the plaintiff might be some hideously ugly or decrepit old woman. Usually she has beguiled a young man into her bed at night, when he is drunk and can't tell the difference. With the morning light he flees in horror, and the old dame prosecutes him out of wounded pride.

Other accusations are physically implausible to the point of absurdity. The defendant is a wheezy old man who can only hobble to the stand. A giantess hauls a dwarf into court: "A strammelling two-handed Harlot, Grenadier-height, and limb'd like a Bacon-fac'd Dutchman, accus'd a little diminutive Taylor once upon a Rape." Result: forty lashes for bringing a false prosecution. This scenario may be lifted from part 2 of *Don Quixote*, where Sancho Panza's detection of a false rape charge is one instance of his wise administration of his island.[9] It is also there in folk traditions. The English trickster Tom Tram hires himself to a justice and takes the master's place in his absence. A "tall and lusty" woman arrives with a complaint against a "little man" whom she accuses of rape. "Alas! Sir, altho' he is little, he is very strong." Tom easily discerns the truth: the woman was a prostitute who had demanded more than the agreed-on price and dragged her customer before the justice out of vengeance. Verdict? "Here, Mr. Constable, give her a hundred lashes at the town whipping post. Which was done, and Tom was applauded for his just proceedings."[10]

To scoff about a rape accusation was to put vocal and resistant women back in their place, to confirm old ideas that women never told the truth, especially when it came to sex. It is tempting to read these jokes as reactions against increasing tendencies to believe and sympathize with women. One important context here is the Charteris case of 1730. Convicted of raping a maidservant in his own house, the disgusting "Colonel" Francis Charteris (ca. 1665–1732) was denounced at every level of society. He became a recurring personification of vice in Scriblerian satire and looms large behind the villain-rapists of sentimental fiction. Although Charteris was swiftly pardoned by the Walpole administration, the conviction and tremendous media event that surrounded it have often seemed like signs of newer standards. Certainly in its age it created enduring perceptions that the English law might punish privileged men for crimes against their social inferiors (thus one shocking aside in Casanova's letters from London: he'd better not actually rape anyone until he returns to the Continent).[11] In these contexts, jokes about rape trials seem to reflect a backlash against the possibility that the law might hang a man on nothing more than a woman's word. An initial look at the evolution of these jokes might confirm the hypothesis: seventeenth-century jestbooks repeat all the ancient jokes about no meaning yes, but fewer about the contested definition of *rape*. Courtroom jokes do become more common over the course of the eighteenth century. The earliest print form of the "nine months later" joke dates from the late 1730s; taken up by *Joe Miller*, it then reappeared in almost every jestbook for the next hundred years.[12] We now know that the fears were misplaced. The Charteris conviction was anomalous in every way, a result less of his monstrous sex crimes than of his dubious political allegiances and a long history of financial swindles that created too many enemies.[13] Nonetheless, the perception existed, and many rape jokes were working against it.

But at least as many false accusation jokes seem hardly to register contemporary concerns. A false rape accusation was an age-old way of humiliating respectable citizens—parsons, schoolmasters, parish clerks, and the like. One finds definite traces of this in Mrs. Slipslop's accusations against Parson Adams, confirmed by Lady Booby's tirade. Adams was "the wickedest of all Men," she declares, furious at him for "chusing her House for the Scene of his Debaucheries, and her own Woman for the Object of his Bestiality." The scene is completed when Adams, self-conscious about his nakedness, gets into bed with Slipslop.[14] An alternative: the false accusation joke combined with the incapable defendant trope. Gay's *The Mohocks* offers two versions of this scenario in quick succession. First, a fussy beau named Gentle is accused of taking a cinder wench into an alley and slitting her nose when she refuses to yield. Soon afterward, a dim-witted watchman called Peter Cloudy is hauled before a judge for raping two women, a pair of prostitutes named Peg Firebrand and Jenny Cracker. "He gagg'd me, and please your Worships," Miss Firebrand tells the court, "then drew his Sword, and threaten'd to kill me, if I did not—." "The Fellow has a confounded Ravishing Look," announces the judge while poor Cloudy quivers in the dock. "Heav'n preserve our Wives and Daughters—away, away, they are dangerous Persons—commit them."[15] In both cases, the trick is enacted by male practical jokers who have enlisted women.

As usual, Smollett pursues the comic implications of these situations further than anyone. One extended night scene early in *Roderick Random* brings together an old miser named Rapine with a pregnant London prostitute who accuses him of rape. "Rape! murder! rape!" screams the woman. "Help! for heaven's sake help!—I shall be ravished—ruined! help!" The entire household enters the room to find her holding the "ancient Tarquin" down on the bed by his ears. Absurd as the charge is, Rapine recognizes his danger and agrees to "make it up" with £5.[16] Such "trickster plaintiff" jokes all too readily adapt themselves to multiple comic scenarios. In this example, the elemental humiliation of a respectable man is combined with the equally universal situation of a miser mumped of his gold. Along the way, it also glances at contemporary suspicions of rape charges as modes of extortion.[17]

There are myriad other possibilities. Often the woman is caught in flagrante delicto and cries out to preserve her reputation. This was an ancient and almost automatic countercharge against any rape plaintiff, one that occurs in darker contexts like the Lucretia story as well as the comic versions I discuss in this chapter. Fielding returns to the joke again and again. A prominent scene in *Tom Jones* has Mrs. Waters crying out to deal with the hero's presence in her room. In *Joseph Andrews*, Mrs. Slipslop is more proactive, shrieking out like a beleaguered maiden in the hope of restoring her reputation with Lady Booby.[18] One cannot overstate the frequency and variability of this set piece. Consider one atrocious example from the *Grub-Street Journal* of 13 July 1732, part of the journal's brief fad for reporting "Irish News" in deliberately bad verse. A young man attacks a sixty-year-old in the fields outside Dublin:

> She cast her eyes round, and could see no assistance;
> So wisely laid still and made little resistance.
> At last on the castle she looking upright,
> Spy'd some Gentlemen laughing at the comical sight:
> Then hideously scream'd out, *A rape, A rape, A rape!*
> The fellow run for his life, and made his escape.[19]

As usual, the old woman screams out only when someone is watching, whether to get money out of him or to protest her virtue, or both at once.

The examples multiply and only get more confusing. One of D'Urfey's quick-witted heroines accuses an innocent man of rape in order to prevent the discovery of her lover, who remains under a table throughout. Emilia's husband, Bubble, is heard beating on the door:

EMILIA: Now help me, Wit, or I am lost. (*She goes and puts the key into* [Ranger's] *coat-pocket, and then lays hold of him, and cries out.*) Help, help there, for Heav'ns sake. I am undone, ruin'd forever. A rape, a rape!—Help, help!

RANGER: Hell and the Devil, what does she mean?

EMILIA: Ah, cruel man, cannot these tears prevail? Will nothing stop barbarity? What have I done that could deserve this usage? O most unfortunate of women.

RANGER: Dam her, I shall be finely catcht if this hold; I must get away.— (*Struggles; she holds him.*)

EMILIA: A rape, a rape! Help there, for Heaven's sake, help—

Emilia eventually drops the charge, and all is well. But Ranger does not leave without a bitter curse: "*Succubus*, farewell; / There is not such a sorceress in Hell."[20] It is a gruesomely pliable comic device. The three London whores, Slipslop, Mrs. Waters, an unnamed Irish grandmother, D'Urfey's Emilia Bubble: alternately ingratiating and despicable, this incongruous band of women all reach for the same farcical charge. At the same time, distinctions about who would or wouldn't use the word produced endless additional laughs—from plain scoffing at any woman who would even use the word to mock-decorous protestations from those who decline to. "Some women she knew would sue him for a Rape," says a chambermaid to the dirty old man with whom she has accidentally spent the night, "but she valued her Character more than to appear in a Court of Justice upon such a filthy Occasion."[21]

Consistency is nowhere. Robust and resourceful women also figure in a wide range of "prevention" jokes, as one might call them. Here, the attacker really does try to force his victim, but she prevents him, and he can then be exposed as a failure (a *pudding*, as one slang term put it). Lady Galliard, the heroine of Behn's *City Heiress* (1682), prevents herself from being raped by the drunken Sir Charles Merriwill—stripped down to his breeches for the act—by promising to marry him the next day. She has only to bide her time while he drinks himself into a stupor. Fielding's Mrs. Heartfree similarly deals with a rough sea captain; to complete the joke he tumbles and dislocates a shoulder. Anne Holland, the celebrated pickpocket, refuses to submit until her attacker at least takes his boots off. She helps him off with one boot but leaves the other one half on and makes her escape.[22]

Confounding as it must seem, prevention humor moved especially easily between imaginary contexts and the world. People made up stories about their friends trying and failing to rape someone. Thus one anecdote about Wilkes and the poet Charles Churchill visiting the second Earl Temple (1711–79) at Stowe. The earl himself orchestrates the fun, sending "every young nobleman who came to Stowe" out to try his luck with his Amazonian dairymaid. First Churchill returns "with his wig pulled all to pieces" and his cheeks beaten "as red as bull beef." Wilkes meets a similar fate; eventually, the joke concludes, the woman "bore a bastard child to the helper of the stables, who had but one eye and one leg."[23] Stories circulated about Swift or George III trying to rape someone during their mad phases. The Swift story is certainly false, but its very invention tells us something. The George III story originated with Caroline, Princess of Wales (hardly a reliable witness). It has something of an analogue in Burney's account of the king chasing her round Kew Gardens in the winter of 1789. But the important point is that the comedy of a fumbling rapist could be so widely and readily adapted—in this case into a jab at George III's celebrated chastity.[24]

Villains who huff and puff but can't blow the house down, as Susan Staves puts it in her analysis of Fielding's failed rapists, "are silly villains who do no real harm."[25] But we don't laugh about attempted rape today—and, given the prominence and gravity of sexual violence in eighteenth-century fiction, modern readers must be surprised by the flippancy of so many episodes. All too often, moreover, a sexual assault serves as the catalyst for some desirable narrative outcome. Again and again, one finds authors resorting to sexual violence as a way to tie up plots or bring the text's central characters together. With disturbing predictability, a brutal attempt on the heroine serves to reunite her with her lover, who just happens to be around for a last-minute rescue. This horrific-sentimental scenario is all too frequent in chivalric romance and the seventeenth-century *romans de longue haleine* (as before that in Heliodorus and Ariosto). In all these contexts, the incident is crucial to the text's sexual plot, exposing flesh and showing women in vulnerable states. In Richardson's *Sir Charles Grandison* (1754), the entire love plot develops from such an incident. Harriet first meets Sir Charles as her rescuer, having been abducted and almost ravished by the villainous Sir Hargrave Pollexfen. "This is indeed bringing good out of evil," Harriet marvels, one of many moments at which Richardson betrays his self-consciousness about the device.[26]

Less familiar, I suspect, is the spectacular forgetability of such incidents in comic fiction. *Young Scarron* (1752) is the lively "history" of a troop of strolling players by Thomas Mozeen (d. 1768), a small-parts member of Garrick's company at Drury Lane. Toward the end of the story, the likable heroine, Diana, is almost raped in a barn by a Squire Western type named Hunter. Fortunately, her long-lost lover, naturally called Ramble, is taking a nap in a neighboring thicket. The tableau is horrible: Ramble races into the barn to find Diana "struggling on the Ground with her Cloaths almost torn off, her Hair in great Disorder about her Head, and screaming out for Help." The would-be rapist scoffs at her alarm. "*Pish, pish*," he cries, it was "*only a little love-Affair; and the foolish Girl is so ignorant, as not to know what's for her good.*" Pressed by Ramble to apologize, Hunter eventually splutters out the following:

> *Madam, my Design was no worse that what is practis'd every day. I love a pretty Girl, and you, being such, struck my Fancy, and then I us'd my best Endeavours to get Possession of you.*

This is good enough for the lady and for her lover, who promptly forgives the attacker (after all, who wouldn't try to rape a beauty like Diana?). Indeed, they both conclude, they should probably be grateful to Mr. Hunter: had Diana not been forced to scream, they might never have been reunited. Let's forget that he tried to rape me, she tells Ramble, "since it has been the means of making us both happy."[27] One can hardly imagine a clearer illustration of the stunning *harmlessness* of sexual violence in this culture. Eighteenth-century novelists use sexual violence to tie up their plots as readily, and as unreflectively, as the Victorians resort to chance encounters in hotels or railway carriages.

MODESTY AND THE IMPOSSIBILITY OF CONSENT

Perhaps the largest body of rape jokes revolves around this culture's impossible standards of sexual modesty. Of course the ideologies were ancient, but along with refinements of manners came increasingly stringent standards. The politest women were forbidden from expressing preferences in courtship, but at every level of society men seem to have expected a show of resistance from any woman who was not completely abandoned. It followed that certain levels of force were an accepted part of mainstream sexuality. Every kiss is "half resisted"; attentions are "half refused"; women were "half willing to be prest," like the "coy maid" in Goldsmith's *Deserted Village*. These ambiguities—or open secrets—supply one of the most charged subjects in French boudoir paintings like Fragonard's *The Lock* (*Le verrou*) or Garnier's *La douce résistance*. And in every local context, as Anna Clark has demonstrated, behaviors that would now be called rape were "seen as an extension of natural, everyday relations between the sexes."[28] "Pleasurable violence," "agreeable rape": these appalling oxymorons are everywhere. Women were always "willing to be ravished." Machiavel that he is, Lovelace is only explicating widely shared assumptions when he generalizes about the sexual practices of his age. Since modest women had to feign such complete ignorance of sex, he writes to Belford, everything depended on the "confidence" of a man who would not take no for an answer. Otherwise the two parties would proceed "as two parallel lines; which, though they run side by side, can never meet." Plainly put: "[I]t is cruel to ask a modest woman for her consent. It is creating difficulties for both."[29] Even Anna Howe, in an unguarded moment, muses: "[O]ur sex are best dealt with by boisterous and unruly spirits."[30] The potentials for misunderstanding or malignant toying are terrifyingly clear. Among so much else, *Clarissa* makes a protracted analysis of the tragic consequences of its culture's extreme standards of delicacy.

In the comic genres, however, cries of resistance are always false. The best-known instance of this joke, now widely cited in modern scholarship, occurs toward the end of Vanbrugh's *The Relapse* (1696), a comedy that both parodies the lurid rape scenes of Restoration tragedy and makes fun of the idea that women could be raped against their will. Vanbrugh's unscrupulous young widow allows herself to be carried into the bedroom by Loveless, the relapsed libertine of the title. "Help, help," she mutters—"*very softly*," as the stage directions put it—"I'm Ravish'd, ruin'd, undone. O Lord, I shall never be able to bear it. (*Exeunt*)."[31] This scenario, along with the stage direction itself, is everywhere. Congreve's Lady Wishfort is delighted to hear that her suitor, Sir Rowland, is a "brisk Man" who will take her "by Storm." "For if he shou'd not be Importunate—I shall never break Decorums," she announces. "I shall die with Confusion if I am forc'd to advance. . . . Oh, I'm glad he's a brisk Man." Perhaps the most exaggerated form of the joke appears in Shadwell's *The Libertine* (1675), where the villain-hero rapes an unnamed "ugly old Woman" as a prank to amuse his friends. "O murder! murder! help! help!" cries the Beldam. "I was never ravish'd in my life." "That I dare swear," replies the hero, but your face won't protect you this time. "Oh my Honour! my Honour, help, help my Honour," she cries as she is carried offstage.[32] With its extravagant burlesque of libertine masculinity, Shadwell's play soon dropped from the repertoire, but *The Relapse* and *The Way of the World* continued to play throughout the eighteenth century. And one finds the same old joke being added to newer compositions: thus *Betty; or, The Country Bumpkins* (1732), a ballad opera by Henry Carey of *Chrononhotonthologos* and the "Namby-Pamby" parodies. Betty resists her lover with the following air:

> Audacious Intruder
> If thus you grow ruder
> I'll raise all the House. (*Very softly*).[33]

As historians of sexuality have now repeatedly demonstrated, the line be-tween rape and a "normal" use of force was a blurred one, in low as well as high contexts.

Closely related is all the knowing humor about women swooning or feigning sleep as ways of enjoying themselves without consent. Lady Wishfort again: "Oh no, I can never advance! I shall swoon if he should expect advances." It was a lewd commonplace in eighteenth-century culture that women always swooned at the right moment—and certainly the heroines of amatory fiction repeatedly do so. Charlotte Lennox was characteristically caustic about the convention. All ladies faint when they are about to be abducted, she jeers, "and seldom recover till they are conveniently carried away; and when they awake, find themselves many Miles off in the Power of their Ravisher." No wonder Richardson had such trouble with his abduction scene, where Clar-issa faints into Lovelace's arms.[34] The mutual role-playing involved in ravish-ing a woman while she sleeps is still more bizarre, yet this situation also shows up in every permutation. It looms large in French pictorial erotica. There were drinking songs: a man finds a young virgin sleeping in the fields, a "yielding state" in which he easily "rifles her charms." Leafing through the fashionable *St James's Miscellany* (ca. 1725), one suddenly comes across "Caelia Enjoy'd in Her Sleep." After several foiled seduction attempts, the narrator steals into Caelia's bedroom at night. Whispering endearments in her ear, he reads her rising breast and lack of "rude Alarms" as consent and wins the "Fort," Cae-lia remaining "insensible and dead" throughout.[35] Coarser versions play up the comic potentials. Smollett is clearly inviting us to laugh when he has his London prostitute declare that the old moneylender has "ruined her in her sleep," and Mrs. Slipslop's accusation of Beau Didapper is even more ludi-crous ("O thou Villain! who hast attacked my Chastity, and I believe ruined me in my Sleep").[36] Yet the claim also comes up occasionally in legal con-texts, suggesting that it was at least conceivable to contemporaries. In June

1730, the papers reported the case of a waterman arrested for rape after the plaintiff deposed that he had "got in at her window, and . . . *done it* in her sleep." The *Grub-Street Journal* added its own rude commentary, joking that breaking in through the window was the only force involved. The case predictably collapsed at the Old Bailey, but it is significant that it made it that far.[37]

These impossible restraints on open consent also account for yet another comic subgenre: the mass of mock complaints from women yearning for the right sort of man to "take [them] by force" or delighting that someone had done so. In style, they range from crude and filthy to elaborate exercises in wit. One finds wry inversions of Surrey's "Complaint by Night" and comparable verses to unresponsive mistresses. Complaints from old maids or lecherous widows are predictably common. But one finds an almost equal number in the voice of young virgins who long to have sex without compromising their virtue. Christopher Smart's *The Midwife* prints "A Ballad: Compos'd by Miss Nelly Pentweazle, a Young Lady of Fifteen" who longs for some hearty man to take her by force:

> Ye Heroes triumphant by Land and by Sea,
> Sworn Vot'ry's to Love, yet unmindful of me,
> You can storm a strong Fort, or can form a Blockade,
> Yet ye stand by, like Dastards, and see me a Maid!

The song "may with great Propriety be sung at Christenings," Mrs. Midnight concludes, offering a sudden insight into the presumed sequence of disgrace and social reintegration. The poem ends with an insult to all fops

> Who answer no End, and to no Sex belong,
> Ye Echoes of Echoes, and Shadows of Shade,—
> For if I had you—I might still be a Maid.

There is much more in this vein. A young countrywoman comes home and casually announces that she has been assaulted in the fields. Her mother tears her hair out, announcing that she is utterly ruined. "O, Mother, says the Girl smiling, I wish I was to be ruin'd every Night of my Life, and live to the Age of Methusalah."[38]

No doubt all this rehearses ancient male fantasies about willing and accessible women. But what must be emphasized is the casual stress on violence as an accepted or even commonsensical reaction to prevailing standards of modesty:

> An elderly Lady was telling a Daughter, a Girl of Sixteen, of the abomi-
> nable Lewdness and Wickedness of the Age, and what Debaucheries were
> daily practised by vicious Men, who made use of Violence as well as Art,
> to satisfy their brutal Appetites; and how Swords and Pistols had been put
> to Women, threatening them with immediate Death, if they refused their
> unlawful Embraces; and then asked Miss, if it should ever happen to be her
> Fate to meet with such a Trial, how she should behave? Says the Girl, *Life
> is sweet, Mamma.*[39]

This is a comic treatment of all the most horrific rape stories of the age—from the Lucretia legend to contemporary sentimental tales and stories about historical rapists like Philip, Duke of Wharton, or the pistol-wielding Charteris. In many contexts, this combines with more mainstream discourses about the decline of British masculinity—the contexts around Miss Pentweazle's abuse of the fops. "I have Reason to bless myself that I am an old Woman," Mrs. Jervis tells Shamela in Fielding's parody. "Ah Child! If you had known the Jolly Blades of my Age, you would not have been left in the Lurch in this manner." In former times, it was said, the men were more vigorous, and women enjoyed themselves without having to consent. Now, however, every young woman was surrounded by puny beaux who couldn't do the deed if they tried and backed off in horror at the slightest gesture of resistance. "O you damn'd rogue, you devil, you dog, how dare you offer such a thing?" shrieks a cobbler's wife to her husband's apprentice, who apologizes and agrees to leave:

> *Nay,* says she, *you did not hear me bid you begone; now you are here, you may
> stay; but if ever you offer to do such another thing, I protest, as I am an honest
> woman, I will tell your master.*[40]

Such jokes condense powerful beliefs that crying rape enabled women to enjoy themselves without loss of honor. Why did Lucretia have to go and kill herself? "'Tis most egregious Nonsense, / To die for being pleas'd, with a safe Conscience," wrote one poet. Since Lucretia never had to consent, there was no dishonor involved. "Pretty Fool!" says Mr. B to Pamela, "how will you forfeit your Innocence, if you are obliged to yield to a Force you cannot withstand?"[41] Of course all this coexisted with contrary and equally powerful beliefs about rape as an irremediable stain. Like Lucretia, the raped heroines of tragedy and sentimental-horrific fiction somehow have to die, at once innocent and polluted.[42] But the comic treatments were relentlessly trivializing, presenting even extreme violence as a favor.

Thus, also, all those peculiar commonplaces about women's alleged excitement reading rape narratives, watching tragic representations, or attending rape trials. "A Rape in Tragedy is a Panegyrick upon the Sex," said the critic John Dennis, proof of the irresistible allure of women and the extremes to which men would go to possess them. In addition, since the woman was "pleas'd without her Consent," female spectators could freely indulge their fantasies of surrendering to a handsome libertine.[43] The same thrills were said to draw women to rape trials, where they sat "impatient for a Smutty Word" ("as reliably as women at a rape trial" was one catchphrase for some regular occurrence).[44] Richard Steele devotes an entire *Tatler* paper to the subject, with Bickerstaff's faux naïveté at its most plodding. Why were there so many women at the Old Bailey for a rape trial? he wonders. Perhaps it was useful for them to learn how to avoid such dangers, but it was probably better for them to stay at home. Rape trials were too distressing:

> I have known a young woman shriek at some parts of the evidence; and how frequently observed, that when the proof grew particular and strong, there has been such an universal flutter of fans, that one would think the whole female audience were falling into fits.[45]

As we shall see, none of this bears any relation to what actually happened in eighteenth-century courtrooms when a rape was tried. And given how rare these trials were, one marvels at their prevalence as imaginative scenarios. Lovelace ceaselessly imagines a courtroom as the scene of his greatest triumphs, a place where every woman would gaze in wonder, "disclaiming prosecution, were the case their own." "There goes a charming handsome man! . . . Who could find it in their hearts to hang such a gentleman as that?"[46]

Equally obscure to modern readers are the constant jokes about fears of rape as signs of vanity or wish fulfillment. Charlotte Lennox is blunt about the gratifications of constantly imagining oneself on the verge of violation. "My Crime," Arabella tells her maid, "is to have Attractions which expose me to these inevitable Misfortunes, which even the greatest Princesses have not escaped." Every man is struck by an unmasterable desire; even Arabella's uncle feels an "impious Flame."[47] Nuns were proverbially prone to such fantasies— at least for the English authors who got away with so much under the guise of anti-Catholicism. Thus Sterne's abbess of Andoüillets and her novice, stuck on the road when their mules refuse to move:

> We are ruin'd and undone, my child, said the abbess to Margarita—we shall be here all night—we shall be plunder'd—we shall be ravish'd—
> —We shall be ravish'd said Margarita, as sure as a gun.
> Sancta Maria! cried the abbess . . . why didst thou not suffer thy servant to go unpolluted to her tomb?
>
> O my virginity! virginity! cried to the abbess.
> —inity!—inity said the novice, sobbing.

Exhausted by tuberculosis, Sterne threw this volume of *Tristram Shandy* together; here we find him reaching almost effortlessly for a standard piece of comedy. (Needless to say, all ends happily when the two women find a way of cursing their mules by saying one syllable each: *bou-ger, fou-ter*.)[48]

The most likely person to worry about rape, it was boorishly suggested, was a woman who had least to fear. One particularly blunt statement of this commonplace comes from Frances, Lady Vane (ca. 1715–88), the scandalous adulteress who included her "Memoirs" as chapter 88 of Smollett's *Peregrine Pickle*. Lady Vane and her unfortunate-looking maid are held up by highwaymen on the way to Paris. Lady Vane is furious about the robbery, but the maid is just terrified of being ravished. "I cannot help observing," concludes Lady Vane, her own spectacular vanity combining with a snort at her ugly companion, "that an homely woman is always more apt to entertain those fears, than one whose person exposes her to much more imminent danger."[49] Consider one final example. One of Johnson's favorite stories about his ramble through the Scottish highlands was an encounter with an elderly crofter on the shores of Loch Ness. Looking around the old woman's "wretched little hovel," he and Boswell ask to see where she slept. Quaking with terror, she refuses to show them—fearing, they joke with each other, that one of them was planning to ravish her.[50] Read from Johnson's point of view, the episode seems like just one more droll encounter with the Scots. But then one recalls that such women *were* vulnerable to rape.

However obscure and varied in their details, these examples all evince the same horribly familiar assumptions about no meaning yes. "Maids say nay and take it," went one old adage; "a woman's nay's a double yea."[51] Here again, the ambiguities produced one of the standard routines of early modern stage comedy: an extended parley between a young woman and the would-be ravisher who simply cannot believe her refusals. In turn, the very possibility of such humor rested on darker assumptions that most women could stop an attacker if they really wanted to. "A Woman's never to be Ravisht against her will," says the rake-hero of Mary Pix's comedy *The Different Widows* (1703).[52] In most everyday situations, it was assumed, there were other people around, and if the woman cried out loudly enough, someone would come to her rescue (after all, women could scream like the devil when they wanted to). Beneath these assumptions lay more specific beliefs that nonconsensual sex was physically impossible. Again and again in the comic and legal sources, one finds the same murky suggestion that women could avoid penetration by crossing their legs firmly, rolling to one side, or refusing to stay still. One proverb put it with hideous referentiality: rape was impossible; how could you thread a moving needle? (In the 1830s, the young Honoré de Balzac offered an extended treatment of this commonplace in his *Contes drolatiques*.) Dubious medical witnesses turned up in courtrooms to assert this "fact," which clearly lies behind countless hostile cross-examinations.[53]

At the same time, Patricia Crawford and other gender historians have found more and more evidence of a distinctly female sexual subculture—a shared knowledge about the male anatomy that probably included techniques for trying to prevent sexual assault. We are only slowly piecing together this traditional wisdom about men, sex, and reproduction; transmitted orally in such all-female contexts as childbed confinements, it only rarely shows up in print sources.[54] Equally important, of course, are the hostile male presumptions that such knowledge existed and was communicated between women. But certain details do recur across male and female contexts. It seems to have been widely understood, for example, that one could stop an attacker by kicking or kneeing him in the groin. One finds "Kick him!" as a piece of advice shouted through doors or out windows to a woman being forced against her will. The question "Did you kick him?" routinely shows up in cross-examinations.[55] Much prevention humor delights in the rudest possible techniques for immobilizing a rapist. Shamela's mother has given her certain "Instructions . . . to avoid being ravished." "[They] soon brought [Mr. Booby] to Terms," she reports, "and he promised me, on quitting my hold, that he would leave the Bed." In case we had any doubt about what exactly Shamela has been squeezing, the mock-Richardsonian declaration that follows makes it clear: "*O Parson* Williams, *how little are all the Men in the World compared to thee.*" This detail further clarifies so many elusive courtroom questions about what the plaintiff was "doing with her hands" at the time (only occasionally does one find such open declarations as "I was forced to take him by the members to save myself").[56] The cumulative impression of all this is a casually violent world in which men were always trying and women were able to prevent them if they really wanted to.

I spell out these particulars only because they shed so much light on the conventions of sentimental rape scenes. With very few exceptions, these literary episodes are set in extravagantly nonrealistic environments: careening carriages, remote castles, cottages in the woods, ships at sea. There are daggers, pistols, brutal assistants with ropes: sentimental authors seem intuitively to have recognized that anything less than overwhelming and brutal force would implicate the victim. Thus, also, the importance of opiates and sleep potions in these texts. Anyone who first encounters the legal sources after reading sentimental fiction will be surprised to find that rape plaintiffs almost never claimed to have been drugged. The forensic reasons will be obvious: a successful prosecutrix had to give a clear account of what had happened. In all sentimental and amatory fiction, however, such anatomical clarity was both unnecessary and detrimental, and the victim's complete unconsciousness worked to dispel any suspicion of complicity. One of Delarivière Manley's novellas states this explicitly: unconsciousness, everyone decides, made the raped Mariana "innocent of the Guilt."[57] In many cases, as with Mrs. Bennet in Fielding's *Amelia* (1751), the villainous rapist informs his victim the following morning. Less fictional accounts of rape, however, had to establish the overwhelming violence that was used. The midcentury courtesan Teresia "Con" Phillips (1709–65), far more remorseful than her contemporary Lady Vane, offers an excruciating circumstantial account of how she was ruined by the mysterious "Mr. Grimes." After long searches, Grimes found out her hiding place, plied her with large quantities of "Barbados Water," and then

> *coming behind her,* while she sat upon an old-fashion'd high-back'd Cane Chair, and, *catching hold of her Arms, drew her Hands behind the Chair,* which he held fast with his Feet: In *this* Position, it was an easy Matter for him with one Hand to secure both hers, and to take the Advantage, he had previously meditated.[58]

Plausible judicial or newspaper accounts of rape depended on such specifics: unusually isolated spots, with firearms, victims tied to trees, monstrous violence, and bruises to show for it.

I return to these evidentiary questions at the end of this chapter. For the moment, one final set of comic texts remains to be discussed: the mass of scornful counterexplanations for the iconic rape stories from sacred history and the classics. This boorish counterdiscourse was so familiar as to be proverbial. Lucretia was a whore and had encouraged Tarquin all along. She killed herself because they were discovered or in a panic that the truth would emerge. Susanna resisted the elders only because they were so old and ugly. Leda was raped "with her own consent."[59] Helen is a tragic figure in Homer and an archetype of wronged femininity, but later Greek and Roman writers cast her as a lecherous bolter; eighteenth-century wits continued to produce *Mock-Iliads* that turned her into a whore. Even serious representations of these mythical attacks are streaked with complicitous mischief, as Norman Bryson has argued in a fascinating essay on visual treatments of Lucretia. In canvas after canvas, he finds, viewers are forced to dwell on the issue of consent, their attention drawn to a faint smile on Lucretia's face as reason gives way to desire.[60] Even in tragic treatments of the myth, one finds the same uncomfortable pull toward bawdry. Witness *The Fall of Tarquin* (1713), a dreary provincial tragedy by a York exciseman named William Hunt. The performance concludes with an epilogue spoken by the middle-aged actress who plays Tarquin's mother, Tullia. She'd rather have played Lucretia and struggled with the manly Tarquin, Tullia tells the audience—not to repel him, but "least he shou'd depart." Such lewd deflations are still clearer in earlier texts like Heywood's *Rape of Lucrece* (1608), where the tragic action is constantly interrupted by bawdy interludes. Even immediately after the rape, Heywood brings a trio onstage to sing a smutty song about the event.[61] But in the mid-eighteenth century, the story still remained too heightened or implausible to appear without deflation.

*

I have reviewed this humor at such length to give at least some idea of its pervasiveness and variability in eighteenth-century culture. Rape jokes are everywhere one looks: in cheap pamphlets and song sheets as well as more literary texts. The same dirty jokes show up in ballad operas and then again as asides in otherwise morbid tragedies. As they migrate across genres, these jokes take every possible form; the only constant, in fact, is that the woman is always lying. The emphasis falls here on a comic humiliation, there on wordplay or a clever conceit. Tone ranges from innuendo and knowing snickers to brasher declarations that "sword and pistol gallantry" was something every woman needed. Yet one finds many other contexts in which the women are resourceful and win our sympathy, enacting favorite jokes against accepted figures of fun.

In all this, the word *rape* itself becomes a sort of empty signifier, easily taking on multiple different meanings. It meant at once much less than it does today—nonconsensual intercourse in any situation—and much more. *Rape* meant that a woman had been caught in bed with someone and was crying out to protect her reputation. To some, the word signified modesty, while others insisted that any woman who used it must already be unchaste. It meant that a lower-class woman was trying to extort money out of a social superior—sometimes this was wicked, but often it was a hugely satisfying joke. Even in consensual situations, it would seem, women used the word to display a suitable level of reluctance, and their seducers accepted the accusation. A woman who fretted about being raped was either indulging her vanity or longing for it. The word conjured up brutal violence, death sentences, and executions. But since it also referred to relatively mainstream sexual behaviors it carried an erotic charge that would now be pathological. It referred to something that was impossible and that happened all the time. These semantic ambiguities produced unending humor, but they also ensured that it was almost impossible for a woman convincingly to accuse someone of rape, let alone convict him. Any serious use of the word perpetually threatened to slip over into one of its countless ironic uses.

Large numbers of male and female readers seem to have accepted rape jokes as mainstream comic fare. More surprising to modern readers is the extent to which women writers themselves fall back on the same comic scenarios. We have seen Aphra Behn and Charlotte Lennox doing so. Mary Pix, Frances Vane, and other women writers repeat the old jokes with even less self-consciousness. Lady Mary Wortley Montagu glibly describes Lucretia's suicide as a "heathenish" act. She positively gloried in the attempted rape case that titillated London society in the autumn of 1721—an attack on the genteel Griselda Murray (1692–1759) by a besotted Scottish footman named Arthur Gray. Murray had energetically repulsed the attack, but suffered immensely from her family's decision to prosecute the man for burglary and the torrent of publicity that ensued. Lady Mary came up with not one but two poetic responses to the incident. The first, an Ovidian epistle in which the imprisoned footman bemoans his impossible love, was first printed in 1747 and became widely known from successive editions of Dodsley's *Collection of Poems* (1748). The second, provocatively titled *Virtue in Danger* after the subtitle of Vanbrugh's *Relapse*, was a smutty ballad to the tune of "Chevy Chase." A broadside version was being hawked about the streets soon after the event. A longer version circulated in manuscript for more than five decades (fig. 11). In

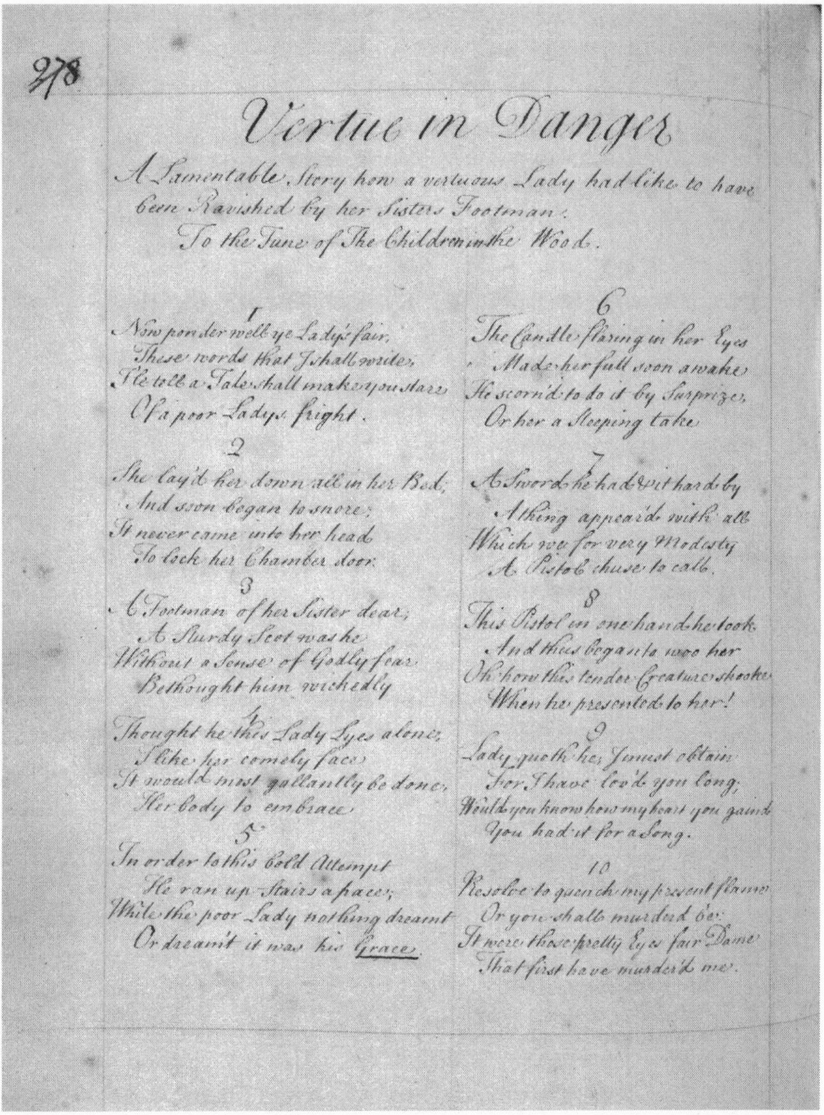

278

Virtue in Danger

A Lamentable Story how a vertuous Lady had like to have been Ravished by her Sisters Footman.

To the Tune of The Children in the Wood.

1
Now ponder well ye Lady's fair,
These words that I shall write;
Ile tell a Tale shall make you stare
Of a poor Ladys fright.

2
She lay'd her down all in her Bed,
And soon began to snore;
It never came into her head
To lock her Chamber door.

3
A Footman of her Sister dear,
A Sturdy Scot was he
Without a Sense of Godly fear
Bethought him wickedly

4
Thought he this Lady Lyes alone,
I like her comely face
It would most gallantly be done,
Her body to embrace

5
In order to this bold Attempt
He ran up Stairs apace;
While the poor Lady nothing dreamt
Or dreamt it was his Grace.

6
The Candle flaring in her Eyes
Made her full soon awake
He scorn'd to do it by Surprize,
Or her a sleeping take

7
A Sword he had & it hard by
A thing appear'd with all
Which we for very Modesty
A Pistol chuse to call.

8
This Pistol in one hand he took
And thus began to woo her
Oh how this tender Creature shooke
When he presented to her!

9
Lady quoth he, I must obtain
For I have lov'd you long;
Would you know how my heart you gain'd
You had it for a Song.

10
Resolve to quench my present flame
Or you shall murder'd be:
It were those pretty Eyes fair Dame
That first have murder'd me.

FIGURE 11. [Lady Mary Wortley Montagu], "Virtue in Danger" (1721), as it circulated in manuscript for more than five decades. Line 20 makes a lewd allusion to the Duke of Athol; stanza 7 initiates an extended analogy between pistols and other "weapons." The poem is here copied by a scribe of Lord Oxford's, clearly from another manuscript version rather than the printed ballad, which omits stanza 7. This full version was later reprinted, openly attributed to Lady Mary, in the 1770s. Photograph © The British Library Board (MS Harley 7316, fol. 137v).

Lady Mary's hands, Mrs. Murray becomes a knowing Amazonian preventor heroine who briefly wonders whether to let the footman have his way ("I thought this fellow was a Fool, / But there's some Sense in this") before leaping out of bed and immobilizing him. Lady Mary gets particular mileage out of the "where were her hands?" joke:

> His Pistol hand she held fast clos'd
>   As She remembers well;
> But how the other was dispos'd
> There's none alive can tell.

Mrs. Murray was supposed to be her friend; this jeu d'esprit understandably put an end to their intimacy.[62]

Behn scholars have been especially troubled by the repeated rape attempts in act 3 of *The Rover*, where the witty rake Willmore several times tries to overcome the heroine's sister Florinda, treating her shrieks as nothing more than the customary show of modesty. Florinda doesn't actually want to be ravished and fortunately survives this and all subsequent threats to her virtue. Were such scenes indulgent treatments of libertine masculinity or more reluctant concessions to the men in her audience?[63] No one seems able to resolve such questions, but there is certainly little to distinguish Behn's attempted rape scenes from those of her male contemporaries. And, crucially for my purposes, these scenes continued to be played throughout the eighteenth century. Behn's fiction became scandalous, but, as Jane Spencer has demonstrated, her drama remained popular and largely unbowdlerized. *The Rover* suffered a few local cuts by the 1740s, but at least until the 1790s, Willmore the would-be rapist "charmed the town."[64]

Surely the most unexpected rape joke in eighteenth-century women's writing appears in Sarah Fielding's *History of Ophelia* (1760), a text that turns repeatedly on the Richardsonian situation of a virgin abducted and threatened with violence. About halfway through the novel, the horrible and hideous Mrs. Herner awakens everyone at an inn with a cry of rape. The lady had come to him, protests her "rapist" from the bed, and then someone comes in with a candle:

> Thou Witch, thou Monster, full Light would better have obtained thy Release than all thy Struggling. Have such a Hag as thee at my Side! I had rather have [a manservant] or my Crop Horse for my Bedfellow.

Ophelia offers an obligatory reaction to the incident ("there seemed such an Enormity of Wickedness in this Man that amazed me"), but even she "could not restrain a Smile" to see Mrs. Herner insulted and humiliated in front of everyone. Sarah Fielding does not just repeat a standard series of jokes; she indulges in and elaborates on them. Ophelia's physical description of Mrs. Herner is like something out of Smollett—a strikingly unsympathetic depiction of female aging from an author who was herself a spinster of fifty. In one particularly odd moment, Ophelia wonders whether she should just leave the door locked and let the nasty crone have it.[65]

At this point, one suddenly notices that early feminist writings say almost nothing about rape. Sarah Fielding, Frances Brooke, Frances Sheridan, and Sarah Scott all return again and again to rape as a sentimental subject, but none of their more programmatic writings raise the subject. None of the other Blue-stockings mention the issue; nor, earlier, had Mary Astell. At the time of her death, Mary Wollstonecraft was taking on the topic with the story of Jemima in *The Wrongs of Woman* (1798), but she never broached the subject in her nonfiction. These women attacked sexual double standards and campaigned about abandoned women and the need for child support, but they had far less to say about sexual violence.[66] Of course there were questions of decorum and strategy. Female sexuality was an impossibly risky subject. Arduous as it was to assert the intellectual equality of women, it was immensely more difficult to take up the question of sexual consent. Even so, modern readers must be surprised that these authors did so little to challenge the widely shared opinion that, with the exception of obviously horrific cases that the law took care of, there was no such thing as genuinely nonconsensual sex.

FUNCTIONS OF AN ASSAULT

But naturally there are no consistencies in any of this, and all the skeptical scenarios appear alongside other comic representations in which nonconsensual sex is precisely the point. In a valuable discussion, Isobel Grundy has described early modern culture's festive or "comic-gallant" attitude toward rape: male force used "in an atmosphere of sport and celebration" "to convince women of their unadmitted desire for sexual penetration." In so many contexts, she finds, rape is "a cure for affected female frigidity, an appropriate prelude to mutual enjoyment," a forcible revelation to women "of the way things truly are": violent subjection was the fate of every woman.[67] In every genre, at every level of discourse, one finds constant rehearsals of the same old stories from Ovid's *Metamorphoses* and ancient history. Leda, Europa, Io, and Andromeda struggled on every decorated surface. They were painted on ceilings, woven into tapestries, and enameled on snuffboxes. There were bas-reliefs on punch bowls and porcelain figurines like the "Rape of the Sabines" advertised in the Chelsea Porcelain catalog for 1755.[68] Beneath the elegant Queen Anne surface of Pope's *Rape of the Lock*, Ellen Pollak finds an elemental fable about the destiny of every woman—about the forcible transformation of an intact and independent virgin into a mutilated and submissive sex object. Pope's metonymic rape is a corrective to prudery or aloofness, its violence only thinly veiled (the Baron's "fatal weapon," the spilling of "virgin blood," the heroine's "fall" or "ruin").[69] Sexual violence was one of this culture's most flexible metaphors, one easily applied to personal circumstances or topical issues. Walpole "rapes" the Exchequer; Pitt "rapes" the Bank of England, the ugly old lady of Threadneedle Street. The great diplomatic and religious conflicts of the age were all easily allegorized as acts of sexual violence. Attacking George II's capitulation to Prussia in 1741, cartoonists showed Frederick the Great throwing himself at the half-naked Queen of Hungary, insisting, "I must have ye low countries."[70]

The same devastating sense of inevitability is captured in countless catchphrases. Violent defloration was "what all women must come to," no more than what your father did to your mother, only "what *Harry* gave *Doll*." "Every Maid is undone" went another maxim.[71] Sexual initiation was assumed to be violent and traumatic, but something that one soon got over. She'll be fine once she knows the worst, says every village matron; you'll get used to it by and by. Pain was thought to be unavoidable, within marriage or without. "Putting to the squeak," "making her roar": it was taken for granted that the loss of virginity made a woman scream (and a cause for suspicion if she didn't).[72] Beyond this lay deep-seated beliefs that women needed a bit of force to liberate their sexuality and that they would be grateful once it was all over. "There is no woman but she will yield in time," ran yet another unpleasant adage. All this was repeated in emerging paramedical and sexological texts as well as the old misogynistic tracts. The law effectively allowed men to "get physical" to overcome initial reluctance—and from here arose further debates about whether rape was still a crime if the victim seemed happy afterward. The old statutes were noticeably ambiguous on this point, defining rape as both "the ravishing of any woman against her will, where she neither consenteth before, nor after," and "the ravishing of her by force, though she consenteth after." Again, Burn feels the need specifically to insist that post facto consent was no defense.[73]

These confusions inevitably bring up debates about changing levels of sexual violence (and behind them, levels of interpersonal violence in general). Taking a cue from cultural anthropology, historians have speculated that different historical moments, like different cultures, can be more or less "rape prone" or "rape free."[74] As so often, the conclusions have tended toward positive or negative poles. At one end, historians like John Gillis and Susan Amussen describe relatively calmer and more equitable gender relations in preindustrial communities, and collective sanctions against wife beaters, adulterers, and rapists. Recent scholarship on politeness and sensibility has tended to compound such impressions.[75] At an opposite extreme, one finds the misogynistic traditions emphasized by Felicity Nussbaum and Phyllis Mack, the violence and legal oppression described by Anna Clark and Garthine Walker, and Randolph Trumbach's controversial argument about high levels of male violence as anxious reassertions of heteronormative masculinity.[76] These less sanguine scholars find entire communities, women as well as men, vilifying anyone who dared to raise a rape charge. They find rapists turning up at alehouses to brag about what they had done and even exhibiting a perverse pride about being tried for the crime.[77] Over time, levels of sexual violence at the lowest social strata may actually have been increasing, as household production involving both genders gave way to more homosocial work environments.[78]

These debates about levels of violence continue as more and more sources come to light. But certainly the comic sources suggest a widespread acceptance of male violence. One particularly revealing genre is the enormous body of mimetic ballads, where music and verse structure mimic the accepted sequence of refusal, violence, and eventual capitulation. A wagoner attacks a young woman on the side of the road:

> His Waggon he stop'd, and his Leg o'er her laid.
> Oh! what are you doing? then whisper'd the Maid,
> She struggl'd, she threaten'd, she vow'd she'd be gone,
> 'Till fainter and fainter, she cry'd out, Drive on,
> *Drive on* Robin, *geeho, geeho.*[79]

Sung over and over in taverns and private drinking parties, such catches worked to normalize beliefs about sex as a terrain of struggle. Rawer still is John Aubrey's story of Sir Walter Raleigh raping a young woman against a tree:

> He loved a wench well; and one time getting up one of the Mayds of Honour up against a tree in a Wood ('twas his first Lady) who seemed at first

boarding to be something fearfull of her Honour, and modest, she cryed, sweet Sir Walter, what doe you me ask; Will you undoe me? Nay, sweet Sir Walter! Sweet Sir Walter! Sir Walter! At last, as the danger and the pleasure at the same time grew higher, she cryed in the extasey, Swisser Swatter Swisser Swatter.

"She proved with child," Aubrey concludes, clearly taking her pregnancy as proof of consent. Nineteenth-century biographers did everything they could to suppress this story, but it remained firmly attached to Raleigh throughout the eighteenth century and was repeated, its brutality only slightly mollified, in a well-known ballad version, set to music by Henry Purcell.[80]

Here again, the less pessimistic historians see these and thousands of similar ballads—with all their analogies about ploughmen, blacksmiths with hammers, storming forts, and razing defenses—as part of a metaphoric war of the sexes. Less ambiguous sexual assaults, Susan Amussen insists, were not a tolerated part of youth culture: "It was not through sexual violence that men acted as men."[81] But other evidence compels us to read in more literal ways and to see fact situations behind the metaphors. One of the most gruesome scenarios across genres involves a mother cooperating with a traveling gentleman in the ruin of her daughter at a roadside inn. The alehouse historian Peter Clark finds general expectations that landladies' daughters would satisfy the sexual demands of guests. Clark's findings provide at least some context for nasty drinking songs like D'Urfey's "The Trooper Watering His Nagg," with its jovial chorus: "It was with the Mother's own Consent / Ho, ho, was it so, was it so, was it so."[82] Captain Smith's *School of Venus* (1716) attributes an extended version of this story to Rochester. Coming across a "pretty wench" on the side of the road, Smith's Rochester arranges with the woman's grandmother to debauch her. The "obstinate Slut" resists his payments for a full twelve months until both he and the old woman are at the end of their patience. Finally, she sends Rochester up to her granddaughter's bedroom, telling him, "[I]f fair means would not make her yield to his Passion, he might use foul if he pleas'd." Sure enough, Rochester finds "that all his *Rhetorick* had not force enough to tempt her to his Embraces" and therefore begins to use violence. What happens next will make any jaw drop. Hearing her granddaughter being "put to the squeak" upstairs, and "being one that lov'd to see Generation Work go forward," the old woman runs upstairs and "piously [gives] an helping Hand, by holding her Legs" until Rochester finishes his business. (One does not need Freud to see the mythic structures lurking behind this ghastly set piece.) Perhaps what most appalls is how easily Smith's narrative voice accommodates the dreadful sequelae: the ruined daughter weeps for a month but finally agrees to "make the best of a bad Market" and accept an annuity from the earl. After his death, she spends eight or nine years as a Fleet Market whore before she is beaten to death by her bully.[83] Contemporaries were clearly not expected to expend much effort squaring up such stories with the announced moral purpose of the book (a pro forma lesson to young women about the consequences of vice). But modern readers must be shocked by the nonchalance with which the text so brutally disposes of this woman, as if this were just the way of things.

At the same time, comic genres also celebrate a range of less consistently violent ways of overcoming women, most of which would be rapes by modern definitions. Sex achieved through opiates or alcohol long remained part of the repertoire of rakish pranks (further complicated by associations with the benigner love potions of folklore). The horrific-sentimental versions of this ruse are now familiar, but comic versions are disarmingly flippant, often going so far as to represent the drugging as an act of kindness to the woman. Peregrine Pickle resolves to rape Emilia Gauntlet with the aid of "a certain elixir" so "that he might spare her the confusion of yielding without resistance." "*Somnivolencies*" Lovelace insists on calling them—"I hate the word *opiates* on this occasion." "I aver that my motive for this expedient was *mercy*."[84] One finds innumerable other ruses: disguises, duplicate keys, conniving chaperones, chests and closets. Inherited from the fabliaux tradition, from Boccaccio, Chaucer, and Bandello, and then from picaresque fiction and late-Restoration sex farces, these devices remained alive and well in the mid-eighteenth century.

Smollett offers a particularly awful range of examples, almost an anatomy of sexual violence. Well before he tries to rape the heroine, Peregrine and her brother take revenge on a recalcitrant farmer's wife who had rebuffed them both. Peregrine easily imitates the husband's voice (trickster rapists are always accomplished mimics), and the pair burst in on her. "With seeming reluctance" she submits to Gauntlet but is afterward happy to repeat the exercise. Our hero, meanwhile, overcomes the housemaid, which makes him "as happy as such a conquest could make him." In such episodes, one recalls all the nastiest Restoration bed tricks—mordant instances like Dryden's *Amphitryon* (1690) or Aphra Behn's *Luckey Chance* (1686), where the ambiguous Gayman wins permission to take Fulbank's place in the marital bed after defeating him at a game of dice. These plays were falling out of the repertoire by the mid-eighteenth century, but Smollett repeats all their situations with no apparent recognition that they might be problematic. Hired as an apprentice to a London apothecary, Roderick Random rapes the man's daughter by pretending to be her lover. *Peregrine Pickle* devotes an entire chapter to the hero's revenge against a woman who had dared to prefer a brawny soldier to him.[85]

Revenge, payment of a gambling debt, first-class nocturnal prank: these examples alert us to the astonishing pliability of sexual violence in early modern culture. Sexual violence in Smollett is explicitly framed as a matter of vengeance rather than lust. Peregrine and his friend attack every woman who refuses their desires. Roderick Random punishes the apothecary's daughter for her haughty disdain, so delighting in the trick that he goes back to bed in a glorious "congratulation of [his] own happiness." Or consider, once again, Behn's *The Rover*: having fought off Willmore, Florinda is then attacked by the oafish Blunt. Blunt has no real desire but wants to take revenge on the entire female sex. "Thou shalt lie with me," he tells her, "not that I care for the enjoyment, but to . . . be revenged on one whore for the sins of another."[86] From here one finds rape being used for any number of other different *functions*, as a sociologist would put it. Getting there first is a glorious joke on a rival lover. Raping an enemy's wife or daughter is one of the sweetest forms of revenge (as Lovelace thinks of his assault on Clarissa as a triumph over the entire Harlowe clan). A single night scene of Wycherley's *Plain Dealer* (1676) offers two distinctly different instances of rape as a sort of diabolical problem-solving act. Manly, Wycherley's Molièrean misanthrope, resolves to rape his former betrothed, Olivia, as a "punishment" for having married someone else and kept his money. He will take his vengeance "upon her honour," elaborate it by informing her the next day, and complete the joke by telling the world what he has done. Only moments later, the villain Vernish tries to rape Fidelia, having stripped her of her male disguise. Here, sexual violence is explicitly compared to torture as a way of extracting the truth. "If I must not know who you are," Vernish tells her, "'twill suffice for me only to know certainly what you are." He then throws her onto the bed, the "rack" on which the truth will finally be forced from her. The scene ends with yet another grisly piece of comic business when Vernish is interrupted by his servant: "You saucy rascal, how durst you come in, when you heard a Woman squeal? that shou'd have been your Cue to shut the door."[87]

Playing in this form into the 1740s and only slightly softened in the bowdlerized version of 1766, *The Plain Dealer* points to everyday assumptions about sexual violence as a way of humbling and controlling women, assumptions that surely require further discussion.[88] Beyond employers' casual attacks on their female servants, for example, one finds instances of sexual assault as a ritual assertion of the master's authority, something that wives tolerated or even openly accepted. In one of the very few servant-master rape prosecutions that made it to the Old Bailey, a maid recalls her mistress's response. "He always served all his servants so the night they came into the house," the wife told her, handing over sixpence. We know that formal defloration practices like the droit du seigneur were largely mythical, but they certainly had their shabbier counterparts in eighteenth-century households.[89] Odder still are all the offhand jokes about landowners "punishing" village women. One squire catches his tenant's daughter stealing firewood and warns that, if he catches her again, he will punish her *"in a way most agreeable to his wishes."* He duly does so. As usual at a rape trial, the court is full of women. The squire should find a different way of protecting his wood, the judge chortles: otherwise, "believe me that the *ladies in the gallery will not leave you a stick in your hedge."*[90] In another version, the peasant girl is stealing beans. "If ever she came again," the farmer warns her, "she should not return without a green gown" (i.e., he would assault her on the grass). Soon she is back in the bean field, and the farmer fulfills his threat. Her prosecution collapses into a similar linguistic joke: "[Y]ou have taken a very good method to *save your bacon, but a very bad method to save your beans."*[91]

Plucked from diverse contexts and all doing different things for different readers, these comic representations are nevertheless affirmed by other sorts of evidence. Among the laboring classes, historians have found rape being used as a routine way of settling scores, avenging insults, or getting something back for an unpaid loan.[92] Above all, violence was at this level of society an accepted last resort with unwilling women, a reliable way of forcing them into marriage. Ceaselessly rehearsed in the ballad and chapbook traditions, this pattern also recurs in surviving judicial records. Persistently rebuffed by a local maiden, a young rustic rapes her on the riverbank:

> With water'd Eyes she pants and crys,
>   I'm utterly undone;
> If you will not be wed to me,
>   E'er the next Morning Sun:
> He answer'd her he ne'er would stir,
>   Out of her Sight till then;
> We'll both clap Hands in Wedlock Bands,
>   Marry, and to't again.[93]

Such verses are no simple form of evidence and no one would now call them *popular*. This version comes from D'Urfey's multivolume collection, where it appealed to upper-class assumptions about plebeian rudeness. Yet to the extent that they survive from this period, genuinely popular texts repeat the same situations. What one cannot avoid in all this is the odd, almost compulsory way in which misery evaporates once the attacker agrees to marry, the irresistible transformation of trauma into relief or even celebration. Historical documents offer ample evidence of practices behind the texts. Reviewing the London parish and hospital records dealing with illegitimacy, Randolph Trumbach concludes that for a significant proportion of the population "marriage was a possible conclusion to a relationship that had begun in rape." Rape, he concludes, "was part of the continuum of courtship."[94]

Less obvious to modern readers is the scattered evidence of violence as an appropriate way of dealing with recalcitrant women at higher levels of society. Where marriage was principally about consolidating private property, sexual violence was part of a continuum of strategies for subduing stubborn women. Locking up, beating, withholding food, forcing marriage: sexual violence was only an extreme version of these routine compulsions. Toward the end of *Tom Jones*, Lady Bellaston readily believes that a raped Sophia would do them all proud and accept Lord Fellamar. Fellamar himself is not at all ashamed to pursue his suit with Western, even immediately after the attempt. Even if they believe Sophia's claims, no one really cares what the wealthy peer tried to do to her. Most baffling of all is Fielding's defense of the man. Fellamar is clearly a pompous fool, but Fielding takes pains to inform us that he is not a complete villain. "His Reputation was extremely clear, and common Fame did him no more than Justice, in speaking well of him." Sophia was "unjust" to call him "that odious Lord." Using violence as a way of convincing a young woman what was best for her was clearly conceivable both to a foolish but relatively harmless young man like Fellamar, and to the society that would judge him. Sophia was dangerously in love with a low fellow, and given that her own relative was encouraging him, the whole thing "appeared in no very heinous Light to his Lordship, (as he faithfully promised, and faithfully resolved too, to make the Lady all the subsequent Amends in his Power by Marriage)."[95] Why such a detailed and sympathetic analysis of a would-be rapist's motives?

The fact that Sophia manages to fight off her attacker allows Fielding's episode to remain within the realm of comedy. More shocking is the insistent pull toward comic outcomes even with accomplished rapes. The logic of benigner Renaissance bed tricks—as exemplified by *Measure for Measure*—remained powerful. In every sort of genre, one finds sexual violence easily remedied by marriage or actively engineered as a means of steering the heroine toward the right husband—as if biological identity would easily displace so transient a thing as the woman's will. Similar patterns are more darkly represented in Restoration comedies and now-opaque novels like Mary Davys's *Reformed Coquette* (1724), where rape or threatened rape is a sharp corrective for women who assert their independence.[96] The strangest of all these literary treatments must be Eliza Haywood's *The Lucky Rape; or, Fate the Best Disposer* (1727). The heroine, Emilia, is almost seduced by her lover when she is abducted and raped by a stranger. This is just as well, since the first lover turns out to be her long-lost brother. All ends happily when her rapist offers his hand. "This rape therefore," Haywood concludes (as if a single adverb could discharge all trauma),

> which had the Appearance of the most terrible Misfortune that Female Virtue cou'd sustain, by the secret Decrees of Destiny, prov'd her greatest Good, since by it she was not only deliver'd from that Manifest Danger of Incest she was falling into, but also gain'd a Husband.[97]

This hasty stitch-up stands out, but any number of milder versions enact the same transformation from horrific to benign. Behn's Lady Fulbank is naturally appalled to find that she has slept with Gayman, but the plot soon takes its inevitable direction. She does not get her lover, but the misadventures of that night do eventually allow her to separate from an idiotic husband. Taken out of context, many of the "lucky" or comedic rapes are indistinguishable from tragic or sentimental ones: all depends on their narrative consequences. The bed trick in Otway's *The Orphan* (1680) leads to three suicides, but in its rudiments it comes close to Behn's. Judging from their writings, at least, these authors seem hardly able to conceive that nonconsensual sex could be traumatic in and of itself, or that it could remain so for long. At once catalytic and empty, rape is a plot device like so many others.

This shocking blindness to a rape victim's psychic experience surely accounts for so many of the hostile early reactions to *Clarissa*—and for the open longing of so many sympathetic readers for a happy ending. There were just so few precedents for representing the miseries of patriarchal subjection, forced marriage, or rape. Few other major authors were seriously suggesting that women should be free to consent or refuse, or that their feelings were worth attending to. These were the expectations that obliged the young Mary Granville (later Mary Delany; 1700–1788) to marry the revolting Alexander Pendarves at eighteen. Richardson of course had his circle of admiring gentlewomen, but others at higher stations objected to the book's exhaustive representation of female miseries. *Clarissa* was "that most stupid book," wrote Lady Kildare (1731–1814) to her father, the Duke of Richmond, who was about to play one of his practical jokes on Richardson. The Duchess of Portland (1715–85) was similarly unmoved. "I was disgusted with their tediousness," she wrote of *Clarissa* and *Sir Charles Grandison*, "and could not read eleven letters with all the effort I could make: so much about my sisters and my brothers, and all my uncles and my aunts!" Of Lady Kildare's reaction, Stella Tillyard concludes that Clarissa's stubborn refusal of an arranged marriage "seemed pig-headed" to a woman who had herself just agreed to such a match. No one denied that Solmes and the Harlowes were monstrous creations or that there might be people like them. But arranged marriages were routine at this level of society and generally worked out well enough, with both parties avoiding each other and taking lovers if necessary. Only two years later, Lady Kildare was writing cheerfully to her sisters about her husband's affairs, concluding: "[M]y turn for getting a lover will come.")[98]

Complex and sympathetic representations of female emotions were only slowly displacing older hostilities. "A woman is a weathercock" ran the old proverb, always swinging from gentleness to vengeance or lust to malice. "Women weep and sicken when they list" went another: they were always ready to swoon, cry, or fall into a fit. And so it goes on. "Trust not a woman when she weeps"—any whore could "pump water out of her eyes." You might as well believe a shopkeeper or expect clarity out of a drunkard.[99] And above all, no one but a fool would believe a woman when it came to sex. It is clearly no accident, as Frances Ferguson has suggested, that the greatest technical advances of early psychological realism occurred in first-person rape narratives.[100] Erotic tension supplied *Pamela* and *Clarissa* with their narrative charge, as it had for Manley and Haywood. But a sympathetic rape plot also required new ways of representing intentional states. Richardson's attempts to elicit sympathy for his victim-heroines demanded an exhaustive focus on their mental state—their repeated refusal of consent.

The length of *Clarissa* offers the clearest proof of the mistrusts Richardson was taking on: anything less would suggest that the heroine had courted her fate. Only an exquisitely detailed record of Clarissa's mental state—the agonizing flux of contradictory passions—could make us think otherwise. So many early feminocentric texts revolve around the same tortured issues of pure and impure motives. Lucretia, Helen, Rowe's Calista: each of these heroines was surrounded by the same hairsplitting debates. *The Fair Penitent* was "one of the most pleasing tragedies on the stage," wrote Johnson, but Calista never truly repented. She killed herself after the affair with Lothario came out:

her pain followed "from the detection rather than from guilt, and expresses more shame than sorrow, and more rage than shame." Johnson's own attempt at she-tragedy, the ill-fated *Irene* (1736/1749), dwells on similar distinctions. Irene was a helpless victim in the original Turkish story; Johnson's heroine is a victim of her own weakness and gradually, if hesitantly, succumbs to her seducer ("Trembling to grant, nor daring to refuse").[101]

After several decades of intensive work on Richardson, it seems crucial to remind ourselves of just how counterintuitive his sympathetic representation of "female" emotions was. It is always surprising to find how little Smith's *Theory of Moral Sentiments* (1759) has to say about the great texts of literary sentimentalism. Characteristically female emotions have almost no place in Smith's account of a society tied together by bonds of sympathy. We too often neglect the stoic inheritance in Smith's thought and his insistence that excessive emotions—let alone the obtrusive bodily symptoms of sentimental fiction—will actually impede sympathy. The constant "whining, and crying, and kneeling is very absurd," objected one reader of *Sir Charles Grandison*, "and no where in practice, except amongst the *Pamelas* and *Clarissas, &c.* of [Richardson's] own making."[102] This aversion also survives in hundreds of now-forgotten parodies: demonic fathers starve daughters to death; a ruined cook wench bemoans her fate like Jane Shore; abandoned market women rave like Bedlamites. Of course there were also the hagiographic traditions, the virgin martyrs of she-tragedy and the idealized heroines of romance. But sympathetic representations of ordinary women who wept and suffered in realistic environments were extraordinary violations of representational decorums.

Revolutionary as it now seems, *Clarissa* was in its time only a moderate success. Compared to *Tom Jones*—which went through four authorized editions within the first year alone, a total of ten thousand copies—*Clarissa* was a disappointment. The fashionable world, as Eaves and Kimpel sum up the situation, found it "very moral and very long and was not inclined to welcome novels with unhappy endings."[103] Richardson comes sixth in James Raven's list of best-selling novelists for the years 1750–69, behind (in order) Sterne, Fielding, Haywood, Smollett, and Defoe. Of this list, the author who remains distinctively absent from modern criticism is Smollett. Contemporary critics rated him below Richardson and Fielding, but he was as popular and as commercially successful as either of them—for which reason I have been stressing examples from *Peregrine Pickle* and *Roderick Random*.[104] Smollett was a direct and caustic opponent of sentimentalism and, for all the exertions of his twentieth-century defenders, vastly less sympathetic to women.

ACCUSING, MAKING UP, AND THE LOCAL MAGISTRATE

It would be perverse not to return to all those courtroom jokes and at least attempt to explore the contexts behind them: the practices and institutions in which uncertainties about refusal or consent became significant. Surviving records of rape trials at the Old Bailey and regional assizes have now been worked over many times. The depressing statistics are all too familiar to anyone working in legal history or the history of sexuality: between 80 and 100 percent of these cases failed, and the figure was usually closer to 100 percent. We also know why: the additional caution that rape was "an accusation easily to be made"; the universal acceptance of sexual history evidence, much of it hearsay; the pitiless cross-examination to which the plaintiff was subjected, generally by the defendant himself. It was also widely thought that death was too harsh a penalty for this crime, and that any woman must be really vindictive to be pursuing the matter so far.[105]

Wretched paradoxes surrounded the case at every point. Resistance was defined as a vigorous physical struggle, but then too much strength itself cast doubt on the charge. If she was that strong, she could have fought him off, no? Courts were increasingly skeptical of cases without medical evidence, but then the very act of having allowed oneself to be examined by a surgeon implied immodesty and, therefore, consent: no honest woman would allow a strange man anywhere near her genitals. Indeed, the very fact of making a rape charge effectively damned one: no respectable woman would ever use the word, let alone go before a judge and repeat the details. Jurists disagreed about exactly what was required to prove a rape, with some requiring both penetration and ejaculation and others, like Hale, accepting "the least penetration" and no ejaculation.[106] But in either case it was easy for the defendant or his counsel to keep demanding more and more smutty details. "You must explain yourself," the plaintiff is told; "you must be more particular." "You must describe it because the man's life is in hazard." "Did you perceive anything come from him?" "Why do you not say what he did?"[107] There was certainly no respectable language for such things. It may also be true, as gender historians have suggested for some time, that the very language of penetrative sex—persistently described as an action performed on a passive being—implied consent.[108]

The result, we now know, is that a successful prosecution depended on exceptional circumstances: either the victim's injuries were so serious that they could not be ignored, or the assault was interrupted by persons of good character who both supported the prosecution and were prepared to testify.[109]

The handful of midcentury Old Bailey convictions involved quite breathtaking brutalities—beating, kicking, stabbing, throttling. In a significant proportion, the victim actually died of her injuries. Even with minors, a successful prosecution depended on hideous bruises, genital lacerations, hemorrhages, attested to by a surgeon or an apothecary, and this testimony was itself vulnerable to hostile cross-examination. Could the surgeon be sure that it wasn't just a normal first time? None of this was consistent—not in doctrine, trial procedures, sentencing, or punishment. Perhaps the only constant was that rape trials reversed the usual prosecutorial biases of early modern English law, which obliged the defendant to explain away the charge (a thief was guilty unless he could explain where the thing came from; beggars were assumed to be vagabonds unless they could "give a good account" of themselves). In a rape trial, the prosecutor had to overcome the presumption that she was lying.

This presumptive mistrust certainly matches a large proportion of rape jokes, which in turn offer striking evidence of the atmosphere in which cases collapsed. But the capital trial records tell only a fraction of the story. Rape trials were never more than a tiny percentage of capital trials—rarely more than 1 percent, and never more than a handful of cases each year at the Old Bailey. For anyone hoping to recover the law's more everyday treatment of sexual violence, capital trials may be a red herring. Far more complaints were dismissed at the pretrial stage, in preliminary hearings before local JPs. In his meticulous analysis of the London Petty Sessions records between 1740 and 1767, Antony Simpson finds less than 15 percent of rape complaints being sent on to the grand jury, which itself selected only the strongest cases for formal trials. Since a large number of complaints were never documented, the true proportion of cases sent on must be much lower. Most were dismissed out of hand, a few were redefined as assaults or attempts, and the rest were "made up" by financial settlements, apologies, or offers of marriage.[110] The London newspapers constantly report rape cases that never appear in official records and must therefore have been settled or decided by local magistrates. What happened in these local summary hearings is therefore far more important than the periodic sessions at the Old Bailey. The problem—one repeatedly complained of in modern scholarship—is that the sources are mere scraps. Only a handful of JPs' notebooks survive. There was no legal obligation to record magistrates' hearings, and even the most detailed records, like the Middlesex Sessions Rolls, leave out complaints that produced no formal action such as a warrant or a jail delivery order (sadly, most rape accusations fall into this category). The newspapers were both selective and cavalier with the facts. But summary hearings do come up repeatedly in the eighteenth-century comic genres, and they come up as fully dramatized scenarios. That such evidence is problematic goes without saying. But read alongside the skeletal official records, comic texts might tell us much about the everyday treatment of rape complaints, and by extension about sexual practices that are otherwise lost to history.

A combination of imaginary and documentary sources yields no easy or consistent conclusions, but it may help us establish the range of possibilities and attitudes. Together, these sources confirm recent arguments that early modern people routinely approached local JPs to settle every sort of dispute. Local summary justice was by far the most routine contact between people and the law, and far more familiar than the awesome theatricality of the assizes. Peter King's analysis of records from one Essex community reveals more than 40 percent of the population involved with one or more summary hearings within a single four-year period. JPs worked as conciliators and peacemakers, resolving vast numbers of local conflicts while protecting the higher courts from trivial charges.[111] What King's work now demonstrates beyond a doubt is how frequently and tactically ordinary people used the law in this period. Read alongside the scattered evidence of real complaints, comic treatments of rape hearings suggest that accusations of sexual violence were being tossed about far more readily than we have suspected, and certainly more frequently than historians have concluded from the capital trial statistics. These accusations were being made from a complex range of motives and with strikingly different levels of determination. Some were clearly made in shock and terror, perhaps at the prompting of a well-meaning surgeon or the better sort of farmer's wife; others reflect a tragically naive belief that the law would protect injured innocence, while others were frankly instrumental attempts to force attackers into marriage or extract damages.

Whatever the motivation, both parties could be almost certain that the complaint would go no further than the summary stage, not least because of the heavy costs of prosecution.[112] In theory, a rape plaintiff had little control over how her case was framed or whether it was even sent on. But in practice these were private actions, and once a prosecutor dropped her charge, it was all over.[113] In this world of accusations and counteraccusations casually made and withdrawn, one is constantly struck by everyone's familiarity with the law. Women knew how to frame a rape charge, sometimes even repeating the statutory definitions word for word. In turn, their alleged attackers were ready with countercharges, to which the plaintiffs had further rebuttals. Upper-class rapists, for example, routinely countercharged that the woman had tried to rob them and dreamed up the rape only after they were found out. But one also finds female theft defendants arguing that their male prosecutor was just trying to force them to drop a rape charge.[114]

The imaginary sources do confirm historians' general arguments about high-low situations. Even if they accepted that a gentleman had forced a low-ranking woman against her will, most JPs concluded that it was a matter to be resolved with a few coins. Still, it is important to stress the range of motives and attitudes behind this one outcome. In the nastiest comic sources, the very idea that the woman would complain to a magistrate or expect to be taken seriously is itself a joke. The plaintiff is told to dry her tears, accept the money, and be satisfied with that. In the jestbooks, the situation dissolves into a bawdy play on words. What satisfaction would she have for the loss of her virginity? asks the plaintiff. "*Pho*, says the Justice, *ne're mind that Child; the first Loss is always the best*" (in modern terms, quit while you're ahead). The fellow would take care of her; it would be the "best Night's Work" she ever did.[115] Waggish gentlemen always have some trifling objection to the charge. Why would he defile his marriage bed? "There was no Bed in the Case," he replies—"it was done in a Field."[116] The unsympathetic atmosphere evoked in these jokes fits with what we know about the venality and incompetence of many local justices. But we also know that other JPs were sympathetic and responsible and that rape plaintiffs came to them supported by their community. In these contexts, monetary compensation could even be a compassionate resolution. Since rape convictions were so impossible to obtain, local magistrates may well have seen prosecutions for this crime as a waste of judicial resources. By informally "making up" the complaint, they were at least securing some sort of modest redress for the victim.

Between the scorn and the sympathetic pragmatism, one finds all sorts of even less comprehensible depictions. Consider one episode from *The History of Will Ramble* (1755), one of the loose comic novels I discuss in the conclusion to this book. Early in the book, on a Sunday morning when everyone else is at church, the young hero rapes Rose Freelove, his guardian's servant and an honest farmer's daughter. It is an attack as brutal as anything in sentimental fiction. "Catching her hold round the Neck, he pulled her down to him," and notwithstanding her "Storm of roaring and crying," he proves too strong for her. In comparison, what happens next is shockingly blasé. Will is not without remorse and hands over a couple of guineas, whereupon she, having wiped the Tears off her Face, and set her Cap and Apparel a little to rights by the Glass that was in his Room, went down Stairs as usual, about her Business.

Atrocious as it must seem to any modern reader, Will Ramble is presented as a likable and amusing character throughout. Nor is this the end of it. Rose soon proves pregnant. Will leaves for Oxford and pays her an allowance, but the poor woman is desperate and looks around for someone else to swear her bastard to. She fixes on Mr. Johnson, the justice's clerk, and allows herself to be seduced by him. The plan succeeds for a time and occasions much incidental humor as the sober clerk, a determined enemy to our hero, is dragged before his employer and humiliated. Yet the tone here is endlessly complex. On one hand, the lack of empathy is stunning, with the woman and her body as little more than a venue or blank space for a string of comic incidents. The episode ends on dark note, when Mr. Johnson discovers that Will had already had his "Finger in the Pye" and refuses Rose any further help. On the other hand, one finds a long and unexpectedly sympathetic discussion of the young woman's motives in laying her child to Mr. Johnson. Johnson was an unpleasant hypocrite and deserved to be exposed. Since Rose wasn't asked to swear a formal oath, no one could accuse her of perjury. She used some of the money to support her mother and three younger siblings.[117] It is an extraordinary moment of evenhandedness.

At such moments, one suddenly catches sight of the intricate web of circumstances behind the painfully terse records of local justice: the tangle of competing moral norms; the compromises, injuries, and partial compensations; small wrongs weighed against greater ones and little deceits practiced on those who could afford to pay. From the literary example, one starts to gloss the cryptic references in JPs' notebooks. One finds women using their local magistrate, or at least threatening to, to extract damages from attackers of higher status. The man pays up, and the case is dismissed. Repugnant as this transactional logic may be, it does at least suggest that ordinary women were not completely helpless. An employer tries to ravish his gardener's daughter: the case is made up by paying her a year's wages.[118] If she became pregnant, a rape victim could go before the JP and win damages or ongoing support payments. Obviously, no woman wanted to declare that she had been sexually assaulted. But we are now learning that appeals to the local JP were far more routine, and more successful, than we have assumed. For those at the bottom of the social heap, "going to law" was one of many survival strategies, part of the adaptive "economy of makeshifts" that British labor historians have recently described.[119] In this context, everyday legal actions take their place alongside neighborly reciprocities, appeals to the parish, and intermittent gleaning, stealing, and poaching, all of them ways of getting by. Ordinary people were reluctant and usually lacked the resources to take charges to the quarter sessions, but they were evidently willing enough to go before magistrates and seek informal arbitration. One finds them doing so with some expertise, selecting their JP according to his well-known sympathy for rape plaintiffs, unwed mothers, or hungry food thieves.

So much for genuine assaults. What is still more unexpected is the baffling variety of attitudes surrounding false accusations. The response could be hateful and vindictive, as we have seen. But the imaginary sources represent a far greater range of responses. A false rape charge can be a first-class trick and create all manner of incidental comedy. Rose Freelove's tactic with Mr. Johnson is typical of many fictional episodes in which a pregnant woman allows herself to be "raped" in order to force someone to pay for her bastard. Usually it is some respectable figure who will be gloriously humiliated by the charge. But some men were evidently flattered to be accused of rape, since it gave one a reputation for vigor. Thus the odd comic set piece of an impotent old man handing over his shillings with a display of delighted mock contrition. Here, from another forgotten comic novel, is Betty, the usual roadside maidservant, accusing an old miser named Squeezum. Betty says all the right things:

> The Chambermaid said, as she hop'd to be saved, she only went for the Gentleman's Candle, and he lock'd the Door and swore horridly he would murder her if she did not comply; and so, to save her Life, she did go to bed to him, that was the truth, if it was the last word she had to say.

Going for the gentleman's candle has its own lewd suggestion, and the complaint quickly evaporates once Squeezum hands over the necessary guinea. Betty then "embraced him, and hoped he would not forsake her, now that he had got his nasty Will of her." Squeezum himself is ecstatic since a report "that he should be so violent in his Love Attack" will help him snare a rich widow once the hated Mrs. Squeezum dies.[120] In other instances, an entire household conspires to entrap a suitable dupe with a rape charge. In the rudest cases, a syphilitic prostitute is hired to perform the role of ruined maiden. To the satisfaction of dragging her "attacker" before the justice and extorting damages is added the still greater joke that he will soon have the pox:

A young buxome Baggage, with a Candle in her Hand, was set upon by a Hot-spur, who by all Means must have a Bout with her; but she vowed, if he meddled with her, she would *burn* him: Will you so, says he, *I'll try that, and thereupon blew the Candle out, thinking himself safe from the Threat; however, not long after, he found she was as good as her Word.*

(Such jokes glance obliquely at another recognized strategy by which poor women tried to avoid sexual violence: a claim, whether true or false, that they had syphilis.)[121] At the same time, getting someone infected with vene-real disease was a familiar prank in this culture, and not necessarily such a nasty one. London bucks played the trick on their friends or gullible country cousins, who were expected to take it all in good fun. The same situation is repeated at startling length in "A Fireship instead of a Maidenhead," one of the annually reprinted tales in *Laugh and Be Fat*. Instead of deflowering his landlord's maid, a "rich Country Curmudgeon" is inveigled into bed with a prostitute, whom the maid enlists to lie in her bed for the night. The old man is immensely pleased with himself for successfully raping the young woman. He fantasizes about consoling the poor creature he has ruined. But then "the Fire which lay smothering in the Gentleman's lower Apartment, began to break out with most astonishing Violence." The whore, meanwhile, "could not Sleep for Laughing in her Sleeve, to think how she had Pepper'd off the Spark, and made him a Partner in Affliction."[122]

Gross exaggerations as they are, such examples do at least bring out the discursive presence of false rape accusations in this culture. Anxiety about malicious prosecutions is certainly one important context: it is prominently foregrounded in Hale's "accusation easily to be made" formula and glossed by every subsequent commentator. By the mid-eighteenth century, there was even talk of organized extortion—gangs that threatened innocent men with a rape charge unless they paid up. One study of 167 London prosecutions be-tween 1730 and 1830 finds the countercharge of extortion being made in more than one-third of them. It appears even where the victim is a minor.[123] It was a successful defense: any suggestion that the plaintiff or her family had initi-ated negotiations was enough to end the case, even though such cash settle-ments were established ways of "making up" for injuries of all sorts. At the higher courts, indeed, poverty itself cast suspicion on a rape plaintiff. As it happens, there is little evidence of blackmail rackets like those that entrapped homosexuals. Any real extortion was amateurish and involved small amounts of money, which may explain the peculiar levity of so many comic treatments. It was simply assumed that such things were going on: they were part of the innate sneakiness of the poor and something that amateurish local justices took for granted. More horrific acts of violence or significant property crimes were taken seriously, but there was nothing terribly important about the cheats of the lower classes.

Unfamiliar as it seems to us, increasingly detailed research is now showing that perjured testimony was almost taken for granted in this world and usually went unpunished. The defendant in a failed criminal case could sue for both false imprisonment and malicious prosecution, but in practice this was rare. False rape complaints were generally stopped at the summary stage: there was some danger of a flogging, but usually not even that.[124] One rape plaintiff to William Hunt, a Wiltshire gentleman-justice, simply admits that she was lying once the accused man disappears. "Upon which recalled my warrant," Hunt concludes.[125] The main thing at this level was that the conflict was resolved and the higher courts were not overburdened. Even at the Old Bailey, one finds the same stunning indifference to perversions of justice. A rape case brought by one London barmaid is dismissed when it comes out that she had already threatened another man with the same charge and had in fact extorted 10s. 6d. out of him. The trial ends with a simple caution: "You should not play these tricks, young woman."[126] Clearly, all the assumptions about artful women conceal numberless instances of horrific violence. But it is also no accident that the circumstances of local justice—even rape charges, perjury, and shabby extortion attempts—translated so easily into jokes. To visit the justice's parlor was to see all the humiliations and dirty secrets of village life. These semipublic hearings were recognized diversions in rural communities, as they certainly were in London. Curses and insults were exchanged across the chamber. A procession of witnesses turned up to announce that they had caught the curate in bed with a kitchenmaid or that the plaintiff was a well-known local harlot.

For all the literary and erotic force of the *Pamela* scenario, we know that lower-class women were far more likely to be raped by social equals. London maidservants were much more often attacked by fellow servants in the same house than by their masters. Farm women were raped by other villagers as they wandered home after dark. Laborers broke into cottages after a night at the alehouse. Such violence between social equals has not always been easy to describe. E. P. Thompson's attack on the "condescension of posterity"—his determination to demonstrate the importance of ordinary people to the movement of history and to discharge assumptions that cast them as brutal and unworthy of notice—still carries immense moral weight. After decades of work on solidarities, collective action, and the formation of class consciousness, we are only beginning to recognize the tensions and conflicts of plebeian life. Anna Clark has starkly reminded us that proletarian class consciousness did nothing to improve the lives of women. Laura Gowing's work on seventeenth-century church court records provides an unforgettable picture of mutual hatreds at the bottom of society, and certainly dispels easy assumptions we might have about solidarity between women. No one can now overlook the nastiness of early modern plebeian life: the violence and long-held grudges, the insults and catfights in alleyways, the elaborate vengeance for unpaid debts or borrowed goods not returned. Litigious spats, threats, and accusations (true or false) were all powerful forms of revenge.[127]

Even so, it is hard for us to imagine a rape charge being used in these ways. In the mid-eighteenth century, however, this was a presumption to be overcome: if she wasn't after money, it was widely assumed, a rape plaintiff must have some private grievance. Especially in prosecutions between social equals, a successful rape plaintiff would have to demonstrate that she had no motive for vengeance. When the London servant Mary Brickinshaw prosecuted an Irish journeyman baker in 1768, she had to establish not only that she had no grudge against the defendant or his master, but also that neither did her master or mistress, who were supporting the prosecution.[128] And now and then one does find rape charges being used in some strikingly unfamiliar ways. An Old Bailey prosecution of 1752 collapses with the plaintiff admitting that she was trying to punish the defendant, who had accused her of sleeping with another man: "[S]he could not tell how to be revenged of him in any other shape, than to swear a rape against him."[129]

In sexual assault cases, this culture of conflict and retribution combined with all the ambiguities and misunderstandings of early modern courtship. By far the most common rape charge at this level of society came from women forced by men who were courting them or had done so. We are still piecing together our understanding of premarital sexuality among the early modern working class. Focusing on deep-seated structures of obligation and oath keeping, John Gillis describes restrained and careful interactions between the sexes, with intercourse allowed only after a solemn "betrothal" or promise of marriage.[130] Plainly the reality was much messier, and newly accessible documents—poor law records, Foundling Hospital petitions, and the like—point to constant ambiguities of language and custom. One finds tragic misunderstandings around consent and compulsion, broken promises, lovers absconding or dragged unwilling to the altar. The confusions were clearly compounded by the fact that even consensual sex was so often understood as an act of violence, by the presumption that sexual initiation was painful for women, and by the blurred line between cries of resistance and the modest reluctance that was so widely expected. Betrothal or the acceptance of a man's promise effectively constituted permission to use force and to ignore subsequent objections.[131]

Yet the miscommunication and misery were all resolved once the man kept his promise to marry: this is the message of repeated comic treatments with their obligatory happy endings. Even if they were absolutely satisfied that the defendant had overcome a virgin against her will, most JPs would conclude that he had just been a little too eager in his wooing. If the parties knew each other, as was usually the case, the justice would generally accept the defendant's claim that the whole thing was no more than a "sweetheart business"— a silly lover's quarrel and certainly nothing to hang a man over. One London summary hearing of 1730 is easily made up when the defendant offers to marry his accuser and sends for a Fleet clergyman, "who married them at a tavern in Smithfield, to the great joy of all parties." The *Grub-Street Journal* reprinted the story with its usual wry critique: "Such precedents may prove of dangerous consequences, by introducing a very easy way of getting immediately either a portion, or a husband."[132] Fielding the magistrate resolves a similar situation: a rape plaintiff accepts a proposal from the defendant, and, "[i]nstead of returning before the Justices, they went directly before the Parson."[133] All this unfolds with the kindly justice chortling at the quaint conflicts of ordinary life.

Consent, refusal, betrothal, and even marriage itself were all ambiguous at this level of society. Hardwicke's famous Marriage Act (1753) only partially clarified the muddle of more customary arrangements—all the semilegal ceremonies, "broomstick" weddings, and cohabitations understood as marriage. These definitions were never so important where there was no property involved. And thus, in social and even legal practice, *rape* was defined less as an act of violence than by what happened or didn't happen before and afterward. In these socially equal situations, as with higher-status attackers, one finds increasing evidence that women were using a rape charge, or a threat of one, to exercise some control over events. Lump-sum compensations, periodic child-support payments, marriage—all these remedies came up repeatedly in JPs' notebooks. Ever conciliatory, William Hunt made up even the most brutal attacks with cash payments (five guineas, three guineas, eight shillings).[134] And often, it would seem, the parties would reach their own agreement. "They agreed as I heard at £2 1s." "It was agreed without a hearing, paying her 2s. 6d."[135] This custom of routine conciliation may explain some of the oddities of rape reporting at the Old Bailey, where so many cases between social equals read like local complaints that have got out of hand, cases in which the usual negotiation process had broken down.

This is not to underestimate the shame or the agonizing sense of compromise that must have surrounded such accusations. Going before the JP was presumably a last resort, something to do only after private threats or community pressure had failed. As for marrying one's rapist, some women might have engineered this outcome, but the level of compulsion becomes clear once one notices how inevitably a woman's complaint collapsed if her attacker was offering to repair the damage by marriage and she was refusing. Presenting oneself as a rape victim was an extraordinarily risky and uncertain thing to do. For a pregnant woman trying to get money out of the parish or to have her child accepted at the Foundling Hospital, it was far better to claim that she had been seduced after a promise of marriage that was later broken (not least because for so many pregnancy implied consent).[136] Thus all the evidence of rape victims testing the community mood or seeking advice about how to frame things.[137] Perhaps some of these women knew what they were doing in confiding in others (a successful prosecution depended on the victim having told someone at the time). Perhaps some were consciously manipulating public opinion against their attackers or hedging their bets in case the man refused to make amends. And certainly one finds neighborhoods rallying around rape plaintiffs, vilifying the attacker or driving him out of town.

But more often, one can be sure, victims were reaching out in confusion and trauma. The most predictable result, at this stage as above, was hostility and disbelief. Read against the JPs' notebooks, literary rape hearings seem to tell us much about what went on in all those parlors and vestry rooms when ordinary women came in to make a rape charge. Elinor Carruthers, a seventeen-year-old woman from Tyneside, accuses two miners of raping her in a field; the complaint is struck out with the annotation "this Elinor Carruthers was proved to be a *common strumpet*."[138] A Hackney laborer and his wife complain "that about 3 weeks or 4 weeks since she was forced &c by Rob. Flemming in his own house." This was clearly a run-of-the-mill extortion case: "[O]n ye relation [it] did not appear to be force."[139] The counteraccusations were automatic, almost instinctual. She was trying to force an unwilling man to marry her. She wanted him to pay for someone else's bastard. Someone had found her having sex in the barn, and she had to say *something*. Maybe, women being what they were, she was just gratifying some dark, spiteful impulse. In the most traditional communities, any woman who dared to raise a rape charge could herself be accused of debauchery and might even be forced to perform penance—dressed in a white sheet and made to confess her depravity in church or at the market cross.[140] The hostility was reflexive. Hadn't she punished him enough? Did she really want the man's blood on her hands? Rural rape trials, whichever way the verdict went, could be followed by weeks of rough music. Obscene effigies of the plaintiff were paraded around town and burned in bonfires; the collective vengeance could last for weeks, if not for the rest of the woman's life.[141] If things got so far as a death sentence, let alone an execution, there was no predicting what might happen.

On the morning of 19 August 1763, a large crowd gathered around the New Gaol in Croydon, determined to prevent the execution of a coachman named Matthew Dodd. Coincidently employed by the courtesan Kitty Fisher (of whom more in the conclusion to this book), Dodd was condemned for raping a farmer's daughter named Ann Dutnell on her way to Croydon market. The mob twice stopped the cart that was to carry Dodd to his execution on Kennington Common, forcing the sheriff to request a military detachment from London. Around noon, a tremendous storm broke out, which the mob interpreted as a sign of divine displeasure: even God thought the man should be spared. The standoff continued until six in the evening, when a detachment of 150 soldiers with fixed bayonets arrived to escort the cart. Dodd's wife then burst out of her lodgings next to the jail and "made several hideous shrieks, which greatly alarmed the unfortunate man, and raised the compassion of the populace." By then an enormous crowd had gathered from all the outlying villages, and the execution could not be completed until 7.30 P.M. A full record of the trial has not survived in the Surrey Assize Proceedings. Dodd confessed that he had dragged the plaintiff off her horse and tried to rape her, but he denied the fact. Whatever actually happened, Ann Dutnell was horribly injured and died five days after her attacker. An aldermanly correspondent from Croydon expressed outrage at both the rescue attempt and Dodd's denial of the crime. It was a "plain and clear case," "one of the vilest rapes ever committed." Besides, he concludes, if they hadn't executed the man, "the country markets must have been hurt." Which farmer's daughter would want to take her eggs to market?[142]

HUMORS OF THE OLD BAILEY

Having said that capital trials are a red herring for anyone interested in the everyday legal treatment of rape, I now return to the Old Bailey Sessions Papers. For all the fine work on these records, much remains to be said about their tone and narrative shaping. The atmosphere and even the procedures of eighteenth-century rape trials are still obscure. Famous prosecutions like those of Charteris (1732) and Lord Baltimore (1768) are atypical in every way. The brutal sex crimes explored by Randolph Trumbach and other historians of sexuality are equally anomalous. The vast majority of Old Bailey rape cases are deliberately expansive comic representations of unsuccessful prosecutions. Distasteful as they are, these comic acquittals tell us much about the haphazard treatment of sexual violence at even London's highest court. In turn, they raise questions about the evidentiary reliability of the Sessions Papers, which have generally been accepted as accurate if incomplete.

It comes as no surprise to find the Sessions Papers covering sex crime trials in greater detail than other felonies. Along with divorce and criminal conversation cases, rape trial reports satisfied an open craving for sensationalism. But smut came in many forms: in spite of all the talk about female spectators swooning in the gallery, there is no erotic melodrama about any of these cases. Most involve rows between highly particularized plebeians: an orange wench accuses a soldier of raping her in a stable; two Irish beggars offer competing accounts of what went on under a bulk at Fleet Market. Slum realism, not pornography, is the genre here. In fact, the most explicit part of the evidence is either glossed over or recorded in the protagonists' own dirty lingo (much of it rendered phonetically). The reports capture an atmosphere of mild excitement; there is little real sexual charge. One can almost feel the fidgeting and smirking as the crowd waits for the first naughty word, chortles while the plaintiff is denounced as the neighborhood harlot, and, finally, bursts into laughter when the poor woman accidentally betrays her consent. How these cases made it through the summary stage and the further filtering of the grand juries is anyone's guess: most are doomed from the start. Perhaps the authorities had waved the case on in a general expectation that the parties would make up before anything got serious.

It helps to recognize that the Old Bailey was one of the great diversions of eighteenth-century London, a destination recommended in guidebooks and a routine fixture of the metropolitan entertainment calendar. For four or five days eight times a year, the old Sessions House was packed with spectators of both sexes and every social rank. For all the rituals and theatricality of the law—the robes and wigs, the grandiose rhetoric and drama of life and death— Old Bailey trials were rowdy and often chaotic affairs. Much of the crowd was often drunk and regularly interrupted proceedings with laughter, heckling, and missiles thrown across the room.[143] To an extent scholars have yet to recognize, the Sessions Papers strove to capture this atmosphere and its inherent social comedy. The papers were always a commercial venture, uncomfortably positioned between their official functions and the demands of the market. For about a decade in the 1720s and early 1730s, the reporters openly elaborated certain cases as comic scenarios, transcribing extended dialogues, and even reproducing dialects, speech impediments, and slips of the tongue. ("Yesh-fait, upon my Shoul," swears every Irish witness, "tat ish very true indeed.") The Sessions Papers, wrote one foreign visitor during this period, "are in the opinion of many one of the most diverting things one can read in London."[144] The humor was somewhat curtailed in the 1730s, after one particularly farci-cal trial attracted official attention and the printer was forced to publish an apology for his "rude and indecent" way of reporting.[145] But the publisher's commercial interests long continued to determine which trials were summa-rized and which were selected for extended treatment. "These little Histo-ries," announces one collected edition of trial reports in 1764, "will afford the curious Peruser, not only Instruction, but an agreeable Amusement." Like so many other print genres, trial records were offered for reading aloud as much as individual enjoyment. "They may be considered as a Collection of Dra-matical Pieces," the preface continues, each of them offering a "new Scene of Action" and gradually moving to "the final Catastrophe."[146]

The most reliably comic trials were (1) anything involving a linguistic mi-nority, where accents and incomprehensions made for such good comic busi-ness, (2) thefts of small animals or food, and (3) the historically specific crime of "private stealing." *Private stealing* meant robbing people without their knowledge, usually prostitutes robbing their clients. The comic potentials of this last scenario will be obvious: a respectable plaintiff accusing a foul-mouthed whore, inevitable questions about how she could pick his pocket without him noticing ("were there any familiarities betwixt ye?"), demands for further specificity about bodily hiding places, and so on.[147] Appalling as it must seem, unsuccessful rape trials drift just as insistently toward comedy. Semiliterate plaintiffs muddle and curse while the defendant's character wit-nesses turn up to destroy their reputation. On the very day mentioned in the indictment, says one witness, he "saw her lay upon the Grass, behind a Hedge, with 3 Boys one on each Side, and the other upon her, &c."[148] He'd seen her drinking with the prisoner for weeks before the alleged attack; one of her neighbors caught her having sex with a strange man on the staircase. "She is a very vile girl. I have seen a young man upon her with his breeches down, and her cloaths up, and another man lie by the side of her in a stable. I have laid with her a great many times myself."[149] Such testimony reveals in an instant the topography of plebeian sex (barns, hedgerows, attics, and haystacks). Almost any plaintiff over the age of nine—and occasionally, more disturbingly, even younger ones—faced a hostile and scoffing cross-examination.[150] Accused of raping a girl of ten, one defendant doesn't even bother to deny the charge, merely claiming that "somebody else had known the Girl before him" and bringing witnesses to denounce her as "a forward wicked Girl."[151]

Merely through the reporter's selection or compression, many cases fall effortlessly into comic patterns. Why did you stay for three months when he was trying to rape you several times a week?[152] What did the cook say when you told her he had raped you? She said if I played my cards right, I could do quite well for myself.[153] Do you have any children? Yes—I had one after Mr. N ravished me last year.[154] You could easily have stopped him if you'd put down the baby. Why did you have to keep holding the baby?[155] Why did you go through the fields with him? Because I was afraid of being ravished in the street with all those people around.[156] These last lines come strikingly close to punch lines. In the original versions of the Sessions Papers, and even more in reedited collections, particularly farcical moments are often set in italics and followed almost instantly by the negative verdict. The plaintiff told me that she "*had rather marry him than hang him*," announces the final witness; "the Jury acquitted him."[157] "The Prisoner in his Defence said that he had been as loving with them both as ever he had been with his own Wife, and met with no more Opposition—The Jury acquitted him."[158] One plaintiff accidentally admits that someone else had raped her the previous week and that she hadn't complained that time.[159] A surgeon admits that he couldn't tell whether the woman had been raped (there was no blood, so unless her attacker was "extremely small . . .").[160] The plaintiff's midwife accidentally incriminates them both: she doesn't know whether the man had actually raped the plaintiff, but, speaking for herself, she would never have done it "*in such a dirty Place*."[161]

Some of the most protracted acquittals are structured as fully developed one-act farces. The average length of acquittals in the Sessions Papers is 150 words; cases like *R. v. Kill* (17 October 1743) extend to almost 4,000.[162] Thomas Kill is a basketmaker of twenty-five, accused of rape by Elizabeth Berry, a hefty and hard-drinking working woman in her fifties, married for thirty-two years with twelve children, and well-known for going to law against her neighbors. The first part of her evidence is printed as an astonishing, unstructured ramble, full of non sequiturs and compromising details, like any of the best stage monologues of this period. She spends pages and pages wandering about Chelsea Common looking for her drunken husband, who keeps lying down in his stupor. At last she arrives at the crucial part of her testimony, only to have the courtroom erupt into laughter: "I held out against him, till I had no strength in me—he pulled my Legs open with his hands." Everyone laughs, and Berry is forced to scold: "I knew these Things before I came here; I expected to be laughed at, but it is not a laughing Matter." Kill was at it for half an hour, she continues—and then he did it again. Afterward, since it was so late, she asked him to see her home. They walked past several taverns, but everyone was going to bed, and she didn't want to make a fuss. Finally she gets her attacker home and locks him up in her own house (the constable "was in Bed and said he could not get up, and could not find the Key of the Cage"). A lengthy cross-examination follows, during which Mrs. Berry repeatedly impugns herself:

Q: What did he say to you after he had done what he did to you?
BERRY: After I got off the bed—
Q: Off the Bed!
BERRY: Off the Ground . . .

On and on it goes. You are an extremely large woman. You managed to lock him up in your house for most of the night; couldn't you protect your chastity? Eventually she loses patience:

COUNSEL: How long might he be penetrating your body?
BERRY: Longer than I desired, as I told you before.
COUNSEL: What did he penetrate you with?
BERRY: With what other People do, and with what you do other People with.

Here the reporter doesn't need to record the howls of laughter—and even this is not the end of it. Finally it emerges that Mr. Berry hates his wife and had tried to lock her up in a private madhouse in Southwark. "She is a vile, sottish, drunken Woman, and a great lieprobate," concludes the last defense witness. "I would not hang a Dog upon her evidence."[163]

Such texts reflect the general skepticism with which early modern justice treated women, whether as plaintiffs, witnesses, or defendants. But it was still infinitely easier for a woman to hang someone for stealing a pocket watch than it was to win a rape case. As a general rule, the Sessions Papers are more sympathetic to prosecutors: testimony from defense witnesses is abridged, while that for the prosecution is given in detail. With rape trials, they do exactly the opposite. The entire parade of character witnesses gets to speak. She used to be my apprentice, declares a neighbor of Sarah Evans. She was "a great Liar, and a Pilferer," and came home drunk every night with mud on her petticoat. She would sleep with anyone, "tho' she did not know him, if he did but say, *Come* Sal *go with me*." After more than two pages of this, the reporter abbreviates all testimony from the other side, stating simply: "Several gave the Prisoner the Character of a sober modest honest Man."[164]

With other crimes, the reporter usually ignored stumblings and repetitions. Evidence produced under cross-examination was integrated into the original testimony, making it appear as a single statement. Thomas Gurney, the official shorthand writer from 1748 to 1769, once testified about his recording practices. "If a question brings out an imperfect answer, and is obliged to be asked over again, and the answer comes out more strong, I take that down as the proper evidence and neglect the other," he declared. "It is not to be expected I should write down every unintelligible word."[165] Question-and-answer sequences were extremely rare: even in the 1780s, notes John Langbein, the Sessions Papers "were still omitting most of what was said at most of the trials they reported."[166] Rape trial records reverse every one of these norms, recording contradictions, verbal tics, and long sequences of dialogue. They take special delight in needless particularities. ("He bolted the Door, and blew out the Candle, but she being a Maid blew it in again, the Prisoner blew it out again, and she again blew it in 2 or 3 Times.")[167]

Here, exactly as it appears, is the testimony of the rustic Sarah Muns, who has somehow been forced into a prosecution:

> He was very rude—and—a—lay with me—once—whether I would or no.— He had the car—nal—use of my Body—without my Con—sent—by— Force—but not—not against my Will.—I did not comply thro' any Fear— He forced me to it by great Per—Persuasion, and not by any Threats.—And indeed, I cannot say whether he had any Thing to—to—do with me or no. He might, or might not,—but he never meddled with me,—so as to do me any Harm; for if he had, I should have cry'd out; but I made no Noise at all.

The editor of *Select Trials* has still more fun, introducing a rustic dialect ("It *mought* be the Prisoner—or it *mought* not") and further slips (he "lay with me once—I think it was once").[168] One acquittal of 1751 offers phenomenal swathes of this absurd dialogue. Again, the plaintiff seems to have been forced into the prosecution—this time as a way of appeasing her husband after she stayed out all night. The whole thing unfolds at a glacial pace:

Q: What did he do to you?
C. KENSEY: He—me.
Q: Did he throw you down?
C. KENSEY: No.
COUNSEL: What, not upon a table?
C. KENSEY: No.
COUNSEL: Not upon a chair?
C. KENSEY: No, neither of them.
Q: Did you cry out?
C. KENSEY: I did not.
Q: What did he say to you?
C. KENSEY: He said he would lie with me.
Q: What did you say?
C. KENSEY: I said he should not.
Q: Did you resist him?
C. KENSEY: I had not strength to do anything.
Q: Had you any marks or bruises?
C. KENSEY: I had none.
Q: Was you hurt?
C. KENSEY: I was not hurt at all. . . .
COUNSEL: Was this mischief done as you was standing?
C. KENSEY: It was.
COUNSEL: Do not you know, that had you made a small resistance in that position you was in, it would have been impossible for him to have committed a rape upon you?
No Answer.[169]

This example offers an extended script for reading aloud, but in the hands of a waggish reporter, every sort of misunderstanding could be recast as comic. Thus the cross-examination of a girl of twelve:

Q: Did you consent or resist at the time?
UPINGTON: Yes.
Q: Did you consent?
UPINGTON: Yes Sir.

Q: Was it with your will or against your will that he lay with you?
UPINGTON: Against my will.[170]

To a modern reader such exchanges conjure up a terrified confusion, yet for the upper- and middle-class consumers who bought these pamphlets and read the trials aloud, it was evidently funny. Why else reproduce the entire exchange when the last two lines would do? A poor knowledge of English was an invariable source of farcical misunderstanding. Here, for example, is the cross-examination of a Welsh woman from Spitalfields, at a time when a majority of the Welsh population knew no English at all:

Q: Did you make an[y] Resistance?
SARAH EVANS: No—I don't know what Resistance is.
Q: Did you struggle, or cry out?
SARAH EVANS: Yes, I struggled as much as I could, and cry'd out as loud as I could all the while.[171]

All these reporting habits and many more are exemplified at astonishing length in the trial of John Ellis, turnkey at the Gatehouse Prison in Westminster (8 December 1731). A thug who operated on every side of the law, Ellis exemplifies the grubby world of bailiffs, thief takers, and sponging-house keepers. But his accuser, Sarah Matts, was hardly the ideal plaintiff. She had already been whipped for stealing a quilt and reappears in at least three more theft cases before she is transported early in 1736. Ellis freely admits that Matts and he had slept together, but insists that she was willing and later came to drink a glass of wine with him (*"Here's to you* John, *you are no fumbler, for you have lain with me 20 times"*). The slum comedy only expands when Matts calls a friend to testify on her behalf. "I was sent to the Gatehouse for striking a Woman a blow with a Frying pan," the woman begins. "I went up into her Room, and found her crying. Sarah, says I to her, I hope he hasn't—yes, says she, but he has, and beat and bruised me too."[172]

The case becomes progressively more bizarre as its sordid back-story comes to light. The defendant asserts that Matts is trying to punish him for having arrested her a few months earlier, when she had helped one John Sherwin escape from Newgate in women's clothes. Sherwin himself then turns up to refute this counteraccusation: "Sarah Matts knew nothing of my going out of Gaol in Women's Clothes. No-body knew of it but my Wife and Daughter." Then begins the usual procession of character witnesses. "Sarah Matts is a common vile Woman. The greatest Blackguard may lie with her for

6d." Neighbors had seen her in bed with the prisoner several times since the alleged rape. Odder still is the testimony of one Henry Williams, who turns up to declare that he had slept with Matts on the very evening of the alleged rape:

> I was committed to the Gatehouse, because my Boy swore Sodomy against me; which I am as innocent of, as I am of going to Heaven. Now Sarah Matts being there, I wanted a Bit of that same—as any other Man may—and so I invited her to the Sport, and lay with her in March and April too. I'll assure you I did not ravish her, any other wise than by talking her over, and making her drink, as a man must always do in such Cases; for you know a Woman must be coax'd a little, though she's never so willing.

At this point Williams is interrupted by the judge. "You say right, my Lord, I am a very impudent Fellow, that's true; but I can't help it—Truth is Truth, and it will come out." Anyway, he knew for a fact that Sarah Matts had never been to bed with the prisoner—he had asked her so before they had their bit of fun. Ellis's gonorrhea was notorious, and Williams certainly didn't want to take the clap home to his wife. Justice De Veil, Fielding's predecessor at the Bow Street Magistrate's Court, is there to announce that it was only a month since the plaintiff's last rape prosecution—this time against Ellis's friend James "One Eye" Sylvester. Even the Middlesex executioner John Hooper (fl. 1728–35), "the Laughing Hangman" as he was known, turns up to denounce Sherwin and Matts for trying to punish Ellis for arresting them both.[173]

In these capital trials, as with so many summary hearings, one is struck by the baffling levity toward perversions of justice. An apprentice accusing his master of sodomy (along with the riddling suggestion that it might be true); a hardened thief in league with a cross-dressing jailbreaker, both of them trying to punish a grubby turnkey (or, failing that, one of his friends) with a charge of rape: all these shabby abuses are presented as little more than the ongoing comedy of plebeian life. In an odd way, the actual truth doesn't seem to matter. Again and again, one finds the same casual references to threats, bribes, informers, spying neighbors, and reckless rape charges being thrown about— all as ways of avenging private enmities. The girl's parents were always taking their neighbors to court, announces one defense witness; they offered to drop the case if the prisoner gave them £100.[174] "*You had better be quiet*," says Elizabeth Berry to Thomas Kill, "*for I know you.*" "*Damn you for a* Newgate *Bitch*," Kill replies, using some now-forgotten term for a litigious matron.[175]

These and dozens of similar cases point to widely shared beliefs about the mendacity of the poor, and to more specific assumptions that they understood and knew how to manipulate the law. Although they rarely say so openly, the reporters consistently imply that the plaintiffs had been instructed or knew exactly what to say. He forced drink on me; I was bruised all over my body; my petticoat was torn to shreds; "a great deal of moisture came from him."[176] Thus the knowing, sardonic tone of so much recorded testimony, often emphasized with italic type. "It was about 7 o'Clock at Night when he *deluded me*."[177] "I awaked and struggled with him as long as I could. No person could ever struggle more than I did."[178] "You would have bless'd yourself to have seen me," begins yet another plaintiff.

> The Blood gush'd out of my Nose, and ran into my Mouth, as I lay upon my back; so that I had like to have been strangled with it. I was all over bloody, from Head to Foot, both within and without—I was in such an Agony!—I struggled and strove, and did all that a Woman could do, till I was quite spent.

The bungled grammar and folkish locutions are all irrelevant to any legal question. As so often, the editor of *Select Trials* points up the irony, adding an emphatic adjective: "all that a *weak* Woman could do."[179] A skilled defense counsel would explicitly confront the plaintiff. You've been practicing, haven't you? "When did you get the story so perfect?"[180]

As the authorities increasingly curtailed the more explicit slum comedy, a skeptical third-person narrative voice came to take its place, by turns arch, mock portentous, and pseudosentimental. Determined to make the room "as dark as his Deeds," the defendant blew out his candle, and then "the Innocent *Elizabeth Smith* was made a Sacrifice." The chair was broken in the very "*middle of the ceremony*."[181] She was a pure, chaste virgin before that fatal night. Where had she sat down after "this mighty affair was over?"[182] Clearly, some of this sarcasm reflects elite fears of entrapment or blackmail. But, since most of these abuses involved ordinary people extorting small sums of money from their social equals, who cared?

Anyone who finds these readings unconvincing might look at the surviving volume of *Humours of the Old Bailey* (for 1720–27). All sixteen private stealing cases are here, along with a couple of droll felony hearings and two bigamy cases in French dialect ("Mine broder, *Jean Gandon*, and dis voman, de preesonar, vas marrie togader at de *Stapaney-shursh*"). And every one of the comic rape acquittals for these years is here. *R. v. Alloway*, with all the plaintiff's stammering and reluctance rendered typographically. *R. v. J——*, where the woman accidentally lets slip that she "*had rather marry him than hang him.*" *R. v. Pritchard*, where she acknowledges that she went into the fields with the defendant—but only "for fear of being ravished in the Publick Street." The volume ends with *R. v. Coventry*, where the midwife announces that she herself would never have done it in that filthy place. Gesturing toward a range of still more distant comic scenarios, *Humours of the Old Bailey* also includes three more rape cases I had not thought to discuss, all of them reprinted verbatim from the Sessions Papers.[183]

At this point, growing concerns about the evidentiary value of the Sessions Papers cannot be ignored. The general consensus among legal historians has long been that the records omit things but don't make them up. John Langbein's comparison between four sets of midcentury Sessions Papers and notes taken by the judge Sir Dudley Ryder found no significant fabrications: "If the OBSP reports that something happened, it did. If the OBSP report does not say it happened, it still may have." These conclusions are supported by observations about the papers' semiofficial functions, about the presence of witnesses, and about the simultaneous publication of other records. For all these reasons, Langbein concludes, the publishers couldn't depart too far from the truth.[184] Yet recent work on the reporters' shorthand system has made it clear the trial records were essentially re-creations. Thomas Gurney acknowledged that a single reporter did not and could not write everything down. When public interest demanded an absolutely verbatim record (as, e.g., with the Elizabeth Canning case of 1754), his publisher hired additional reporters to assist him.[185] In such cases as *R. v. Ellis*, one finds definite proof of fabrication—of specific comic additions. One can be certain that Henry Williams did say he was "as innocent of sodomy as [he was] of going to Heaven" (to spell it out, being innocent of going to heaven meant going to hell). Real Irishmen do not talk in Irish bulls, but they routinely do so in the Sessions Papers ("O' my Shoul, I wash got pretty drunk, and wash going very shoberly along the *Old-Baily*").[186] Gurney's own moderate literary gifts are demonstrated in several volumes of poetry and some fanatical anti-Methodist tracts. Surely we need to pay more attention to the literary shaping of all these records.

In turn, these long, semifarcical acquittals might provide further insights into the atmosphere of many more compressed cases and, beyond them, of the briefest summary hearings. One cannot avoid, in all this, the sound of collective laughter. Some of this is the laughter of a roomful of men as a threat to widely shared standards is so easily and predictably broken down. But at least as much is laughter at the petty world of litigious spats, bribes, perjured witnesses, insults, and revenge. Of course, there are other much more sympathetic cases: horrific acts of violence that no one could ignore. Occasionally one finds an entire community united behind a rape plaintiff. But the statistics speak for themselves: the less sympathetic reactions predominated.

*

Sentimental representations of rape and the reality of social and legal attitudes have almost nothing in common. I have used these trials as a sort of limit or test case—a venue in which female sentimental symptoms are completely out of place. Almost none of these rape plaintiffs, and certainly none of the successful ones, faints away in the courtroom. Nor would it do to claim that one had swooned at the moment of attack. This would obviously make it difficult then to give a detailed account of what had happened. But surely more important, the claim that one had "fainted away in terror," "had no strength to resist," or was "insensible through fright" inevitably recalled all the old sayings about women always fainting at the right moment. General claims that an attacker had overpowered one were not sufficient either. What was required was a convincing account of a major struggle and usually some horrible injuries to prove it. A successful plaintiff would specify a period of time for this struggle (half an hour seems to be the accepted minimum). Some of these struggles are almost unimaginable: one successful plaintiff "scuffed with [her attacker] for almost three hours, but being at last spent with loss of blood, was forced to submit to his inhuman lust."[187]

In the courtroom, too, the successful rape plaintiff was stoical, not sentimental. It would not do to faint, weep, or tremble; all these symptoms were contaminated with ancient prejudices about women as emotional manipulators. It followed that there was no place in the courtroom for psychic trauma, which makes no appearance in the records except as an occasional compressed euphemism. "I was quite outrageous"; "I was deeply shamed": women sometimes volunteer such information, but no one asks for it, and it is irrelevant. The case failed immediately if the victim had not reported the attack at the time or at least told someone—a "stale Complaint" was always dubious, said Blackstone.[188] The notion that a rape victim might be silent through trauma, confusion, or shame seems hardly to have existed. (The exception that proves the rule is the trauma of younger plaintiffs—thus a conviction of 1748 where the court accepts a thirteen-year-old's claim that she didn't tell anyone because

her stepfather threatened to kill her.)[189] Women's inner states might have become more representable and more credible, but, when a man's life was at
stake, few were prepared to trust them. In judicial contexts, at least, women
and their bodies were empty signifiers. Activity, passivity, speech, silence—all
were open to lewd interpretation. All implied consent.

Without taking up the tangled subject of *Clarissa* and eighteenth-century
rape law, recall the heroine's reasons for declining to prosecute Lovelace.
When she contemplates a public trial, Clarissa imagines being laughed at. Her
tragic story, she recognizes, would easily be displaced by Lovelace's comic
one—the ancient and culturally more plausible story of a woman who at first
consents and then cries rape. He would charm all the women, be admired by
the men, and repeatedly offer to repair the damage by marriage, while Clarissa
would seem irrational and vindictive. Even her description of his "infamous
methods"—the opiates conveyed in a foul-tasting mug of "London milk"—
would be "bandied about and jested profligately with." Her experience, as she
tells the naive Doctor Lewin, could be properly reported only to a "*private
and serious* audience."[190]

Were these things changing? Could a rape victim tell her story and expect to be taken seriously? John Beattie, acknowledging the limitations of his
sample size, nevertheless describes victims' increasing willingness to come
forward and, by implication, a greater readiness of courts and communities
to believe them. In a fascinating recent article, Lincoln Faller describes a
"*Clarissa* effect" in records of the Baltimore prosecution of 1768. Richardson scholars have long taken this case as an analogue for Clarissa Harlowe's
plight; Faller's innovation is to speculate about the novel's influence on a case
and its reporting. Long passages of the official Baltimore trial record read like
sentimental fiction. The testimony of Sarah Woodcock, Baltimore's victim, is
a uniquely detailed and circumstantial record of psychological and physical
torment: the cruel trick by which Baltimore and his servants lure her into
his house; her fruitless pleading, weeping, and struggles to escape; and the
horrifying final days at his country house, where he repeatedly tries to rape
her and eventually succeeds. At almost three hundred pages, it is probably the
longest rape trial record to date. The trial itself lasted from 7 A.M. one morning
to 3 A.M. the following day.[191]

Baltimore was widely vilified. Even before the trial, a torrent of pamphlets
appeared telling Sarah Woodcock's pitiful story and calling for the full vengeance of the law. After his death in the autumn of 1771, a furious mob sacked
the undertaker's rooms in Exeter Change where his body was displayed to
the public. But all this was accompanied by an equally powerful body of pro-

Baltimore publications—from lighthearted celebrations of Baltimore's erotic exploits to virulent attacks on his accuser. One of the oddest writings on the affair is an anonymous line-by-line gloss of Woodcock's testimony—printed, like a legal commentary, in parallel columns. To even the slightest utterance of this simple young woman, the author responds with snide asides or long, pedantic demonstrations that she just had to be lying. Above all, every sentimental symptom is perverted into obscenity:

TRIAL	OBSERVATIONS
He began to commit indecencies, such as putting his tongue into her mouth, &c.	This is very unlikely for him to have done at first seeing her, and her mouth is in too bad a condition for such a kiss.
I was quite outrageous.	This seems as if she was a great hypocrite; some of whom can kiss and kill, laugh and cry, in the same breath; this part is quite a romance, like Bluebeard.
I was in such a tremble.	Might not she tremble with eagerness and desire?
His fingers in my mouth.	Where were Sarah W——k's hands at that time?
Run along with him.	One would not imagine a woman, so sore as she is represented to be, could have run, or even walked.

Here, predictably, were all the usual jokes (what was she doing with her hands?). She'd got into the bed herself, the author continues. Maybe she had cried out—but only to ask him to be gentle. Afterward, it wasn't out of exhaustion or despair that she had stayed in bed; she probably just didn't want to catch cold.[192]

More illuminating, finally, than either empathy or hatred is the detached perspective of such mainstream publications as *The Gentleman's Magazine*. None of them doubts that Woodcock was kidnapped and forced against her will, but at the same time none seriously suggests that Baltimore should be convicted of rape. As so often, Woodcock's complaint was destroyed by her behavior after the rape. She had begun to comply with Baltimore's desires, the court concluded; she had appeared "chearful, and even playful," and ate with a healthy appetite. All this, she insisted, was only to avoid worse violence. But then she accepted gifts from him and passed up several chances to escape. She had obviously been raped, *The Gentleman's Magazine* coolly concluded, but once it was all over she had probably decided, as "generally happened," that staying with her wealthy violator was the lesser of two evils.[193] A rape victim's trauma could now be seriously represented, and at enormous length. But this certainly did not translate into convictions.

The Forgotten Best-Sellers
of Early English Fiction

Few discoveries have remained so striking throughout this project as the volume of comic fiction in the midcentury print market. Well-known sentimental or didactic novels—*Clarissa, David Simple, Millenium Hall, The Vicar of Wakefield*—were surrounded if not swamped, when they first appeared, by playful "lives" and "adventures." Some titles from just one decade:

Adventures of Mr Loveill, Interspers'd with Many Real Amours of the Modern Polite World (2 vols., 1750);
Memoirs of Lydia Tongue-Pad, and Juliana Clack-It (1750);
Adventures of Shelim O'Blunder, Esq.; The Irish Beau (1751);
Adventures of the Revd. Mr. Judas Hawke (1751);
Memoirs of a Coxcomb (1751);
Adventures of a Valet (2 vols., 1752);
The Female Rambler, Being the Adventures of Madam Janeton de ***** (1753);
The History of Sophia Shakespear (1753);
The History of Pudica, A Lady of N——RF——LK (1754);
Adventures of Dick Hazard (1754);
Adventures of Jerry Buck (1754);
The History of Jasper Banks, Commonly Call'd, the Handsome Man (2 vols., 1754);
Memoirs of the Noted Buckhorse (2 vols., 1756);
Adventures of Jack Smart (1756);
The History of Two Orphans (4 vols., 1756);
Adventures of a Rake: In the Character of a Public Orator (2 vols., 1759);
The History of Tom Fool (2 vols., 1760).

Few scholars have read any of these books, but there are dozens, if not hundreds, more where they came from—cheerful memoir novels in which a skeletal plot and a rudimentary central character are used to string together a sequence of broad comic incidents. *Ramble novels* they were often called, after the name of so many central characters and their careless progress through the world. And this term—with its glance at the eighteenth-century diversion of the ramble or aimless excursion—seems better than *picaresque*, which was not yet used in this period and too easily connotes the bleak survivalism of premodern rogue literature. Ramble fiction is firmly rooted in the metropolitan culture of its day; its realist details are there not to mock the artificialities of romance but because they were funny. I have referred intermittently to these texts—*Young Scarron* (1752), *The History of Will Ramble* (1754), and others—and used them to shed light on some of the darker corners of eighteenth-century culture. In conclusion, it seems important to gather these scattered discussions and establish the prominence of this genre in its time. In the process, I take up questions that have recurred since chapter 1: the central mystery of ownership, the ongoing need for more nuanced accounts of early modern reading practices, and the paradoxical place of nondramatic comic genres in literary history (always such a major part of production yet rarely given more than a nod in professional scholarship). Distinctly trashy as most now seem, ramble novels were in no way distinguished—neither by the book trade nor by reviewers or readers—from what are now accepted as literary novels. They were published in the same duodecimo format and sold for the same price of 3s. per volume as the canonical fiction of these years.

The "rise of the novel" has for so long dominated our understanding of eighteenth-century literature, and so consistently produced the most searching theoretical scholarship, that it is shocking to discover how little we still know about the noncanonical fiction of the age. The statistics and catalogs have now been available for more than two decades: more than seven hundred new novels were published between 1740 and 1770 (including texts that have not survived and therefore make no appearance in the *English Short Title Catalogue*). Add a similar number of reprints, and we have a total of fifteen hundred novels for these thirty years.[1] No working canon does more than scratch the surface. Analyzing the numbers for 1750–70, James Raven finds the traditional male foursome of Richardson, Fielding, Smollett, and Sterne accounting for just 7 percent of titles. Adding the sixteen next most popular authors (including Cervantes, French authors, and the four best-selling women novelists) brings the total to 25 percent. That leaves three-quarters of all texts unaccounted for: more than eight hundred novels, written by two hundred authors who can be identified and many others who will never be known—and this just for a twenty-year period.[2] Of course we have filled many gaps. Criminal biographies, erotic or pornographic fiction, travel memoirs, and playful "it" narratives have provided invaluable raw material for changing scholarly questions. Thomas Keymer has explored Sterne's debt to midcentury self-conscious fiction, including whimsies like *Ephraim Tristram Bates* (1756) and imitations of Fielding like *Charlotte Summers* (1750) and *The Adventures of Captain Greenland* (1752).[3] Identifiably Scottish, Irish, or transatlantic texts have found their places in specialist studies. Above all, several decades of feminist scholarship have recovered the dozens of neglected women authors who produced about 17 percent of all novels in the two decades of Raven's study and somewhat fewer in the 1740s.[4]

But no one has much to say about the hundreds of less definable, appealing, or polemically useful texts: piles and piles of droll narratives about sailors, orphans, rascally apprentices, and Irish fortune-hunters. There were odd histories of prizefighters, fairground orators, quack doctors, dandy apothecaries, and a surprising range of trickster heroines. It was a "*life-writing age*," said Francis Coventry, justifying the dog hero of *Pompey the Little* (1751). Even the "lowest and most contemptible Vagrants, Parish Girls, Chamber-maids, Pick-Pockets, and Highwaymen find Historians to record their Praises, and Readers to wonder at their Exploits."[5] As an abstract category, this surge of pseudo-biographical fiction at first seems to confirm inherited arguments about the rise of the novel—Ian Watt's view that readers experiencing the world in modern ways were demanding more realistic representations of that experience, or J. Paul Hunter's further suggestions that novels emerged to satisfy the needs and fantasies of isolated urban youngsters.[6] On closer inspection, one finds these functions almost irrelevant to ramble fiction. The mimetic techniques of these novels are so crude that identification and instruction are beside the point. Even the most firmly English texts—those set in the world of taverns, stableyards, and London streets—offer no more than the most basic representations of consciousness. These books are far more interested in amusement and incident. Their protagonists are stock comic types rather than unique individuals in particular circumstances; their plots are little more than scaffolds for humor and silliness.

Mainstream terminologies tell us nothing about such fiction. Normative assumptions about what literature or a novel should be, about the teleologies of literary history, about psychological realism or the cultural work of fiction get us nowhere. All produce partial and deceptively familiar impressions, both of individual texts and of the overall literary landscape of the age.[7] Of course the same is true of my own categories, which I use heuristically—as a necessity for talking about a vast and ever-changing body of texts. In what follows, I discuss one major narrative pattern and three variations on it: male-centered ramble novels, feminocentric versions, humorous "lives" of public figures, and an unexpected number of comic novels about low life. In form, they range from forty or fifty pages to four duodecimo volumes (I have followed Raven in excluding anything that looks like a chapbook). What unites these texts are their predominantly comic energies and their overt indifference to the emerging sentimentalism of the age.

RAMBLE NOVELS AND SLUM COMEDY

Without question, the most neglected subgenre of midcentury fiction is the male-centered ramble novel that emerged in the wake of *Tom Jones* (1749) and *Roderick Ramble* (1748). From 1750 on, each season saw seven or eight comic coming-of-age novels, most of them brasher variations on Fielding and Smollett's picaresque-cum-romance formula. Among these now-forgotten novels are some spectacular best-sellers—texts like Edward Kimber's *Life and Adventures of Joe Thompson* (1750), which went through at least six editions before 1800, reprints into the nineteenth century, and translations into French and German. We now know very little about Kimber (1719–69), but between 1750 and 1765 this industrious autodidact published seven original novels and a translation from Crébillon fils (he was also a major contributor to the *London Magazine* and its editor from 1755).[8] Along with general assumptions that novelists were falling into line behind Richardson, Fielding's late turn toward sentimentalism has obscured this comic tradition, though it remained a major part of the fiction market for decades. As the *Critical Review* complained in 1756, the runaway success of *Tom Jones* had "fill'd half the world with imitating fools."[9]

Along the way, such imitations confirm just how emphatically Fielding was in this culture associated with broad humor. Fistfights at roadside inns, comic humiliations and misunderstandings, the cast of high-written comic characters: these were the things that made Fielding "the English Cervantes," the greatest humorist of his age. After years of attacks on his low humor, Fielding conspicuously dropped it in *Amelia* (1751). But the profitable formula was established by *Tom Jones*. "Now the Humour, or Manners, of this Age are to laugh at every Thing," he complained when everyone sneered at his final novel, "and the only Way to please them is to make them laugh."[10] Making people laugh often seems like the primary goal of ramble fiction, and in this authors strove to outdo Fielding. Most ramble protagonists are active practical jokers rather than mere witnesses of humor like Tom. Will Ramble, Joe Thompson, Jerry Buck, and Peregrine Pickle are tricksters and accomplished mimics, skilled from an early age with itching powders, laxatives, firecrackers, and the rest. Their stories follow a series of standard episodes with deep roots in early modern comic literature. (And to read these subcanonical texts is to recognize how Fielding had refined his raw and nasty source material while his contemporaries continued to elaborate on it.)

First comes an unusual birth or parentage, the clearest indication of what the hero's relation to the world will be. Tom is found in Allworthy's bed; the hero of a ramble novel shows up in a barn or a basket of turnips. He is born in a boat (like Lazarillo de Tormes) or a moving cart (like Smollett's *Ferdinand Count Fathom*). The expectant mother has strange dreams or vile cravings like Mrs. Pickle's demand for frog fricassée. Will Ramble's mother dreams that she is "delivered of a Roe-Buck which gored its Way through her Side"— and sure enough she dies in cesarean section.[11] Other heroes are born with sharp teeth or terrify the household with their unworldly cackle. Then come the childhood mischiefs: leaking chamber pots, loosened floorboards, and little turds showing up in all the wrong places. Bunions, chilblains, asthma, and incontinence all cry out for boyish malignities. Meddling housekeepers are the victims of much of it, but naturally no one gets it worse than clergymen and schoolmasters. The pranks continue into adulthood, now alternating with a string of amours and increasingly serious misfortunes before the hero settles down with a wealthy heiress (Miss Rich, Miss Charlotte Lovely) who has been waiting in the wings all along.

It was a capacious and adaptable formula, something anyone in need of a few guineas could try their hand at. Ever alert to an opportunity, John Hill jumped on the bandwagon with *The Adventures of Mr Loveill* (1750) and *Adventures of George Edwards, a Creole* (1751). Hot on the heels of the *Fanny Hill* scandal, John Cleland came out with *Memoirs of a Coxcomb* (1751). *Jerry Buck* is the work of John Slade (d. 1760), a bachelor infantry lieutenant who also produced an old-fashioned tragedy on the love-versus-duty theme and a Lucianic satire called *The Transmigrating Soul* (1760). The interminable *History of Two Orphans* (4 vols., 1756) was the labor of William Toldervy (1721–62), a traveling linen salesman from the Welsh marches and hack writer for the bookseller William Owen.[12] Some of the earliest Irish novels are exercises in this genre, most notably William Chaigneau's best-selling *History of Jack Connor* (1752), which soon entered the national folklore. No one seems to know anything about Adolphus Bannac (if there ever was such a person), but under this name Francis Noble put out eight novels between 1755 and 1757. And on it went: *The History of James Lovegrove* (1761), *The Amours and Adventures of Charles Careless* (1764), *The Adventures of Jack Wander* (1766), *Adventures of a Kidnapped Orphan* (1767), and many, many more.

By no means was it all rubbish. As much as other subgenres, ramble fiction attracted skilled authors who tried out different types of protagonists and variations in tone, structure, and point of view. Kimber's Joe Thompson and other good-natured but impulsive young men might be considered one end of a spectrum. Their histories conclude with suggestions that the hero has learned from experience, leaving readers cheered and consoled in the mode of *Tom Jones* and *Gil Blas*. At an opposite extreme are rebarbative heroes like Judas Hawke, an astonishingly depraved clergyman who prostitutes his wife for a living, consistently reads pornography when he should be studying the scriptures, and takes particular joy in literally terrifying nice people to death. Still nastier is B—— Tracey, "the Notorious Libertine" (1757), whose shocking career of sexual violence begins at thirteen when he rapes his cousin Lucia. Such stories surely help make sense of texts like *Ferdinand Count Fathom* (1753). Swindler, ingrate, and heartless destroyer of virtuous women: none of Smollett's heroes has so confounded scholars, but Fathom easily finds his place alongside the experimental protagonists of the 1750s and 1760s.

Between the benign and the repugnant stretch a dazzling range of possibilities. Witty survivors drift into crime without being the active con men of criminal biography. Feckless students torment college proctors and bring goats to matins but otherwise do no harm. *The Adventures of Dick Hazard* (1754) is one of many tales about ingratiating cads, in this case a shameless but likable Irish rascal. Dick's disgraces progress from a blasphemous academy in Dublin to eloping with the unhappily married Mrs. B., who robs her husband to pay for their flight to Paris. The couple is later captured by pirates and taken to Algiers, where Dick happily allows his mistress to sleep with their captor. Back in London, the hero progresses from one fraud to another before being rescued from the King's Bench prison by Mrs. B., now a wealthy widow.[13] Such texts reduce their obligatory romance plot to its most cursory and profane. Clearly in a hurry to wrap things up, the author of *Jack Smart* (1756) has his drunken hero find an open window in Essex Street and reel upstairs to surprise a young lady going to bed. Naturally the lady screams in terror, but she is soon "very well pleased at my Humour"—"and really," Smart boasts, "when I am a little elevated with Liquor, my Wit is always the keener." By dawn, the lady has promised to marry him with her fortune of £10,000.[14] This sort of bluff male confidence evidently charmed many readers; not even the ugliest behavior broke the spell. Packed with vicious torments and ghastly acts of vengeance, *The Adventures of Jerry Buck* went through three editions in 1754 alone.

As season followed season, authors experimented with more and more eccentric protagonists. Idiot heroes, for example, are almost fondly presented. George Stevens's *The History of Tom Fool* (1760) is the deliriously silly story of a handsome simpleton. (Running joke: "You're a fool." "Thank you, Sir, I certainly am.") Here, the romance element appears in a series of seduction attempts that poor Tom never understands until he is snared by Lady Greensy, the heaving-bosomed widow of Sir Pansy Greensy, who wants a second fool for a husband. The anonymous *Adventures of Oxymel Classic* (1768) introduces a different sort of idiot, this time a dunderhead scholar who manages with Greek and Latin but has trouble in English and makes a hilariously incompetent clergyman. (And even Oxymel produced the requisite comic episodes, bullying an apple woman and banging a carter on the head with Ainsworth's *Dictionary*.)[15] Other texts develop a notably sardonic perspective—texts like *The Temple Beau* (1754), the scornful story of yet another Mr. Smart, this one a lawyer of base origins who tries to behave like a courtier. The romance plot sees the hero wooing Miss Jenny Gripe, the daughter of an upstart solicitor (to round out the action, an evil viscount turns up to rape someone in an alley).[16] Equally scorned but ultimately harmless is Shelim O'Blunder, "the Irish Beau" (fig. 12). Shelim is a rascal, but as an Irishman "his mental Endowments were not the most accomplished." The novel ends with him in prison, all his schemes come to naught.[17]

Comic novels about women have in general attracted greater scholarly attention, with stories of pluckish pickpockets, actresses, female soldiers, and courtesans proving invaluable to feminist criticism. But even here one finds many neglected texts. The prattling *Memoirs of Lydia Tongue-Pad, and Juliana Clack-It* (1750) is one of many uncategorizable exercises in silliness. *The History of Pudica* (1754) is a deliberately lumbering saga about a young countrywoman and her five hapless suitors, from Dick Merryfellow and 'Squire Fog of Dumpling Hall to the lucky Miles Dinglebob of Popgun-Hall, not the best catch with his dull "gooseberry" eyes (fig. 13). No one knows quite what to do with all the really nasty heroines—brutal and unrepentant women who shove old men into fireplaces and punch rivals in the teeth. Witness the critical silence around *The Fortunate Transport* (ca. 1740–42), the bewildering story of Polly Haycock and her career of ruthless fraud and violence on both sides of the Atlantic. As the novel ends, Polly still "rolls in Ease, Splendor, and

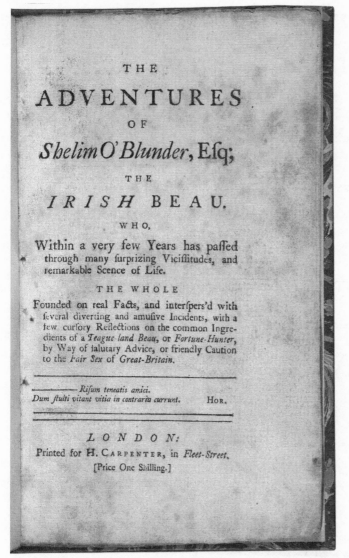

THE

ADVENTURES

OF

Shelim O'Blunder, Efq;

THE

I R I S H B E A U,

WHO,

Within a very few Years has paffed
through many furprizing Viciffitudes, and
remarkable Scence of Life.

THE WHOLE

Founded on real Facts, and interfpers'd with
feveral diverting and amufive Incidents, with a
few curfory Reflections on the common Ingredients of a *Teague-land Beau*, or *Fortune-Hunter*,
by Way of falutary Advice, or friendly Caution
to the *Fair Sex* of *Great-Britain*.

———— *Rifum teneatis amici.*
Dum ftulti vitant vitia in contraria currunt.   HOR.

L O N D O N:
Printed for H. CARPENTER, in *Fleet-Street*,
[Price One Shilling.]

FIGURE 12. Title page from *The Adventures of Shelim O'Blunder, Esq.* (London, ca. 1751), the short life of a hilariously unsuccessful Irish fortune hunter. O'Blunder is one of a wide range of despicable or unsympathetic protagonists that began to appear in the early 1750s: every sort of caddish clerk, upstart linen draper, and "Holborn beau." All exemplify the deep social conservatism of so much early fiction. Rambling, sardonic, and poorly written, *Shelim O'Blunder* is the labor of an anonymous hack who keeps pleading for compassion from the critics. Cribbed from standard school texts, the bungled lines from Horace attempt to legitimate the book's narrative perspective. Reproduced by permission of the Huntington Library, San Marino, California (349504).

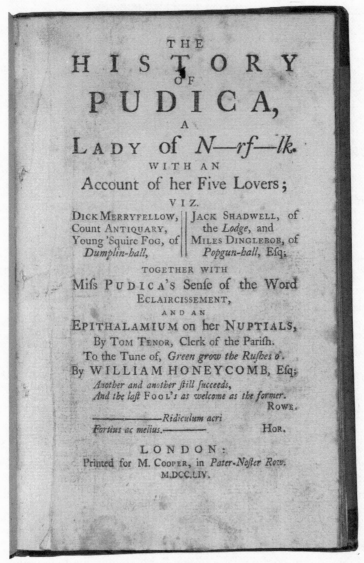

THE

HISTORY
OF

PUDICA,
A

LADY of *N—rf—lk.*

WITH AN

Account of her Five Lovers;

VIZ.

DICK MERRYFELLOW,	JACK SHADWELL, of
Count ANTIQUARY,	the *Lodge,* and
Young 'Squire FOG, of	MILES DINGLEBOB, of
Dumplin-hall,	*Popgun-hall,* Esq;

TOGETHER WITH

Miss PUDICA's Sense of the Word
ECLAIRCISSEMENT,

AND AN

EPITHALAMIUM on her NUPTIALS,
By TOM TENOR, Clerk of the Parish.
To the Tune of, *Green grow the Rushes o'.*
By WILLIAM HONEYCOMB, Esq;

Another and another still succeeds,
And the last FOOL's as welcome as the former.
ROWE.

———————————*Ridiculum acri*
Fortius ac melius.——————
HOR.

LONDON:
Printed for M. COOPER, in *Pater-Noster Row.*
M.DCC.LIV.

FIGURE 13. Title page from [Richard Gardiner], *The History of Pudica, a Lady of N——rf——lk* (London, 1754). An established instance of the semiautobiographical character of so much midcentury fiction. Gardiner (1723–81) represents himself as Dick Merryfellow, the unlucky first suitor. Sometime Cambridge student, deacon, army officer, political satirist, and hack on demand, Gardiner typifies the lesser-known authors of so many ramble novels. Even with this relatively unified narrative, the title page stresses variety and the mixing of genres. Reproduced by permission of the Huntington Library, San Marino, California (124997).

Luxury; and laughs at dull Moralists, who would persuade Mankind that the Way to be happy is to be good." Though almost ignored by modern critics, *The Fortunate Transport* was sufficiently popular in its day to be commemorated in a high-quality copper engraving by George Bickham the Younger.[18]

Among these less recuperable texts one finds another forgotten best-seller: the anonymous *Secret History of Betty Ireland* (1741 and up to nine more editions before 1800). While clearly influenced by Defoe, *Betty Ireland* is insistently comic and exuberantly amoral. Wholly immune to Christian and every other moral principle, the heroine prospers as a mistress and cheat for more than forty years. Betty is a brilliant manipulator of men and a wildly successful fraud, at one point being kept simultaneously by three brothers and the usual "rich Jew." She robs the Jew and marries all three brothers under different names; after almost ruining each husband with her extravagance, she agrees to legal separations, gaining £1,400 from one and £500 each from the other two. And so it continues, the prose crackling throughout with gleeful malignity—page after page of Betty's vindictive tricks and insults. "Lord! What a nasty Smell is here of sour *small Beer*!" she suddenly exclaims to an uppity brewer's daughter: the lady must have soiled herself (done a *"Brewer's Fart"*). Shoplifter, strolling player, procuress, adoring companion to Smutty Will the Irish con man—Betty triumphs through it all. Even when robbed by highwaymen, she manages to kill one of them first. "If you like that, you shall have more," she tells the dying man.[19]

For all the apparent familiarity of such plots, *Betty Ireland* offers little of the existential perspective of early picaresque. The heroine is a figure of static immorality: unlike Lazarillo or Moll Flanders, Betty is not hardened by misfortune but abandons herself, from the earliest age, to every inclination. She drinks and swears like a fishwife, guiltlessly seduces any man she takes a fancy to, and callously casts up her accounts before each lover's corpse is cold. At one point, she knowingly sleeps with her own son—a real *"Chip of the old Block"* who impregnates her the very first time.[20] Yet even this incident is so casually dropped into the narrative as to obviate anything like the shock functions of early scandal fiction or the gothic, let alone eroticism. All Betty's enormities retain the same peculiar harmlessness. Odd and appalling as it must seem, Betty is an enjoyable character—a pluckish, brassy survivor and the orchestrator of much high comedy.

At the shifting boundary of fact and fiction, one finds all these narrative patterns being used for comic "histories" of public figures. A few years after his success with *Joe Thompson*, Kimber rolled out his familiar formula in *The Ju-*

venile Adventures of David Ranger (1756), which thinly disguises David Garrick under the name of his most celebrated comic role (the affable Ranger in Hoadly's *Suspicious Husband* [1747]). While bearing little resemblance to the historical Garrick—for extra fun the book even turns him into an Irishman—Kimber's Ranger is nevertheless witty and likable, the sort of figure London readers might associate with their favorite actor. Born in Cork to a mother who behaves like a tragic queen and even scolds her servants in couplets, the infant Davy already declaims the word *farewell!* Soon he is wooing his sister like Otway's Castalio and practicing Garrick's trademark death agonies on every carpet. Most of the adventures that follow (two long volumes of them) are entirely invented; only in its final chapter does the novel come closer to a roman à clef, with clear allusions to Lord Burlington and Garrick's marriage to Eva Maria Veigel (the "most enchanting" Miss Tulip). The critics were scornful, but *David Ranger* and other heavily fictionalized lives do tell us about this culture's tolerance of fancy. A few known facts are combined in all these texts with other incidents that seem plausible enough and much more that is openly fictitious. Probability and empirical realism—the very qualities that made other early novels so important to literary history—are clearly unimportant.[21]

The repertoire of ready-made comic incidents also made it possible for authors to capitalize quickly on causes célèbres. A striking range of persons and events invited such comic treatment. One important if unpleasant precedent, given the subject of chapter 5, is the six full-length histories of the rapist Francis Charteris that suddenly appeared in the winter of 1729–30. Each of these promises the truth about the man, even as they pad out the facts with scatological pranks or turn him into Don Francisco, an archetypal Spanish seducer. As one midcentury comic life that was rushed to press in a matter of weeks, consider the *Juvenile Adventures* of the courtesan Kitty Fisher (ca. 1741–67). This text characteristically combines a handful of well-known details (German father, early career as a milliner, vanity and extravagance) with much that is completely fanciful. As with some of the Charteris texts, *Kitty Fisher* transfers the action from London to Madrid; Kitty's career of vice begins with a lesbian encounter at a convent school; there are spells in prisons and madhouses and the usual bawds, fortune-tellers, and lecherous friars. Several chapters tell the story of an unfortunate "little lover"—three foot one, hopelessly attracted to tall women, and probably a reference to the tiny Baron Montfort (1733–99), whom Fisher once hid under her petticoat. Kitty almost kills the little man with her amateur medical experiments, leaving him "physicked and purged . . . till the poor devil was scarce visible."[22]

Fisher was already famous before the afternoon of 12 March 1759, when she fell from her horse in St. James's Park. This accident, all too ripe for lewd analogies, was soon on everyone's lips. By morning a ballad "to the Tune of Kitty Fell" was being hawked about the streets, followed by smutty verses "On K—— F——'s Falling from Her Horse." A satiric print showed Kitty sprawled indecently on the ground.[23] By 30 March, *The Juvenile Adventures of Miss Kitty Fisher* must already have been advertised in the London press. On that date, the *Public Advertiser* ran a letter from one C. Fisher, complaining that she had been "abused in the public papers [and] exposed in print-shops"—and, to cap it off, a group of "wretches" was trying to "impose upon the public, by daring to publish her memoirs." These memoirs may have been in preparation before the accident, but when they finally appeared in the bookshops, volume 2 ended with an extended treatment of Fisher's recent accident. All Madrid goes about singing "Kitty Fell"; there were lampoons and epigrams on every tongue. The women were triumphant, but gentlemen stood up to defend her in coffeehouses. The author even adds two "letters" from rival courtesans, including the celebrated Fanny Murray (1729–78), who urges Kitty to reflect "upon the transitory reign of beauty and success." The fictional Kitty feels obliged to defend herself in the public papers—and here the author includes a garbled version of Fisher's actual complaint in the *Public Advertiser*:

> She has been *disabused* in public papers, *apposed* [examined] in print-shops, and to *blow* up the *hole*, some mean, ignorant, *venereal* wretches, would dispose *of her in public*, by DARING TO PRETEND TO DARE, (*though they have not yet dared or pretended any thing*) about her Memoirs.

It was all a forgery, the fictional Kitty insists: her memoirs had been kept "so extreamly *secret*, that even she herself is unacquainted with them."[24] This last jest was a bookseller's in-joke, a brazen acknowledgment of the fabrications behind this and many similar texts, all of them knowing, facetious, stuffed with comic filler, reading in places like romans à clef, and including real documents along with the fiction and fun.

My final cluster of texts is characterized less by protagonist type (male or female, fictional or real) than by its distinct narrative perspective. *Slum comedy* one might call it, a sustained amusement not just in the proverbial ignorance of the lower orders, but in every base detail of their lives. The endurance of such attitudes should by now be no surprise, but they play no major part in discussions of early realist fiction. The central action of many ramble novels is surrounded by an army of rustic idiots and illiterate footmen (Chaigneau's gallery of English and Irish dolts was much the best thing about *Jack Connor*, said the *Monthly Review*).[25] Again and again, the narrative is interrupted by slummy comic set pieces. Domestic rows spill onto the street. Most texts include at least one ferocious kitchen brawl—all curses, chairs broken over heads, volleys of cooking pots and half-picked pork bones. Great swathes of text are devoted to foolish omens and superstitions (moles, birthmarks, village fortune-tellers), none of it there for any reason except the inherent humor of plebeian credulity. Wry narrators consistently strive to echo the language world they are describing, with slang terms for the chattels of common life and all manner of folkish catchphrases: "Love and a Cough cannot be hid"; "Hungry Dogs eat dirty Puddings." Long swearing matches are printed verbatim, great clusters of asterisks and printers' blanks that explode off the page even as they lay on their performance of restraint. The predictable damning and poxing alternates with compound epithets that only get richer as the years go on: "stinking good-for-nothing jade" or "pitiful cuckoldly scrub" are nothing beside "poor, pitiful, lousy Pickle-herring Dog."[26]

Authors and readers clearly enjoyed the mutual nastiness of households and small communities—the spats and petty hierarchies, the gossip, grudges, and furtive sex. The early chapters of *Will Ramble* alternate between its main plot and parallel melodramas below stairs. Everyone is trying to court Mrs. Norris, the mean, foul-tempered housekeeper. Mr. Snarl the tutor is rejected with scorn. The same happens to old Ebenezer Doughty from the stables, who promptly tries to drown himself. The whole household gathers round the horse pond: Ned and Betty, Jack the stableboy, Deborah the fat, weepy cook, and poor Esther, who cries to go along with the other women. Naturally it all comes out, with Ebenezer and Mrs. Norris becoming the laughingstock of the village.[27] Such contents point to a prevailing source of amusement in many upper-class households, and beyond it to a major readership of these texts. They also raise much larger questions about the genealogy of formal realism as a medium for representing ordinary life and demotic speech in serious ways. Both features appear in ramble novels to be laughed at.

A surprising number of novels make slum realism their defining trait (the grimiest whore biographies, e.g., had always fallen into this mode).[28] *The Authentic Memoirs of Nancy Dawson* (ca. 1765) tells the story of a celebrated midcentury dancer. The historical Nancy Dawson (ca. 1728–67) was irascible, violent, and mercenary. But she was also a wildly popular performer and still going in the 1760s, now grossly fat. The *Authentic Memoirs* finds its idiom and setting in the squalor around Clare Market, which it presents with an almost forensic level of detail. The daughter of a drunken basket woman and a shiftless "pimp and porter," Nancy is born in a stable—behind a grubby curtain "which formed a bed-chamber for her mamma." Soon she is cursing other children during games ("B[la]st your eyes for a b[itc]h!") and is always the first to know when the local boys start fooling around with the butcher's daughter: "[A]nd when once she catched them in the fact, all came out." Nancy grows up with thieves and beggar women and is easily deflowered by a chimney sweep ("indeed, she was now so ripe that the least shake would bring her down"). Then comes the usual variety of adventures before Nancy takes up with the actor Ned Shuter, whose touching proposal is printed in full:

My dear Nancy; thou hast been long enough a hackney-jade, and I'm sure must now be tired of being spurred and galled by every rider that pleases to mount thee: Come, in the name of love, then, O my Nancy, forsake the common whore thou now art, shelter thyself in the warm stable of my arms, and I swear to thee, by the immortal powers, thou shalt never be turned out to graze again.

The text leaves Ned and Nancy in their shabby idyll, still cooing like turtle-doves. To be sure, Nancy did drink like a fish, but she definitely had "a certain sprightliness in her conversation when she was sober, which she sometimes was once or twice a week."[29]

As with other subgenres, the male-centered examples of this mode consistently receive less attention. Consider Christopher Anstey's *Memoirs of the Noted Buckhorse* (2 vols., 1756), a fanciful life of the prizefighter John "Buckhorse" Smith (fl. 1720–50). Anstey (1724–1805) would eventually become famous for his *New Bath Guide* (1766); this early text sheds light on his apprentice years and situates ramble fiction alongside the jumble of epistles, dialogues, and verse satires with which every aspiring hack tried to earn a living. By 1756 Buckhorse himself had retired from the ring but remained a well-known sight in Covent Garden, working as a peddler and linkman, so fantastically ugly that provincial visitors came to gawk at him. *Memoirs of Buckhorse* offers fascinating glimpses into a world where all but the most fastidious gentlemen went slumming in taverns and chophouses and delighted in rough vulgarians for their sheer entertainment value.

Especially important for my purposes in this book are this text's cartoonish representations of lower-class emotions. *Memoirs of Buckhorse* might as well be an explicit riposte to the *Pamela* strain and its sympathetic depiction of plebeian distress. Even more deliberately than *Nancy Dawson*, Anstey's Buckhorse scoffs at every suggestion that ordinary people had feelings. "Having as noble Sentiments of Love as a Horse, a Dog [or] an Ass," Buckhorse falls in love with a cinder wench named Rachael Ragged-Rump, whom he courts with an appropriate string of metaphors ("The Suns of your bright Eyes having burnt my Heart to a Cinder, permit me to lay it in the Dust-cart of your Affection"). The fortunate woman immediately agrees ("hif u intends tow mari me, I am redy—yurs till Deathe, *Rachel Ragged Rump*, ✛ her Mark"). They are tacked together by a good-natured parson, who for a couple of shillings rents them his bed for the night. The wedding feast (bread, cheese, and many pints of gin) takes a sad turn with everyone drunk and the landlord raping the new Mrs. Buckhorse in her stupor. No matter: husband and wife are placated with more gin, and just nine weeks later they are rewarded with a strapping boy, "as like the Father as if he had been spit out of his Mouth." Mrs. Buckhorse is soon transported for theft, but Buckhorse easily consoles himself with a suitable gallows widow (sixty-three years old, two yards around the waist, great shaggy eyebrows, and most importantly, plenty of gin on the shelves). And so it goes on—a consistent skepticism about anything like tender feelings in the vulgar, ending only when the hero dies in a gutter.[30]

Powerful arguments about the novel as an agent of social mobility—or at least the first genre to present sympathetic characters from ordinary life—sometimes make it hard to recognize the snobbery and conservatism of so much eighteenth-century fiction.[31] Putative connections between literary innovations and historical change have so matched the intellectual zeitgeist of the past thirty years that counterarguments still struggle to be heard. In a wide-ranging recent article, Nicholas Hudson takes on the tenacious association between the novel and "the rise of the middle class," pointing to the antiprogressivism of so much early fiction and stressing the singularity of the *Pamela* scenario. Ramble novels overwhelmingly confirm Hudson's thesis, with middling social aspirants consistently mocked from *The Temple Beau* and *Shelim O'Blunder* to the pretentious burghers of *Tom Fool* and *Joe Thompson*. But such texts also invite us to press the point and recognize the deeper conservatism of so many scornful representations of the lower classes. The miseries of common life are always ludicrous in ramble fiction, as they are in *Will Ramble*'s weepy scene around the horse pond. Consider the death of Nancy Dawson's mother: having drunk her daily pint of gin, Mrs. Dawson "mistook the kennel for her own bed-chamber, where, laying herself down, the night proved so very rainy and cold, that she never got up again, being froze to death." This was a shame for young Nancy, but such things happened.[32]

As usual, *Memoirs of Buckhorse* points up the antisentimentalism most clearly of all. Early in volume 1, we meet the hero's landlady, Mrs. Diver, whom Fortune seems determined to destroy. "Her Husband condemned to die, her Friend to Transportation! Could any Thing add to Mrs. *Diver's* Distress?" No wonder the unhappy woman falls into a swoon, Anstey continues—or "something like a Swoon, that is, being oppressed with Grief, and Gin, [she] had reclined her Head on the Back of the Seat, and was fallen fast asleep."[33] There is also much satire, in this text and throughout the genre, on upper-class vice. Buckhorse learns all his worst habits from the high-swearing bucks and smarts of the age. But none of it, here or anywhere else, amounts to much of a critique.

READING FOR THE FILLER

How bad are these books? Judged by formal-realist standards, they inevitably fall short. One finds glaring chronological and geographic mistakes (Madeira in the Caribbean, Milan in the Low Countries) and inconsistencies in the occupations and even names of important characters. The heroine is introduced as Lucy but then reappears in volume 3 as Louisa. After ten years as a slave in Algiers, the hero somehow returns a younger man. Authors evidently felt no shame in admitting that they had forgotten to plan for a recognition scene or other major plot twist ("I should have mention'd before, that, at parting, he had made her a Present of a Tortoiseshell Snuff-box set in Gold, and his Picture in the Lid of it").[34] Huge sections of one novel reappear in other titles, with no more than superficial changes. The Fleet Street printer Henry Woodgate reissued most of *The Adventures of Jack Smart* (1756) as *The Fortunate Imposter* (1759), simply renaming the central character and hardly caring whether anyone noticed. Such practices reveal in an instant the intensely seasonal nature of the midcentury fiction market. "From the trade's point of view," says the book historian John Feather, "the significance of the novel lay not in its literary merit but in its essential triviality," the way it so quickly made room for more of the same.[35] These were disposable texts, intended to be read once, discussed for six or seven months, and then forgotten.

Nevertheless, these conditions also elicited much good writing. *Betty Ireland, Will Ramble, David Ranger,* and *Joe Thompson* are witty and well written, however repugnant individual episodes may be. In their gloriously seedy way, *Nancy Dawson* and *Memoirs of Buckhorse* clearly satisfied the readers who bought them in such quantities. But understanding this enjoyment—appreciating ramble fiction within the culture where it was so successful—is not easy. We must set aside normative expectations not just about the novel,

but about reading and the usual mechanisms of narrative. Plot is so rudimentary in these texts, and characterization so shallow, that the usual motors
of narrative are just not there. Ramble novels are almost without desire, as
a narratologist might say. There are no important mysteries to be resolved,
no hermeneutic plot. Who left the infant heroine on the woodpile? Will Jack
ever find his father? Such questions inevitably cross our minds, but identity
is never the ongoing enigma that it is in *Tom Jones* or *Evelina*. Will the hero
recover his lovely Lydia? Will she forgive him for trying to assault her in the
hackney coach? It hardly matters: the heroines of these novels are so flat and
unproductive of sympathy that any young woman with £12,000 will tie up the
plot just as well.

What really sticks in the mind is the riotous, anarchic comedy of these
books, most of it entirely irrelevant to plot. Neither narratology nor our everyday critical vocabulary offers any positive terminology for such noninstru-
mental content. Neither *digression* nor *comic relief* is the right term (digression or relief from what?). *Filler* might be better, with the proviso that this
filler—the static comic stuffing that fills pages and chapters—is the very substance of these novels. The flimsy plots soon fade, but one long remembers
the collective cast of comic characters. The foulmouthed Merry Andrew in
Will Ramble, so good at kicking people in the jaw. That horrid landlady in
Nottingham, lying awake with the colic after stuffing herself on pickled cu-
cumbers. Kitty Fisher spanking her besotted "little lover." Buckhorse putting
out a fire with his piss pot and then angrily insisting, "[T]he Water could not
smell, as it had not been long made." Mrs. Thrum, the village shopkeeper in
Tom Fool, who wants to redecorate the parish church "in the *Chinese* manner."
Father Kelly, the dirty Irish priest in *Jack Connor*, fondling Mrs. Connor's
breasts in front of her blind husband (after which he visited regularly "and
always left something behind").[36]

Long after the volumes have gone back to the stacks, one can still hear the
shrieks, thuds, and wallops. Mad bulls on the loose. Terrified old ladies tumbling into privies. Biting, scratching, scaldings, and broken noses. Who could
forget the raucous quarrel with a London coachman in *Nancy Dawson* ("one
of the whores whipt off his wig, pissed in it, and knocked it in his face")? Such
frantic episodes tell us everything about the world that produced them—its
intolerance, misogyny, xenophobia, anti-Semitism, and frank delight in misery and pain. *Joe Thompson* takes on an appalling gusto once the hero starts
tormenting Mr. Prosody, that novel's obligatory schoolmaster. Pistols and firecrackers, brimstone, cats going crazy from pepper up the anus, all of it end-

ing only when old Prosody defecates in terror (buttered eggs in the breeches was the eighteenth-century term for this mishap, a Kimber specialty that also shows up in *David Ranger*). Protracted acts of vengeance are the most energetic sequences in many texts. Witness Betty Ireland's revenge on the London magistrate who had her whipped through the streets. Looking about for "one of the pockiest Fellows she could get," Betty deliberately infects herself with syphilis and seduces the judge in disguise. Having *"pickled"* him handsomely, she follows him to take the waters at Scarborough, where she convinces the whole town that he is an escaped lunatic.[37]

Much of this comic stuffing was plagiarized from other texts (*Jack Smart*, sniffed the *Critical Review*, simply lifted everything from *Laugh and Be Fat*).[38] The more self-conscious authors wryly apologize for having to repeat so many tired old conventions. "We are obliged to introduce a Night Scene, for which we must beg the Reader's Pardon," begins Christopher Anstey's chapter-length example of that set piece: if he left it out, no one would believe him.[39] Ramble fiction catered to a significant demand for more of the same: comic set pieces were nourishing or even comforting, like milk puddings or an old cushion. Such ingenuity as there is appears not in the technical innovations of formal realism but in variations on established scenarios, ever more outlandish or disgusting incidents. One protracted episode in *Jerry Buck* recounts a naked dance at a London brothel—the bucks and their doxies stripped to the skin and even the prodigiously fat madam "in buff" to accompany them on the fiddle. With such incidents, remarked the *Monthly Review*, Slade had "outdone the greatest outdoings of the whole tribe" of hack novelists.[40] Grotesque set pieces, in particular, seem to get more and more repulsive as the years wore on. Early in Toldervy's *History of Two Orphans*, we find a bullish parson named Drill drinking buttered ale at a tavern. The reverend's digestion proves delicate, and he vomits his ale up into the mug. He swallows again, and again brings the ale up into his vessel. At this instant, a stout carter walks in, and our waggish parson offers him the mug:

"Here, my lad, said the parson, do'st love butter'd ale?" "Yes, sir, God Bless you," cried the fellow; "here then," returned the parson, "drink it up, my lad, for thou art very welcome to it." The fellow . . . taking the pint from the parson, drank the liquor off; gave the pot to the parson again, who, setting his hands to his sides, said, "Well, my lad, how dost like it? does it lay well on thy stomach?" "yes, very well, I thank you, Sir," replied the fellow: "B— G—d" (for he could not swear) cried the parson, "I am

glad of it, much good may do thee; for it has been twice already in my stomach, but it would not stay there at all." In an instant the man grew pale; he
was seized with a trembling, threw that into the road, which Mr. *Drill* had
been so careful to save, and departed, cursing the parson for a nasty son
of a b——h.[41]

Sublimely vile as it is, the prank must have satisfied the sort of readers who
shelled out 12s. for the four volumes of this text. With its detailed circum-
stantiality and prolonged transcription of everyday speech, the passage is as
mimetic as anything in Defoe or Richardson, and again forces us to wonder
about possible comic sources for novelistic realism. With its mock-decorous
circumlocutions ("that . . . which Mr. *Drill* had been so careful to save") and
then the wry aside and typographic joke about parsons not being allowed to
swear, it is a fine example of how these expensive texts took the basest fairground pranks and elaborated them for educated readers. But none of it was
anomalous. Vomit, urine, excrement, and dead animals were the raw materials
of so much early modern humor, and people wanted to read about them.

Perhaps half these texts—a surprising proportion given so much recent
emphasis on the instructive functions of early fiction—make no claim to be
anything more than cures for the spleen or diversions for "vacant hours."
Long titles and advertisements persistently stress the books' "sundry humourous Anecdotes," their abundance of "laughable Incidents" and "Entertaining
Characters." Another half include a stock didactic preface and intermittent
moralizing for those who needed it. *Joe Thompson* told a useful story, Edward
Kimber announces: a young man struggling with his passions but "at length,
thro' a Series of Temptations, getting the better of Vice." Even the ribald *History of Jasper Banks* presents itself as "a Caution to our Youth," a warning
"*not to engage too early in the* ensnaring Pleasure of Love."[42] And there were
all manner of other defenses, between the sardonic and the sincere. All those
brothel scenes were attacks on the shocking sexual standards of the age; the
scuffles and humiliations of *Jack Connor* were there only to help the medicine
of instruction go down; *Shelim O'Blunder* was a caution to the fair sex, advising them how to avoid "a *Teague-land Beau*" (fig. 12 above).

Yet the repentance phase in *Joe Thompson* is plenty long enough to justify
Kimber's didactic claims, which are also sustained by routine admonitions to
his readers ("Ye Youths, beware how ye yield to the first Attacks of Vice!").[43]
There seems no reason to be suspicious of the attacks on gambling or homilies on charity that show up in so many texts. More starkly than most genres,

ramble novels exemplify the baffling heterogeneities I have been exploring throughout this book—the coexistence of what seem to us the most incompatible behaviors and tastes. Even beside the digressions and interpolations of other early fiction, the disjunctions of ramble novels can be extreme. Bawdy stories appear alongside grave sermons or condensed theological discourses; the narrative suddenly stops for five chapters about Abyssinia or the mishaps of a little French cook. There are passages of literary criticism and evaluations of contemporary actors. Animal fables rub shoulders with Oriental tales and coldly methodical descriptions of Arab torture techniques. Dream visions and voyages to the moon alternate with Royal Society–style reports on toads and fossils. Sober travel narratives come complete with fantastic natural-historical finds like the "Dog-Bird," a ferocious oversized griffin that had everyone talking in the winter of 1753–54.[44]

Most unsettling of all, even the nastiest rambles might include genuinely sentimental episodes. Alongside the slummy mock sympathy of Anstey's *Memoirs of Buckhorse*, one finds the sentimental set piece of a ruined clergyman's daughter. The vicious *Jerry Buck* devotes five long chapters to this scenario, introducing a Miss Firetail to tell her pitiable story. In spite of the stock whore's name, the sentimentalism of this digression seems sincere, with horrific accounts of Miss Firetail's drugging, rape, and fall into prostitution and impassioned denunciations of the world. Yet the context could hardly be stranger, with the story immediately preceded by the hero's torture of the foppish Mr. Dapper and followed by his pitiless pranks as a London buck. As for Miss Firetail, her major role in the text so far has been to seduce the hero's pedantic tutor and infect him with a good clap. She is hugely amused by this act of revenge and happily accepts five guineas for it.[45]

With the high costs and narrow profit margins of eighteenth-century book production, authors and publishers clearly needed to attract as many readers as possible. The more haphazard of these novels read almost like miscellanies, themselves such a profitable part of the midcentury print market. But even more unified texts include wildly inconsistent materials without the slightest narrative pretext. As if it wasn't long enough already, William Toldervy fattened up *The History of Two Orphans* with odes, ballads, and snatches of funerary poetry from his earlier publication, *Select Epitaphs* (1755). And one would be wrong to attribute such diversity to lack of skill: abundance and variety were important selling points. Title pages and advertisements promise plenitude: the main narrative is "interspers'd with" additional attractions, "A great Variety of Incidents," "Sundry very curious Particulars." The anonymous author of *Will Ramble* candidly acknowledges that he wants to make money and will therefore "endeavour to engage all Attentions, whatever the Object may be that is sought after."[46]

The earliest reviews of ramble fiction make it clear that these crude, jumbled texts nevertheless remained within the bounds of educated taste. *Jack Connor* was unquestionably the best comic novel since *Pompey the Little*, wrote the *Monthly Review* in June 1752; in spite of "certain slight crudities," it was "a truly moral tale." *Will Ramble* was "better worth reading than some of the late productions of the kind": while a libertine "as to women and gaming," Ramble was otherwise a man of principle. *The History of Pudica* was written "with a good deal of pleasantry." *David Ranger* was "by no means the most contemptible" text of 1756; at least Kimber was "so much of a Scholar as to understand Latin."[47] Even such mixed reviews began to disappear in the summer of 1756, when Smollett's *Critical Review* began its condemnation of everything and the *Monthly* hurried to imitate it.[48] "It is impossible to conceive anything more stupid, incoherent, and indelicate" began the *Critical's* review of *The History of Two Orphans*. "Lay aside thy pen till it hath pleased God to work a miracle upon thy understanding," it entreated another author. *Memoirs of Buckhorse* was "such a strange compound of sense and nonsense," complained the *Monthly* in November 1756, that it was hard to tell whether the author was "a sorry scribbler, or a smart fellow."[49] From this point, the reviews' negative commentary on ramble fiction only goes to confirm recent cautions that these sources tell us little or nothing about reception and purchasing.[50] Whatever the reviewers said about them, ramble novels continued to sell in large quantities.

So who was reading these muddled texts, and how? Ramble novels seem almost designed for the "extensive" readers so long thought to be emerging in this period—those who carelessly consumed multiple books rather than intensively reading a small number. Certainly midcentury essayists never ceased to complain about this hasty and distracted way of reading.[51] In one of her contributions to Lyttelton's *Dialogues of the Dead* (1760), Elizabeth Montagu imagines a dialogue between Plutarch and a modern bookseller who explains why nobody bothers with the classics anymore:

> Would you present a modern fine gentleman, who is negligently lolling in an easy chair, with the *labours of Hercules* for his recreation? or make him climb the Alps with Hannibal, when he is expiring with the fatigue of last

night's ball? Our readers must be amused, flattered, soothed; such adventures must be offered to them as they would like to have a share in.[52]

Ramble novels were perfectly suited to this scenario: they gave readers a good laugh, enabled them to imagine the favorable part they might play in events, and allowed them to skip ahead or doze off when they got bored. The near-universal division into books and chapters effectively invited readers to dip in or skim as interest came and went. The author of *Will Ramble*, so frank in pandering to his readers, compares his chapter titles to the playbills handed out in front of fairground booths, offering the reader "an Account of what he is to expect in the Representation." Chapter titles worked as promises ("A Comical Revenge," "A Very Entertaining Adventure upon the Road") or warnings ("Rules for the Education of Youth," "Melancholy Reflections"). Many alluded playfully to selective reading practices: a chapter "contains no great matter" or "may be passed over, without Prejudice to the Story."[53]

Ramble fiction thus substantiates recent arguments about the diversity of early modern reading practices. Fiction once seemed inextricably tied to a semimythical population of idle young ladies, overheated by romances and always about to run off with soldiers. Only recently have we come to see that novels were read like other books: intermittently and in combination at the interstices of busy lives. *Clarissa* and *Joe Thompson* were read alongside newspapers, periodical essays, travel narratives, and books of sermons. *Sidney Biddulph* and *Dick Hazard* were consumed alongside Pope's Homer, bits of natural history, Shakespearean monologues, and contemporary farces. All these books were read while traveling, in stagecoaches or on horseback; they were listened to while doing accounts, needlework, or even reading something else. Then as now, reading was a consolation or a distraction, a way of procrastinating or relieving loneliness. More surprising, we are only now discovering just how much novels were dipped into, read in bits and pieces, and started but never finished (certainly the case with *Sir Charles Grandison*). Circulating library records even show volumes of novels being read out of order.[54] Single chapters or individual letters were evidently far more self-contained than we have imagined—the characteristic that also made early fiction so suitable for excerpting into anthologies or magazines. This is not to say that absorptive or intensive reading had died out. Certain books always compelled attention and were read straight through; others were treasured and reread time and again. But these practices coexisted with much more desultory modes of consumption.

Ramble fiction draws particular attention to the lost practice of reading aloud. As much as the detachable episodes of sentimental fiction or the three-page periodical essay, the freestanding comic set pieces of ramble fiction easily lent themselves to oral performance. Once one starts looking for it, the evidence of this practice is everywhere to be found. Ladies' companions read to their mistresses after supper. Visitors were asked to read to everyone over tea, as Mr. Collins reads to the Bennett sisters. Reading aloud went on all day at circulating libraries, above all in resort towns. Families or local communities often had a recognized best reader—someone with good timing, a talent for accents, waggish commentary, and questions to the company. So there you are, gentlemen and ladies—you see what happens when a young lady runs away with an Irishman. What would they like to hear next? In mixed company, a male reader would generally read anything risqué, supposedly censoring the worst affronts to feminine modesty. But here too, it does not take much to imagine the tone of nudging suggestiveness, the parade of reticence itself such an invitation to lewd thoughts, and then the fatal word slipping out anyway. And one can almost hear the loud objections to anything tedious, the cries of "sad stuff!" and calls to move on to something more cheerful. Inscrutable as these practices may be, they survive in the sudden shifts of ramble fiction and even in the physical characteristics of the printed page. In all that heavy punctuation, the promiscuous mixing of italic and roman type, the phonetic rendering of dialects, and the semidramatic layout of so many episodes, one suddenly encounters those most fugitive beings, historical readers and auditors.[55]

These readers created a surprising demand for mainly entertaining fiction that could be taken up and put aside without regret. "I like a Book well enough," announces the belching Sir Goutly Scutcheon in the opening pages of *Tom Fool*. "Just to amuse, to kill time, when one has no Company, and it rains,—or—a Book then is the Thing." Nothing but amusement would do, carped the critics; serious and useful works were scarcely read. "The ridiculous" was so much the rage, bemoaned one midcentury essayist, "that no sooner a droll rogue touches that foible, but he commands all our affections." Moralists could put on their grave face, critics could complain, parsons could harangue from the pulpit, but it was all no use. Readers wanted entertainment, and anyone who wanted to stop them "may as well think of stemming a flood-tide in the river *Humber*."[56] The profitable thing for every bookseller was to swim with the tide. Readers evidently didn't care about probability, morality, unity, or stylistic decorum, the critical standards against which reviewers found ramble novels wanting. They bought the book anyway, and both authors and booksellers were confident in that knowledge. The preface to *Sophia Shakespear* (1753) dismisses in advance the objections that would inevitably come from "grave Pedants who have not Humour enough to divert others, nor Wit to please themselves." Introducing *Jerry Buck*, John Slade scorns any "low or groveling animadversions, which many mongrels in criticism may think proper to produce."[57]

The more self-reflexive ramble novels maintain a consistent tone of delight that they had so easily defied the literary and ethical standards of the day, that anyone would buy such trash. (And here one pauses to reconsider *Tristram Shandy* and the balance between subverting realist conventions and Sterne's giddy triumph that he was getting away with it.) By the late 1750s, increasing numbers of defiantly worthless and stupid novels began to appear, many of them printed in enormous fonts with huge margins, all an open insult to readers. Thus *A Book without a Title Page* (1761) or the brazenly titled *Did You Ever See Such Damn'd Stuff? or, So Much the Better*, subtitled *A Story without Head or Tail, Wit or Humour* (London, 1760). "*Rantum-skantum* is the Word / And *Nonsense* shall ensue" runs the epigraph, and the author's chapter titles keep up the joke. Chapter 1 "promises more than it performs." Chapter 2: "In which there is not much." Chapter 3: "All nonsense: so much the better." "Worse and worse" runs the next one: "Is that possible?" There was much more in this vein. Among other things, *The History of Tom Fool* (1760) is a hugely satisfying spoof on contemporary commercial fiction, a two-volume collection of deliriously amusing rubbish that consistently recognizes itself as such. Its goal, Stevens tells us, is to fill that empty "half Hour immediately preceding Dinner" when people don't know what to do with themselves. It was necessary to "all Families, Unchristian, as well as Christian," by whom one chapter a day is to be "served up, by Way of Whet."[58]

Still, the question remains. Who exactly was buying this shameless rubbish? Some things are easy to establish. Ramble novels were far too expensive for the lowest of readers—the orphaned apprentices and young women from the provinces who loom so large in the sociogenetic theories of Ian Watt and J. Paul Hunter. At 12s. for four volumes, *The History of Two Orphans* cost as much as *Amelia* or Frances Brooke's *Emily Montague* (1767). At 6s. for two duodecimo volumes, *Will Ramble* and *Kitty Fisher* cost the same as *Pamela* or Scott's *Sir George Ellison* (1766). This in a period when £12 was a good annual salary for laborers, domestic servants, and even curates or schoolmasters.[59] Watt and other postwar scholars clearly overestimated both the levels of reading at these lower reaches of society and the influence of such readers on production.[60] No doubt literate servants read employers' copies, with or without permission. Perhaps they occasionally picked up something second-hand. Probably they were reading library copies, but servants could never have joined the libraries on their own account: at 15s. or a guinea, the annual membership fees were much too high. They would have had to read books borrowed by their employer or use their employer's membership to take things out for themselves.

Production was obviously not determined by such incidental or furtive reading. Nor, despite the histrionics, was it directly determined by membership levels and borrowing habits at the circulating libraries. Even if all the circulating libraries in London (twenty by 1760) bought one or two copies of each novel, the proceeds would come nowhere near the cost of a minimum print run. Add provincial libraries and bookshops that lent on the side, and one doesn't come much closer. Clearly there was also a large retail market among those with money to spend, unthinkingly, on any new novel that came out. As James Raven has demonstrated, the libraries' role in stimulating purchase was at least as important to their proprietors as the profits to be made from lending. Certainly the infamous Noble brothers worked this way, using their two circulating libraries to promote duds like *The Jilts; or, Female Fortune-Hunters* (3 vols., 1756), *Memoirs of the Shakespear's Head* (2 vols., 1755), and dozens that are much worse—texts like *The Fortune-Teller; or, Footman Ennobled* (1756) and *The Life and Distresses of Simon Mason, Apothecary*, which somehow went through three editions between 1752 and 1756.[61]

Men or women? If nothing else, ramble fiction helps dispel lingering generalizations about the novel as a female genre, written for women and concerned with female subjects. The bluff mannishness of many texts invites us to imagine a class of male readers with time on their hands and money to spend—men like Elizabeth Montagu's "modern fine gentleman" lolling in his armchair. The young James Boswell would be one of these, keeping himself "well supplied" with novels from Francis Noble throughout his first stay in London (1762–63). Bookplates and auction catalogs point to legions of other male readers, from lords to rural schoolmasters and everything in between. Laurence Sterne owned *David Ranger*, *The Adventures of a Valet*, and Cleland's *Memoirs of a Coxcomb*, and he definitely read *The History of Two Orphans* (which turns out to have demonstrable influences on *Tristram Shandy*).[62] But here, as with every eighteenth-century genre, modern gender inferences soon start to collapse. Just as men read romances, domestic fiction, and sentimental lyrics in this period, so women read bawdy farces, low comic periodicals, and all the coarsest ramble novels. Most of the earlier ramble novels are on the list of two hundred books that George Colman attaches to his preface to *Polly Honeycombe* (1760)—the "greasy" and "much thumbed" catalog of a London circulating library. *Dick Hazard* and *Jerry Buck*, Colman implies, were the sort of books that led Polly to run away with the rascally Mr. Scribble.[63] But one would be wrong to generalize from such satires: keeping up with all the latest novels was a necessity for participating in polite conversation.

One of the most detailed records of midcentury fiction reading—if hardly a typical one—comes in the 1928 Sotheby's catalog of Lady Mary Wortley Montagu's library, complete with facsimiles of the marginalia she left in many copies.[64] The catalog alternates oddly between expensive editions of Epictetus and Voltaire and "the Gay part of reading," as she called it.[65] There are popular plays, scandal memoirs, and miscellanies like D'Urfey's *Stories* or Jane Barker's *Patch-Work Screen for the Ladies*. And there are dozens of midcentury novels. During her Italian years (1746–61), Lady Mary would scour English newspapers and booksellers' catalogs and compile lists of recent titles, which would then be sent by her dutiful daughter, the Duchess of Bute. Fielding, Richardson, and Smollett are on the lists, as are Lennox, Coventry, Haywood, and Sarah Fielding. But Lady Mary also ordered a striking proportion of the ephemeral fiction that appeared each year—all sorts of trash from Francis Noble and the other London fiction factories. Here, for example, is her order for April 1757:

> I see in the newspapers the names of the following books: *Fortunate Mistress, Accomplished Rake, Mrs. Charke's Memoirs, Modern Lovers, History of Two Orphans, Memoirs of David Ranger, Miss [?Kat]ty N, Dick Hazard, History of a Lady Platonist, Sophia Shakespear, Jasper Banks, Frank Hammond, Sir Andrew Thompson, Van a Clergyman's Son, Cleanthes and Celimena.* I do not doubt at least the greatest part of these Trash, Lumber, &c.; however, they will serve to pass away the idle time, if you will be so kind to send them to your most affectionate mother.[66]

Lady Mary knew what she was ordering: the booksellers' advertisements gave long titles and often a table of contents or commentary. Given this level of information, she is a strikingly undiscriminating purchaser of books. She detested Defoe, but nevertheless sent away for *Roxana. Jasper Banks* (subtitled *The Handsome Man*) and *The Accomplished Rake* were obviously going to be bawdy, as was *The Modern Lovers; or, The Adventures of Cupid, the God of Love* (1756). She orders Katherine Maxwell's scandalous *History of Miss Katty N——*. In *Sir Andrew Thompson*, she was ordering a butchered version of *Le paysan parvenu* (yet another production of the shadowy Adolphus Bannac).

Once the books arrived, Lady Mary's predictions were largely confirmed. *Roxana* was "vulgar"; *Sophia Shakespear* was "trash." *The Adventures of Frank Hammond* was "flat," while the "History of a Lady Platonist" was "insufferable."[67] These are characteristic of the annotations in Lady Mary's copies: *Captain Greenland* was "impertinent"; others were "foolish," "humdrum," or "riff-raff"; she tired of their shallow characterization and "abominable insipidities." Other comments are ambiguous: *Dick Hazard* was "pert" (lively?); when she called *Young Scarron* "risible," she seems to have meant that it was amusing; *The Adventures of Jack Smart* was "Smart tho' ordinary." *Joe Thompson* evidently got worse: volume 1 was "tolerable," but volume 2 was "intolerable." But many others she seems to have thoroughly enjoyed. She could not put down *Charlotte Summers*. Benjamin Victor's *Widow of the Wood*, a scandalous roman à clef of 1755, was "wonderfull." *Jack Connor* offered "many Pictures well drawn." With its satiric portrait of herself, Cleland's *Memoirs of a Coxcomb* was "instructif." The important point is that Lady Mary kept asking for these histories of "Cobblers and Kitchin Wenches"—and that she enjoyed them without shame. "Wiser people may think it triffling," she concedes to her daughter, "but it serves to sweeten Life to me, and is, at worst, better that the Generality of Conversation." "Daughter, Daughter," she replies to another scolding letter from London, "don't call names":

> You are always abusing my Pleasures, which is what no mortal will bear. Trash, Lumber, sad stuff, are the Titles you give to my favorite Amusements. . . . We all have our Playthings; happy are they tha[t] can be contented with those they can obtain.[68]

Aristocratic and astonishingly thriftless, Lady Mary is no representative figure. Few readers could have ordered every book in the papers, scrawled their contempt, and then tossed them aside after a few pages. Lady Mary's letters show her working through an entire case of books in a matter of days (cost of the shipment above: £3 15s.).[69] Still, her guiltless recreational reading does remind us that even the most discerning readers purchased and enjoyed the trash fiction of the age—and that even the crudest novels were not entirely unsuitable reading for genteel women. Her own changing tastes in fiction—from the *contes de fée* and French romances of her youth to the native comic realism of her later years—exemplify general shifts in taste and the print market. For diversion and passing time, male and female readers at every level of the reading public now turned less to the older narrative genres than to low and disposable fiction, much of it comic.

*

Jerry Buck, David Ranger, Betty Ireland: why are these popular and profitable texts so entirely absent from working assumptions about early English fiction? As with jestbooks or comic periodicals, material survival is itself a major factor: many ramble novels are now exceptionally rare, surviving in single or imperfect copies, with pages missing and covers torn off. Some have been used as small-scale scrapbooks, with doodles in the margins and newspaper clippings glued on top of the text. A striking number, perhaps 12–15 percent, haven't survived at all, being known only by reviews or advertisements.[70] At the same time, the selection processes of literary history were already beginning in the late eighteenth century. None of these texts, not even blockbusters like *Joe Thompson*, make it into early nineteenth-century collections or histories of the novel by Scott, Barbauld, and John Dunlop. A century later, when the first professional English literature scholars began their rehabilitation of eighteenth-century fiction, they obviously had no use for hackwork. It was hard enough to convince people that Defoe, Fielding, and Smollett were worth reading, let alone these coarse and amoral formula fictions. A half century later, ramble fiction had no place in teleologies like Ian Watt's—arguments that made eighteenth-century texts respectable by relating them forward to the great realist and modernist novels.

Times have now changed. Few professional scholars talk about literature in the old exalted sense, and aesthetic judgments are seldom relevant. We know what forward-looking perspectives do to the past. The fiction canon has now been expanded to admit all manner of minority voices, most notably the dozens of women writers who made such major contributions to early fiction. But no one has had much to say about ramble novels, and this silence reveals just how few adequate methods we still have for dealing with frankly distasteful parts of the historical record. Recovery projects and calls to expand the canon depend on empathetic perspectives. As John Guillory pointed out more than a decade ago, they conceive of texts as representing a community in the way that politicians represent their constituents. The critic's job is to speak for each marginalized author and the marginalized communities they represent.[71]

Two major studies of forgotten fiction—both important models when I started work on ramble novels—reveal the currently available tropes for

FIGURE 14. Francesco Bartolozzi after John Mortimer, engraving for *Evelina*, 4th ed. (London, 1779), vol. 3. The foppish Mr. Lovel is being bitten on the ear by a monkey. Captain Mirvan, Burney's boorish practical joker, stands on the left. While a number of readers objected to the old women's footrace earlier in volume 3, no one took issue with this scene. Photograph © The British Library Board (1484.e.11).

FIGURE 15. Thomas Rowlandson, *Feast after the Manner of the Antients*, engraving for *Peregrine Pickle* (London, 1796). One of Smollett's most celebrated comic sequences, it depicts a staggering concatenation of head knocking, fallen periwigs, upset tables, scalding, nausea, and vomiting. Courtesy of the Special Collections Research Center, Earl Gregg Swem Library, The College of William and Mary.

accumulative scholarship of this sort. Monographs by Margaret Cohen and Katie Trumpener both champion unrecognized precursors of canonical authors and suggest that this suppressed tradition would have been preferable to what actually developed. Cohen's *Sentimental Education of the Novel* is a deeply empathetic recuperation of early nineteenth-century women's fiction, a tradition all but obliterated by the triumph of Balzac and Stendhal, whom she casts as literary bullies, perpetrators of a "hostile takeover" of the genre. In romantic era national tales, Katie Trumpener discovers not just important precursors to Scott's imperial fiction but a deeply appealing alternative: a glimpse of "how differently some of Scott's contemporaries imagined a critical, cosmopolitan fiction of empire."[72] None of this rhetoric is available for ramble fiction. Who wants to champion *Jack Smart* or *The History of Pudica*? Claiming long-term influence is not an option either. One might no doubt trace connections to Egan, Marryat, or Bulwer Lytton, but in truth these texts are dead ends—without influence and stubbornly of their time. Few readers of midcentury comic fiction—or any of the other forgotten rubbish of this study—could feel much regret that literary history left them behind.

Yet beyond their obvious interest as historical documents, ramble novels may still have much to tell us about the canonical fiction of this age, the literature that they both imitated and influenced. In a strict sense, as Pierre Bourdieu points out in his fascinating analysis of minor novelists around Flaubert, any critic who fails to explore the forgotten publications around a canonical text is doomed to an "unknowing poetics"—destined to take up the book with modern expectations rather than the norms of its own time.[73] This is not to say that a fully knowing poetics could ever be possible, or that anyone could read every minor text around an accepted literary one. But once approached from the minor comic writings of their age, the odder moments of many canonical novels start to make sense. By now it should be clear how true this is of Fielding, Smollett, and Burney—and, after working through so many ramble novels, one begins to notice other details (figs. 14–15). The heavy-handed vulgarity of the Seagrim family in *Tom Jones*. Stupefying gay-bashing episodes in *Amelia* and *Peregrine Pickle*. The furious Mrs. Delvile bursting her blood vessel in *Cecilia*. And why all the frenetic action in *Camilla*—the dogfight, the orchestra of monkeys at Northwick Fair, the disastrous provincial *Othello* (straight out of *Young Scarron* and *Le roman comique* before it)? One easily thinks of other episodes in Lennox, Sarah Fielding, Edgeworth, and, by way of the juvenilia, Austen.

And then one starts to notice odd comic traces in so much broadly sentimental writing. Sterne's notorious mingling of bawdy and high feeling surely obliges us to look for this sort of mischief. Take the kitchen scene in volume 5 of *Tristram Shandy*: Trim announcing the death of Bobby, Susanna instantly thinking of Mrs. Shandy's green satin nightgown, Obadiah of the ox moor, the coachman announcing that Bobby used to be alive, the "fat foolish scullion" squatting in her filth. "Is not all flesh grass?" says Trim, in his best oratorical posture. "'Tis clay,—'tis dirt.—They all looked directly at the scullion,—the scullion had just been scouring a fish kettle.—It was not fair." Trim drops his hat, and all weep as if by animal reflex. From here one thinks of Yorick's encounter with the dwarf in *A Sentimental Journey*. "I cannot bear to see one of them trod upon," he begins, only to offer a droll description of that very thing: an archetypal squabble between a slow-witted giant and an increasingly peevish little dwarf. What of the enclosure of rescued freaks in *Millenium Hall*? Five dwarfs, one giantess, one case of premature aging, and one seven-foot hunchback who is happy enough to be bent down to a normal size, and all of them bickering about who had been most successful as a fairground exhibit. One hundred years later, Henry James was deriding Dickens's habit of assigning his sentimental business to a "troop of hunchbacks, imbeciles, and precocious children."[74] And today one wonders whether the mysterious transformation of comic sufferings into pitiable ones may not be perpetually incomplete. The loudest laughter may have died down, but let us not be too proud of our humanity. Our most malicious, petty, brutal, egotistical, defensive impulses have not disappeared. We just satisfy them in other ways.

ABBREVIATIONS

BL	British Library
BM	British Museum
BM Satires	British Museum, Department of Prints and Drawings, as numbered and explicated in M. Dorothy George and Frederic George Stephens, eds., *Catalogue of Political and Personal Satires, Preserved in the Department of Prints and Drawings in the British Museum*, 10 vols. (London: British Museum Publications, 1978)
BM Satires undescribed	Not explicated in George and Stephens, eds. (see BM Satires); cited by date and registration number
Bodleian	Bodleian Library, Oxford
ESTC	*English Short Title Catalogue*
Harding	Harding Collection, Bodleian Library
HL	Huntington Library, San Marino, CA
HMC	Publications of the Historical Manuscripts Commission, London
LMA	London Metropolitan Archives
ODNB	*Oxford Dictionary of National Biography* (Oxford: Oxford University Press, 2004–10); updates accessed online
OBSP	Old Bailey Sessions Papers as available online (www.oldbailey online.org), verified against originals; cited by cause, date, and online reference number

NOTES

INTRODUCTION

1. See esp. John Mullan, *Sentiment and Sociability: The Language of Feeling in the Eighteenth Century* (Oxford: Clarendon, 1988); Barbara Benedict, *Framing Feeling: Sentiment and Style in English Prose Fiction, 1745-1800* (New York: AMS, 1944); Markman Ellis, *The Politics of Sensibility: Race, Gender and Commerce in the Sentimental Novel* (Cambridge: Cambridge University Press, 1996); Lawrence Klein, *Shaftesbury and the Culture of Politeness: Moral Discourse and Cultural Politics in Early Eighteenth-Century England* (Cambridge: Cambridge University Press, 1994); and John Brewer, *The Pleasures of the Imagination: English Culture in the Eighteenth Century* (New York: Farrar Straus Giroux, 1997).

2. Paul Langford, *A Polite and Commercial People: England, 1727-83* (Oxford: Oxford University Press, 1992).

3. Terry Eagleton, *The Rape of Clarissa* (Minneapolis: University of Minnesota Press, 1982), vii.

4. This change is explored in a searching article by Robert Griffin, "The Age of 'the Age of' Is Over: Johnson and New Versions of the Late Eighteenth Century," *Modern Language Quarterly* 62, no. 4 (2001): 377-91.

5. David Fairer, *English Poetry of the Eighteenth Century* (London: Longman, 2003), ix, 2-3, and the extended discussion in chap. 2; Helen Berry, "Rethinking Politeness in Eighteenth-Century England," *Transactions of the Royal Historical Society*, 6th ser., 11 (2001): 65-81.

6. Paul Langford, "British Politeness and the Progress of Western Manners," *Transactions of the Royal Historical Society*, 6th ser., 7 (1997): 53-57, and *Englishness Identified* (Oxford: Oxford University Press, 2000). For an exhaustive analysis of French attitudes toward the British during the precise period of my study, see Edmond Dziembowski, *Un nouveau patriotisme français, 1750-1770* (Oxford: Voltaire Foundation, 1998).

7. Vic Gatrell, *City of Laughter: Sex and Satire in Eighteenth-Century London* (New York: Walker, 2006).

8. Robert D. Hume, "Drama and Theatre in the Mid- and Later Eighteenth Century," in *The Cambridge History of English Literature, 1660–1780*, ed. John Richetti (Cambridge: Cambridge University Press, 2005), 324 and n; Roger Lonsdale, ed., *The New Oxford Book of Eighteenth-Century Verse* (Oxford: Oxford University Press, 1989), xxxvi–xxxvii. The myth of sentimental dominance is especially remarkable with the drama, since counterstatistics have been available since the 1960s.

9. Jane Spencer, *The Rise of the Woman Novelist* (Oxford: Blackwell, 1986), chap. 3. For a useful revisionist analysis of these midcentury authors and their shrewd professionalism, see Betty S. Schellenberg, *The Professionalization of Women Writers in Eighteenth-Century Britain* (Cambridge: Cambridge University Press, 2005).

10. Amanda Vickery, *The Gentleman's Daughter: Women's Lives in Georgian England* (New Haven, CT: Yale University Press, 1998); Linda Colley, *Britain: Forging the Nation, 1707–1837* (New Haven, CT: Yale University Press, 1992), esp. chap. 6; Charlotte Sussman, *Consuming Anxieties: Consumer Protest, Gender, and British Slavery, 1713–1833* (Stanford, CA: Stanford University Press, 2000); Harriet Guest, *Small Change: Women, Learning, and Patriotism, 1750–1810* (Chicago: University of Chicago Press, 2000); Karen O'Brien, *Women and Enlightenment in Eighteenth-Century Britain* (Cambridge: Cambridge University Press, 2009). For a valuable range of perspectives across disciplines, see Elizabeth Eger, Charlotte Grant, Clíona Ó Gallchoir, and Penny Warburton, eds., *Women, Writing and the Public Sphere, 1700–1830* (New York: Cambridge University Press, 2001).

11. John Gregory, *A Father's Legacy to His Daughters* (London, 1774), 30–31.

12. George L. Justice and Nathan Tinker, eds., *Women's Writing and the Circulation of Ideas: Manuscript Publication in England, 1550–1800* (Cambridge: Cambridge University Press, 2002).

13. Laura J. Rosenthal, "Recovering from Recovery," *The Eighteenth Century: Theory and Interpretation* 50, no. 1 (March 2010): 1–11.

14. Terminology first proposed in Raymond Williams's famous essay "Base and Superstructure" (1973), reprinted in *Culture and Materialism* (London: Verso, 2005), 31–49. For an Olympian analysis of the patterning of historical time, see Penelope J. Corfield, *Time and the Shape of History* (New Haven, CT: Yale University Press, 2007).

15. Marc Bloch, *The Royal Touch: Sacred Monarchy and Scrofula in England and France* (1924), trans. J. E. Anderson (London: Routledge, 1973).

16. Lynn Hunt has lucidly synthesized these developments in *Inventing Human Rights: A History* (New York: Norton, 2007).

17. For influential programmatic statements from this time, see the introduction to Felicity Nussbaum and Laura Brown, *The New Eighteenth Century* (New York: Routledge, 1987); and John Bender, "A New History of the Enlightenment?" in *The Profession of Eighteenth-Century Literature*, ed. Leo Damrosch (Madison: University of Wisconsin Press, 1992), 62–83.

18. Lawrence Lipking, "Inventing the Eighteenth Centuries," in Damrosch, ed., *The Profession of Eighteenth-Century Literature*, 7–25. The periodization problem is discussed as an annual ritual in the "Recent Studies" essays in the journal *Studies in English Literature*.

19. Terms proposed by William St. Clair, *The Reading Nation in the Romantic Period* (Cambridge: Cambridge University Press, 2004), 2.

20. Eric Hobsbawm, "Introduction: Inventing Traditions," in *The Invention of Tradition*, ed. Eric Hobsbawm and Terence Ranger (Cambridge: Cambridge University Press, 1993), 13n17.

21. See Thomas Keymer, *Sterne, the Moderns, and the Novel* (Oxford: Oxford University Press, 2002), 55–56.

22. Christopher Hill, *Reformation to Industrial Revolution* (New York: Pantheon, 1968), 19–20; Lawrence Stone, *The Crisis of the Aristocracy, 1558–1641* (Oxford: Oxford University Press, 1965), 4.

23. Roy Porter, "English Society in the Eighteenth Century Revisited," in *British Politics and Society from Walpole to Pitt, 1742–1789*, ed. Jeremy Black (Basingstoke: Macmillan, 1990), 29–52, esp. 36–37.

24. See esp. Peter Goodrich, "A Short History of Failure," in *Languages of Law* (London: Weidenfeld & Nicolson, 1990), 15–52.

25. T. J. Clark, *Farewell to an Idea: Episodes from a History of Modernism* (New Haven, CT: Yale University Press, 1999); Denis Hollier, ed., *A New History of French Literature* (Cambridge, MA: Harvard University Press, 1989).

26. Keith Luria and Romulo Gandolfo, "Carlo Ginzburg: An Interview," *Radical History Review* 35 (1986): 89–111, 105.

27. Jean Starobinski, *1789: The Emblems of Reason*, trans. Barbara Bray (Cambridge, MA: MIT Press, 1988); Hans-Robert Jauss, "*La douceur du foyer*: Lyric Poetry of the Year 1857 as a Model for the Communication of Social Norms," in *Aesthetic Experience and Literary Hermeneutics*, trans. Michael Shaw (Minneapolis: University of Minnesota Press, 1982), 263–93. The last twenty years have seen a run of these single-year studies, some of them recognized turning points, others deliberately choosing historically unimportant years. For an acute analysis of this mode and its possibilities, see Michael North, "Virtual Histories: The Year as Literary Period," *Modern Language Quarterly* 62, no. 4 (December 2001): 407–25.

28. For a suggestive recent commentary on these conventions, see Clifford Siskin, "More Is Different: Literary Change in the Mid- and Late Eighteenth Century," in Richetti, ed., *The Cambridge History of English Literature, 1660–1780*, 795–823.

29. Walter Benjamin, "Abfall der Geschichte," in *Das Passagen-Werk*, ed. Rolf Tiedemann, 2 vols. (Frankfurt: Suhrkamp, 1983), 1:575 (N 2,6).

30. See, e.g., Steven Zwicker, "Recent Studies in the Restoration and Eighteenth Century," *Studies in English Literature, 1500–1900* 44, no. 3 (2004): 640.

31. Stephen Greenblatt and Catherine Gallagher, *Practicing New Historicism* (Chicago: University of Chicago Press, 2000), esp. chap. 2. I make these distinctions in sympathy with Peter de Bolla, Nigel Leask, and David Simpson, *Land, Nation, and Culture, 1740–1840* (New York: Palgrave, 2005), introduction, esp. 6–7.

CHAPTER ONE

1. *Coffee-House Jests* (London, 1760), 42 (no. 80).

2. *The Jests of Beau Nash* (London, 1763), 65–66.

3. *Joe Miller's Jests; or, The Wit's Vade-Mecum*, 12th ed. (London, [ca. 1755]), 40 (no. 234).

4. *England's Witty and Ingenious Jester*, 17th ed. (London, n.d. [BL Cup. 406. g. 5]), 37; cf. *Oxford Jests* (London, n.d. [Bodleian Harding E 197]), 41–42.

5. *The Merry Miscellany* (Bristol, n.d. [BL 12316.bb.37.2.]), n.p.

6. *Joe Miller's Jests*, 75 (no. 439).

7. Thomas Hobbes, *Leviathan*, ed. Richard Tuck (Cambridge: Cambridge University Press, 1991), 3 (1.6).

8. Deaf jokes were sufficiently common in early modern culture to merit their own category in Stith Thompson's *Motif-Index of Folk Literature*, 6 vols. (Bloomington: Indiana University Press, 1955–58). The Finnish folklorist Antti Aarne devoted an entire monograph to the subject: *Schwänke über schwerhörige Menschen* (Helsinki: HSTK, 1914).

9. See, e.g., *The Laugher; or, The Art of Jesting*, 2nd ed. (London, 1755).

10. See Keith Thomas, *Man and the Natural World* (New York: Pantheon, 1983), 32.

11. *The Complete London Jester*, 3rd ed. (London, 1766 [Bodleian Harding E268]), 16; cf. *Tom Brown's Complete Jester*, 4th ed. (London, n.d. [Bodleian Harding E276]), 2.

12. *The Nut-Cracker* (London, 1751), 12 (cf. 43, 46).

13. Ibid., 33.

14. *Joaks upon Joaks; or, No Joak Like a True Joak* (Worcester, n.d. [HL 150742]), 3.

15. These debates and the changes they produced were richly explored fifty years ago in Stuart Tave, *The Amiable Humorist* (Chicago: University of Chicago Press, 1960). Among the most encompassing recent studies, see Ronald Paulson, *Don Quixote in England: The Aesthetics of Laughter* (Baltimore: Johns Hopkins University Press, 1998).

16. Adam Smith, *The Theory of Moral Sentiments*, ed. D. D. Raphael and A. L. Macfie (Oxford: Clarendon, 1976), 13; James Beattie, "An Essay on Laughter and Ludicrous Composition," in *Essays* (Edinburgh, 1776), 665.

17. David Hume, *An Enquiry concerning the Principles of Morals*, ed. L. A. Selby-Bigge, 3rd ed., rev. P. H. Nidditch (Oxford: Clarendon, 1975), 226 (5.2.184); Hester Chapone, *Letters on the Improvement of the Mind, Addressed to a Young Lady* (London, 1777), 166–67.

18. Jonathan Swift, *A Tale of a Tub and Other Works*, ed. Marcus Walsh (Cambridge: Cambridge University Press, 2010), 40.

19. See, e.g., Barry Reay, *Popular Cultures in England, 1550–1750* (London: Longman, 1998); and the essays in Tim Harris, ed., *Popular Culture in England, c. 1500–1850* (New York: St Martin's, 1995).

20. H. R. French, *The Middle Sort of People in Provincial England, 1600–1750* (Oxford: Oxford University Press, 2007); Margaret Hunt, *The Middling Sort: Commerce, Gender and the Family in England, 1680–1780* (Berkeley and Los Angeles: University of California Press, 1996); Peter Borsay, *The English Urban Renaissance: Culture and Society in the Provincial Town, 1660–1770* (Oxford: Clarendon, 1989). On the smudging of identities in later decades, see Dror Wahrman, *Imagining the Middle Class: The Political Representation of Class in Britain, c. 1780–1840* (Cambridge: Cambridge University Press, 1995).

21. *The Agreeable Companion; or, An Universal Medley of Wit and Good Humour* (London, 1745), e.g., appeared in eight weekly parts. On the serial publication of *Joe Miller* and other comic texts, see R. M. Wiles, *Serial Publication in England before 1750* (Cambridge: Cambridge University Press, 1957), 349.

22. The only sustained discussion of eighteenth-century jestbooks is Ronald Paulson, "The Joke and *Joe Miller's Jests*," in *Popular and Polite Art in the Age of Hogarth and Fielding* (South Bend: University of Notre Dame Press, 1979), 64–84. Paulson treats jestbooks as popular texts and focuses his discussion on subversive humor; he has little to say about the pitiless jokes that interest me here.

23. See Victor Neuberg, "The Diceys and the Chapbook Trade," *The Library* 24 (1969): 219–31.

24. *Polly Peachum's Jests* (London, 1728, etc.); *Tristram Shandy's Bon Mots, Repartees, Odd Adventures, and Humourous Stories* (London, 1760); *Tristram Shandy's Jests* (London, 1760); *Sterne's Witticisms; or, Yorick's Convivial Jester* (London, n.d. [BL 12316.bb.31]); *Tristram Shandy at Ranelagh* (London, 1760); and several others.

25. *The Sailor's Jester* (London, 1788), title page; *The Female Jester; or, Wit for the Ladies* (London, n.d. [Bodleian Douce HH 139(4)]); *Woman's Wit, a Jest-Book for the Ladies* (London, n.d. [Houghton Library 25267.32]).

26. *The Irish Miscellany; or, Teagueland Jests* (London, 1746, etc.); *The Theatrical Jester; or, Green-Room Witticisms* (London, 1770); *The Macaroni Jester and Pantheon of Wit* (London, 1764).

27. *Polly Peachum's Jests*, title page.

28. *Jack Smart's Merry Jester*, 2nd ed. (London, n.d. [BL 1607/3945]), 1.

29. Samuel Johnson, *Lives of the Most Eminent English Poets*, ed. Roger Lonsdale, 4 vols. (Oxford: Clarendon, 2006), 2:42 (Waller) (cf. 3:45 [Sheffield]).

30. *The Muse in Good Humour: A Collection of Comic Tales*, 8th ed., 2 vols. (London, 1785), 2:136–41 (the swearing contest).

31. *Rochester's Jests* (London, 1766), 77; *Ben Johnson's Last Legacy to the Sons of Wit, Mirth, and Jollytry* (London, 1756), 43–46.

32. *The Wit's Miscellany* (London, 1762); *The Merry Medley* (London, [ca. 1750]), title page. For more Christmas volumes, see *The Medley, or Universal Entertainer* (London, 1748); *The Tell-Tale* (London, 1755); *The Hotch-Potch* (London, 1774); *The Winter Evenings Entertainment* (London, 1737); *Winter's Wit; or, Fun for Cold Weather* (London, 1770); and *The Christmas Treat; or, Gay Companion* (Dublin, 1767).

33. *Coffee-House Jests*, 71 (no. 128); *The Merry Medley*, 294.

34. *England's Witty and Ingenious Jester*, 23; cf. *Joe Miller's Jests*, 4 (no. 23).

35. Compare *The Harangues; or, Speeches, of Several Celebrated Quack-Doctors* (London, 1762, 1778, etc.).

36. *The Entertaining Companion; or, The Merry Jester* (London, n.d. [Bodleian Harding E54]), 5, 7; *England's Witty and Ingenious Jester*, 58.

37. *The Agreeable Companion*, 16–18.

38. *Joe Miller's Jests*, 9 (no. 51).

39. *England's Witty and Ingenious Jester*, 8–9; cf. "How Eulenspiegel Shitted on an Innkeeper's Table in Cologne" and "How Eulenspiegel Shitted in His Bed and Convinced His Innkeeper That a Priest Had Done It," in *Till Eulenspiegel: His Adventures*, trans. Paul Oppenheimer (Oxford: Oxford University Press, 1995), chaps. 78, 84.

40. *Joe Miller's Jests*, 105 (no. 585).

41. *England's Witty and Ingenious Jester*, 59–60.

42. Ibid., 60.

43. *Joe Miller's Jests*, 6 (no. 38). This was identified as a particular favorite in the BL twelfth edition (1507/670), with a big cross in the margin.

44. *The Muse in Good Humour*, 7th ed., 2 vols. (London, 1766), 1:123–37.

45. *The Jests of Beau Nash*, 4, 30, 65–66, 68–71, and passim.

46. *The Merry Medley*, 10, 17–18, 21–22, etc.

47. For the library catalogs of Goldsmith and Wilkes, see A. N. L. Munby, ed., *Sale Catalogues of Libraries of Eminent Persons*, 12 vols. (London: Mansell Information, 1971–75), vols. 7, 8. For Walpole's texts, see Horace Walpole, *The Yale Edition of Horace Walpole's Correspondence*, ed. W. S. Lewis et al., 48 vols. (New Haven, CT: Yale University Press, 1937–83), 9:35, 16:253, 35:565. James Woodforde, *The Diary of a Country Parson*, ed. John Beresford, 5 vols. (Oxford: Oxford University Press, 1981), 3:353 (1792).

48. Henry Fielding, *The History of Tom Jones*, ed. Martin C. Battestin and Fredson Bowers (Oxford: Clarendon, 1977), 528. On Fielding's use of *Joe Miller's Jests*, see Hollis Rinehart, "Fielding's Chapter 'Of Proverbs,'" *Modern Philology* 77, no. 3 (1980): 291–96. On the Nell Gwyn anecdote, see Tom Keymer, "*Tom Jones*, Nell Gwyn and the *Cambridge Jest Book*," *Notes and Queries* 51, no. 4 (2004): 408–9.

49. On Sterne's use of *The Muse in Good Humour* and other comic collections, see Melvyn New, "Sterne's Bawdry: A Cautionary Tale," *Review of English Studies* 62, no. 253 (2011): 80–89.

50. Jan Fergus, *Provincial Readers in Eighteenth-Century England* (Oxford: Oxford University Press, 2006). I am grateful to Jan Fergus for looking into her notes (Jan Fergus, personal communication, 18 May 2010).

51. Fergus, *Provincial Readers*, 69, and personal communication, 18 May 2010; Vic Gatrell, *City of Laughter: Sex and Satire in Eighteenth-Century London* (New York: Walker, 2006); *The Complete London Jester*, title page. For Mrs. Thrale's library catalog, see Munby, ed., *Sale Catalogues*, vol. 5.

52. Fergus, *Provincial Readers*, passim.

53. Of the large scholarship on this topic, see esp. Jacqueline Pearson, *Women's Reading in Britain, 1750–1835: A Dangerous Recreation* (Cambridge: Cambridge University Press, 1999); James Raven, Helen Small, and Naomi Tadmor, eds., *The Practice and Representation of Reading in England* (Cambridge: Cambridge University Press, 1996); and, more recently, Stephen Colclough, *Consuming Texts: Readers and Reading Communities, 1695–1870* (New York: Palgrave, 2007).

54. John Gregory, *A Father's Legacy to His Daughters* (London, 1774), 58.

55. *Fun for the Parlour; or, All Merry above Stairs* (London, 1771).

56. *The Tell-Tale; or, Anecdotes Expressive of the Characters of Persons Eminent for Rank, Learning, Wit, or Humour . . . for the Improvement of Youth in Conversation* (London, 1762), vi.

57. *The Diverting Muse; or, The Universal Medley* (London, 1707).

58. *The Buck's Bottle Companion* (London, 1772); "Roger Rubyface," in *The Frisky Jester; or, The Cream of the Jest, and the Marrow of the Tale* (London, n.d. [BL 1080.k.36]).

59. Place Papers, BL Add. MSS 27828, fol. 29; David H. Solkin, *Painting for Money: The Visual Arts and the Public Sphere in Eighteenth-Century England* (New Haven, CT: Yale University Press, 1993), 99–102; Gatrell, *City of Laughter*, esp. chap. 4; Brian Cowan, *The Social Life of Coffee: The Emergence of the British Coffeehouse* (New Haven, CT: Yale University Press, 2005); Markman Ellis, *The Coffee House: A Cultural History* (London: Weidenfeld & Nicolson, 2004).

60. Peter Clark notes the staggering consumption of alcohol almost in passing, preferring to stress the condemnation it attracted. See his *British Clubs and Societies, 1580-1800: The Origins of an Associational World* (Oxford: Oxford University Press, 2000), esp. 2, 10, 225–26.

61. *The Jests of Beau Nash*, i.

62. Oliver Goldsmith, *The Vicar of Wakefield*, in *Collected Works of Oliver Goldsmith*, ed. Arthur Friedman, 5 vols. (Oxford: Clarendon, 1966), 4:78; Ann Thwaite, *Glimpses of the Wonderful: The Life of Philip Henry Gosse* (London: Faber, 2002), 34–35.

63. *The Nut-Cracker*, 1–10; cf. *The Merry Medley*.

64. William H. Sherman, *Used Books: Marking Readers in Renaissance England* (Philadelphia: University of Pennsylvania Press, 2008), chap. 2.

65. See, e.g., *The Merry Philosopher; or, Thoughts on Jesting* (London, 1764).

66. See *Thraliana: The Diary of Mrs. Hester Lynch Thrale*, ed. Katherine C. Balderston, 2 vols. (Oxford: Clarendon, 1942), 1:323. The jests and anecdotes are concentrated at the beginning of vol. 1.

67. *Memoirs of Richard Cumberland, Written by Himself*, 2 vols. (London, 1807), 1: 194–95.

68. Sir Nicholas LeStrange, "Merry Passages and Jeasts" (BL Harley 6395), also available as a modern edition: *Merry Passages and Jeasts*, ed. H. F. Lippincott, Elizabethan and Renaissance Studies 29 (Salzburg: Universität Salzburg, 1974).

69. *The Letters of Philip Dormer Stanhope, 4th Earl of Chesterfield*, ed. Bonamy Dobrée, 6 vols. (London: Eyre & Spottiswoode, 1932), 3:1036 (16 October 1747).

70. *England's Genius; or, Wit Triumphant* (London, 1734), title page; *The Jests of Beau Nash*, title page.

71. On gentlemen and aristocrats at the Inns of Court—i.e., the large proportion of lodgers who were not law students—see David Lemmings, *Gentlemen and Barristers: The Inns of Court and the English Bar, 1680-1730* (Oxford: Clarendon, 1990), chaps. 1–2.

72. *Joe Miller's Jests*, 3 (no. 16); *The Merry Miscellany*, n.p.; *The Laugher*, 161.

73. *Woman's Wit*, title page.

74. *The Delicate Jester* (London, n.d. [BL 12331.f.37(1)]), title page, 55.

75. *The Female Jester*, [i], 31, 37.

76. *The Jests of Beau Nash*, 65–66.

77. *Joe Miller's Jests*, 3 (no. 16); Jonathan Swift, "Verses on the Death of Dr Swift," in *Jonathan Swift: The Complete Poems*, ed. Pat Rogers (New Haven, CT: Yale University Press, 1983), 497 (lines 471–72).

78. *The Merry Medley* (London, 1745), v.

79. Solkin, *Painting for Money*, 99–102; cf. Philip Carter, *Men and the Emergence of Polite Society, Britain 1660-1800* (London: Longman, 2001).

80. Sigmund Freud, *Jokes and Their Relation to the Unconscious*, in *The Standard Edition of the Complete Psychological Works of Sigmund Freud*, ed. and trans. James Strachey, 24 vols. (London: Hogarth, 1953–74), 8:103.

81. I take my terminology here from Norbert Elias, *The Civilizing Process* (1939), trans. Edmund Jephcott, 2 vols. in 1 (Oxford: Blackwell, 1982). One scholar, at least, has argued that the punch line has a historical moment of origin. "The punch-line, which is nowadays believed to be the heart and soul of the joke," argues Gershon Legman, "is actually just a modern accretion. . . . The important and universal elements of the joke have all been delivered before the punch-line is reached" (*The Rationale of the Dirty Joke: An Analysis of Sexual Humor, First Series* [New York: Grove, 1968], 139).

82. Cited in Keith Thomas, "The Place of Laughter in Tudor and Stuart England," *Times Literary Supplement*, 21 January 1977, 80.

83. Robert Halsband, "New Anecdotes of Lady Mary Wortley Montagu," in *Evidence in Literary Scholarship*, ed. René Wellek and Alvaro Ribeiro (Oxford: Clarendon, 1979), 241–46. For contemporary commentary on Charlotte Grandison, see Francis Plumer, *A Candid Examination of the History of Sir Charles Grandison*, 3rd ed. (London, 1754), 49.

84. Stella Tillyard, *Aristocrats: Caroline, Emily, Louisa and Sarah Lennox 1740–1832* (London: Chatto & Windus, 1994), 242, 156–60.

85. *Boswell's Life of Johnson*, ed. George Birkbeck Hill, rev. L. F. Powell, 6 vols. (Oxford: Clarendon, 1964–71), 2:337.

86. Chapone, *Letters on the Improvement of the Mind*, 166–69.

87. See William St. Clair, *The Reading Nation in the Romantic Period* (Cambridge: Cambridge University Press, 2004), 27; and, most recently, Michael F. Suarez S.J., "Towards a Bibliometric Analysis of the Surviving Record, 1701–1800," in *The Cambridge History of the Book in Britain*, vol. 5 (1695–1830), ed. Michael F. Suarez S.J. and Michael L. Turner (Cambridge: Cambridge University Press, 2009), 39–65.

88. On Douce, see *The Gentleman's Magazine*, 2nd ser., 2 (1834): 215–16. On Hazlitt, see Samuel Schoenbaum, *Shakespeare's Lives*, rev. ed. (Oxford: Clarendon, 1991), 492. Walter Newton Henry Harding wrote about his passion in "British Song Books and Kindred Subjects," *The Book Collector* 11, no. 4 (1962): 448–59.

CHAPTER TWO

1. An intense theoretical debate surrounds all these issues. For useful starting points, see Lennard J. Davis, ed., *The Disability Studies Reader*, 2nd ed. (New York: Routledge, 2006); and Helen Deutsch and Felicity Nussbaum, eds., *"Defects": Engendering the Modern Body* (Ann Arbor: University of Michigan Press, 2000). (*"Defects"* is part of the important series Corporealities: Discourses of Disability, from the University of Michigan Press.) A valuable overview is Sharon L. Snyder, Brenda Jo Bruggemann, and Rosemarie Garland-Thomson, eds., *Disability Studies: Enabling the Humanities* (New York: Modern Language Association, 2002).

2. See Felicity Nussbaum's discussion of these developments in her *The Limits of the Human: Fictions of Anomaly, Race and Gender in the Long Eighteenth Century* (Cambridge:

Cambridge University Press, 2003), 2. See also two useful articles from the British disability movement: Colin Barnes, "Disability Studies: New or Not So New Directions?" *Disability and Society* 14, no. 4 (1999): 577–80; and Tom Shakespeare, "The Social Model of Disability," in Davis, ed., *The Disability Studies Reader*, 197–204.

3. *Pinkethman's Jests*, 2nd ed. (London, 1721), 7.

4. *The Laugher; or, The Art of Jesting*, 2nd ed. (London, 1755), 158.

5. *The Laugher*, 158; *The Gentleman's Magazine* 5 (1735): 97.

6. "The Foolish Beggars," in *Doctor Merryman; or, Nothing but Mirth* (London, n.d. [Bodleian Douce PP 179(12)]), 22–24.

7. Francis Grose, *A Classical Dictionary of the Vulgar Tongue*, 3rd ed. (1796), ed. Eric Partridge (New York: Barnes & Noble, 1963), 224–25.

8. *The Laugher*, 165.

9. *The Gentleman's Magazine* 5 (1735): 97 (a prize-winning epigram on this subject).

10. Ned Ward, *The London Spy: The Vanities and Vices of the Town Exposed to View*, ed. Arthur L. Hayward (London: Cassell, 1927), 36–37.

11. *The Life and Adventures of Lazarillo de Tormes*, 2nd ed. (London, 1726).

12. Francisco de Quevédo, *The Life of Paul, the Spanish Sharper (El Buscón)*, in *Comical Works of Don Francisco de Quevédo* (London, 1742), 173–82 (bk. 2, chap. 2).

13. Paul Scarron, *The Whole Comical Works of Mons. Scarron*, trans. Thomas Brown et al., 2 vols. (London, 1700, and five more editions); Richard Head, *The English Rogue*, 4 vols. (London, 1665–80).

14. Tobias Smollett, *The Adventures of Peregrine Pickle*, ed. James L. Clifford (London: Oxford University Press, 1969), 20, 171, 59.

15. Ibid., 76, 200.

16. *Miss C——y's Cabinet of Curiosities; or, The Green Room Broke Open, by Tristram Shandy, Gent.* (London, 1765 [BL 641.e.24.(6.)]), 5–10. Published under a fictitious imprint: "Utopia: Printed for William Whirligig, at the *Maiden's Head*, in *Wind-mill-street*."

17. In general, see Roger Lonsdale, ed., *The New Oxford Book of Eighteenth-Century Verse* (Oxford: Oxford University Press, 1987); David Fairer, *English Poetry of the Eighteenth Century* (London: Longman, 2003); J. Paul Hunter, "Political, Satirical, Didactic and Lyric Poetry (I)," in *The Cambridge History of English Literature, 1660–1780*, ed. John Richetti (Cambridge: Cambridge University Press, 2005), 160–208; Paula Backscheider, *Eighteenth-Century Women Poets and Their Poetry* (Baltimore: Johns Hopkins University Press, 2005).

18. Poetry statistics from Hunter, "Political, Satirical, Didactic and Lyric Poetry"; David Foxon, *English Verse, 1701–1750: A Catalogue of Separately Printed Poems with Notes on Contemporary Collected Editions*, 2 vols. (London: Cambridge University Press, 1975); and *ESTC*. Prose fiction numbers for 1740–70 from James Raven, *British Fiction, 1750–1770: A Chronological Check-List of Prose Fiction Printed in Britain and Ireland* (Newark: University of Delaware Press, 1987); and *ESTC*.

19. *A Collection of Jests, Epigrams, Epitaphs, &c.* (Edinburgh, 1753), 80–81. A loose adaptation of Martial 1.19.

20. William Wycherley, *Miscellany Poems* (London, 1706), 220; *St. James's Miscellany; or, The Citizens Amusement* (London, n.d. [BL Cup.700.m.86]), 4–5; etc.

21. *A Collection of Jests, Epigrams, Epitaphs, &c.*, 85.

22. [Samuel Johnson], *A Pastoral Ballad*, 2nd ed. (London, 1774), reprinted in editions of *A Collection of Songs* (London, 1782) and anthologies like *The Comick Magazine* (London, 1797).

23. William S. Baring-Gould and Ceil Baring-Gould, eds., *The Annotated Mother Goose* (New York: Bramhall, 1962), 258.

24. Iona Opie and Peter Opie, eds., *The Oxford Dictionary of Nursery Rhymes* (Oxford: Oxford University Press, 1997), 219 (no. 184), 340 (no. 324).

25. Baring-Gould and Baring-Gould, eds., *Annotated Mother Goose*, 148n30, 156n51; Opie and Opie, eds., *Nursery Rhymes*, 340 (no. 324). "As I was going to sell my eggs" was first printed in 1805 but is evidently much older (ibid., 259–60 [no. 242]).

26. Opie and Opie, eds., *Nursery Rhymes*, 520–21 (no. 543).

27. John Gay, *Trivia*, 2.389–93, in *Poetry and Prose of John Gay*, ed. Vinton Dearing and Charles Beckwith, 2 vols. (Oxford: Clarendon, 1974), 1:154. Dearing and Beckwith rightly note that "this unpleasant story reads like a real incident" but find no source (2:561n). The severed head must surely be Gay's own addition.

28. Ward, *London Spy*, 59.

29. *The Merry Medley* (London, [ca. 1750]), 74, etc.

30. *Tom Brown's Complete Jester*, 4th ed. (London, n.d. [Harding E276]), 46–47; *Garrick's Jests* (London, n.d. [BL 12314.bbb.31]), 8.

31. *Tom Brown's Complete Jester*, 86; *Garrick's Jests*, 8; *Ben Johnson's Jests* (London, n.d. [BL 1607/4679]), 83.

32. *The Court and City Jester* (London, 1770), 74.

33. *Tom Brown's Complete Jester*, 24.

34. *Joe Miller's Jests; or, The Wit's Vade-Mecum*, 12th ed. (London, n.d. [Bodleian Harding E 101]), 14–15 (no. 82); cf. *The Merry Medley*, 23–24; and many others.

35. *The Laugher*, 158; "On an Old Scold," in *A Collection of Jests, Epigrams, Epitaphs, &c.*, 92.

36. All from Grose, *Classical Dictionary*.

37. Compare *Joe Miller's Jests*, 79 (no. 460).

38. Grose, *Classical Dictionary*, 325.

39. Samuel Butler, *Hudibras* (London, 1663), 1.1.285–302; Quevédo, *The Life of Paul, the Spanish Sharper*, 2.2.

40. Ned Ward, *The Secret History of Clubs* (London, 1709), 81; Tobias Smollett, *The Expedition of Humphry Clinker*, ed. O. M. Brack Jr. (Athens: University of Georgia Press, 1990), 52–53.

41. Miguel de Cervantes, *Don Quixote*, trans. P. A. Motteux (1700 etc.; New York: Knopf, 1991), 120 (1.3.2).

42. Henry Fielding, *Joseph Andrews*, ed. Martin C. Battestin (Middletown, CT: Wesleyan University Press, 1967), 32.

43. *Nixon's Cheshire Prophecy* (Edinburgh, 1730), which also includes a crude woodcut of these misfortunes.

44. *Spectator*, no. 17 (20 March 1711); cf. *Tatler*, no. 89 (3 November 1709); and Richard Head, *The Life and Death of Mother Shipton* (London, 1684), 10.

45. *London Magazine*, June 1753, 304.

46. The definitive study of these changes remains Stuart Tave, *The Amiable Humorist* (Chicago: University of Chicago Press, 1960), esp. chap. 1–3.

47. James Beattie, "An Essay on Laughter and Ludicrous Composition," in *Essays* (Edinburgh, 1776), 665.

48. John Dennis, *Critical Works*, ed. E. N. Hooker, 2 vols. (Baltimore: Johns Hopkins University Press, 1939–43), 2:384; William Congreve, "Concerning Humour in Comedy" (1696), in *Restoration and Eighteenth-Century Comedy*, ed. Scott McMillin, 2nd ed. (New York: Norton, 1997), 475; William Whitehead, *An Essay on Ridicule* (London, 1743), 13.

49. See Tave, *Amiable Humorist*, chap. 4, esp. 75.

50. Fielding, *Joseph Andrews*, 9.

51. The first of the "Maxims and Moral Reflections" in William Wycherley, *Posthumous Works* (London, 1728), 9; John Vanbrugh, *The Relapse; or, Virtue in Danger* (London, 1697), 27 (2.1).

52. Morris Palmer Tilley, *A Dictionary of the Proverbs in England in the Sixteenth and Seventeenth Centuries* (Ann Arbor: University of Michigan Press, 1950), 129 (C827); Matt. 7:3–5.

53. Samuel Richardson's version is *Aesop's Fables: With Instructive Morals and Reflections* (London, 1739, 1760, 1775, etc.).

54. John Vanbrugh, *Esop; a Comedy* (1697; London, 1753), passim. As further evidence of more local performances and the jokes that clustered around them, consider a performance of November 1724 at the Castle Tavern in Paternoster Row, advertised "At the Desire of Several of the Inhabitants of Cripplegate Parish." See Emmett L. Avery et al., eds., *The London Stage, 1600–1800*, 5 pts. in 11 vols. (Carbondale: Southern Illinois University Press, 1960–68), pt. 5, vol. 2, p. 796.

55. David Garrick, *Lethe; or, Aesop in the Shades* (London, 1749), 28–33.

56. Earl of Chesterfield to George Faulkner, 22 May 1766, in *The Letters of Philip Dormer Stanhope, 4th Earl of Chesterfield*, ed. Bonamy Dobrée, 6 vols. (London: Eyre & Spottiswoode, 1932), 6:2737–38.

57. *Universal Museum and Complete Magazine*, June 1776, 294–95.

58. *The Little Hunch-Back; or, A Frolic in Bagdad* (London, 1789). Twenty performances by 1800. On West's pop-up kits, see George Speaight, *A History of the English Toy Theatre* (London: Studio Vista, 1969), 197.

59. R[obert] Fabian, *Trick for Trick* (London, 1735), passim. There were also two Glasgow editions of 1757 and 1761, published to accompany performances at the Royal Theatre. There is no relation to D'Urfey's 1678 comedy of the same name.

60. Thomas D'Urfey, *The Fond Husband; or, The Plotting Sisters*, in *Two Comedies by Thomas D'Urfey*, ed. Jack A. Vaughn (Rutherford, NJ: Fairleigh Dickinson University Press, 1976), 156. Fumble is yet another deformed threatened suitor.

61. Compare *1 Henry IV*, 2.4.149, an extended exchange of insults between Falstaff and Prince Hal.

62. Charles Coffey, *The Devil to Pay* (1731), in *Ten English Farces*, ed. Leo Hughes and A. H. Scouten (Austin: University Press of Texas, 1948), 189–90.

63. On Falstaff, see William Chetwood, *A General History of the Stage* (London, 1749), 153. On Foote, see *The European Magazine, and London Review*, January 1794, 15.

64. *The Poetical Works of Charles Churchill*, ed. Douglas Grant (Oxford: Oxford University Press, 1956), 14 (lines 401–4); L. W. Conolly, "Personal Satire on the Eighteenth-Century Stage," *Eighteenth-Century Studies* 9, no. 4 (1976): 599–607.

65. On Corbaccio, see Tave, *Amiable Humorist*, 50. On George Powell's Falstaff, see Chetwood, *A General History of the Stage*, 153.

66. Richard Steele, *The Conscious Lovers* (London, 1723), 26 (2.1); *Whitehall Journal*, 11 December 1722. For other voices in this debate, see Tave, *Amiable Humorist*, 51, 256n25.

67. See George Speaight, *History of the English Puppet Theatre*, 2nd ed. (Carbondale: Southern Illinois University Press, 1990), esp. 21, 168. The blind beggar appears in the Payne Collier text of 1828, reprinted as an appendix to George Speaight, *Punch and Judy: A History* (London: Studio Vista, 1970).

68. As noted in Avery et al., eds., *The London Stage*, esp. pt. 3, vol. 1, pp. 15–17, and pt. 4, vol. 2, pp. 1475, 1518, 1532.

69. Henry Lucas, *Coelina: A Mask* (London, 1795), 41.

70. Avery et al., eds., *The London Stage*, pt. 3, vol. 1, pp. clv–clix, and pt. 4, vol. 1, pp. cxxxv–cxliii; Emmett L. Avery, "Dancing and Pantomime on the English Stage," *Studies in Philology* 31 (1934): 417–52.

71. Gregorio Lambranzi, *A New and Curious School of Theatrical Dancing* (1716), trans. Derra de Moroda, ed. Cyril W. Beaumont (New York: Dance Horizons, 1966), pt. 1, no. 15, pp. 32–33.

72. On crutch dances at puppet theaters and fairground booths, see Speaight, *History of the English Puppet Theatre*, 121.

73. Ward, *London Spy*, 193. Something similar is clearly meant in "The Wapping Landlady," a dance first performed at Covent Garden on 26 April 1768 (Avery et al., eds., *The London Stage*, pt. 4, vol. 3, p. 1324).

74. Reprinted, probably from a scrapbook, in John Ashton, *Social Life in the Reign of Queen Anne* (London, 1883), 194–95.

75. See, e.g., *The Diseases of Bath: A Satire* (London, 1737), 17–19; and *Second Thoughts on the Present Ministry* (London, 1785), 80.

76. Compare Ariosto, *Satire V* (a play performed by a lunatic, a dwarf, and a fool); and Ben Jonson, *Volpone*, 1.2 (Nano, Androgyno, Castrone, and Mosca). On European carnival traditions and comic tournaments of hunchbacks or dueling dwarfs, see Barry Wind, *Images of "Freaks" in Baroque Art: "A Foul and Pestilent Congregation"* (Brookfield, VT: Scolar, 1998).

77. "Prologue for Timbertoe," in *The Miscellaneous and Whimsical Lucubrations of Lancelot Poverty-Struck* (London, 1758), 86–87. This was much reprinted in other contexts.

78. *Public Advertiser*, 1 January 1753, 13 March 1753, etc.

79. *General Advertiser*, 29 April 1746, and over the next two weeks.

80. Ward, *London Spy*, 131–32.

81. *Public Advertiser*, 21 September 1761.

82. *Public Advertiser*, 1 January 1753; *Daily Advertiser*, 3, 5, 6 September 1753; *General Advertiser*, 31 August 1754, etc.

83. *Public Advertiser*, 21 September 1761.

84. Andrea Perrucci, *Dell'arte representiva* (1699), cited and translated in Allardyce Nicoll, *The World of Harlequin: A Critical Study of the Commedia dell'Arte* (Cambridge: Cambridge University Press, 1963), 149–50.

85. "On Seeing the Incomparable Mons. Timbertoe Dance at Mother Midnight's Oratory," *General Advertiser*, 22 May 1752.

86. The complex conjunctions between disability and performance in different contexts are beyond the scope of this discussion. For a useful starting point, see Philip Auslander and Carrie Sandahl, *Bodies in Commotion: Disability and Performance* (Ann Arbor: University of Michigan Press, 2005).

87. Aristotle, *Poetics*, ed. and trans. Stephen Halliwell, Loeb Classical Library 199 (Cambridge, MA: Harvard University Press, 1995), 45.

88. Crucial to my thinking on these matters have been Jacques Le Goff, "Mentalities: A History of Ambiguities," trans. David Denby, in *Constructing the Past: Essays in Historical Methodology*, ed. Jacques Le Goff and Pierre Nora (Cambridge: Cambridge University Press, 1985), chap. 8; and Roger Chartier, *Cultural History: Between Practices and Representations*, trans. Lydia G. Cochrane (Cambridge: Polity, 1988), esp. chaps. 1–2. Among Anglophone adaptations of this tradition, I am indebted to Vic Gatrell, *The Hanging Tree* (Oxford: Oxford University Press, 1994).

89. Whitehead, *Essay on Ridicule*, 13; William Hay, *Deformity: An Essay* (1754), ed. Kathleen James-Cavan, ELS Monograph no. 92 (Victoria, BC: University of Victoria, 2004), 26.

90. Frances Burney, *Camilla* (1796), ed. Edward A. Bloom and Lillian D. Bloom (Oxford: Oxford University Press, 1983), 305–6 (4.6).

91. Pierre-Jean Grosley, *A Tour to London*, trans. Thomas Nugent, 2 vols. (London, 1772), 1:85.

92. *Memoirs of the First Forty-Five Years of the Life of James Lackington*, 7th ed. (London, 1794), 30–32; "Peter Pindar," *Ode to the Hero of Finsbury Square* (London, 1795), 30.

93. For ample documentation of such seasonal misrule, see Guildhall Library, Bartholomew Fair Scrapbook, MS 1514. For Anna Clark's reminder that the emergence of proletarian class consciousness did little to improve the lives of women, see *The Struggle for the Breeches: Gender and the Making of the British Working Class* (Berkeley and Los Angeles: University of California Press, 1995), 82.

94. See Paula McDowell, *The Women of Grub Street: Press, Politics, and Gender in the London Literary Marketplace, 1678–1730* (Oxford: Clarendon, 1998), 58–62.

95. David Dabydeen, *Hogarth's Blacks: Images of Blacks in Eighteenth-Century English Art* (Manchester: Manchester University Press, 1987). The pictorial sources are expertly discussed in Sean Shesgreen, *Images of the Outcast: The Urban Poor in the Cries of London* (Manchester: Manchester University Press, 2002).

96. Ruth McClure, *Coram's Children: The London Foundling Hospital in the Eighteenth Century* (New Haven, CT: Yale University Press, 1981), 229.

97. See *Spectator*, no. 436 (21 July 1712).

98. See "On the Benefit of Laughing," *Mist's Weekly Journal*, 3 August 1728.

99. See Tim Hitchcock, *Down and Out in Eighteenth-Century London* (London: Hambledon & London, 2004), esp. chap. 2.

298 Notes to Pages 70—74

100. Smollett, *Humphry Clinker*, 120.

101. "The Old Pudding-Pye Woman Set Forth in Her Colours, *&c*" (BL Rox.II.388), a broadside of 1680.

102. J. S. Müller, "Blind Musician" (ca. 1740, Metropolitan Museum, New York), reproduced in Shesgreen, *Images of the Outcast*, [95].

103. See, e.g., James Hulett, *Owen Farrell, the Irish Dwarf* (1742 [Lewis Walpole Library]); Marcellus Laroon, "Cudgelling" (1770 [Ashmolean Museum, Oxford, Cat. 65]); *Richard III*, 1.1.

104. *Daily Advertiser*, 30 May 1752.

105. *Mist's Weekly Journal*, 6 August 1726.

106. *Grub-Street Journal*, 4 February 1731, reprinted from the *St. James's Evening Post*.

107. Francis Grose, *The Grumbler: Containing Sixteen Essays by the Late Francis Grose, Esq.* (London, 1791), 35–36.

108. *London Chronicle*, 16 February 1768.

109. Daniel Defoe, *Second Thoughts Are Best* (London, 1729), 1; cf. *The Jovial Companion* (London, n.d. [Bodleian Harding E 65]), 26.

110. *Pinkethman's Jests*, 4th ed. (London, 1735), 81. These bands of dwarfs and linkboys are also much illustrated in comic street scenes. See Robert Dighton's *Return from a Masquerade* (1784 [BM Satire no. 6763]), James McArdell's *Teague's Ramble at Charing Cross* (1747 [Westminster City Libraries]), and many more.

111. *The Laugher*, 155–56. Both are from the dedicated section of jokes "Of Faces and Scars."

112. Jonathan Swift, *Journal to Stella*, ed. Harold Williams, 2 vols. (Oxford: Clarendon, 1963), 1:98 (18 November 1710).

113. Ibid., 2:581. On the "innumerable quiet charities" that underlay such peevish statements, see Irvin Ehrenpreis, *The Personality of Jonathan Swift* (London: Methuen, 1958), 122, 139.

114. George Winchester Stone and George M. Kahrl, *David Garrick: A Critical Biography* (Carbondale: Southern Illinois University Press, 1979), 434.

115. *England's Witty and Ingenious Jester*, 15th ed. (London, n.d. [Bodleian Douce W 30]), 16–17.

116. As described in Gédéon Tallemant des Réaux, *Historiettes*, 6 vols. (Paris, 1834), 2:360.

117. Laurence Sterne, *The Life and Opinions of Tristram Shandy, Gentleman*, ed. Melvyn New and Joan New, 3 vols. (Gainesville: University of Florida Press, 1978), 1:430 (5.7).

118. For a well-documented study of such footraces, see Earl R. Anderson, "Footnotes More Pedestrian Than Sublime: A Historical Background for the Foot-Races in *Evelina* and *Humphry Clinker*," *Eighteenth-Century Studies* 14, no. 1 (1980): 56–68. I owe the second Garrick story to Arthur Sherbo's "Addenda to 'Footnotes More Pedestrian Than Sublime,'" *Eighteenth-Century Studies* 14, no. 3 (1981): 313–16, 313.

119. "On Whimsical Notions and Practical Jokes," *Spectator*, no. 371 (6 March 1712).

120. Horace Walpole, *The Yale Edition of Horace Walpole's Correspondence*, ed. W. S. Lewis et al., 48 vols. (New Haven, CT: Yale University Press, 1937–83), 33:554 (27 April 1742); Bernard Falk, *The Way of the Montagues: A Gallery of Family Portraits* (London: Hutchinson,

1947), 269; *Aristophanes, Being a Classic Collection of True Attic Wit* (London, 1778), 139–40, etc.

121. For a print of Whitehead's 1742 procession and full commentary, see BM Satire no. 2546. On the Garrat elections, see John Brewer, "Theatre and Counter-Theatre in Georgian Politics: The Mock Elections at Garrat," *Radical History Review* 22 (1979): 7–40.

122. Henry Fielding, *Amelia*, ed. Martin C. Battestin (Oxford: Clarendon, 1984), 450; Adam Smith, *The Theory of Moral Sentiments*, ed. D. D. Raphael and A. L. Macfie (Oxford: Oxford University Press, 1979), 29.

123. Joshua Gee, *The Trade and Navigation of Great Britain Considered* (London, 1729), 38.

124. The Slavic suffix alluded to Tory charges that Shaftesbury wanted to make England an elective monarchy like Poland. See Tim Harris, "Cooper, Anthony Ashley, First Earl of Shaftesbury," *ODNB*.

125. John Dryden, "Absalom and Achitophel," in *The Works of John Dryden*, ed. E. N. Hooker and H. T. Swedenburg Jr., 20 vols. (Berkeley and Los Angeles: University of California Press, 1956–2000), 2:10.

126. *A Supplement to the Last Will and Testament of Anthony, Earl of Shaftesbury* (1683), in *Poems on Affairs of State*, vol. 3, *1682–1685*, ed. Howard H. Schless (New Haven, CT: Yale University Press, 1968), 407 (lines 58–59, 102–7).

127. Lady Mary Wortley Montagu, "Verses Address'd to the Imitator of the First Satire of the Second Book of Horace," in *Essays and Poems and Simplicity, a Comedy*, ed. Robert Halsband and Isobel Grundy (Oxford: Clarendon, 1977), 265–70 (lines 110–12, 19).

128. See BM Satires (and commentaries) nos. 1502–3, 1533–35, 1549.

129. Samuel Foote, *The Minor* (London, 1760).

130. See Diana Donald, *The Age of Caricature: Satirical Prints from the Age of George III* (New Haven, CT: Yale University Press, 1996), 31–32.

131. *The Jovial Companion*, 26; *The Laugher*, 165. For the linkboy joke, see *The Complete London Jester*, 3rd ed. (London 1766), 48; it is still there in the twelfth edition of 1786.

132. Smollett, *Peregrine Pickle*, 658–59; cf. *Habbakkuk Hilding* (London, 1752); BM Satires nos. 2479–83; and George Townshend's caricature of Lyttelton, Henry Fox, and the Duke of Cumberland (BM Department of Prints and Drawings).

133. The second earl is described in Philip Woodfine's article on his father ("William Stanhope, First Earl of Harrington," *ODNB*).

134. Samuel Foote to David Garrick, 26 February 1766, cited in Philip H. Highfill, Kalman A. Burnim, and Edward A. Langhans, eds., *A Biographical Dictionary of Actors, Actresses, Musicians, Dancers, Managers and Other Stage Personnel in London, 1660–1800*, 16 vols. (Carbondale: Southern Illinois University Press, 1973–93), 6:343. Garrick came to Foote's defense with the verses "Upon Some Attempts (Weak, as Inhuman) to Jest upon Mr. Foote's Late Accident," printed in the *London Chronicle*, 18–20 February 1766.

135. John O'Keeffe, *Recollections of the Life of John O'Keeffe*, 2 vols. (London, 1826), 1:144.

136. Smollett, *Humphry Clinker*, 46.

137. Charles Lucas, *An Essay on Waters*, 3 pts. in 1 (London, 1756), 3:259.

138. Smollett, *Humphry Clinker*, 48, 37; cf. *The Diseases of Bath*, 17–19.

139. Smollett, *Humphry Clinker*, 54; Thomas Rowlandson, "Comforts of Bath: Gouty Persons Fall on Steep Hill," in *The Drawings of Thomas Rowlandson in the Paul Mellon Collection*, ed. John Baskett and Dudley Snelgrove (New York: Brandywine, 1978), no. 303.

140. Smollett, *Humphry Clinker*, 48. For his admiration of Henley, see Tobias Smollett, *A Continuation of the Complete History of England*, 5 vols. (London, 1762–65), 4:222.

141. *England's Witty and Ingenious Jester*, 21. These lines make no appearance in Harold Love's edition of Rochester (*The Works of John Wilmot, Earl of Rochester* [Oxford: Oxford University Press, 1999]), not even as a disputed attribution.

142. See Harold Love, *Scribal Publication in Seventeenth-Century England* (Oxford: Oxford University Press, 1995), and *English Clandestine Satire, 1660–1702* (Oxford: Oxford University Press, 2004).

143. *A Collection of Jests, Epigrams, Epitaphs, &c.*, 84.

144. *Spectator*, no. 17 (20 March 1711).

145. William Pattison, "*Upon a Lame*, Latin Elegaic, *Bard*," in *The Poetical Works of Mr. William Pattison, Late of Sidney College Cambridge*, 2 vols. (London, 1727), 2:229.

146. Ibid., 134–35.

147. Ibid., 223. The poem was reprinted in *A Collection of Jests, Epigrams, Epitaphs, &c.*, 110, and other places.

148. This recuperation was the life's work of Wilmarth Lewis (1897–1979). See, most recently, Morris R. Brownell, *The Prime Minister of Taste: A Portrait of Horace Walpole* (New Haven, CT: Yale University Press, 2001).

149. Walpole, *Correspondence*, 39:12 (2 October 1765).

150. Part of Horace Walpole's "Anecdotes of Lady Mary Wortley Montagu and Lady Pomfret," in Walpole, *Correspondence*, 14:246–47; Horace, *Odes*, 1.3.

151. Walpole, *Correspondence*, 18:136 (17 September 1741), 86–87 (30 October 1742), 289 (20 August 1743).

152. Robert James, *A Medicinal Dictionary*, 3 vols. (London, 1743–45), vol. 3, s.v. "Scorbutus."

153. Lady Mary Wortley Montagu, *Complete Letters*, ed. Robert Halsband, 3 vols. (Oxford: Clarendon, 1965–67), 2:121–12 ([September] 1738).

154. Montagu, *Letters*, 2:131 ([November] 1738). On the generally scornful accounts of illness and marriage in these letters, see Isobel Grundy, *Lady Mary Wortley Montagu: Comet of the Enlightenment* (Oxford: Oxford University Press, 1999), 387.

155. Montagu, *Letters*, 2:37 ([March 1724]).

156. See Grundy, *Lady Mary Wortley Montagu*, 419–21.

157. Hester Lynch Piozzi (née Thrale), *The Piozzi Letters*, ed. Edward A. Bloom and Lillian D. Bloom, 6 vols. (Newark: University of Delaware Press, 1989–2002), 2:312–13.

158. See *Spectator*, no. 17 (20 March 1711); *The Guardian*, no. 91 (25 June 1713); Ned Ward, *Apollo's Maggot in His Cups; or, The Whimsical Creation of a Little Satyrical Poet* (London, 1729), n.p.; cf. Samuel Richardson, *Clarissa; or, The History of a Young Lady* (1747–48, 1st ed.), ed. Angus Ross (London: Penguin, 1985), 1130 (Belford to Lovelace).

159. Montagu, *Letters*, 2:122 ([September 1738]).

160. Frances Burney, *Early Journals and Letters*, ed. Lars E. Troide et al., 2 vols. (Oxford: Clarendon, 1988–90), 2:106, 1:231, 2:203, 2:4, 2:70–71.

161. Ibid., 2:4.

162. *The Early Diary of Frances Burney, 1768–1778, with a Selection from Her Correspondence*, ed. Annie Raine Ellis, 2 vols. (London, 1889), 2:298 (24 June 1782?). The word *clunch* (lumpy, thickset) was a Burney family favorite.

163. *Thraliana: The Diary of Mrs. Hester Lynch Thrale*, ed. Katherine C. Balderston, 2 vols. (Oxford: Clarendon, 1942), 1:113, 129.

164. Goldsmith biographers cited in John Dussinger, "Oliver Goldsmith," *ODNB*; *Johnsonian Miscellanies*, ed. G. B. Hill, 2 vols. (Oxford, 1897), 2:268.

165. *The Nut-Cracker* (London, 1751), 38.

166. Pattison, *Poetical Works*, 2:229.

167. See Chetwood, *A General History of the Stage*, 153 (Pinkethman tormenting D'Urfey).

168. Vanbrugh, *Esop*, 17–18 (2.1); Samuel Foote, *The Lame Lover* (London, 1770), 12 (1.1).

169. Priscilla Pointon, "Address to a Bachelor on a Delicate Occasion," in *Eighteenth-Century Women Poets*, ed. Roger Lonsdale (Oxford: Oxford University Press, 1989), 274–75.

170. Mrs. Delany, *Autobiography and Correspondence*, ed. Lady Llanover, 6 vols. (London, 1861–62), 2:6. On Chesterfield's wager, see Judith Milhous, "Johann Jakob Heidegger," *ODNB*; and cf. the joke collected by Christopher Smart (*The Nut-Cracker*, 37).

171. For the fullest account of this prank, see John Nichols and George Steevens, *The Genuine Works of William Hogarth, Illustrated with Biographical Anecdotes*, 3 vols. (London, 1810), 2:322–25.

172. Kenny Fries, ed., *Staring Back: The Disability Experience from the Inside Out* (New York: Penguin, 1997), and *Body Remember: A Memoir* (New York: Dutton, 1997); Simi Linton, *Claiming Disability: Knowledge and Identity* (New York: New York University Press, 1998). For a useful commentary on the promise as well as the problems of life writing in this field, see G. Thomas Couser, "Signifying Bodies: Life Writing and Disability Studies," in Snyder, Brueggemann, and Garland-Thomson, eds., *Disability Studies*, 109–17.

173. See Lorraine Daston and Katherine Park, *Wonders and the Order of Nature, 1150–1750* (New York: Zone, 1998); and Marie-Hélène Huet, *Monstrous Imagination* (Cambridge, MA: Harvard University Press, 1993).

174. Lennard J. Davis, *Enforcing Normalcy: Disability, Deafness and the Body* (New York: Verso, 1995), esp. chap. 2.

175. Leslie Fiedler, *Freaks: Myths and Images of the Secret Self* (New York: Simon & Schuster, 1978); Dennis Todd, *Imagining Monsters: Miscreations of the Self in Eighteenth-Century England* (Chicago: University of Chicago Press, 1995); Huet, *Monstrous Imagination*; Felicity Nussbaum, *Torrid Zones: Maternity, Sexuality, and Empire in Eighteenth-Century English Narrative* (Baltimore: Johns Hopkins University Press, 1995), and *Limits of the Human*.

176. Among the considerable scholarship on this topic, see Lennard J. Davis, *Bending over Backwards: Disability, Dismodernism, and Other Difficult Positions* (New York: New York University Press, 2002), chaps. 3 and 5, and *Enforcing Normalcy*, chap. 2; Nussbaum, *Torrid Zones*, chap. 6, and *Limits of the Human*, chaps. 1 and 4; Robert W. Jones, "Obedient Faces: The Virtue of Deformity in Sarah Scott's Fiction," in Deutsch and Nussbaum, eds., *"Defects,"* 280–302; and Rosemarie Garland-Thomson, *Extraordinary Bodies: Figuring Physical Disability in American Culture and Literature* (New York: Columbia University Press, 1997).

177. Helen Deutsch, *Resemblance and Disgrace: Alexander Pope and the Deformation of Culture* (Cambridge, MA: Harvard University Press, 1996), and *Loving Dr. Johnson* (Chicago: University of Chicago Press, 2005); Jill Campbell, "Lady Mary Wortley Montagu and the 'Glass Revers'd' of Female Old Age," in Deutsch and Nussbaum, eds., *"Defects,"* 213–51; Grundy, *Lady Mary Wortley Montagu,* esp. chap. 7; Devoney Looser, *Women Writers and Old Age in Great Britain, 1750–1850* (Baltimore: Johns Hopkins University Press, 2008); Richard Wendorf, *Sir Joshua Reynolds: The Painter in Society* (Cambridge, MA: Harvard University Press, 1996), 38–45. On Duncan Campbell, see Nussbaum, *Limits of the Human*, chap. 1.

178. Roger Lund, "Laughing at Cripples: Ridicule, Deformity and the Argument from Design," *Eighteenth-Century Studies* 39, no. 1 (2005): 91–114.

179. Widely printed well into the nineteenth century, Harrison has been almost single-handedly revived for modern critics by Paula Backscheider (*Eighteenth-Century Women Poets*, chap. 4). In their new *Anthology of Long Eighteenth-Century Women's Poetry* (Baltimore: Johns Hopkins University Press, 2009), Paula Backscheider and Catherine Ingrassia gather most of these poems under the category *life writing.*

180. Priscilla Pointon, "Consolatory Reflections That Have Occasionally Occurred on That Most Lamentable Incident, My Loss of Sight" and "The Following Lines, Extempore, to a *Blind* Young Gentleman, Who Was So Obliging to Send the Author a Song of Her Own Composing Set to Music," both in *Poems on Several Occasions* (Birmingham, 1770), 84–85, 99–105.

181. Esther Clark, "A Mirror for Detractors" (1754), in Lonsdale, ed., *Women Poets*, 226; Priscilla Pointon, "To the Critics," in Lonsdale, ed., *Women Poets,* 273–74, and *Poems on Several Occasions*, lxiii, 8; Mary Chandler, *A Description of Bath . . . with Several Other Poems*, 8th ed. (London, 1767), [1].

182. Mary Chandler, "My Own Epitaph" and "A True Tale," both in Lonsdale, ed., *Women Poets*, 152–55.

183. Lady Mary Wortley Montagu, "Satturday: The Small Pox: Flavia," in *Essays and Poems*, 201–4. For a wide-ranging discussion, see Nussbaum, *Limits of the Human*, esp. 116–20.

184. Elizabeth Teft, "On Viewing Herself in a Glass" (1747), in Lonsdale, ed., *Women Poets*, 218.

185. Mary Barber, "To Mrs. Frances-Arabella Kelly," in ibid., 125–26.

186. Principles set out in Tim Hitchcock, Peter King, and Pamela Sharpe, ed., *Chronicling Poverty: The Voices and Strategies of the English Poor, 1640–1840* (London: Macmillan, 1997). Notable monographs include Hitchcock, *Down and Out in Eighteenth-Century London*; Robert Shoemaker, *The London Mob: Violence and Disorder in Eighteenth-Century England* (London: Hambledon & London, 2004); and two meticulous studies by Peter King: *Crime, Justice and Discretion in England, 1740–1820* (Oxford: Oxford University Press, 2000) and *Crime and Law in England, 1750–1840* (Cambridge: Cambridge University Press, 2006). Some valuable sources are reprinted in Alysa Levene et al., ed., *Narratives of the Poor in Eighteenth-Century Britain*, 5 vols. (London: Pickering & Chatto, 2006). For a cogent critique, see Nicholas Rogers, "London's Marginal Histories," *Labour/Le travail* 60 (Fall 2007): 217–34.

187. *London Journal*, 13 February 1731.

188. Montagu, *Letters*, 1:249 (3 August 1716).

189. The extent of old-age disability has not, to my knowledge, been studied for the eighteenth century. I am here using, as a rough comparator, Margaret Pelling's work on sixteenth-

century Norwich: "Old Age, Poverty, and Disability in Early Modern Norwich," in *Life, Death and the Elderly: Historical Perspectives*, ed. Margaret Pelling and R. H. Smith (London: Routledge, 1991), 74–101. Andrea Rusnock's *Vital Accounts: Quantifying Health and Population in Eighteenth-Century England and France* (Cambridge: Cambridge University Press, 2002) is mainly about the history of statistics but gathers much useful information along the way.

190. Matthew Martin, *Letter to the Right Hon. Lord Pelham on the State of Mendicity in the Metropolis* (London, 1803).

191. See Smith, *Theory of Moral Sentiments*, 29; Oliver Goldsmith, "On the Distresses of the Poor," in *Citizen of the World* (London, 1762), letter 116; Beattie, "An Essay on Laughter and Ludicrous Composition," 665.

192. Tilley, *Proverbs*, 28 (B54).

193. E. Cobham Brewer, *Brewer's Dictionary of Phrase and Fable*, 14th ed., rev. Ivor H. Evans (London: Cassell, 1989), 1079; Tilley, *Proverbs*, 649 (T23); Opie and Opie, eds., *Nursery Rhymes*, 479–80 (no. 495).

194. Friedrich Hoffmann and Bernardino Ramazzini, *A Dissertation on Endemial Diseases . . . together with a Treatise on the Diseases of Tradesmen* (1700; London, 1746), 408, 232, 63. See also M. Dorothy George, *London Life in the Eighteenth Century* (New York: Capricorn, 1965), 202–5.

195. See Michael MacDonald and Terence R. Murphy, *Sleepless Souls: Suicide in Early Modern England* (Oxford: Clarendon, 1990), 256–57; and, more recently, Kevin Siena, "Suicide as an Illness Strategy in the Long Eighteenth Century," in *Histories of Suicide*, ed. John Weaver and David Wright (Toronto: University of Toronto Press, 2009), 53–72.

196. Susannah R. Ottaway, *The Decline of Life: Old Age in Eighteenth-Century England* (Cambridge: Cambridge University Press, 2004), 14.

197. Donna Andrew, *Philanthropy and Police: London Charity in the Eighteenth Century* (Princeton, NJ: Princeton University Press, 1989). On the severity of legal and institutional structures, see Nicholas Rogers, "Policing the Poor in Eighteenth-Century London: The Vagrancy Laws and Their Administration," *Histoire sociale/Social History* 24, no. 47 (1991): 127–47.

198. Hoffmann and Ramazzini, *Diseases of Tradesmen*, 174.

199. Roy Porter, *English Society in the Eighteenth Century* (Harmondsworth: Penguin, 1991), 86.

200. See, however, Jonas Hanway's extraordinary *Sentimental History of Chimney Sweepers* (London, 1785).

201. Adam Smith, *Wealth of Nations*, ed. R. H. Campbell, A. S. Skinner, and W. B. Todd, 2 vols. (Oxford: Oxford University Press, 1976), 2:100.

202. Examples from William Forster, *A Treatise on the Causes of Most Diseases Incident to Human Bodies*, 2nd ed. (London, 1746), 356, 358.

203. See Alice Bertha Gomme, *The Traditional Games of England, Scotland, and Ireland*, 2 vols. (London, 1894–98), 2:305–6 ("Trades"). The game is also described in Charles Sorel, *Récréations galantes* (Paris, 1642), 73–74; and T. F. Crane, *Italian Social Customs of the Sixteenth Century* (New Haven, CT: Yale University Press, 1920), 269.

204. See Bibliothèque nationale, Cabinet des estampes, "Métiers réunis." I owe this lead to Sheila McTighe's fascinating article on Carracci, "Perfect Deformity, Ideal Beauty, and the 'Imaginaire' of Work," *Oxford Art Journal* 16, no. 1 (1993): 75–91.

205. Henry Fielding, *An Enquiry into the Causes of the Late Increase of Robbers and Related Writings*, ed. Malvin R. Zirker (Oxford: Clarendon, 1988), 109.

206. For Ward's "Beggars' Club," see Ward, *Secret History of Clubs*, chap. 21. For the false wound recipes, see Grose, *Classical Dictionary*, 151; and George Parker, *A View of Society and Manners in High and Low Life* (London, 1781), 155–59.

207. See Tim Hitchcock, "Cultural Representations: Rogue Literature and the Reality of the Begging Body," in *A History of the Human Body in the Age of Enlightenment*, ed. Carole Reeves (Oxford: Berg, 2010), 175–92.

208. Henry Mackenzie, *The Man of Feeling* (London, 1771), 32; *Anecdotes and Egotisms*, ed. Harold William Thompson (Oxford: Oxford University Press, 1927), 68.

209. Useful commentary in Richard Sennett, *The Craftsman* (New Haven, CT: Yale University Press, 2008), 88–94.

210. On which, see Shesgreen, *Images of the Outcast*, 73–76; and Marcellus Laroon, *The Criers and Hawkers of London*, ed. Sean Shesgreen (Stanford, CA: Stanford University Press, 1990).

211. Hay, *Deformity*, 26, 25.

212. *Encyclopedia of Wit and Anecdote; or, The Punster's Last Legacy* (Dublin: n.d. [Bodleian Harding E3(1)]), 9, s.v. "A Poetical Shape."

213. See, e.g., *Ephraim Tristram Bates* (London, 1759), chap. 26.

214. *Quin's Jests* (London, 1766), 39–40.

215. Ibid., 74–75. The accident was reported in *Mist's Weekly Journal*, 19 February 1726.

216. For a useful discussion, see Mahadev L. Apte, *Humor and Laughter: An Anthropological Approach* (Ithaca, NY: Cornell University Press, 1985), chap. 1.

217. Erving Goffmann, *Stigma: Notes on the Management of Spoiled Identity* (Englewood Cliffs, NJ: Prentice-Hall, 1963), 19.

218. Davis, *Bending over Backwards*, chap. 2.

219. See Davis, *Enforcing Normalcy*, 3; Michael Oliver, *Politics of Disablement* (London: Macmillan, 1990); and James Trent, *Inventing the Feeble Mind: A History of Mental Retardation in the United States* (Berkeley and Los Angeles: University of California Press, 1984). See also Douglas Baynton, *Forbidden Signs: American Culture and the Campaign against Sign Language* (Chicago: University of Chicago Press, 1996).

220. Robert Erikson, *Mother Midnight* (New York: AMS, 1986).

221. Mikhail Bakhtin, *Rabelais and His World*, trans. Hélène Iswolsky (Bloomington: Indiana University Press, 1984), 161. On the ludic associations of gout, see Roy Porter and G. S. Rousseau, *Gout: The Patrician Malady* (New Haven, CT: Yale University Press, 1998).

222. Ward, *Secret History of Clubs*, 36.

223. On which, see Donald, *Age of Caricature*, 10–11.

224. *Spectator*, no. 32 (6 April 1711) (cf. nos. 17 [20 March 1711], 48 [25 April 1711], 52 [30 April 1711], 78 [30 May 1711], 86 [8 June 1711], and 87 [9 June 1711]); Edward Howell, ed., *Ye Ugly Face Clubb Leverpoole, 1743–1753: A Verbatim Reprint from the Original Manuscript* (Liverpool: Edward Howell, 1912). For the more sanguine interpretation of these phenomena ("a cheerful, rational view of ugliness"), see Donald, *Age of Caricature*, 10.

225. Hay, *Deformity*, 27.

226. Notably the extended comic dialogue *Wit for Money; or, Poet Stutter* (London, 1691).

227. *Diary of Dudley Ryder, 1715–16*, ed. William Matthews (London: Methuen, 1939), 240; cf. *The Reminiscences of Henry Angelo*, ed. H. Lavers Smith, 2 vols. (London: Kegan Paul, 1904), 1:309. On the *Esop* association, see Philip Carter, "Richard Nash," *ODNB*.

228. *Memoirs of Dr. Burney*, 3 vols. (London, 1832), 2:18.

229. *Thraliana*, 1:4.

230. Henri Bergson, *Laughter*, in *Comedy*, ed. Wylie Sypher (Baltimore: Johns Hopkins University Press, 1980), 64.

231. David Morris, *The Culture of Pain* (Berkeley and Los Angeles: University of California Press, 1991), 93–94.

232. *Iliad*, bk. 6, lines 483–84; Michel de Montaigne, "How We Laugh and Cry for the Same Thing," in *The Complete Essays of Montaigne*, trans. Donald M. Frame (Stanford, CA: Stanford University Press, 1965), 1:38; Pierre-Augustin Caron de Beaumarchais, *The Barber of Seville*, 1.1; George Gordon, Lord Byron, *Don Juan*, 4.4.

233. For an acute transhistorical discussion of these parallels, see Helmuth Plessner, "Lachen und Weinen," in *Philosophische Anthropologie* (1941; reprint, Frankfurt: Fischer, 1970), chap. 1. For a succinct discussion of the physiology of laughter, see William F. Fry, "The Biology of Humor," *Humor* 7, no. 2 (1994): 111–26.

234. Simone de Beauvoir, *Old Age*, trans. Patrick O'Brian (London: André Deutsch, 1972), 5.

235. Norbert Elias, *The Civilizing Process* (1939), trans. Edmund Jephcott, 2 vols. in 1 (Oxford: Blackwell, 1982), vol. 2, pt. 2, esp. pp. 441–91; Friedrich Nietzsche, *On the Genealogy of Morality*, trans. Carol Diethe, ed. Keith Ansell-Pearson (Cambridge: Cambridge University Press, 1994), 39 (2.2).

236. A fuller exploration of these differences would take in recent research on historical changes in the experience of time, on differing levels of uncertainty, and the emergence of probabilistic reasoning—territory first explored in Ian Hacking, *The Taming of Chance* (Cambridge: Cambridge University Press, 1991). Still fascinating is Lucien Febvre's speculative essay on historical differences in the sense of security, "Pour l'histoire d'un sentiment: Le besoin de sécurité," *Annales E.S.C.* 11 (1956): 244–47. Behind it all are long-term advances in medical science—the perspective of Roy Porter's *The Greatest Benefit to Mankind: A Medical History of Humanity* (New York: Norton, 1997).

237. Lund, "Laughing at Cripples."

238. Bergson, *Laughter*, 77 and passim.

239. See Gomme, *Traditional Games*, 1:37–40, 402–4.

240. Quoted names from Anthony Van Assen's print *The Ugly Club: A New Comic Song* (Liverpool, 1805 [Library of Congress, British Cartoon Collection, PC3-1805; not in BM]). The Johnson reference is from Wendorf, *Sir Joshua Reynolds*, 44.

241. *Johnsonian Miscellanies*, 2:268.

242. [Robert Shiels], *The Lives of the Poets of Great Britain and Ireland*, 5 vols. (London, 1753), 5:351.

243. Jane Austen, "Frederic and Elfrida, a Novel," in *Volume the First*, ed. R. W. Chapman (Oxford: Clarendon, 1933), 9. A full analysis of this theme in Austen's work would look ahead to *Persuasion*—to the roly-poly Mrs. Musgrove with her "large fat sighings" and the counter-figure of Mrs. Smith.

244. *Spectator*, no. 17 (20 March 1711); Hay, *Deformity*, 32. See also Lund, "Laughing at Cripples," 95–97.

245. Vanbrugh, *Esop*, 7.

246. In *The Merry Companion; or, Humorous Miscellany* (Dublin, 1752), 10–12.

247. *Nothing Irregular in Nature; or, Deformity a Mere Fancy* (London, 1734). This was one of Francis Douce's early acquisitions (Bodleian Douce HH 223).

248. *The Midwife; or, The Old Woman's Magazine*, 3 vols. (London, 1751–53), 1:242–45.

249. Smith, *Theory of Moral Sentiments*, 29.

250. *Encyclopédie; ou, Dictionnaire raisonné des sciences, des arts et des métiers*, 17 vols. (Paris, 1751–65), 9:176, s.v. "Laideur."

251. Denis Diderot, *Paradox of Acting*, trans. W. H. Pollack (New York: Hill & Wang, 1957), 20, 23.

252. Gotthold Ephraim Lessing, *Laocoön*, trans. Edward Allen McCormick (Baltimore: Johns Hopkins University Press, 1984), chaps. 23–25.

253. See esp. David Marshall, *The Figure of Theater: Shaftesbury, Defoe, Adam Smith, and George Eliot* (New York: Columbia University Press, 1986), chap. 7.

254. Judith Milhous, "The Ideal Body on the Eighteenth-Century English Stage: The Tension between Pragmatic Limits and Noble Aspirations" (typescript). On Aldridge and persistent associations between racial otherness and ugliness or deformity, see Nussbaum, *Limits of the Human*, pt. 2, esp. 169.

255. Colley Cibber, *Apology for the Life of Colley Cibber*, 2 vols. (London, 1740), 2:109, cited in Milhous, "Ideal Body"; Joseph Knight, "Charles Coffey," rev. Yvonne Noble, *ODNB*.

256. All from Milhous, "Ideal Body."

257. On Macklin, see Fielding, *Joseph Andrews*, 262; and Samuel Foote, *A Treatise on the Passions* (London, 1747), 37–39.

258. On Norris, Spiller, and Cibber, see Highfill, Burnim, and Langhans, eds., *Biographical Dictionary*, 11:50–53, 14:219–23, 3:242–60. Mynheer Broomstickado appeared at the Little Haymarket Theatre 2 and 8 September 1757.

259. Samuel Foote, *Roman and English Comedy* (London, 1747), 40; William Chetwood, *The British Theatre* (London, 1752), 177. Other anecdotes from John Genest, *Some Account of the English Stage*, 10 vols. (Bath, 1832), 4:253. Highfill, Burnim, and Langhans, eds., *Biographical Dictionary*, 7:333, 335, reproduces two likenesses: an engraving by J. H. Green and an oil portrait in the Garrick Club (Matthews Collection, no. 300).

260. See Anton Zijderveld, *Reality in a Looking-Glass: Rationality through an Analysis of Traditional Folly* (London: Routledge & Kegan Paul, 1982).

261. On Tarleton and Fiorillo, see M. Willson Disher, *Clowns and Pantomimes* (London: Constable, 1925), 29, 72–73. On Belleroche, see Anthony Caputi, *Buffo: The Genius of Vulgar Comedy* (Detroit: Wayne State University Press, 1978), 135.

CHAPTER THREE

1. Erich Auerbach, *Mimesis: The Representation of Reality in Western Literature*, trans. Willard R. Trask (Princeton, NJ: Princeton University Press, 1953).

2. Samuel Taylor Coleridge, *Biographia Literaria*, 2 vols., ed. James Engell and W. Jackson

Bate (Princeton, NJ: Princeton University Press, 1983), 2:48–49. The entire chapter is a fascinating reflection on the enduring comic associations of ordinary life and low speech.

3. K. M. Briggs, *A Dictionary of British Folk-Tales in the English Language*, 2 vols. in 4 (London: Routledge & Kegan Paul, 1970), 2:3 ("Folk Narratives").

4. *Thraliana: The Diary of Mrs. Hester Lynch Thrale*, ed. Katherine C. Balderston, 2 vols. (Oxford: Clarendon, 1942), 1:57, 139. For a suggestive analysis of this widespread form of laughter, see Carolyn Steedman, "Servants and Their Relationship to the Unconscious," *Journal of British Studies* 42, no. 3 (July 2003): 316–50.

5. *The Jovial Companion* (London, n.d. [Bodleian Harding E 65]), 19.

6. *Rochester's Jests* (London, 1766), 26; *Joe Miller's Jests; or, The Wit's Vade-Mecum*, 12th ed. (London, n.d. [Bodleian Harding E 101]), 19 (no. 519); *The Merry Miscellany* (Bristol, n.d. [BL 12316.bb.37.2.]), n.p.

7. *The Merry Medley* (London, [ca. 1750]), 15.

8. Statistics from Nicholas Rogers, "London's Marginal Histories," *Labour/Le travail* 60 (Fall 2007): 221; *Irish Miscellany; or, Teagueland Jests* (London, 1746), [v] (see also later editions: 1747, 1749, 1750, etc.).

9. Tobias Smollett, *The Expedition of Humphry Clinker*, ed. O. M. Brack Jr. (Athens: University of Georgia Press, 1990), 225–26.

10. *Coffee-House Jests* (London, 1760), 7 (nos. 2–3).

11. Morris Palmer Tilley, *A Dictionary of the Proverbs in England in the Sixteenth and Seventeenth Centuries* (Ann Arbor: University of Michigan Press, 1950), 75 (B781); *Coffee-House Jests*, 24 (no. 44).

12. Jane Cave, "Written by Desire of a Lady on an Angry, Petulant Kitchen-Maid" (1783), in *Eighteenth-Century Women Poets*, ed. Roger Lonsdale (Oxford: Oxford University Press, 1989), 375. The biographical complexities around this poem are beyond the scope of my discussion: Cave was herself of humble origins, and like so many of her other poems, this was something of a commissioned piece.

13. See Amanda Vickery, *The Gentleman's Daughter: Women's Lives in Georgian England* (New Haven, CT: Yale University Press, 1998), chap. 4.

14. David Hume, *A Treatise of Human Nature*, ed. L. A. Selby-Bigge, 2nd ed., rev. P. H. Nidditch (Oxford: Clarendon, 1978), 402 (2.3.1). For a detailed exploration of this topic in Smith, Hume, and the Scottish physiologists, see Christopher Lawrence, "The Nervous System and Society in the Scottish Enlightenment," in *Natural Order: Historical Studies of Scientific Culture*, ed. Barry Barnes and Steven Shapin (Beverly Hills, CA: Sage, 1979), 19–40.

15. BL, Add. MS 27825, "Place Papers, xxxvii, Manners and Morals," i, fol. 158. The last two examples are "The Sandman's Wedding" and "The Wheel Barrow Cantata," both in *The Apollo: Being the First Volume of the Masque or Collection of Songs* (Dublin, 1772).

16. *The Nut-Cracker*, new ed. (London, 1760), 15. There is no evidence for the Swift attribution.

17. John Gay, "Friday," in *Poetry and Prose of John Gay*, ed. Vinton Dearing and Charles Beckwith, 2 vols. (Oxford: Clarendon, 1974), 1:118 (lines 159–64). For a masterful discussion of these contexts, see John Barrell, *The Dark Side of the Landscape: The Rural Poor in English Painting, 1730–1840* (Cambridge: Cambridge University Press, 1980), 54–57.

18. *The Diverting Muse; or, Universal Medley* (London, 1707), 171–81.

19. See Samuel N. Bogorad and Robert Gale Noyes, eds., "Samuel Foote's *Primitive Puppet-Shew* Featuring *Piety in Patterns*: A Critical Edition," special issue, *Theatre Survey* 14, no. 1a (1973).

20. See Eric Partridge, *A Dictionary of Slang and Unconventional English*, 8th ed., rev. Paul Beale (London: Routledge, 2002), 936.

21. *The Muse in Good Humour*, 7th ed., 2 vols. (London, 1766), 98–103.

22. *Merry Miscellany*, n.p.

23. *England's Witty and Ingenious Jester*, 15th ed. (London, n.d. [Bodleian Douce W 30]), 76.

24. Thomas D'Urfey, *Pills to Purge Melancholy*, 6 vols. in 3 (1719–20; New York: Folklore Library, 1959), 6:120.

25. See *Tom Gay's Comical Jester* (London, 1765), 5–6; *Tristram Shandy's Bon Mots* (London, 1760); and Henry Fielding, *Tom Jones*, ed. Martin C. Battestin (Oxford: Clarendon, 1974), 229 (5.5). Specifics are amply described in Emily Cockayne, *Hubbub: Filth, Noise, and Stench in England, 1600–1770* (New Haven, CT: Yale University Press, 2007).

26. On which, see Barrell, *The Dark Side of the Landscape*; and the more recent discussions in Ann Birmingham, *Sense and Sensibility: Viewing Gainsborough's "Cottage Door"* (New Haven, CT: Yale University Press, 2005).

27. *Joe Miller's Jests*, 5 (no. 26); cf. *Merry Medley*, 18.

28. *The Complete London Jester*, 3rd ed. (London 1766), 98.

29. *Coffee-House Jests*, 37–38 (no. 69).

30. *Oxford Jests*, 14th ed. (London, n.d. [HL 145868]), 105 (no. 396); *England's Witty and Ingenious Jester*, 10.

31. *Ben Johnson's Last Legacy to the Sons of Wit, Mirth, and Jollytry*, 2nd ed. (London, n.d. [Bodleian Harding E41]), 5–6. Compare *The Banquet of Wit* (Gosport, n.d. [Huntington 308430]), 50.

32. *Aristophanes, Being a Classic Collection of True Attic Wit* (London, 1778), 45.

33. "Jack Is Accused by a Wench of Being the Father of a Bastard Child," in *The Birth, Life, and Death of John Franks, with the Pranks He Played Though a Meer Fool* (London, n.d. [BL 1079.i.14(2)]), chap. 3, pp. 7–8.

34. *Ben Johnson's Jests* (London, n.d. [BL 1607/4679]), 31.

35. *Rochester's Jests*, 57; *Ben Johnson's Last Legacy to the Sons of Wit, Mirth, and Jollytry*, 16; *Coffee-House Jests*, 23 (no. 43).

36. *London Jests* (London, 1720), 121–22; cf. *Coffee-House Jests*, 146 (no. 264).

37. *The Nut-Cracker* (London, 1751), 53. This joke is frequently repeated (cf. *Quin's Jests* [London, 1766], 47–48, etc.).

38. *The Irish Miscellany*, 37, 73, 89, etc.

39. *Tom Brown's Complete Jester*, 4th ed. (London, n.d. [Harding E276]), 57; *London Jests*, 121.

40. *The Laugher; or, The Art of Jesting*, 2nd ed. (London, 1755), 83.

41. *London Jests*, 135; *Miss C——y's Cabinet of Curiosities; or, The Green Room Broke Open, by Tristram Shandy, Gent.* (London, 1765), 8; *Jack Smart's Merry Jester*, 2nd ed. (London, n.d. [BL 1607/3945]), 51; *Encyclopedia of Wit and Anecdote* (Dublin, n.d. [Harding E 3[1]), 5.

42. *Merry Medley*, 26–27.

43. *Merry Miscellany*, n.p.

44. *Jack Smart's Merry Jester*, 5.

45. *Joe Miller's Jests*, 18 (no. 99).

46. *England's Witty and Ingenious Jester*, 73.

47. *Tristram Shandy's Bon Mots*, 33; cf. *Coffee-House Jests*, 42 (no. 81).

48. Ronald Paulson, "The Joke and *Joe Miller's Jests*," in *Popular and Polite Art in the Age of Hogarth and Fielding* (South Bend, IN: University of Notre Dame Press, 1979), 68.

49. Henry Mackenzie, *Anecdotes and Egotisms*, ed. Harold William Thompson (Oxford: Oxford University Press, 1927), 68.

50. *Tristram Shandy's Bon Mots*, 33.

51. *England's Witty and Ingenious Jester*, 77.

52. Paul Langford, *A Polite and Commercial People: England, 1727–83* (Oxford: Oxford University Press, 1992), 154.

53. John Langbein, "Albion's Fatal Flaws," *Past and Present* 98 (February 1983): 96–120; Peter King, *Crime, Justice, and Discretion in England, 1740–1820* (Oxford: Oxford University Press, 2003), 125.

54. K. D. M. Snell, *Annals of the Labouring Poor: Social Change and Agrarian England, 1660–1900* (Cambridge: Cambridge University Press, 1985), esp. 107–8; Peter King, "The Poor, the Law, and the Poor Law: Pauper Strategies in Eighteenth and Early Nineteenth-Century England," in *Poverty and Relief in England, 1500–1800*, ed. Steven King and R. M. Smith (Woodbridge: Boydell & Brewer, forthcoming); and H. R. French, *The Middle Sort of People in Provincial England, 1600–1750* (Oxford: Oxford University Press, 2007), passim.

55. Auerbach, *Mimesis*, 22.

56. Stuart Tave, *The Amiable Humorist* (Chicago: University of Chicago Press, 1960), 57–58.

57. [James Ralph], *Sawney: An Heroic Poem Occasion'd by the Dunciad* (London, 1728), vii.

58. Among the many accounts of these concerns, see the richly detailed discussion in Vickery, *The Gentleman's Daughter*, chap. 4.

59. Tim Hitchcock, Peter King, and Pamela Sharpe, eds., *Chronicling Poverty: The Voices and Strategies of the English Poor, 1640–1840* (London: Macmillan, 1997), 1–18; Tim Hitchcock and John Black, eds., *Chelsea Settlement and Bastardy Examinations, 1733–1766* (London: London Record Society, 1999), introduction; Paul Slack, *Poverty and Policy in Tudor and Stuart England* (London: Longman, 1988), 192; Steven Hindle, *On the Parish? The Micro-Politics of Poor Relief in Rural England c. 1550–1750* (Oxford: Clarendon, 2004).

60. On these and other mendicant strategies, see Tim Hitchcock, "Begging on the Streets in Eighteenth-Century London," *Journal of British Studies* 44, no. 3 (July 2005): 478–98, and, more emphatically, "Cultural Representations: Rogue Literature and the Reality of the Begging Body," in *A History of the Human Body in the Age of Enlightenment*, ed. Carole Reeves (Oxford: Berg, 2010), 175–92.

61. *The Gentleman's Magazine* 1 (1731): 15.

62. King, *Crime, Justice, and Discretion*, 252–57.

63. Tobias Smollett, *A Continuation of the Complete History of England*, 5 vols. (London, 1760–65), 1:56.

64. *An Elegy Written in Covent-Garden* (London, n.d. [BL 11630.e.13(18)]), much reprinted and anthologized (e.g., *The Repository*, 4 vols. [London, 1777–83]). James Lackington seems to quote the poem from memory (*Memoirs of the First Forty-Five Years of the Life of James Lackington*, 7th ed. [London, 1794], 289).

65. Anthony Hilliar, *The Brief and Merry History of Great Britain* (London, 1730), 42.

66. Sandby's watercolors were lost until 1961, when they were sold and dispersed. They are reproduced in Sean Shesgreen, *Images of the Outcast: The Urban Poor in the Cries of London* (Manchester: Manchester University Press, 2002), pls. 1–10. The comic-mordant tradition continued in such artists as Thomas Heaphy, on whom see a fascinating recent article by David Solkin: "The Other Half of the Landscape: Thomas Heaphy's Watercolour Nasties," in *Land, Nation, and Culture, 1740–1840*, ed. Peter de Bolla, Nigel Leask, and David Simpson (New York: Palgrave, 2005), 63–98.

67. Tilley, *Proverbs*, 39–41 (B222–B252).

68. Celina Fox, *Londoners* (London: Thames & Hudson, 1987), 186; Tim Hitchcock, *Down and Out in Eighteenth-Century London* (London: Hambledon & London, 2004).

69. Peter King, "Edward Thompson's Contribution to Eighteenth-Century Studies: The Patrician-Plebian Model Re-Examined," *Social History* 21, no. 2 (1996): 218. For influential arguments on overall increases in aristocratic power and the efficiency of the state, see J. A. Cannon, *Aristocratic Century: The Peerage of Eighteenth-Century England* (Cambridge: Cambridge University Press, 1984); and John Brewer, *The Sinews of Power: War, Money and the English State, 1688–1783* (Cambridge, MA: Harvard University Press, 1988).

70. Harold Perkin, *The Origins of Modern English Society, 1780–1880* (London: Routledge & Kegan Paul, 1969); J. C. D. Clark, *English Society, 1688–1832* (Cambridge: Cambridge University Press, 1985).

71. Garthine Walker, *Crime, Gender, and Social Order in Early Modern England* (Cambridge: Cambridge University Press, 2003); Susan Amussen, *An Ordered Society: Gender and Class in Early Modern England, 1560–1725* (New York: Columbia University Press, 1993).

72. *Rochester's Jests*, 55–56.

73. Earl of March, *A Duke and His Friends: The Life and Letters of the Second Duke of Richmond*, 2 vols. (London: Hutchinson, 1911), 1:264.

74. Jonathan Swift, *Journal to Stella*, ed. Harold Williams, 2 vols. (Oxford: Clarendon, 1963), 1:307 (3 October 1711).

75. *The Laugher*, 116–17; *Jemmy Twitcher's Jests* (Paisley, 1776), 43, etc.

76. See Tobias Smollett, *The Adventures of Peregrine Pickle*, ed. James L. Clifford (London: Oxford University Press, 1969), 577 (cf. 90, 205, 208, 214, 246–47, 745, etc.).

77. LMA MJ/SR 3358/9 (Middlesex Sessions Rolls, 1778). Lennox appeared before Sir John Hawkins at Hicks Hall; Laetitia Hawkins recalls the hearings in her *Memoirs, Anecdotes, Facts, and Opinions, Collected and Preserved*, 2 vols. (London, 1824), 1:331.

78. J. J. Hecht, *The Domestic Servant Class in Eighteenth-Century England* (New York: Routledge & Kegan Paul, 1956), 78–80; and, more recently, Tim Meldrum, *Domestic Service and Gender, 1660–1750: Life and Work in the London Household* (New York: Longman, 2000),

39; and Kristina Straub, *Domestic Affairs: Intimacy, Eroticism, and Violence between Servants and Masters in Eighteenth-Century Britain* (Baltimore: Johns Hopkins University Press, 2009). On a violent mistress hissed at the Nottingham Assizes, see Vickery, *The Gentleman's Daughter*, 146. On Victorian contexts and the act of 1861, see Leonore Davidoff, "Class and Gender in Victorian England," *Feminist Studies* 5, no. 1 (1979): 86–141.

79. *Boswell's London Journal, 1762–63*, ed. Frederick A. Pottle (New Haven, CT: Yale University Press, 1992), 272–73 (4 June 1763).

80. Robert Stanley Forsythe, *A Noble Rake: The Life of Charles, Fourth Lord Mohun* (Cambridge, MA: Harvard University Press, 1928), 27.

81. Swift, *Journal to Stella*, 1:322 (28 July 1711).

82. Samuel Richardson, *Clarissa; or, The History of a Young Lady* (1748, 1st ed.), ed. Angus Ross (London: Penguin, 1985), 449, 637, 1203, 276.

83. For full reports, see *Fog's Weekly Journal*, 12 June 1731; and *Daily Advertiser*, 11 June 1731.

84. *Joe Miller's Jests*, 21–22 (no. 116); *Coffee-House Jests*, 84–85 (no. 156) (and cf. 39–40 [no. 74], 119 [no. 226]). The scenario has its own category (J1184.2) in Stith Thompson's *Motif-Index of Folk Literature*, 6 vols. (Bloomington: Indiana University Press, 1955–58).

85. Richardson, *Clarissa*, 1048, 573, 758.

86. *Hob; or, The Country Wake* (London, 1711, etc.).

87. William Kenrick, *Fun: A Parodi-Tragi-Comical Satire: As It Was to Have Been Perform'd . . . but Suppressed, by a Special Order from the Lord-Mayor and Court of Aldermen* (London, 1752), 14.

88. *Public Advertiser*, 20 July 1764, 4; *Gazette; or, London Daily Advertiser*, 20 August 1764, 2.

89. See Thomas Sheridan, *An Humble Appeal to the Public* (Dublin, 1758), 14–15.

90. Among many journalistic reports, see *World*, no. 23 (7 June 1753), no. 29 (19 July 1753); *Connoisseur*, no. 22 (27 June 1755), no. 54 (6 February 1755); *Oxford Magazine*, May 1772, 186–89; *Adventurer*, no. 68 (30 June 1753), no. 100 (20 October 1753); and *Public Advertiser*, 20 July 1764. For an old but useful synthesis, see Louis C. Jones, *The Clubs of the Georgian Rakes* (New York: Columbia University Press, 1942).

91. *Connoisseur*, no. 54 (6 February 1755); *Oxford Magazine*, May 1772. The anecdotes are still incautiously repeated.

92. John Gay, *Trivia*, 3.331–32, in *Poetry and Prose of John Gay*, ed. Vinton Dearing and Charles Beckwith, 2 vols. (Oxford: Clarendon, 1974), 1:169.

93. *Spectator*, no. 324 (12 March 1712): on "Tumblers"; *Spectator*, no. 332 (21 March 1712): on "Sweaters."

94. See Daniel Statt, "The Case of the Mohocks: Rake Violence in Augustan London," *Social History* 20, no. 2 (May 1995): 179–99; and Neil Guthrie, "'No truth or very little in the whole story?'—a Reassessment of the Mohock Scare of 1712," *Eighteenth-Century Life* 20, no. 1 (1996): 33–56.

95. See Robert Shoemaker, *The London Mob: Violence and Disorder in Eighteenth-Century England* (London: Hambledon & London, 2004), 164–66. Donna Andrew's eagerly anticipated study of London newspapers (provisionally titled *The Attack on Aristocratic Vice*) is

revealing consistent complaints. On Oxford, see V. H. H. Green, "University and Social Life," in *The History of the University of Oxford*, ed. T. H. Aston et al., 8 vols. (Oxford: Clarendon, 1984–2000), 5:309–58.

96. Keith Thomas, "Age and Authority in Early-Modern England," *Proceedings of the British Academy* 62 (1976): 205–48, esp. 217–22. On "The Prince's Frolick," as he calls it, see John, Earl of Egmont, *Diaries, 1730–1747*, 3 vols. (London: HMC, 1920–23), 2:471; and Morris Marples, *Poor Fred and the Butcher: Sons of George II* (London: Michael Joseph, 1970), 17. On Dashwood, see esp. Ronald Fuller, *Hell-Fire Francis* (London: Chatto & Windus, 1939).

97. Anna Clark, *The Struggle for the Breeches: Gender and the Making of the British Working Class* (Berkeley and Los Angeles: University of California Press, 1995), 31. See, more recently, Shoemaker, *The London Mob*, chaps. 6–7.

98. The misemphasis is somewhat remedied in James G. Turner, *Libertines and Radicals in Early Modern London: Sexuality, Politics, and Literary Culture, 1630–1685* (Cambridge: Cambridge University Press, 2002), esp. 156–66, where Turner proposes the term *savage nobles*. On codes of aristocratic violence enduring into the nineteenth century, see Leonore Davidoff and Catherine Hall, *Family Fortunes: Men and Women of the English Middle Class, 1780–1850* (Chicago: University of Chicago Press, 1987), 110.

99. Richardson, *Clarissa*, 419.

100. *The Court and City Jester* (London, 1770), 36; *The Banquet of Wit*, 10, etc.; Smollett, *Peregrine Pickle*, 114; Kenrick, *Fun*, 15–16, 25–32. The scenario endured into the nineteenth century and was widely illustrated. See, e.g., John Cawse, *Birds of a Feather Flock Together; or, Bond Street Loungers Attending the Examination of Their Fellow Scarecrows!!!* (1800, BM Satires undescribed [1948,0214.628]).

101. Horace Walpole, *The Yale Edition of Horace Walpole's Correspondence*, ed. W. S. Lewis et al., 48 vols. (New Haven, CT: Yale University Press, 1937–83), 19:387 (10 April 1747), where full details are collected in the notes.

102. See esp. Andrew, *The Attack on Aristocratic Vice*.

103. "A Letter from a London Buck," *Adventurer*, no. 100 (20 October 1753); *The Buck: A Poem* (London, 1767); "The Buck's Grammar," in *The Comet; or, Meteor of Mirth* (London, 1772), 28–38.

104. Prints include BM Satires nos. 2186–87, 4334; *High Life at Midnight* (1769, LMA p5428808); *He and His Drunken Companions Raise a Riot in Covent Garden* (1735, LMA p5434772); George Bickham, *The Queen of the Mohocks* (ca. 1745; Lewis Walpole Library 745.00.00.05); and Robert Dighton's *Twelve at Night* (Huntington Library, BMX 1795 Pr.Box 211.11/47).

105. "The Disabled Debauchee," in *The Works of John Wilmot, Earl of Rochester*, ed. Harold Love (Oxford: Oxford University Press, 1999), 45.

106. *Connoisseur*, no. 71 (5 June 1755).

107. *Connoisseur*, no. 54 (6 February 1755).

108. *Spectator*, no. 332 (21 March 1712). Other papers on the topic are *Spectator*, nos. 324 (12 March 1712), 335 (25 March 1712), and 347 (8 April 1712).

109. Charges were traded to and fro, with Swift and other Tories insisting that the Mohocks were Whigs determined to overthrow the government, and Whigs countercharging that

the Tories had exaggerated a few common street crimes in order to discredit their opponents. Steele's type of irony is most clearly exemplified in John Gay's mock-apocalyptic pamphlet *An Argument Proving from History, Reason and Scripture That the Present Race of Mohocks and Hawkabites Are the Gog and Magog Mentioned in the Revelation* (London, 1712).

110. *Adventurer*, no. 68 (30 June 1753); *Connoisseur*, no. 54 (6 February 1755).

111. *Mist's Weekly Journal*, 20 February 1720; Hilliar, *Brief and Merry History of Great Britain*, 55.

112. *Public Advertiser*, July 20, 1764.

113. See Gay's warning: *Trivia*, 3.140–42, in Dearing and Beckwith, eds., *Poetry and Prose of John Gay*, 1:164.

114. On this tacit appointment of comedians in human societies, see Peter Berger, *Redeeming Laughter: The Comic Dimension of Human Experience* (New York: Walter de Gruyter, 1997), chap. 5. For a fascinating and still-useful discussion of this role, see Enid Welsford, *The Fool: His Social and Literary History* (London: Faber & Faber, 1935).

115. Much reprinted: James Love, *Cricket: An Heroic Poem . . . To Which Is Added an Epilogue, Call'd Bucks Have at Ye All* (London 1770); *The Young Spouter, Being a New Collection of Prologues and Epilogues* (London, n.d. [BL RB.23.a.9947]); etc.

116. Forsythe, *A Noble Rake*, 4; Delarivière Manley, *Secret Memoirs and Manners of Persons of Quality of Both Sexes: From the New Atalantis, an Island in the Mediterranean*, 4 vols. (London, 1720), 2:290–300.

117. See, e.g., *The Entertaining Companion; or, The Merry Jester* (London, 1760).

118. David Farley-Hills is careful to separate out these three distinct reputations in his introduction to *Rochester: The Critical Heritage*, ed. David Farley-Hills (New York: Barnes & Noble, 1972).

119. John Dennis, *A Defence of Sir Fopling Flutter* (London, 1722), 19; George Etherege, *The Man of Mode*, 1.1. *The Man of Mode* was attacked by Steele (*Spectator*, no. 65 [15 May 1711]), but Dennis's *Defence* reflected widespread opinions, and the play was regularly performed into the 1750s. Note that other contemporaries disputed Dennis's identification of Rochester as Etherege's model for Dorimant.

120. Fielding, *Tom Jones*, 155.

121. Thomas Hearne, *Remarks and Collections*, ed. C. E. Doble et al., 11 vols. (Oxford: Oxford Historical Society, 1885–1921), 9:78.

122. See *The Whole Life and History of My Lord Mohun and the Earl of Warwick, with the Comical Frolicks That They Play'd* (London, 1711); *Pills to Purge Melancholy* (Worcester, n.d. [HL 150742]); and *Joaks upon Joaks; or, No Joak like a True Joak* (Worcester, n.d. [HL 150742]), 3–5. The last two texts are some of the rarest to have survived, preserved by the collector Robert Hoe, who bound them up as "Beggar's Balderdash."

123. *The History of the Frolicksome Courtier and the Jovial Tinker* (London, n.d. [BL 1079. i.13 (14)]), 7–8. Such episodes were quickly removed in nineteenth-century antiquarian reprints like John Ashton's *Chapbooks of the Eighteenth Century* (London, 1882).

124. See Michael Harris, "A Few Shillings for Small Books: The Experience of a Flying Stationer in the Eighteenth Century," in *Spreading the Word: The Distribution Networks of Print, 1550–1850*, ed. Michael Harris and Robin Myers (Winchester: St. Paul's Bibliographies, 1990),

83–108; and Victor Neuberg, "The Diceys and the Chapbook Trade," *The Library* 24 (1969): 219–31. On the conservatism of popular prints, see Sheila O'Connell, *The Popular Print in England, 1550–1850* (London: British Museum Press, 1999), esp. 51–53.

125. A term first proposed by Roger Chartier, *The Cultural Uses of Print in Early-Modern France*, trans. Lydia G. Cochrane (Princeton, NJ: Princeton University Press, 1987).

126. A point emphatically made by Victor E. Neuberg, *Popular Education in Eighteenth-Century England* (London: Woburn, 1971), 2.

127. See William Coles, *Adam in Eden; or, Nature's Paradise* (London, 1657), 66.

128. *Lloyd's Evening Post*, 18–20 January 1762; Francis Grose, *A Classical Dictionary of the Vulgar Tongue*, 3rd ed. (1796), ed. Eric Partridge (New York: Barnes & Noble, 1963), 128–29; Fielding, *Tom Jones*, 301.

129. Smollett, *Peregrine Pickle*, 541. On Godfrey and his business, see John Emsley, *The Shocking History of Phosphorous* (London: Macmillan, 2000), 207–11.

130. Rev. John Sharp to Rev. John Denne, 12 March 1756, cited in R. W. Ketton-Cremer, *Thomas Gray: A Biography* (Cambridge: Cambridge University Press, 1955), 137–38.

131. The same standards that made Chesterfield and others deplore loud and open-mouthed laughter (*The Letters of Philip Dormer Stanhope, 4th Earl of Chesterfield*, ed. Bonamy Dobrée, 6 vols. [London: Eyre & Spottiswoode, 1932], 3:1115–16 [9 March O.S. 1748]). For a fascinating transhistorical survey, see Angus Trumble, *A Brief History of the Smile* (New York: Basic, 2004).

132. Maria Edgeworth, *Belinda*, ed. Kathryn J. Kirkpatrick (Oxford: Oxford University Press, 1994), 58–60 (chap. 4).

133. Grose, *Classical Dictionary*, 322; Keith Thomas, *Man and the Natural World* (New York: Pantheon, 1983), 148 and n.

134. Francis Askham, *The Gay Delavals* (London: Cape, 1955), 74–75. Askham worked from family papers in the Northumberland Record Office.

135. *Old England's Journal*, 10 March 1753.

136. *Boswell's London Journal, 1762–63*, 236n1.

137. Contexts expertly drawn out in Lance Bertelsen, *The Nonsense Club: Literature and Popular Culture, 1749–1764* (Oxford: Clarendon, 1986), 155–60.

138. John Hill, *The Inspector*, 2 vols. (London, 1753), 1:275–78. On calling surgeons and midwives, see *Tatler*, no. 143 (9 March 1709).

139. *Daily Post*, 26 August 1737; *Daily Gazetteer*, 26 August 1737.

140. *Connoisseur*, no. 54 (6 February 1755).

141. See, e.g., Charles Johnstone, *Chrysal; or, The Adventures of a Guinea* (1760–65), ed. E. A. Baker (London: Routledge, 1907), 45, 48.

142. For full contexts, see Jenny Uglow, *Hogarth: A Life and a World* (New York: Farrar Straus Giroux, 1997), 510–12.

143. *The Reminiscences of Henry Angelo*, ed. H. Lavers Smith, 2 vols. (London: Kegan Paul, 1904), 1:314–15.

144. See *Aristophanes, Being a Classic Collection of True Attic Wit*, 139–40; *The Cabinet of True Attic Wit* (London, 1783); etc.

145. Bernard Falk, *The Way of the Montagues: A Gallery of Family Portraits* (London:

Hutchinson, 1947), chap. 8. For Montesquieu's comments, see Henry Fielding, *Joseph Andrews*, ed. Martin C. Battestin (Middletown: Wesleyan University Press, 1967), xxivn.

146. Contemporary reports are reviewed in Emmett L. Avery et al., eds., *The London Stage, 1600-1800*, 5 pts. in 11 vols. (Carbondale: Southern Illinois University Press, 1960-68), pt. 4, vol. 1, pp. cxcvii-viii.

147. Cited in Askham, *Gay Delavals*, 15.

148. *Opinions of Sarah, Duchess Dowager of Marlborough* (London, 1788), 58.

149. John, Lord Hervey, *Some Materials towards Memoirs of the Reign of King George II*, 3 vols. (London: Eyre & Spottiswoode, 1931), 3:828.

150. Hill, *Inspector*, 1:275-78.

151. This increasing psychological difference between children and adults is a major theme in Norbert Elias, *The Civilizing Process* (1939), trans. Edmund Jephcott, 2 vols. in 1 (Oxford: Blackwell, 1982). See esp. vol. 1 ("The History of Manners"), pp. xiii, 115.

152. John Nichols, *Illustrations of the Literary History of the Eighteenth Century*, 8 vols. (London, 1817-58), 8:574; *Lord Hervey and His Friends, 1726-38*, ed. Earl of Ilchester (London: John Murray, 1950), 207.

153. Walpole, *Correspondence*, 20:79 (24 July 1749).

154. Nichols, *Illustrations*, 8:574; *The Jests of Beau Nash* (London, 1763), 65; Oliver Goldsmith, *The Life of Richard Nash of Bath, Esq.* (1762), in *Collected Works of Oliver Goldsmith*, ed. Arthur Friedman, 5 vols. (Oxford: Clarendon, 1966), 3:334.

155. On Pearce, see *Lloyd's Evening Post*, 18-20 January 1762. On Richmond, see John Nichols, *Literary Anecdotes of the Eighteenth Century*, 9 vols. (London, 1812-16), 4:636.

156. Sarah Fielding, *The History of Ophelia*, 2 vols. (London, 1760), vol. 1, chap. 29.

157. Falk, *The Way of the Montagues*, 274-75; *The Entertaining Medley* (London, 1767), 2-7.

158. Richardson, *Clarissa*, 1209-16.

159. Biographical details from T. C. Duncan Eaves and Ben D. Kimpel, *Samuel Richardson: A Biography* (Oxford: Oxford University Press, 1971), 521-23.

160. Richardson, *Clarissa*, 1274.

161. Marginalia transcribed by Janine Barchas, *The Annotations in Lady Bradshaigh's Copy of Clarissa*, ELS Monograph no. 76 (Victoria, BC: University of Victoria, 1998), 124. Richardson's reply appears below.

162. Comment written by the prompter Richard Cross in his diary. Cited in Avery et al., eds., *The London Stage*, pt. 4, vol. 2, p. 503 (31 October 1755).

163. Adam Smith, *Lectures on Rhetoric and Belles Lettres*, ed. John M. Lothian (London: Thomas Nelson & Sons, 1963), 120 (14 January 1763).

CHAPTER FOUR

1. Henry Fielding, *Joseph Andrews*, ed. Martin C. Battestin (Middletown, CT: Wesleyan University Press, 1967), 3-11. Page numbers for subsequent citations are given parenthetically in the text.

2. Sarah Fielding, *The Cry: A New Dramatic Fable*, 3 vols. (London, 1754), 3:120-24.

3. The fullest account of this reputation and the early reception history of *Joseph Andrews* remains Frederic Blanchard, *Fielding the Novelist* (New Haven, CT: Yale University Press, 1926), chap. 1. For an indispensable selection of documents, see Ronald Paulson and Thomas Lockwood, eds., *Henry Fielding: The Critical Heritage* (London: Routledge & Kegan Paul, 1969).

4. "Porcupinus Pelagius," *Old England*, 5 March 1748, 2.

5. Arthur Murphy, *Gray's-Inn Journal*, 2 vols. (London, 1756), 2:276 (no. 96). Allan Ramsay, similarly, could see nothing but "strokes of . . . *Ridicule*" in the character. See *An Essay on Ridicule* (London, 1753), 78n.

6. Henry Knight Miller, *Essays on Fielding's Miscellanies* (Princeton, NJ: Princeton University Press, 1961), 269; J. Paul Hunter, *Occasional Form: Henry Fielding and the Chains of Circumstance* (Baltimore: Johns Hopkins University Press, 1972), 45; William Empson, "*Tom Jones*," *Kenyon Review* 20 (1958): 217–49; Jill Campbell, *Natural Masques: Gender and Identity in Fielding's Plays and Novels* (Stanford, CA: Stanford University Press, 1995); Lance Bertelsen, *Henry Fielding at Work: Magistrate, Businessman, Writer* (London: Palgrave, 2000).

7. William Forsythe, *Novels and Novelists of the Eighteenth Century* (New York, 1871), 255–64.

8. William Shenstone to Richard Graves, 17/18 May 1742, cited in Paulson and Lockwood, eds., *Critical Heritage*, 120.

9. See Paul McPharlin, ed., *The Tragical Comedy or Comical Tragedy of Punch and Judy* (New York: Limited Editions Club, 1937), xv.

10. See Martin C. Battestin, *Henry Fielding: A Life* (London: Routledge, 1989), 48.

11. "Solon's Song," from *The Marriage-Hater Matched* (London, 1693), 2.1. See Arthur Sherbo, "Fielding's Dogs," *Notes and Queries* 17, no. 8 (1970): 302–3.

12. See Claude Rawson, *Henry Fielding and the Augustan Ideal under Stress* (London: Routledge & Kegan Paul, 1972), 232, 234.

13. See Edmond McAdoo Gagey, *Ballad Opera* (New York: Columbia University Press, 1937), esp. chap. 5–6.

14. For just one contemporary text that strikes the same tone of tolerant amusement—down to the ubiquitous detail of the boozing, gluttonous Parson—see Elizabeth Amherst, "The Welford Wedding," in *Eighteenth-Century Women Poets*, ed. Roger Lonsdale (Oxford: Oxford University Press, 1989), 181–83.

15. Judith Frank, *Common Ground: Eighteenth-Century Satiric Fiction and the Poor* (Stanford, CA: Stanford University Press, 1997), 48 (chap. 1). Paula McDowell's more recent exploration of the topic reaches rather different conclusions. See her "Why Fanny Can't Read: *Joseph Andrews* and the (Ir)relevance of Literacy," in *The Blackwell Companion to the Eighteenth-Century English Novel*, ed. Paula Backscheider and Catherine Ingrassia (Oxford: Blackwell, 2004), 167–90.

16. William Chetwood, *The Generous Free-Mason* (London, 1730), 11, 21.

17. Ibid., 26–28 (2.2).

18. Campbell, *Natural Masques*, 103 (see chap. 3 passim). Note that Campbell's emphasis falls on the gendering of these concerns, with the squire's brutal masculinity and aggressive sense of humor set against the more virtuous manliness of Adams and Joseph.

19. Ibid., 276n19.

20. See, e.g., Henry Fielding, *Jonathan Wild*, in *Miscellanies, Volume Three*, ed. Hugh Amory and Bertrand A. Goldgar (Oxford: Clarendon, 1997), 144, 170, 178, 185, 186.

21. Campbell, *Natural Masques*, 106 and 276n19.

22. See, e.g., "Dramaticus," review of *The Modern Husband*, *Grub-Street Journal*, no. 132 (13 July 1732).

23. "Philalethes," *Daily Post*, 31 July 1732.

24. Henry Fielding, *The Covent-Garden Journal and A Plan for the Universal Register-Office*, ed. Bertrand A. Goldgar (Oxford: Clarendon, 1988), 73–74 (no. 10 [4 February 1752]).

25. Henry Fielding, *The Modern Husband*, in *Plays, Volume II*, ed. Thomas Lockwood (Oxford: Clarendon, 2007), 214 (prologue).

26. Paulson and Lockwood, eds., *Critical Heritage*, 2.

27. Henry Fielding, *The Covent-Garden Tragedy*, in *Plays, Volume II*, 368, 403.

28. Martin C. Battestin and Clive T. Probyn, eds., *The Correspondence of Henry and Sarah Fielding* (Oxford: Clarendon, 1993), 18.

29. Henry Fielding, "An Essay on the Knowledge of the Characters of Men," in *Miscellanies, Volume One*, ed. Henry Knight Miller (Oxford: Clarendon, 1972), 159.

30. Compare Sophia's ineradicable love for Tom: "one of those secret spontaneous Emotions of the Soul, to which Reason is often a Stranger" (Henry Fielding, *The History of Tom Jones*, ed. Martin C. Battestin and Fredson Bowers [Oxford: Clarendon, 1977], 580).

31. Fielding, "Essay on the Knowledge of the Characters of Men," 159–60; Henry Fielding, *Shamela*, in *The Journal of a Voyage to Lisbon, Shamela, and Occasional Writings*, ed. Martin C. Battestin (Oxford: Clarendon, 2008), 164.

32. Henry Fielding, *Contributions to The Champion and Related Writings*, ed. W. B. Coley (Oxford: Clarendon, 2003), 230–32 (13 March 1739/40).

33. Henry Fielding, "Of Good Nature," in *Miscellanies, Volume One*, 30; Battestin, *Henry Fielding*, 465.

34. *Daily Gazetteer*, 9 October 1740. I owe the biographical details to Battestin (*Henry Fielding*, 151–60) and relevant *ODNB* essays.

35. Walter Arnold, *The Life and Death of the Sublime Society of Beefsteaks* (London, 1871), 16. There is no record of Fielding's involvement in this club, but one finds close friends and acquaintances among the founding members: Hogarth, Ellys, John Rich, and others.

36. *The Gentleman's Magazine* 62 (1792): 30.

37. Anthony Henley to Thomas Cooke, 17 November 1733, cited in Battestin, *Henry Fielding*, 158.

38. Fielding, "Essay on the Knowledge of the Characters of Men," 160–61.

39. *Tatler*, no. 45 (22 July 1709).

40. On which, see Deidre Lynch, *The Economy of Character* (Chicago: University of Chicago Press, 1998), chap. 3.

41. *1 Henry 4*, 2.2.78–84.

42. Hunter, *Occasional Form*, 111–16; Claude Rawson, "Henry Fielding," in *The Cambridge Companion to the Eighteenth-Century Novel*, ed. John Richetti (Cambridge: Cambridge University Press, 1996), 136, and *Henry Fielding and the Augustan Ideal under Stress*, 247.

43. See, e.g., *Coffee-House Jests*, 91 (no. 168). Compare Erasmus's ridicule of philosophers who claimed to discern universal ideas while unable to see a stone or a ditch in their path: *Praise of Folly*, trans. Clarence Miller (New Haven, CT: Yale University Press, 1979), 85ff.

44. On these long-term changes, see Stuart Tave, *The Amiable Humorist* (Chicago: University of Chicago Press, 1960), 273ff.; and Ronald Paulson, *Don Quixote in England: The Aesthetics of Laughter* (Baltimore: Johns Hopkins University Press, 1998), passim.

45. See Wilbur Cross, *The History of Henry Fielding*, 3 vols. (New Haven, CT: Yale University Press, 1918), 1:346.

46. Henry Fielding, *The Jacobite's Journal and Related Writings*, ed. W. B. Coley (Oxford: Clarendon, 1974), 266 (30 April 1748).

47. See Battestin, *Henry Fielding*, 157 and passim.

48. Fielding, *Champion and Related Writings*, 86 (25 December 1739).

49. Frederick G. Ribble and Anne G. Ribble, *Fielding's Library* (Charlottesville: Bibliographical Society of the University of Virginia, 1996), xxvi.

50. Martin C. Battestin, *The Moral Basis of Fielding's Art* (Middletown, CT: Wesleyan University Press, 1959), chap. 7. Battestin restated these views in his preface to his edition of *Joseph Andrews* and in his *Henry Fielding*.

51. In addition to Claude Rawson's *Henry Fielding and the Augustan Ideal under Stress*, see his *Order from Confusion Sprung* (London: Allen & Unwin, 1985), chap. 15; and his review of Martin C. Battestin, *Henry Fielding: A Life*, *London Review of Books*, 5 April 1990, 20–23. For a detailed critique of Battestin's handling of the evidence, see Arthur Sherbo, *Studies in the Eighteenth-Century English Novel* (East Lansing: Michigan State University Press, 1969), chap. 5.

52. Ronald Paulson, *The Life of Henry Fielding* (Oxford: Blackwell, 2000), 92, 309, and passim. See also Paulson's earlier considerations of this question: "Henry Fielding and the Problem of Deism," in *The Margins of Orthodoxy*, ed. Roger Lund (Cambridge: Cambridge University Press, 1995), 240–70; and *The Beautiful, Novel, and Strange* (Baltimore: Johns Hopkins University Press, 1996), chap. 5.

53. In response to Paulson, Battestin has restated his evidence. Apart from Wilson's account of the freethinkers' club and the conversion of Square in *Tom Jones*, this evidence comes from Fielding's nonfictional writings (periodical essays, the posthumous *Fragment* on Bolingbroke) and his posthumous library catalog. See Martin C. Battestin, "Fielding and the Deists," *Eighteenth-Century Fiction* 13, no. 1 (October 2000): 67–76.

54. Henry Fielding, *Pasquin*, in *Plays, Volume III*, ed. Thomas Lockwood (Oxford: Clarendon, in press), 301.

55. Battestin, *Henry Fielding*, 199; "Marfario," *Grub-Street Journal*, nos. 330 (22 April 1736) and 332 (6 May 1736).

56. "Miso-Cleros," *Grub-Street Journal*, no. 132 (13 July 1732).

57. Writing as "Philalethes" in the *Daily Post*, 31 July 1732, cited in Paulson and Lockwood, eds., *Critical Heritage*, 62.

58. Henry Fielding, *The Old Debauchees*, in *Plays, Volume II*, 310, 327, 311, 315, 326.

59. Ibid., 332.

60. Ibid., 323.

61. Ibid., 318.

62. William Hazlitt, "On the Clerical Character," in *The Complete Works of William Hazlitt*, ed. P. P. Howe, 21 vols. (London: Dent, 1930–34), 7:247–48.

63. Oliver Goldsmith, *The Vicar of Wakefield*, in *Collected Works of Oliver Goldsmith*, ed. Arthur Friedman, 5 vols. (Oxford: Clarendon, 1966), 4:145.

64. On this tradition, see Robert D. Hume, *Henry Fielding and the London Theatre, 1728–1737* (Oxford: Clarendon, 1988), 132.

65. Thomas Stackhouse, *The Miseries and Great Hardships of the Inferior Clergy* (London, 1722), 12.

66. The incident is recounted, from original papers, by the 8th Earl of March. See *A Duke and His Friends: The Life and Letters of the Second Duke of Richmond*, 2 vols. (London: Hutchinson, 1911), 1:264–73.

67. Ibid., 266–67.

68. Samuel Richardson, *Pamela* (1740, 1st ed.), ed. Thomas Keymer and Alice Wakely (Oxford: Oxford University Press, 2001), 150–51.

69. All from March, *A Duke and His Friends*, 269–73.

70. Henry Fielding, *Amelia*, ed. Martin C. Battestin (Oxford: Clarendon, 1984), 364, 367. Compare Richardson, *Pamela*, 297, where the jest is put into the mouth of Sir Simon.

71. Jeremy Collier, *A Short View of the Immorality and Profaneness of the English Stage* (London, 1698), 109.

72. Henry Fielding, *The Tragedy of Tragedies; or, The Life and Death of Tom Thumb the Great*, in *Plays, Volume I*, ed. Thomas Lockwood (Oxford: Clarendon, 2004), 575.

73. Fielding, *Shamela*, 169.

74. Literally, "You have hit the nail on the fingernail" (Fielding, *Tom Jones*, 830).

75. Oliver Goldsmith, "Of Eloquence," in *Collected Works*, 1:480.

76. See James Downey, *The Eighteenth-Century Pulpit* (Oxford: Clarendon, 1969), esp. chap. 1; and Richard Foster Jones, "The Attack on Pulpit Eloquence in the Restoration," in *The Seventeenth Century*, ed. Richard Foster Jones et al. (Stanford, CA: Stanford University Press, 1951), 111–42.

77. "Sterne's Rabelaisian Fragment," ed. Melvyn New, *PMLA* 87, no. 5 (1972): 1083–92. For one particularly exuberant midcentury mock sermon, see Christopher Smart, *The Midwife; or, The Old Woman's Magazine*, 3 vols. (London, 1753), 1:54–58. More distantly, one might recall the famous speech of old Janotus in Rabelais, a glorious parody of Sorbonne eloquence. According to Pepys, the Duke of Buckingham once preached an obscene sermon, based on certain passages in the *Canticles*, before Charles I; in their new edition of Buckingham, Robert D. Hume and Harold Love include the text of a mock sermon that is traditionally attributed to the duke. See *Plays, Poems, and Miscellaneous Writings Associated with George Villiers, Second Duke of Buckingham*, 2 vols. (Oxford: Oxford University Press, 2007), 2: 400–402. For a useful comparative study of the genre, see Sander Gilman, *The Parodic Sermon in European Perspective* (Wiesbaden: Franz Steiner, 1974).

78. On Sandwich, see Ronald Fuller, *Hell-Fire Francis* (London: Chatto & Windus, 1939), 65. The lecture on continence appears in Tobias Smollett, *The Adventures of Peregrine Pickle*, ed. James L. Clifford (London: Oxford University Press, 1969), 133–34.

79. Fielding, *Jonathan Wild*, 181 (bk. 4, chap. 14). Fielding may also be the author of *The Crisis: A Sermon* (London, 1741), an odd hybrid between a mock sermon and a serious attack on Walpole. See Fielding, *Champion and Related Writings*, cvi–xi and app. 5.

80. Fielding, *The Old Debauchees*, 312–13.

81. Smollett, *Peregrine Pickle*, 188.

82. See, e.g., Alexander Pope, *A Full and True Account of a Horrid and Barbarous Revenge by Poison, on the Body of Mr. Edmund Curll* (London, 1716), and *The Narrative of Dr Robert Norris* (London, 1713); and Fielding, *Tom Jones*, 229.

83. Henry Fielding, "Essay on the Remedy of Affliction for the Loss of Our Friends," in *Miscellanies, Volume One*, 212–25 and passim.

84. See the "Epistle Dedicatory" to bk. 4 of *Pantagruel* in François Rabelais, *Gargantua and Pantagruel*, trans. Thomas Urquhart and Peter Motteux (1653–94; New York: Everyman, 1994). Motteux mistranslates *agélastes* as *eavesdroppers*.

85. Fielding first battled with the antitheatricalists late in 1729, when they attempted to close the theater at Goodman's Fields while he was presenting *The Temple Beau*. In 1736–37, they tried to stop him performing *Pasquin* and *Tumble-Down Dick* on the "forbidden" days of Lent and finally succeeded in having his theater closed during Passion Week (further evidence of the young Fielding's indifference to the regular observances of the church). See Paulson, *Life of Henry Fielding*, 28; and Battestin, *Henry Fielding*, 217.

86. Henry Fielding, *The Author's Farce* (1730 version), in *Plays, Volume I*, 282.

87. Fielding, *Covent-Garden Journal*, 87–88 (no. 12 [11 February 1752]). Compare *Spectator*, nos. 269 (8 January 1712) and 329 (18 March 1712); and *The History of Pompey the Little; or, The Life and Adventures of a Lap-Dog* (London, 1751), 93. Compare also Fielding's *Tom Jones*, where Partridge offers to tell "a true Story" of how the devil "took a Man out of Bed from another Man's Wife, and carried him away through the Key-hole of the Door" (466 [8.12]).

88. On sailors' love of the "Ambassador" trick, see Francis Grose, *A Classical Dictionary of the Vulgar Tongue*, 3rd ed. (1796), ed. Eric Partridge (New York: Barnes & Noble, 1963), 15–16.

89. Pope, *A Full and True Account*, n.p.; Tobias Smollett, *The Expedition of Humphry Clinker*, ed. O. M. Brack Jr. (Athens: University of Georgia Press, 1990), 291.

90. See John Loftis, *Comedy and Society from Congreve to Fielding* (Stanford, CA: Stanford University Press, 1959), 37ff. Not far behind, of course, is Erasmus's Folly in her pulpit.

91. An argument first made in George Sherburn, "*The Dunciad*, Book IV," *Texas Studies in English* 24 (1944): 174–90.

92. Thomas Shadwell, *The Virtuoso* (London, 1676), 53; *The Works of John Dryden*, ed. E. N. Hooker and H. T. Swedenburg Jr., 20 vols. (Berkeley and Los Angeles: University of California Press, 1956–2000), 2:60.

93. Samuel Coleridge to Thomas Poole, March 1797, in *Collected Letters of Samuel Taylor Coleridge*, ed. Earl Leslie Griggs, 6 vols. (Oxford: Oxford University Press, 1956), 1:310.

94. Fielding, "Essay on the Knowledge of Characters of Men," 158.

95. Anna Laetitia Barbauld, *The British Novelists; with an Essay; and Prefaces, Biographical and Critical, by Mrs. Barbauld*, 50 vols. (London, 1810–20), 18:xiv; William Hazlitt, "Lectures on the English Comic Writers," in *Complete Works*, 6:115.

CHAPTER FIVE

1. This chapter does not address same-sex violence, which was treated and experienced in very different ways. It does, however, take in assaults on female victims who would now be considered minors. On the legal anomalies by which ten rather than twelve was taken as the age of consent, see Antony E. Simpson, "Vulnerability and the Age of Female Consent: Legal Innovation and Its Effect on Prosecutions for Rape in Eighteenth-Century England," in *Sexual Underworlds of the Enlightenment*, ed. G. S. Rousseau and Roy Porter (Manchester: Manchester University Press, 1987), 181–205.

2. *The Nut-Cracker* (London, 1751), 42; cf. *Joe Miller's Jests; or, The Wit's Vade-Mecum*, 12th ed. (London, n.d. [Bodleian Harding E 101]), 31 (no. 185); and *The Merry Fellow* (London, 1754), 49.

3. On this and other early modern folk beliefs about sex, see G. R. Quaife, *Wanton Wenches and Wayward Wives* (London: Croom Helm, 1979). The belief was mainstream among sixteenth- and seventeenth-century jurists and remained in eighteenth-century reprints of their work (see, e.g., Michael Dalton's *Country Justice* [London, 1746], 366). Hale and Burn feel the need explicitly to reject the doctrine. See Matthew Hale, *The History of the Pleas of the Crown*, 2 vols. (London, 1736), vol. 1, chap. 58; and Richard Burn, *The Justice of the Peace, and Parish Officer*, 2 vols. (London, 1755), 1:315.

4. *The Jovial Companion; or, The Alive and Merry Fellow* (London, n.d. [Bodleian, Harding E 65]), 22.

5. *Rusted's Humorous and Entertaining Jester* (London, n.d. [HL 288760]), n.p.; *The Entertaining Companion; or, The Merry Jester* (London, n.d. [Bodleian, Harding E 54]), 27; François Rabelais, *Gargantua and Pantagruel*, trans. Thomas Urquhart and Peter Motteux (1653–94; New York: Everyman, 1994), 372.

6. *The Merry Fellow*, 120.

7. See John Beattie, *Crime and the Courts in England, 1660–1800* (Princeton, NJ: Princeton University Press, 1986), 124–32; and William Blackstone, *Commentaries on the Laws of England*, 4 vols. (London, 1765–69), 4:213.

8. William Kenrick, *Fun: A Parodi-Tragi-Comical Satire: As It Was to Have Been Perform'd . . . but Suppressed, by a Special Order from the Lord-Mayor and Court of Aldermen* (London, 1752), 26–30.

9. *Pinkethman's Jests*, 2nd ed. (London, 1721), 94; Miguel de Cervantes, *Don Quixote*, trans. P. A. Motteux (1700, etc.; New York: Knopf, 1991), pt. 2, chap. 45.

10. *The Mad Pranks of Tom Tram*, 3 vols. in 1 (London, n.d. [BL 1076.1.11]), 3:18.

11. Giacomo G. Casanova, Chevalier de Seingalt, *History of My Life*, trans. Willard R. Trask, 12 vols. (New York: Harcourt Brace Jovanovich, 1966–71), 9:295 (1764).

12. *A Ramble through London: Containing Observations on Men and Things* (London, 1738), 57.

13. Antony E. Simpson, "Popular Perceptions of Rape as a Capital Crime in Eighteenth-Century England: The Press and the Trial of Francis Charteris in the Old Bailey, February 1730," *Law and History Review* 22, no. 1 (2004): 27–70.

14. Henry Fielding, *Joseph Andrews*, ed. Martin C. Battestin (Middletown, CT: Wesleyan University Press, 1967), 332–33.

15. John Gay, *The Mohocks: A Tragi-Comical Farce* (1712), in *John Gay: Dramatic Works*, ed. John Fuller, 2 vols. (Oxford: Clarendon, 1983), 1:90.

16. Tobias Smollett, *Roderick Random*, ed. Paul-Gabriel Boucé (Oxford: Oxford University Press, 1979), 52-53.

17. On which, see Antony E. Simpson, "The 'Blackmail Myth' and the Prosecution of Rape and Its Attempt in 18th Century London: The Creation of a Legal Tradition," *Journal of Criminal Law and Criminology* 77, no. 1 (1986): 101-50.

18. Henry Fielding, *The History of Tom Jones*, ed. Martin C. Battestin and Fredson Bowers (Oxford: Clarendon, 1977), bk. 10, chaps. 2-3, and *Joseph Andrews*, 331.

19. *Grub-Street Journal*, no. 132 (13 July 1732).

20. Thomas D'Urfey, *A Fond Husband; or, The Plotting Sisters* (1676), in *Two Comedies by Thomas D'Urfey*, ed. Jack A. Vaughn (Cranbury, NJ: Associated University Presses, 1976), 223-24 (4.4). The device is imitated in Thomas Otway's *Soldier's Fortune* (1681) and other farces. *A Fond Husband* was performed well into the eighteenth century and reprinted five times (1677, 1678, 1685, 1711, 1735).

21. [Christopher Anstey], *Memoirs of the Noted Buckhorse*, 2 vols. (London, 1756), 1:168.

22. Smith, *A Compleat History of the Lives and Robberies of the Most Notorious Highway-Men, Foot-Pads, Shop-Lifts, and Cheats, of Both Sexes*, 5th ed., 3 vols. (London, 1719), 1:164-65.

23. *Aristophanes, Being a Classic Collection of True Attic Wit* (London, 1778), 132-33. The joke was published while Temple (1711-79) was still alive.

24. On Swift, see Irvin Ehrenpreis, *The Personality of Jonathan Swift* (Cambridge, MA: Harvard University Press, 1958), 126. On George III, see Christopher Hibbert, *George III: A Personal History* (London: Viking, 1998), 351.

25. Susan Staves, "Fielding and the Comedy of Attempted Rape," in *History, Gender, and Eighteenth-Century Literature*, ed. Beth Fowkes Tobin (Athens: University of Georgia Press, 1994), 87. From his early comedy *Rape upon Rape* (1732) to repeated episodes in his fiction and his wry analysis of the rape cases that came before him as a magistrate, Fielding was preoccupied to the point of obsession with sexual violence. I have taken up these questions in a companion article, "Fielding's Rape Jokes," *Review of English Studies* 61, no. 251 (2010): 572-90.

26. Samuel Richardson, *Sir Charles Grandison*, ed. Jocelyn Harris (Oxford: Oxford University Press, 1986), 145.

27. *Young Scarron* (London, 1752), 126-27, "172-73" (mispaginated).

28. Oliver Goldsmith, *The Deserted Village*, in *Collected Works of Oliver Goldsmith*, ed. Arthur Friedman, 5 vols. (Oxford: Clarendon, 1966), 4:296; Anna Clark, *Women's Silence, Men's Violence: Sexual Assault in England, 1770-1845* (London: Pandora, 1987), 34-35, 42.

29. Samuel Richardson, *Clarissa; or, The History of a Young Lady* (1748, 1st ed.), ed. Angus Ross (London: Penguin, 1985), 802. The second formulation appears in the 3rd ed. (8 vols. [London, 1750-51], 3:229).

30. Richardson, *Clarissa*, 3rd ed., 3:130.

31. John Vanbrugh, *The Relapse; or, Virtue in Danger* (London, 1697), 74 (4.3). Sheridan removed the mock rape when he adapted the play as *A Trip to Scarborough* (1777), but it remained in performing copies and the *Bell's British Theatre* edition (London, 1797).

32. William Congreve, *The Way of the World* (1700), in *The Complete Plays of William Congreve*, ed. Herbert Davis (Chicago: University of Chicago Press, 1967), 429 (3.1); Thomas Shadwell, *The Libertine*, in *The Complete Works of Thomas Shadwell*, ed. Montague Summers, 5 vols. (London: Fortune, 1927), 3:46.

33. Henry Carey, *The Songs, as They Are Sung in Betty; or, The Country-Bumpkins* (London, n.d. [BL C.116.i.4.(28)]), 1.

34. Congreve, *Way of the World*, 429; Charlotte Lennox, *The Female Quixote; or, The Adventures of Arabella*, ed. Margaret Dalziel (Oxford: Oxford University Press, 1970), 300.

35. *A Collection of Bacchanalian Songs* (Edinburgh, 1768), 146–47; *St James's Miscellany; or, The Citizens Amusement* (London, n.d. [BL Cup.700.m.86]), 14–15. On graphic traditions, see Philip Stewart, *Engraven Desire: Eros, Image and Text in the French Eighteenth Century* (Durham, NC: Duke University Press, 1992), 175–233. The motif is sufficiently frequent to merit its own category (T475.2.1, "Intercourse with sleeping girl") in Stith Thompson's *Motif-Index of Folk Literature*, 6 vols. (Bloomington: Indiana University Press, 1955–58).

36. Smollett, *Roderick Random*, 52; Fielding, *Joseph Andrews*, 331.

37. *Evening Post*, 18 June 1730; *Grub-Street Journal*, no. 25 (25 June 1730); *R. v. West*, 4 July 1730 (OBSP t17300704-62).

38. Christopher Smart, *The Midwife; or, The Old Woman's Magazine*, 3 vols. (London, 1753), 1:36; *The London, Oxford, Cambridge, Coffee-House, and England's Jests* (London, ca. 1760 [Bodleian, Harding E 124]), 14.

39. *The Merry Fellow*, 89–90.

40. Henry Fielding, *Shamela*, in *The Journal of a Voyage to Lisbon, Shamela, and Occasional Writings*, ed. Martin C. Battestin (Oxford: Clarendon, 2008), 164; *England's Witty and Ingenious Jester*, "17th ed." (London, n.d. [Bodleian Harding E55]), 60–61; cf. *Ben Johnson's Jests*, "5th ed." (London, ca. 1755 [Bodleian Harding E5.1]), 64.

41. Thomas Southerne, epilogue to *The Fatal Marriage* (London, 1694), cited in Ian Donaldson, *The Rapes of Lucretia: A Myth and Its Transformations* (Oxford: Clarendon, 1982), 87; Samuel Richardson, *Pamela* (1740, 1st ed.), ed. Thomas Keymer and Alice Wakely (Oxford: Oxford University Press, 2001), 31–32.

42. For valuable analysis of Restoration rape tragedy, see Elizabeth Howe, *The First Modern Actresses: Women and Drama, 1660–1700* (Cambridge: Cambridge University Press, 1992), 43–49; and Jean I. Marsden, *Fatal Desire: Women, Sexuality, and the English Stage, 1660–1720* (Ithaca, NY: Cornell University Press, 2006).

43. John Dennis, *Original Letters, Familiar, Moral, and Critical*, 2 vols. (London, 1721), 1:63–64.

44. William Hunt, *The Fall of Tarquin* (Newcastle, 1713), 60 (epilogue); *A Trip from St. James's to the Royal-Exchange* (London, 1744), 46. The actual presence of women at rape trials varied: increasingly, it would seem, courts were cleared of women for the sake of decency. See Vic Gatrell, *The Hanging Tree* (Oxford: Oxford University Press, 1994), 468.

45. *Tatler*, no. 84 (22 October 1709).

46. Richardson, *Clarissa*, 3rd ed., 4:257–58, a passage restored in this edition from the original manuscript.

47. Lennox, *Female Quixote*, 92–93, 164.

48. Laurence Sterne, *The Life and Opinions of Tristram Shandy, Gentleman*, ed. Melvyn New and Joan New, 3 vols. (Gainesville: University of Florida Press, 1978), 2:611–12 (7.23).

49. Tobias Smollett, *The Adventures of Peregrine Pickle*, ed. James L. Clifford (London: Oxford University Press, 1969), 525. The authorship of the "Memoirs"—or, more precisely, the balance between Lady Vane and her collaborator—remains uncertain. See Neil Guthrie, "New Light on Lady Vane," *Notes and Queries* 49, no. 3 (September 2002): 372–78.

50. James Boswell, *A Journal of a Tour to the Hebrides*, 3rd ed. (London, 1786), 120–21.

51. Morris Palmer Tilley, *A Dictionary of the Proverbs in England in the Sixteenth and Seventeenth Centuries* (Ann Arbor: University of Michigan Press, 1950), 405 (M34), 742 (W660).

52. Mary Pix, *The Different Widows; or, Intrigue All-a-Mode* (London, 1703), 34.

53. Randolph Trumbach, *Sex and the Gender Revolution: Heterosexuality and the Third Gender in Enlightenment London* (Chicago: Chicago University Press, 1998), 301–2. All these objections appear in one particularly hostile cross-examination from the early defense-counsel era: *R. v. Curtis*, 20 February 1793 (OBSP t17930220-48). Balzac's story is "La belle fille de Portillon" (*Contes drolatiques*, 3.5).

54. See esp. Patricia Crawford, "Sexual Knowledge in England, 1500–1750," in *Sexual Knowledge, Sexual Science: The History of Attitudes to Sexuality*, ed. Roy Porter and Mikuláš Teich (Cambridge: Cambridge University Press, 1994), 82–106. For invaluable source materials, see Patricia Crawford and Laura Gowing, eds., *Women's Worlds in Seventeenth-Century England* (London: Routledge, 2000).

55. See, e.g., *Kick Him, Jenny* (London, 1733) and *Kick Him, Nan* (London, 1734), both discussed in Karen Harvey, *Reading Sex in the Eighteenth Century: Bodies and Gender in English Erotic Culture* (Cambridge: Cambridge University Press, 2004), 194–95.

56. Fielding, *Shamela*, 177; Garthine Walker, "Rereading Rape and Sexual Violence in Early Modern England," *Gender and History* 10, no. 1 (1998): 12; Quaife, *Wanton Wenches and Wayward Wives*, 167; *R. v. Winch and Tatham*, 26 June 1776 (OBSP t17730626-76); *R. v. Phillips*, 15 May 1771 (OBSP t17710515-6).

57. Delarivière Manley, *The Physician's Strategem*, in *The Power of Love: In Seven Novels* (London 1720), 162.

58. Teresia Constantia Phillips, *An Apology for the Conduct of Mrs. Teresia Constantia Phillips*, 3 vols. (London, 1748–49), 1:35–38.

59. See *The Restor'd Maidenhead: A New Satyr against Woman* (London, 1691), 9. On jokes and travesties of the Lucretia story, see Donaldson, *The Rapes of Lucretia*, chap. 5. For one instance from the mock-romance tradition, see Adrien Perdou de Subligny, *The Mock-Clelia* (London, 1678), 14.

60. Norman Bryson, "Narratives of Rape in the Visual Arts: Lucretia and the Sabine Women," in *Rape: An Historical and Social Enquiry*, ed. Sylvana Tomaselli and Roy Porter (New York: Blackwell, 1989), 165–71.

61. On which, see Donaldson, *The Rapes of Lucretia*, 86–87.

62. "Epistle from Arthur Gray to Mrs. Murray" and "Virtue in Danger: A Lamentable Story How a Virtuous Lady Had Like to Have Been Ravished by Her Sister's Footman," both in Lady Mary Wortley Montagu, *Essays and Poems and Simplicity, a Comedy*, ed. Robert Halsband and Isobel Grundy (Oxford: Clarendon, 1977), 217–24.

63. See, e.g., Anita Pacheco, "Rape and the Female Subject in Aphra Behn's *The Rover*," *English Literary History* 65, no. 2 (1998): 323–45.

64. Jane Spencer, *Aphra Behn's Afterlife* (Oxford: Oxford University Press, 2000), chap. 5 (199).

65. Sarah Fielding, *The History of Ophelia*, 2 vols. (London, 1760), 2:179–86.

66. A point glanced at in Roy Porter, "Rape—Does It Have a Historical Meaning?" in Porter and Tomaselli, eds., *Rape*, 222.

67. Isobel Grundy, "Seduction Pursued by Other Means? The Rape in *Clarissa*," in *Clarissa and Her Readers: New Essays for the Clarissa Project*, ed. Carol Houlihan Flynn and Edward Copeland (New York: AMS, 1999), 256, 263.

68. On which, see Elizabeth Adams, *Chelsea Porcelain* (London: British Museum Press, 1989), 126.

69. Ellen Pollak, *The Poetics of Sexual Myth: Gender and Ideology in the Verse of Swift and Pope* (Chicago: University of Chicago Press, 1985), chap. 3.

70. BM Satires nos. 2513, 9016. Pursuing these allegories, Toni Bowers finds sexual force working as a powerful metaphor for political persuasion, religious conversion, and indeed any interaction between unequal parties (*Force or Fraud? British Seduction Stories and the Problem of Resistance, 1660–1760* [Oxford: Oxford University Press, 2011]).

71. Tilley, *Proverbs*, 404 (M15).

72. For Susan Brownmiller's analysis of "the pain of defloration" as a universal myth of patriarchy, see her *Against Our Will: Men, Women and Rape* (New York: Fawcett Columbine, 1975), 318–19.

73. Burn, *Justice of the Peace, and Parish Officer*, 1:315.

74. Porter, "Rape—Does It Have a Historical Meaning?" and Peggy Reeves Sanday, "Rape and the Silencing of the Feminine," in Porter and Tomaselli, ed., *Rape*, 84–101.

75. John Gillis, *For Better, for Worse: British Marriages, 1600 to the Present* (New York: Oxford University Press, 1985); and Susan Amussen, *An Ordered Society: Gender and Class in Early Modern England* (Oxford: Polity, 1988). Both build on Alice Clark's work on pre-industrial household economies, *The Working Life of Women in the Seventeenth Century* (1919; reprint, with an introduction by Amy Louise Erickson, London: Routledge, 1992]).

76. Felicity Nussbaum, *The Brink of All We Hate: English Satires on Women, 1660–1750* (Lexington: University Press of Kentucky, 1984); Phyllis Mack, *Visionary Women: Ecstatic Prophecy in Seventeenth-Century England* (Berkeley and Los Angeles: University of California Press, 1992); Trumbach, *Sex and the Gender Revolution*; Garthine Walker, *Crime, Gender and Social Order in Early Modern England* (Cambridge: Cambridge University Press, 2003).

77. Clark, *Women's Silence, Men's Violence*, 36; cf. *R. v. Togwell and Mattews*, 11 September 1735 (OBSP t17350911-55), where one of the defendants is heard bragging at a tavern in Drury Lane.

78. An argument developed in Anna Clark's second book, *The Struggle for the Breeches: Gender and the Making of the British Working Class* (Berkeley and Los Angeles: University of California Press, 1995), chap. 1–2.

79. *The Fond Mother's Garland* (London, 1770), 6.

80. The story is suppressed in A. H. Clark's standard edition (Oxford, 1898) but reprinted

in Oliver Lawson Dick, ed., *Aubrey's Brief Lives* (London: Secker & Warburg, 1949), 255–56. For an excellent overview of long-term changes in Raleigh's reputation, see Mark Nicholls and Penry Williams, "Sir Walter Raleigh," *ODNB*. Purcell's "Sir Walter" appears in *The Second Book of the Pleasant Musical Companion* (London, 1701), n.p. (no. 57); cf. *The Catch Club; or, Merry Companions* (London, 1762).

81. Susan Amussen, "'The part of a Christian man,'" in *Political Culture and Cultural Politics in Early Modern England: Essays Presented to David Underdown*, ed. Susan Amussen and Mark A. Kishlansky (Manchester: Manchester University Press, 1995), 213–33, 220. Joy Wiltenburg accepts more ambiguity: *Disorderly Women and Female Power in the Street Literature of Early Modern England and Germany* (Charlottesville: University of Virginia Press, 1992), 199.

82. Peter Clark, *The English Alehouse: A Social History, 1200–1830* (London: Longman, 1983), 288; Thomas D'Urfey, *Wit and Mirth; or, Pills to Purge Melancholy* (1719–20), 6 vols. in 3 (New York: Folklore Library, 1959), 5:13–14.

83. Alexander Smith, *The School of Venus; or, Cupid Restored to Sight*, 2 vols. (London, 1716), 1:142–51.

84. Smollett, *Peregrine Pickle*, 405–8; Richardson, *Clarissa*, ed. Ross, 896–97.

85. Smollett, *Roderick Random*, chap. 19, and *Peregrine Pickle*, chap. 78.

86. Smollett, *Roderick Random*, 103; Aphra Behn, *The Rover*, in *The Works of Aphra Behn*, ed. Janet Todd, 7 vols. (London: Pickering & Chatto, 1992), 5 (4.5).

87. William Wycherley, *The Plain Dealer*, 4.2, in *The Plays of William Wycherley*, ed. Arthur Friedman (Oxford: Oxford University Press, 1979), 469–82.

88. On editions and stage history, see ibid., 360–64.

89. *R. v. Carter*, 9 December 1772 (OBSP t17721209-112). I owe this reference to Simpson, "The 'Blackmail Myth,'" 112n48. Compare Tim Meldrum, "London Domestic Servants from Depositional Evidence, 1660–1750: Servant-Employer Sexuality in the Patriarchal Household," in *Chronicling Poverty: The Voices and Strategies of the English Poor, 1640–1840*, ed. Tim Hitchcock, Peter King, and Pamela Sharpe (London: Macmillan, 1997), 47–69, 56; and Clark, *Women's Silence, Men's Violence*, 41.

90. *Old Joe Miller: Being a Complete and Correct Copy from the Best Edition of His Celebrated Jests* (London, 1800), 169.

91. *Laugh and Be Fat* (London, 1796), 49, 52–53.

92. Trumbach, *Sex and the Gender Revolution*, 303; Quaife, *Wanton Wenches and Wayward Wives*, 172.

93. Thomas D'Urfey, "The Surpriz'd Nymph," in *Pills to Purge Melancholy*, 3:96–98. Compare *Kick Him, Jenny* (London, 1733), where the rape of a housemaid is made up by marriage.

94. Trumbach, *Sex and the Gender Revolution*, 234, 301–22.

95. Fielding, *Tom Jones*, 788–94.

96. For an ample taxonomy of early modern bed tricks, see Marliss Desens, *The Bed-Trick in English Renaissance Drama* (Newark: University of Delaware Press, 1994). For Wendy Doniger's controversial transcultural study, see her *The Bedtrick: Tales of Sex and Masquerade* (Chicago: University of Chicago Press, 2000). On the familial-economic contexts of Restoration bed tricks, see J. Douglas Canfield, *Tricksters and Estates: On the Ideology of Restoration Comedy* (Lexington: University Press of Kentucky, 1997), 137–39. Mary Davys, *The Reformed Coquette; or, The Adventures of Amoranda*, in *Works*, 2 vols. (London, 1724), 2:80–84.

97. Eliza Haywood's *The Lucky Rape* was printed with her *Cleomelia; or, The Generous Mistress* (London, 1727 [two eds.]), 94.

98. For Lady Kildare's letter, see Earl of March, *A Duke and His Friends: The Life and Letters of the Second Duke of Richmond*, 2 vols. (London: Hutchinson, 1911), 2:638. For the Duchess of Portland, see T. C. Duncan Eaves and Ben D. Kimpel, *Samuel Richardson: A Biography* (Oxford: Oxford University Press, 1971), 186. Stella Tillyard, *Aristocrats: Caroline, Emily, Louisa and Sarah Lennox, 1740–1832* (London: Chatto & Windus, 1994), 241.

99. Tilley, *Proverbs*, 741–49 (W653, W720, W638, etc.).

100. Frances Ferguson, "Rape and the Rise of the Novel," *Representations* 20 (Fall 1987): 88–112.

101. Samuel Johnson, *Lives of the Most Eminent English Poets*, ed. Roger Lonsdale, 4 vols. (Oxford: Clarendon, 2006), 2:200, and *Irene*, in *Poems*, vol. 6 of *The Yale Edition of the Works of Samuel Johnson*, ed. E. L. McAdam Jr. with George Milne (New Haven, CT: Yale University Press, 1964), 125 (1.2).

102. Francis Plumer, *A Candid Examination of the History of Sir Charles Grandison*, 3rd ed. (London, 1754), 11.

103. Eaves and Kimpel, *Samuel Richardson*, 306.

104. James Raven, *British Fiction, 1750–1770: A Chronological Check-List of Prose Fiction Printed in Britain and Ireland* (Newark: University of Delaware Press, 1987), 14; Frederick W. Boege, *Smollett's Reputation as a Novelist* (Princeton, NJ: Princeton University Press, 1947), 33.

105. Scholarship on the treatment of rape in early modern law is now voluminous. My discussion of legal contexts in the remainder of this chapter is especially indebted to Beattie, *Crime and the Courts*, 124–32; Clark, *Women's Silence, Men's Violence*; Gatrell, *The Hanging Tree*, chap. 17; John Langbein, *The Origins of Adversary Criminal Trial* (Oxford: Oxford University Press, 2003); Trumbach, *Sex and the Gender Revolution*; Walker, "Rereading Rape"; and the invaluable work of Antony Simpson: "The 'Blackmail Myth,'" "Rape as a Capital Crime," and "Vulnerability and the Age of Female Consent."

106. Hale, *The History of the Pleas of the Crown*, 1:635.

107. *R. v. J——*, 1722 (not published in OBSP), cited from *Select Trials at the Sessions-House in the Old-Bailey*, 4 vols. (London, 1742), 1:344–46; *R. v. Foy*, 4 December 1782 (OBSP t17821204-26).

108. Walker, "Rereading Rape," 6. See also Lyndal Roper, *Oedipus and the Devil: Witchcraft, Sexuality and Religion in Early Modern Europe* (London: Routledge, 1994), 60.

109. Beattie, *Crime and the Courts*, 126–27.

110. Antony E. Simpson, "Rape as a Capital Crime," and "The 'Blackmail Myth,'" 50–52. Anna Clark's work on the Guildhall Justice Room minute books suggests still lower figures (*Women's Silence, Men's Violence*, 51–53).

111. Peter King, "The Summary Courts and Social Relations in Eighteenth-Century England," *Past and Present* 183 (2004): 125–72. See also Gwenda Morgan and Peter Rushton, "The Magistrate, the Community and the Maintenance of an Orderly Society in Eighteenth-Century England," *Historical Research* 76, no. 191 (2003): 54–77. The complex arrangements of summary justice in London are usefully mapped out in Faramerz Dabhoiwala, "Summary Justice in Early Modern London," *English Historical Review* 121, no. 492 (2006): 796–822.

112. These included fees for arrest warrants and witness subpoenas, traveling costs and other compensation for witnesses, and all sorts of payments to court officers, even the doorman. John Beattie estimates the costs of prosecuting a felony at the Surrey Quarter Sessions as 10s.–£1, far beyond the resources of working people (*Crime and the Courts*, 41–48).

113. See Simpson, "Rape as a Capital Crime," 50–52; and Beattie, *Crime and the Courts*, 274–75.

114. *R. v. Noble*, 14 January 1726 (OBSP t17260114-5).

115. *England's Genius; or, Wit Triumphant* (London, 1734), 18; [Anstey], *Memoirs of the Noted Buckhorse*, 1:167.

116. *Joe Miller's Jests; or, The Wits Vade-Mecum*, 9th ed. (London, 1747), 58.

117. *The History of Will Ramble, a Libertine*, 2 vols. (London, 1755), 1:292–300.

118. *The Justicing Notebook (1750–64) of Edmund Tew, Rector of Boldon*, ed. Gwenda Morgan and Peter Rushton (Woodbridge: Boydell, 2000), 50 (26 July 1754), 70 (24 October 1756).

119. A term developed in Steven King and Alannah Tompkins, *The Poor in England, 1700–1850: An Economy of Makeshifts* (Manchester: Manchester University Press, 2003).

120. [Anstey], *Memoirs of the Noted Buckhorse*, 1:168.

121. Tim Hitchcock, *Down and Out in Eighteenth-Century London* (London: Hambledon & London, 2004), 95–96; *R. v. Duell*, 15 October 1740 (OBSP t17401015-53).

122. *The Merry Fellow*, 48; *Laugh and Be Fat* (London, 1761), 81–90.

123. See Simpson, "The 'Blackmail Myth,'" 110 and n. 42 (reviewing 167 cases in which the defense is sufficiently detailed to assess the presence or absence of blackmail). On minors, see Julie Gammon, "A Denial of Innocence," in *Childhood in Question*, ed. Anthony Fletcher and Stephen Hussey (Manchester: Manchester University Press, 1999), 75–76. On malicious prosecution in general, Douglas Hay's article remains authoritative: "Prosecution and Power: Malicious Prosecution in the English Courts, 1750–1850," in *Policing and Prosecution in Britain 1750*, ed. Douglas Hay and Francis Snyder (Oxford: Clarendon, 1989), 343–95.

124. Points well documented in Simpson, "Rape as a Capital Crime," 46 and n. 66.

125. *The Justicing Notebook of William Hunt, 1744–1749*, ed. Elizabeth Crittall (Devizes: Wiltshire Record Society, 1982), no. 145 (18 September 1744).

126. Simpson, "The 'Blackmail Myth,'" 111; notes to *R. v. Foy*, 4 December 1782 (OBSP t17821204-26).

127. Clark, *Struggle for the Breeches*; Laura Gowing, *Domestic Dangers: Women, Words and Sex in Early-Modern London* (Oxford: Clarendon, 1996), esp. chap. 4. Still useful is Iain MacCalman's reminder of the brutality and the misogyny of the Jacobin radicals: *Radical Underworld: Prophets, Revolutionaries and Pornographers in London, 1795–1840* (Cambridge: Cambridge University Press, 1988).

128. *R. v. Sheridan*, 13 April 1768 (OBSP t17680413-30).

129. *R. v. Dale*, 26 October 1752 (OBSP t17521026-49).

130. See Gillis, *For Better, for Worse*, passim.

131. See Clark, *Women's Silence, Men's Violence*, 83–85.

132. *Weekly Journal*, 13 June 1730; *Grub-Street Journal*, no. 24 (18 June 1730).

133. *The Covent-Garden Journal and A Plan for the Universal Register-Office*, ed. Bertrand A. Goldgar (Oxford: Clarendon, 1988), 431 (no. 36 [5 May 1752]).

134. *Justicing Notebook of William Hunt*, nos. 239, 262, 300; *Justicing Notebook of Edmund Tew*, 174 (2 July 1763).

135. *Justicing Notebook of Edmund Tew*, 87 (4 November 1757); *Justicing Notebook of William Hunt*, no. 107.

136. See the petitions reprinted in Alysa Levene et al., eds., *Narratives of the Poor in Eighteenth-Century Britain*, 5 vols. (London: Pickering & Chatto, 2006), vol. 3. J. A. Sharpe's study of bastardy hearings in seventeenth-century Essex finds none who claim to have been raped (*Crime in Seventeenth-Century England* [Cambridge: Cambridge University Press, 1983]).

137. *Deposition Book of Richard Wyatt, JP, 1767–1776* (Guildford: Surrey Record Society, 1978), no. 213, 240.

138. *Justicing Notebook of Edmund Tew*, 201 (the emphasis in the original, a transcription of a manuscript copy, was indicated by underlining).

139. *Justice in Eighteenth-Century Hackney: The Justicing Notebook of Henry Norris and the Hackney Petty Sessions Book*, ed. Ruth Paley (London: London Records Society, 1991), 22–23.

140. For useful cautions against overestimating the decline of ecclesiastical discipline in this period, see Susan Staves, "British Seduced Maidens," *Eighteenth-Century Studies* 14, no. 2 (1980–81): 109–34, 122–23; and R. B. Outhwaite's authoritative *The Rise and Fall of the English Ecclesiastical Courts, 1500–1860* (Cambridge: Cambridge University Press, 2006), esp. 95–96.

141. For two early nineteenth-century instances, see E. P. Thompson, *Customs in Common: Studies in Traditional Popular Culture* (New York: New Press, 1991), 517; and Gatrell, *The Hanging Tree*, chap. 17.

142. See *London Chronicle*, 18, 25 August 1763; *St James's Chronicle*, 25 August 1763. On the storm and its effects across southern England, see *The Annual Register . . . for the Year 1763* (London, 1764), 95–96.

143. For John Beattie's caution against overestimating the solemnity and order of eighteenth-century courtrooms, see his *Crime and the Courts*, 399.

144. Béat-Louis de Muralt, *Letters Describing the Character and Customs of the English and French Nations . . . Translated from the French*, 2nd ed. (London, 1726), 72.

145. Michael Harris, "Trials and Criminal Biographies: A Case Study in Distribution," in *Sale and Distribution of Books from 1700*, ed. Michael Harris and Robin Myers (Oxford: Oxford Polytechnic Press, 1982), 9; John Langbein, "Shaping the Eighteenth-Century Criminal Trial: A View from the Ryder Sources," *University of Chicago Law Review* 50, no. 1 (1983): 15–16.

146. *Select Trials . . . at the Sessions-House in the Old-Bailey*, 4 vols. (London, 1764), 1:n.p. (preface).

147. *R. v. Mordant*, 16 October 1723 (not published in OBSP), quoted from *Select Trials* (1742), 1:371.

148. *R. v. Bateman*, 16 October 1728 (OBSP t17281016-50).

149. *R. v. Norton*, 4 December 1751 (OBSP t17511204-36).

150. On the anomalies by which ten rather than twelve was taken as the age of consent, see Simpson, "Vulnerability and the Age of Female Consent."

151. *R. v. Sibley*, 28 August 1728 (OBSP t17280828-26).

152. *R. v. Medows*, 14 September 1763 (OBSP t17630914-13).

153. *R. v. Bright*, 15 July 1747 (OBSP t17470715-26).

154. *R. v. Medows*, 14 September 1763 (OBSP t17630914-13).

155. *R. v. Green*, 10 May 1769 (OBSP t17690510-15).

156. *R. v. Pritchard*, 27 August 1725 (OBSP t17250827-74).

157. *R. v. J——*, 1722 (not published in OBSP), cited from *Select Trials* (1742), 1:344–46.

158. *R. v. Kelly*, 12 April 1727 (OBSP t17270412-47).

159. *R. v. Remue*, 8 December 1742 (OBSP t17421208-41).

160. *R. v. Page*, 15 January 1748 (OBSP t17480115-4).

161. *R. v. Coventry*, 13 January 1727 (OBSP t17270113-21).

162. Statistics calculated in a valuable article by Robert Shoemaker, "The Old Bailey Proceedings and the Representation of Crime and Criminal Justice in Eighteenth-Century London," *Journal of British Studies* 47, no. 3 (July 2008): 567.

163. *R. v. Kill*, 17 October 1743 (OBSP t17431012-15).

164. *R. v. Jones*, 10 December 1735 (OBSP t17351210-70).

165. Testimony in the trial of Elizabeth Canning, as cited in Shoemaker, "The Old Bailey Proceedings and the Representation of Crime and Criminal Justice," 566.

166. Langbein, *The Origins of Adversary Criminal Trial*, 185.

167. *R. v. Kelly*, 12 April 1727 (OBSP t17270412-47).

168. *R. v. Alloway*, 13 May 1725 (OBSP t17250513-53); *Select Trials* (1742), 2:202–3.

169. *R. v. Adkins*, 11 September 1751 (OBSP t17510911-57).

170. *R. v. Page*, 15 January 1748 (OBSP t17480115-4).

171. *R. v. Jones*, 10 December 1735 (OBSP t17351210-70). Even in 1800, 70 percent of the Welsh population remained entirely monolingual. See Geraint H. Jenkins, Richard Suggett, and Eryn M. White, "The Welsh Language in Early-Modern Wales," in *The Welsh Language Before the Industrial Revolution*, ed. Geraint H. Jenkins (Cardiff: University of Wales Press, 1997).

172. *R v. Ellis*, 8 December 1731 (OBSP t17311208-58).

173. Ibid.

174. *R. v. Jones*, 10 December 1735 (OBSP t17351210-70).

175. *R. v. Kill*, 17 October 1743 (OBSP t17431012-15).

176. *R. v. White*, 19 September 1765 (OBSP t17650918-29).

177. *R. v. Coventry*, 13 January 1727 (OBSP t17270113-21).

178. *R. v. Dale*, 26 October 1752 (OBSP t17521026-49).

179. *R. v. Pritchard*, 27 August 1725 (OBSP t17250827-74); *Select Trials* (1742), 2:297 (emphasis added).

180. *R. v. Phillips*, 15 May 1771 (OBSP t17710515-6).

181. *R. v. Kelly*, 12 April 1727 (OBSP t17270412-47); *R. v. Medows*, 14 September 1763 (OBSP t17630914-13).

182. *R. v. Adkins*, 11 September 1751 (OBSP t17510911-57).

183. *R. v. Lander*, 27 August 1725 (OBSP t17250827-84); *R. v. Simmons*, 2 March 1726 (OBSP t17260302-17); *R. v. Yates and Jessup*, 31 August 1726 (OBSP t17260831-39).

184. Langbein, "Shaping the Eighteenth-Century Criminal Trial," 25. See also, more recently, *The Origins of Adversary Criminal Trial*, chap. 4.

185. See esp. Shoemaker, "The Old Bailey Proceedings and the Representation of Crime and Criminal Justice."

186. *R. v. Grimes*, 7 April 1725 (OBSP t17250407-66).

187. *Weekly Journal; or, British Gazeteer*, 8 April 1727.

188. Blackstone, *Commentaries*, 4:212.

189. *R. v. Garner*, 7 September 1748 (OBSP t17480907-50).

190. Richardson, *Clarissa*, ed. Ross, 1253.

191. Beattie, *Crime and the Courts*, 131–32; Lincoln Faller, "The *Clarissa* Effect," *The Eighteenth-Century Novel* 5 (2006): 197–247; *The Trial of Frederick Calvert, Esq., Baron of Baltimore . . . for a Rape upon the Body of Sarah Woodcock* (London, 1768).

192. *Observations on S. W******k's Own Evidence, Relative to the Pretended Rape, as Printed in the Trial* (London, 1768).

193. *The Gentleman's Magazine* 38 (1768): 180–88.

IN CONCLUSION

1. Jerry C. Beasley, *A Check List of Prose Fiction Published in England, 1740–1749* (Charlottesville: University Press of Virginia, 1972); James Raven, *British Fiction, 1750–1770: A Chronological Checklist of Prose Fiction Printed in Britain and Ireland* (Newark: University of Delaware Press, 1987).

2. Points I make in sympathy with Franco Moretti, "The Slaughterhouse of Literature," *Modern Language Quarterly* 61, no. 1 (2000): 207–27.

3. Thomas Keymer, *Sterne, the Moderns, and the Novel* (Oxford: Oxford University Press, 2002), chap. 2, exploring territory first charted in Wayne Booth, "The Self-Conscious Narrator in Comic Fiction before *Tristram Shandy*," *PMLA* 67, no. 2 (1952): 163–85.

4. Statistics from Raven, *British Fiction*, 14–25; Jane Spencer, "Women Writers and the Eighteenth-Century Novel," in *The Cambridge Companion to the Eighteenth-Century Novel*, ed. John Richetti (Cambridge: Cambridge University Press, 1996), 233n3; and Cheryl Turner, *Living by the Pen* (London: Routledge, 1992), chap. 3. The old mistake that a majority of eighteenth-century novels were written by women evidently originated with Ian Watt himself (*The Rise of the Novel: Studies in Defoe, Richardson and Fielding* [Berkeley: University of California Press, 1957], 298).

5. Francis Coventry, *The History of Pompey the Little* (London, 1751), 8.

6. J. Paul Hunter, *Before Novels: The Cultural Contexts of Eighteenth-Century English Fiction* (New York: Norton, 1992).

7. For valuable discussions of these terms and their genealogy, see Deidre Lynch and William B. Warner, eds., *Cultural Institutions of the Novel* (Durham, NC: Duke University Press, 1996); and Homer Brown, *Institutions of the English Novel: From Defoe to Scott* (Philadelphia: University of Pennsylvania Press, 1997).

8. See Frank Gees Black, "Edward Kimber: Anonymous Novelist of the Mid-Eighteenth Century," *Harvard Studies and Notes in Philology and Literature* 17 (1935): 27–42; and Jeffrey Herrle, "Edward Kimber," *ODNB*.

9. *Critical Review*, no. 2 (October 1756): 276.

10. Henry Fielding, *The Covent-Garden Journal and A Plan of the Universal Register-Office*, ed. Bertrand A. Goldgar (Middletown, CT: Wesleyan University Press, 1988), 58 (no. 7 [25 January 1752]).

11. *The History of Will Ramble, a Libertine*, 2 vols. (London, 1755), 1:22–23.

12. Thomas Keymer gathers the surviving biographical details on Toldervy in "William Toldervy and the Origins of Smart's *A Translation of the Psalms of David*," *Review of English Studies* 54, no. 213 (2003): 52–66.

13. *The Adventures of Dick Hazard* (London, 1754). *The Fortunate Imposter; or, The Very Entertaining Adventures of Dick Hazard* (London, 1759) bears no resemblance to the earlier text; it is a reset version of *The Adventures of Jack Smart* (London, 1756).

14. *Jack Smart*, 219.

15. *The Adventures of Oxymel Classic, Esq; Once an Oxford Scholar*, 2 vols. (London, 1768), 1:19–20.

16. *The Temple Beau; or, The Town Coquets*, 2nd ed. (London, 1754).

17. *The Adventures of Shelim O'Blunder, the Irish Beau* (London, n.d. [BL 1076.g.48]), 2–3.

18. *The Fortunate Transport; or, The Secret History of the Life and Adventures of Polly Haycock* (London, n.d. [BL 635.f.11(10)]), 4; BM Satire no. 2511.

19. *The Secret History of Betty Ireland* (London, 1741), 38–39.

20. Ibid., 21–22.

21. Edward Kimber, *Juvenile Adventures of David Ranger*, 2nd ed., 2 vols. (London, 1757); *Critical Review*, no. 2 (November 1756): 379.

22. *The Juvenile Adventures of Miss Kitty F[ishe]r* (London, 1759), 1:160, 2:7–8.

23. "On K—— F——'s Falling from Her Horse," *Universal Magazine*, March 1759; *The Merry Accident; or, A Print in the Morning* (1759; photograph in BM).

24. *Kitty Fisher*, 2:168–72.

25. *Monthly Review*, no. 6 (June 1752): 447.

26. *Will Ramble*, 1:241.

27. *Will Ramble*, vol. 1, chaps. 5–10.

28. See the ample selection in Julie Peakman, ed., *Whore Biographies, 1700–1825*, 8 vols. (London: Pickering & Chatto, 2006–7).

29. *Authentic Memoirs of the Celebrated Miss Nancy D[a]ws[o]n* (London, n.d. [BL G.14248]), 7, 11, 27–28.

30. [Christopher Anstey], *Memoirs of the Noted Buckhorse*, 2 vols. (London, 1756), vol. 1, chap. 2.

31. Nicholas Hudson, "Social Rank, 'the Rise of the Novel,' and Whig Histories of Eighteenth-Century Fiction," *Eighteenth-Century Fiction* 17, no. 4 (July 2005): 1–36.

32. *Nancy Dawson*, 9.

33. [Anstey], *Memoirs of the Noted Buckhorse*, 1:47–48.

34. *The Fortunate Transport*, 20.

35. John Feather, *A History of British Publishing* (London: Routledge, 1988), 97.

36. *Will Ramble*, 1:230, 243; *Kitty Fisher*, 2:3–4; [Anstey], *Memoirs of the Noted Buckhorse*, 1:19–20; George Stevens, *The History of Tom Fool*, 2 vols. (London, 1760), 1:22; William Chaigneau, *The History of Jack Connor* (London, 1752), 22.

37. *Nancy Dawson*, 24; Edward Kimber, *The Life and Adventures of Joe Thompson*, 2 vols. (London, 1750), vol. 1, chap. 4; *Betty Ireland*, 27–37.

38. *Critical Review*, no. 1 (March 1756): 127.

39. [Anstey], *Memoirs of the Noted Buckhorse*, 1:159–60.

40. *Monthly Review*, no. 10 (March 1754): 238.

41. William Toldervy, *The History of Two Orphans*, 4 vols. (London, 1756), 1:116–17.

42. Kimber, *Joe Thompson*, 1:iv; *The History of Jasper Banks, Commonly Call'd the Handsome Man*, 2 vols. (Dublin, 1754), preface.

43. Kimber, *Joe Thompson*, 1:63.

44. See *The Travels and Adventures of William Bingfield, Esq, . . . with an Accurate Account of the Shape, Nature, and Properties of That Most Furious, and Amazing Animal, the Dog-Bird*, 2 vols. (London, 1753).

45. *The Adventures of Jerry Buck* (London, 1754), chap. 7–9, 14–18.

46. *Will Ramble*, 1:1–2.

47. *Monthly Review*, nos. 6 (June 1752): 447–49; 11 (December 1754): 466–67; 10 (February 1754): 160; and 15 (December 1756): 655–66.

48. A process described in Frank Donoghue, *The Fame Machine: Book Reviewing and Eighteenth-Century Literary Careers* (Stanford, CA: Stanford University Press, 1996), chap. 1.

49. *Critical Review*, nos. 2 (November 1756): 340; and 8 (November 1759): 408–9; *Monthly Review*, no. 15 (November 1756): 534–35.

50. See, in particular, William St. Clair, *The Reading Nation in the Romantic Period* (Cambridge: Cambridge University Press, 2004), 6. For meticulous analysis of midcentury records, see Jan Fergus and Ruth Portner, "Provincial Subscribers to the *Monthly* and *Critical Reviews*, and Their Book Purchasing," in *Writers, Books, and Trade*, ed. O. M. Brack Jr. (New York: AMS, 1994), 157–76.

51. Donoghue, *The Fame Machine*, 28.

52. [George, Lord Lyttelton,] *Dialogues of the Dead* (London, 1760), no. 28.

53. *Dick Hazard*, v.

54. For two distinct stages of this developing scholarship, see James Raven, Helen Small, and Naomi Tadmor, eds., *The Practice and Representation of Reading in England* (Cambridge: Cambridge University Press, 1996); and Stephen Colclough, *Consuming Texts: Readers and Reading Communities, 1695–1870* (New York: Palgrave, 2007). On the unread later volumes of *Sir Charles Grandison*, see Jan Fergus, *Provincial Readers in Eighteenth-Century England* (Oxford: Oxford University Press, 2006), 111 and passim.

55. For a fascinating transhistorical discussion of these connections between punctuation and reading aloud, see M. B. Parkes, *Pause and Effect: A History of Punctuation in the West* (Berkeley and Los Angeles: University of California Press, 1993).

56. Stevens, *Tom Fool*, 1:viii–ix; "A Censure on the Present Reigning Taste for Novels and Romances, and How to Cure It," *London Magazine*, no. 18 (May 1749).

57. *The History of Sophia Shakespear* (London, 1753), viii; *Jerry Buck*, xii.

58. Stevens, *Tom Fool*, vol. 1, front matter.

59. Raven, *British Fiction*, 27–28.

60. See the cautions in Richard Altick, *The English Common Reader: A Social History of the Mass Reading Public, 1800–1900* (Chicago: University of Chicago Press, 1957), 62; and Jan

Fergus, "Provincial Servants' Reading in the Late Eighteenth Century," in Raven et al., eds., *Practice and Representation of Reading*, 202–25.

61. James Raven, "From Promotion to Proscription: Arrangements for Reading in Eighteenth-Century Libraries," in Raven et al., eds., *Practice and Representation of Reading*, 175–201, and "The Noble Brothers and Popular Publishing, 1737–89," *The Library*, 6th ser., no. 12 (1990): 291–345.

62. *Boswell's London Journal, 1762–1763*, ed. Frederick A. Pottle (London: Harborough, 1950), 187; Keymer, *Sterne, the Moderns, and the Novel*, 59–60.

63. *Polly Honeycombe: A Dramatick Novel of One Act* (London, 1760), [v]–xiii.

64. See A. N. L. Munby, ed., *Sale Catalogues of Libraries of Eminent Persons*, 12 vols. (London: Mansell Information, 1971–75), 7:51–75. On Lady Mary's fiction reading in general, see Robert Halsband, "Lady Mary Wortley Montagu and Eighteenth-Century Fiction," *Philological Quarterly* 45, no. 1 (1966): 145–56; and Isobel Grundy, "'Trash, Trumpery, and Idle Time': Lady Mary Wortley Montagu and Fiction," *Eighteenth-Century Fiction* 5, no. 4 (1993): 293–310.

65. Lady Mary Wortley Montagu, *Complete Letters*, ed. Robert Halsband, 3 vols. (Oxford: Clarendon, 1965–67), 2:473 (24 December 1750).

66. Montagu, *Letters*, 3:125–26 (3 April 1757). With "Miss [?Kat]ty N" I have followed Hugh Amory's reading of the MS, rather than Halsband's "Miss [?Mos]tyn" (Munby, ed., *Sale Catalogues of Libraries*, 7:53–54).

67. Properly *The Memoirs of a Young Lady of Quality, a Platonist*, 3 vols. (London, 1756).

68. Montagu, *Letters*, 3:35–38 (23 July 1753), 2:473 (24 December 1750), 3:134 (30 September 1757).

69. Compare Montagu, *Letters*, 3:2–9 (16 February 1752), in which she seems to work through another large case of books in less than two weeks.

70. See Raven, *British Fiction*, introduction. Even for the period 1770–99, the survival rate is only 90 percent (James Raven and Antonia Forster, eds., *The English Novel, 1770–1829: A Bibliographical Survey of Prose Fiction Published in the British Isles*, 2 vols. [Oxford: Oxford University Press, 2000], 1:18). For one instance of the scrapbook treatment, see the British Library copy of *The Midnight Ramble* (1754 [8285.cc.40]).

71. John Guillory, *Cultural Capital: The Problem of Literary Canon Formation* (Chicago: University of Chicago Press, 1993). For valuable analysis of the reigning tropes of feminist literary history, see the introduction to Susan Staves, *A Literary History of Women's Writing in Britain, 1660–1789* (Cambridge: Cambridge University Press, 2006).

72. Margaret Cohen, *The Sentimental Education of the Novel* (Princeton, NJ: Princeton University Press, 1999), 6 and passim; Katie Trumpener, *Bardic Nationalism: The Romantic Novel and the British Empire* (Princeton, NJ: Princeton University Press, 1997), 291.

73. Pierre Bourdieu, "Flaubert's Point of View," in *The Field of Cultural Production: Essays on Art and Literature*, ed. and trans. Randall Johnson (New York: Columbia University Press, 1993), 202.

74. Henry James, review of *Our Mutual Friend*, *The Nation*, November 21, 1865.

INDEX

Most works are listed under their author or artist, except anonymous texts or those for which the title is the more important piece of information.

uted to, 167–68; loud/open-mouthed as indecorous, 170, 314n131. *See also* humor and laughter

law, justice system: comic sources as evidence, 191; doctrines v. practice, 136, 196; perjury taken for granted, 228, 231; used by all levels of society, 125–26, 135, 226, 228. *See also* bastardy hearings; courtrooms, eighteenth-century; Justices of the Peace; poor law; rape trials

laxatives (as practical joke), 21, 146, 254

Lazarillo de Tormes (anon.), 48, 254; translations, xiii

Legman, Gershon (joke collector), 292n80

Le Goff, Jacques, 297n88

Lennox, Charlotte: assaults housemaid, 131, 310n77; rape jokes, 7, 202, 205, 210, 280

Lennox, Charles, 2nd Duke of Richmond: love of hoaxes, 131, 150, 180–81; odd mixture of buffoonery and kindness, 151–52, 169–70; prank against Richardson, 222; and Fielding, 169–70

Le Sage, Alain René: *Le Diable boiteux*, 60; *Gil Blas*, 255

Lessing, Gotthold Ephraim, 108

L'Estrange/LeStrange, Nicholas (manuscript jestbook compiler), 37

Lewis, Wilmarth S., 300n148

Life and Adventures of Joe Thompson, The (Kimber), 264, 265, 271, 276, 277; acknowledged imitation of *Tom Jones*, 253; didacticism, 255, 268; phenomenal best-seller, 253; picaresque-cum-romance formula, 253–54; scatology, 266–67

life writing (term), 301n172, 302n179

Light Summer Reading for the Ladies (novel), 31

linkboys: commonly deformed or malnourished, 72; mistrusted, 128, 142; subjects of laughter and practical jokes, 72, 115; illustrations of, 298n110. *See also* plebeians/the poor

Linton, Simi, 88

literary history: continuity and change in, 7–14; digitization projects, xii, 44; new historicism, 15; *parliament* v. *parade* models, 10; periodization and dialectical patterning, 13–14, 116. *See also* antisentimentalism; the novel; reading, history of; sentimentalism

London Magazine, The, 57, 253

Lonsdale, Roger, 4, 90

lottery prints. *See* popular genres

Love, Harold, 80, 300n142

Lucretia (legendary rape victim): in feminocentric texts, 222; scornful counter-explanations, 197, 204–5, 209; suicide as heathenish act, 210; visual treatments, 209

Lund, Roger, 90, 102

Lysons, Daniel (antiquarian), 92

Lyttelton, George, 1st Baron Lyttelton, 77, 299n132; *Dialogues of the Dead*, 270

MacCalman, Iain, 328n127

Mack, Phyllis, 215

Mackenzie, Henry: *The Man of Feeling*, 96–97; *The Man of the World*, 133; stories of beggars and fishwives, 123

Macklin, Charles (actor), 109, 148

Manley, Delarivière: on Lord Mohun, 143; rape scenes, 208, 222

Mann, Horace (diplomat and letter writer), 82–83, 136

manuscript circulation, 6, 80, 210, 211 fig. 11, 286n12, 300n142. *See also* commonplace books; poetry, unpublished; women's writing

market women: objects of mixed appreciation and disgust, 70; usually frail and disabled, 52–53, 64; victims of violence, 71, 135, 223, 235. *See also* butterwives; food vendors

Marlborough, Duchess of. *See* Churchill, Sarah

marriage: "broomstick" weddings and customary arrangements, 233; as insistently

Printed in Great Britain
by Amazon.co.uk, Ltd.,
Marston Gate.